Civil War
Prisoner of War
Camps
Union States
Confederate States
Union Camps
Confederate Camps
Prisoner Exchange Sites
N
S
W
E
Elmira Prison
Fort Warren
ohnson's
Island
amp
hase
Fort Delaware
Point Lookout
Belle Isle &
Libby Prisons
Danville Prisons
Aiken's Landing
Salisbury
Prison
Castle
Sorghum
Florence Stockade
Camp
wton
Castle Pinckney
sonville
Blackshear Prison
I0759773

Additional Praise for *A Fate Worse Than Hell*

"W. Fitzhugh Brundage has taken on the fraught subject of Civil War prisons and has come out a winner. His mastery of sources, critical and balanced evaluations of Union and Confederate policies, and governance of prisons and prisoners, clear and lucid writing, and empathetic treatment of prisoners' traumatic experiences lift this book head and shoulders above other works on the topic." —James M. McPherson, author of *Battle Cry of Freedom: The Civil War Era*

"Walt Whitman famously observed that the real Civil War would 'never get in the books.' Nevertheless, there occasionally appears a book that brings us closer to that impossible goal. Such a work is W. Fitzhugh Brundage's meticulously crafted exploration of prison life in the war, *A Fate Worse Than Hell.* Steadily and unflinchingly, Brundage leads us into the darkest regions of America's most tragic war, fearlessly illuminating every corner of his subject: the horrors of the camps; the valiant, if ineffectual efforts to reform them; and above all, the courage and tenacity of those who found the will to survive them. *A Fate Worse Than Hell* deserves a place of honor on every Civil War bookshelf."

—John Matteson, Pulitzer Prize winner for *Eden's Outcasts: The Story of Louisa May Alcott and Her Father*

"Perhaps no image of the American Civil War underscores the brutality of the conflict more than that of Andersonville prisoners. For generations, Americans have recoiled from photographs depicting these living skeletons, but few have attempted to explain how a 'civil' war became so uncivil. In powerful and moving prose, W. Fitzhugh Brundage does just that. He offers the first comprehensive exploration of how and why prisoner of war camps developed, challenging the reader to consider the degree of innovation and evolution involved in the process, and shining a light on one of the darkest aspects of war." —Caroline Janney, author of *Ends of War: The Fight of Lee's Army after Appomattox*

"From the pen of one of the most astute chroniclers of the past comes the first comprehensive modern history of prisoners of war during the Civil War. Taking a long approach, W. Fitzhugh Brundage starts with its global history, its awful denouement in horrific Confederate camps like Andersonville, as well as the long afterlives of captivity into the twentieth century. *A Fate Worse Than Hell* is the work of a master of the craft."

—Manisha Sinha, author of *The Rise and Fall of the Second American Republic: Reconstruction, 1870–1920*

"Riveting! Written like a novel and bursting with historical insight, *A Fate Worse Than Hell* tells the story of the Civil War's POW system and the men who struggled—and often failed—to survive it. Brilliant, original, and deeply humane, this is an essential book for anyone seeking to understand war and its long-lasting impact."

—Yael Sternhell, author of *Routes of War: The World of Movement in the Confederate South*

# A Fate Worse Than Hell

**ALSO BY W. FITZHUGH BRUNDAGE**

*Civilizing Torture:*
*An American Tradition*

*The Southern Past:*
*A Clash of Race and Memory*

# A Fate Worse Than Hell

## American Prisoners *of the* Civil War

W. Fitzhugh Brundage

W. W. NORTON & COMPANY
*Independent Publishers Since 1923*

Printed in the United States of America
First Edition



Manufacturing by Lakeside Book Company
Book design by Daniel Lagin
Production manager: Julia Druskin

ISBN 978-0-393-54109-0

W. W. Norton & Company, Inc., 500 Fifth Avenue, New York, NY 10110
www.wwnorton.com

W. W. Norton & Company Ltd., 15 Carlisle Street, London W1D 3BS

Authorized EU representative: EAS, Mustamäe tee 50, 10621 Tallinn, Estonia

10 9 8 7 6 5 4 3 2 1

*To Steve Schmidt*

Free among the dead, like the slain that lie in the grave,

whom thou rememberest no more: and they are cut
off from thy hand.

Thou hast laid me in the lowest pit, in darkness, in the deeps.

Psalm 88

# CONTENTS

# A Fate Worse Than Hell

CHAPTER ONE

# A Photographer Visits Andersonville

## (August 1864)

We may never learn why Andrew Jackson Riddle decided to visit Andersonville in far southwestern Georgia on August 16, 1864. With his bulky camera, fragile photographic plates, and chemical solutions in tow, he trekked sixty miles from his home in Macon to an isolated prison facility that had not existed six months earlier. No other photographer took the trouble to do so during its existence. His hurried tour that day had a significance that he almost certainly did not expect or would ever fully appreciate. It made only a fleeting impression on some of the prison's inhabitants. But the pictures he took that day conferred immortality and importance on scenes that otherwise would have been preserved, inadequately, only in words. While creating some of the few photographs of any prison camp in the Confederacy, he produced the sole photographic record of the most remarkable prison pen of the American Civil War. When he trained his camera lens on the tens of thousands of forlorn Union prisoners of war, Riddle enabled viewers to experience, if only vicariously, imprisonment on a scale and of a kind wholly outside of their experience.

Neither the trajectory of Riddle's life nor his circumstances in 1864 foretold his expedition to Andersonville. He left no record of ardent sectional or political loyalties. Nor had he displayed any evident ambition to distinguish himself, like his famous contemporaries Mathew Brady and Alexander Gardner, as a war photographer. Riddle instead aspired to be a savvy artisan and small businessman, cobbling together a lucrative career that would have passed without notice had he not trained his photographer's eye on Andersonville.

Like many of the photographers active in the region before the Civil War, Riddle had migrated to the South. He was born in 1828 in Delaware, but his family made their home in Baltimore. There, in 1846, he began to master the first widely available and commercially successful photographic process—daguerreotypy. He launched his career by opening a studio in Baltimore before moving to Columbus, Georgia, in 1856. As one of the comparatively few daguerreotypists in the state, his business flourished, and by the start of the war he had three studios. The prestige of his trade enabled him to transcend his humble origins and marry the daughter of a well-to-do slaveholder and mill owner.

Despite being of military age and in good health, Riddle eluded military service when the Civil War erupted. Instead, he moved to Richmond, Virginia, where the steady transit of soldiers and functionaries through the Confederate capital presented a robust market for his services. By 1864 he was back in Macon, where he was finally conscripted into the Confederate army. His technical skills were exploited duplicating military maps using

Andrew Riddle, ca. 1864, assured his place in history by photographing the Confederate prison at Andersonville. (Atlanta History Center)

photographic processes. He also served as staff photographer to General Joseph E. Johnston and the armies under his command.

Riddle's expedition to Andersonville appears to have been a private undertaking. There is no evidence that he made it at the behest of his military superiors. He may have used the pretext of taking portraits of the superintendent of eastern Confederate prisons, Brigadier General John H. Winder, and one of his subalterns, Captain Henry Wirz, to justify his visit and secure permission to photograph the camp. Once there, Riddle displayed little interest in his military hosts and instead devoted his time to photographing the prison itself.

No mere whim would have inspired him to invest his time and skills honed on portraiture to render images with no immediate commercial value. To photograph anything in Riddle's era was laborious and expensive. Photographic supplies, moreover, were so scarce in the blockaded Confederacy that Riddle had twice made furtive trips to the North to smuggle supplies back into the rebel nation. Both times he had been captured by Union troops and briefly imprisoned.

Curiosity rather than profit probably attracted Riddle to Andersonville. His experience of imprisonment, however brief, may have awakened his interest in the plight of the prisoners there. More likely, his years as a portrait photographer had engendered a documentarian's sensibility and he concluded that some record should be made of the most populous prison facility to ever loom on the American landscape. During the same week as Riddle's visit, an editor of an Atlanta newspaper in search of an "interesting and novel spectacle" visited the camp. His subsequent testimony that "the spectacle surpasses description" prompted the *Richmond Whig* to exhort that a photograph of the site "ought to be made and preserved." The newspaper vouched, "Such a picture was never before seen on earth." An opportunity to capture previously unimaginable scenes is the likeliest explanation for Riddle's arrival in Andersonville.

Once there, Riddle faced a multitude of challenges. By all accounts, the day of his visit was mercilessly hot. To secure vantage points of the prison pen, Riddle had to repeatedly hoist his equipment up ladders to platforms along the perimeter of the sixteen-foot-high prison stockade. Once in position, Riddle then had to scurry up and down the ladders and back and forth to his supplies as he exposed each image. The heat must have made the intricate process of preparing the photographic plates for exposure, which had to be executed in darkness and with dispatch, especially taxing. While preparing such plates, another war photographer recalled, "perspiration started from every pore and the sense of relief was great when it was possible to open the door and breathe." Breathing the air at Andersonville, however, offered no relief. An overpowering stench wafted from the fetid creek that provided drinking water and served as an open-air latrine for more than thirty thousand prisoners, assailing anyone within two miles of the camp, especially on the hottest days.

Riddle had previously earned his livelihood by making portraits. In the comfort of his studio, he could use fashionable props, tables, and iron clamps to steady his subjects for the ten or more seconds required to expose a photographic plate. No comparable means allowed him to constrain the movements of the thousands of prisoners who were certain to populate any photograph of the interior of the prison. One prisoner later recalled that he and others had been shunted away from the areas of the prison pen that Riddle photographed. Such measures, however, seem unlikely. There was no vacant space in the stockade to sequester prisoners, even temporarily. Nor were there any permanent structures within the camp where the prisoners could have been hidden from Riddle's lens.

The spectacle of Andersonville, as captured by Riddle, was the teeming human tableau within the stockade that some observers compared to a giant anthill in the midst of rural Sumter County, where fewer than ten

The view from the southeast corner of the Andersonville camp reveals the barrenness of the stockade. (Library of Congress)

thousand inhabitants lived at the war's start. Setting up his camera in the southeastern corner of the stockade, Riddle captured distant panoramas of seemingly endless seas of improvised shelters, haphazard pathways, and faceless prisoners.

In a few instances, Riddle cajoled prisoners to freeze their movements long enough to expose his plates. In his sixth photograph of the day, which Riddle took from a sentry post at the northeast corner of the stockade, dozens of listless men peer into the lens. His eighth photograph, taken late in the afternoon, frames a huge crowd of prisoners swarming the ration wagon. Momentarily still, the men squint into the sunlight that streamed over Riddle's shoulders. In the foreground, a man halts while distributing the daily allocations of beans and slabs of coarse cornbread upon which prisoners subsisted. More than any other image, this photograph conveys the claustrophobic conditions in the stockade, which had a population density many times greater than that of the worst slums in any twenty-first-century city.

Riddle's final photograph of the camp was the most carefully composed. In it, a squad of prisoners assigned to burial duty pause their Sisyphean task of filling a mass grave with more than one hundred corpses that had accumulated since the previous day. Each day, several times a day, wagons loaded with twenty to thirty bodies transported the dead from the prison hospital to the burial grounds. Then, as Riddle's photograph recorded, the burial

A crush of prisoners surrounds the wagon distributing the daily rations at Andersonville. (Library of Congress)

Black and white prisoners on the burial detail burying Leander Farnham in a mass grave at Andersonville. (Library of Congress)

squad lowered the corpses into deep trenches and buried them under dirt, without any covering. The location of each body was marked with a stake at the head identifying the soldier and his date of death. With the banks of removed earth framing either side of the image, Riddle placed in the center of it two men preparing to entomb the body of Leander Farnham, who had died that morning of severe malnutrition. Another eight thousand corpses would come to rest beside his in the burial grounds.

Perhaps no other photograph conveyed so completely or poignantly the dehumanization of prisoners of war that occurred during the Civil War. Riddle's image of the casual disposal of the dead at Andersonville made visible the toll of the human tragedy that was unfolding there. In this and other images, Riddle and fellow photographers of the war enabled contemporaries to be voyeurs of military death. Images of disfigured bodies littering battlefields and of rushed burials adorned the pages of popular magazines. Having never witnessed such an abundance of death as occurred during the Civil War, Americans displayed a grim fascination with it that was only partially satisfied through picture taking.

When Riddle focused his lens on the scenes at Andersonville, he became a witness to one of the singular spectacles of the war—the mass prison pen. His images became iconic depictions of the prisoner-of-war experience and acquired an authority attained by few written descriptions of Andersonville. As the editor of the *Richmond Whig* had acknowledged when he urged someone to photograph the camp, contemporaries granted unique credibility to witnesses. To see an event was to be uniquely qualified to understand it and perceive its truth. Photographs, which froze moments in time with uncanny detail and immediacy, had an unmatched capacity for "certifying experience." They enabled others to become witnesses after the fact. Alexander Gardner, one of the most influential photographers of the war, summed up contemporary wisdom when he affirmed that photography presented an incontrovertible image of reality with a fidelity unattainable by any other means. "Verbal representations of places and scenes," he vouched, "may or may not have the merit of accuracy; but photographic presentments of them will be accepted by posterity with an undoubting faith."

Because the mass-prison-pen experience was so far outside the experience of most Americans, veracity assumed particular importance. Prisoners themselves, whose letters were strictly censored, scribbled descriptions in carefully safeguarded diaries or drew furtive sketches on random scraps of paper, anticipating that those who had not seen Andersonville would greet descriptions of it with distrust. Prisoners repeatedly lamented that they lacked sufficient craft to render their prison experience in words. In later years, they would strive to establish their authority by pledging that their accounts were humble testimonials free of artifice. This aim almost certainly explains why Robert H. Kellogg opened his account of his tenure in Andersonville by invoking the New Testament verse "We speak that we do know, and testify that we have seen."

Riddle's photographs provided unassailable confirmation of the prose portraits of the camp composed by prisoners. Years after the war, his images would incite reverie among former prisoners, who marked up copies of them like so many tourist postcards. Jottings and numbers identified recalled places of note, faces of friends, hovels of acquaintances, and myriad other memories of life within the stockade. Publishers, who likewise grasped the power of the visual, adorned Andersonville memoirs with etchings inspired by Riddle's photographs.

Riddle's photographs (and the etchings they made of them) exposed acute deprivation that could not be dismissed as exaggerated or unsubstantiated. No permanent structures to accommodate prisoners can be seen in his panoramas. None existed. Instead, the viewer sees landscapes cluttered with improvised shelters fashioned of tattered blankets, discarded clothing, random scraps of wood, and any other materials that offered protection against the elements. Prisoners who were unable to scrounge building materials resorted to burrowing earthen shebangs in the ground, which one prisoner recalled "were alive with vermin and stank like charnel houses." The week before Riddle visited the camp a torrential downpour had inundated many of these burrows, drowning and burying some of the prisoners who occupied them.

A conspicuous feature in several of Riddle's prison-scapes was the broad, swampy basin in the southeastern portion of the stockade. In the absence of any sanitary facilities, the earliest inmates of the camp had resorted to using it as an impromptu latrine and bathing spot. Subsequently, prisoners erected a rudimentary plank latrine there. In short order the sink, as the latrine was known, degenerated into an open-air sewer that flooded the basin with a slurry of excrement and "a putrefying mass of fragments of bread and meat and bones" whenever it rained. By the time

Prisoners in the Andersonville stockade are barely discernible on the cluttered landscape beyond the sinks in the foreground. (Library of Congress)

The absence of privacy at the latrine, in the foreground, contributed to the spectacle of Andersonville prison life. (Library of Congress)

Riddle visited the camp, prisoners evidently had surrendered conventional notions of privacy, including any inhibitions they may have had about relieving themselves in view of thousands. Indeed, Riddle's photographs recorded prisoners in the very act at the latrine and on the distant slopes of the basin.

While prisoners struggled to find words to describe the uncanny bleakness of the stockade interior, Riddle's photographs vividly depicted it. Prisoners can be seen struggling to adapt to an environment wholly unsuited to their presence. Apart from the low-lying sink, the remainder of the site was reddish sandy loam that had been pounded hard by the feet of tens of thousands of inmates. Birds, squirrels, rabbits, and other wildlife were wholly absent, but flies, lice, and maggots abounded. Parched of water yet fertile with decay, the stockade was too congested for prisoners to grow anything, even if they had the wherewithal to do so. It was denuded of living plants by prisoners in search of food and firewood. So desperate were many for kindling that, as seen in Riddle's photographs, they took to burrowing in the ground in search of roots that might be combustible. Equally acute was the need for potable water. The principal source in the site was the creek that flowed through two Confederate encampments and the prison bakehouse before reaching the stockade. There, as Riddle recorded, prisoners washed themselves and their clothes while the creek flushed the latrine. Frantic for alternative sources of water, prisoners dug improvised wells on the slopes of the same basin that bordered the latrine.

Riddle's photographs recorded the boundaries that defined the known world of the prisoners at Andersonville. In half of his images the stockade wall and an arbitrary boundary—the so-called dead line—are the most conspicuous manifestations of Confederate authority. Pieces of scantling nailed to stakes driven into the ground formed a primitive fence parallel to the stockade wall. Anyone who ventured too close to it or scrambled over or under it risked being shot by the sentries. So severe was overcrowding within the stockade that, as Riddle's views recorded, many prisoners incorporated this dead line into their ramshackle shelters. Their apparent disregard for the dangers of the dead line was a calculated risk in an environment where habitable space was as precious as life itself.

With more than thirty thousand prisoners caged on the equivalent of ten city blocks, an oppressive sense of overcrowding defined life within the stockade. Riddle's photographs reveal endless vistas of hovels scattered across every fraction of the prison pen, including some areas self-evidently unfit for habitation. On the same day as Riddle's visit, a former prisoner recorded his impressions when he and his comrades had first entered the camp three months earlier. "We found it crowded. . . . By crowded I mean that it was difficult to move in any direction without jostling or being jos-

Livable space was so precious in the Andersonville stockade that prisoners erected their shelters pressing against the rustic fence marking the dead line. (Library of Congress)

tled." Another prisoner groused that there was "hardly room to lie down." Had the interior of the stockade been evenly divided, each prisoner could have staked out about eighteen square feet, or the equivalent of the area of a coffin, for his living space.

The dystopian cityscape that Riddle depicted had emerged with breathtaking speed. Every week during its first few months, the camp had added several hundred new inhabitants. A measure of this frenetic growth is evident in Riddle's sixth photograph, taken from the northeast corner of the stockade. It portrays roughly ten acres of the camp that had opened to prisoners only seven weeks earlier. Yet by mid-August it was jam-packed full of ramshackle lean-tos up to the dead line. By then, Andersonville had surpassed Norfolk, Memphis, Mobile, Savannah, and Nashville and trailed only New Orleans, Richmond, and Charleston as the largest community in the Confederacy.

In addition to a ballooning population, the prison possessed other attributes of a city. Although lacking any meaningful design by Confederate authorities, the city within the stockade acquired a Broadway, a South Street, and numerous improvised byways. It had distinct neighborhoods, some of which can be discerned in Riddle's photographs. Captive entrepreneurs traded anything that might have value to men deprived of basic necessities and every creature comfort. Inhabitants hustled to exploit any skill they possessed. One enterprising prisoner traded haircuts for daily rations. (Decades later, a former prisoner would pinpoint the site of the barber shop on a reproduction of one of Riddle's photographs.) In Riddle's images inhabitants cope in myriad ways with the challenge of living in a teeming prison pen: a few prisoners wander around pants-less, others curl up in fetal positions on the ground, some grub in the earth for roots, a few muck about in the quagmire, while still others clamor for rations.

If, as Susan Sontag suggested, photographs imprison reality, Riddle succeeded in capturing the prison world defined by the dead line and stockade walls. Yet, his photographic inventory was incomplete. In none of his photographs did Riddle depict the prison as it was seen by its inhabitants. In an act of trespass, he turned Union prisoners into objects of scrutiny viewed from the very vantage points their captors used to surveil them.

The captors—prison guards and officers—remain invisible, leaving the impression that Confederate authority rested lightly on the prisoners. The exact number of Confederate soldiers stationed at the prison on August 16 is

*A YANKEE IN ANDERSONVILLE.*

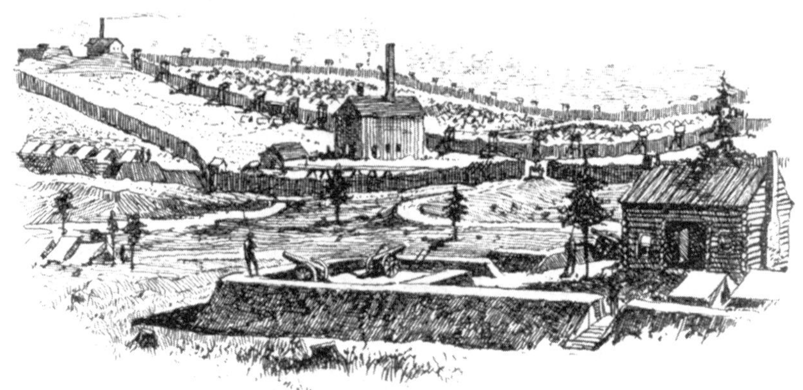

VIEW FROM WIRZ'S HEADQUARTERS OF THE STOCKADE AT ANDERSONVILLE.
(FROM A SKETCH MADE AT THE TIME BY R. K. SNEDEN.)

Riddle ignored the Confederate fortifications overlooking the Andersonville stockade, but prisoners did not. (Library of Congress)

unknown, but three weeks earlier nearly twenty-five hundred had been present. They had caught the eye of an Atlanta editor, G. W. Adair, who visited the camp and described "formidable batteries of artillery" and "a strong force of infantry" positioned on-site to suppress any prison tumult or fend off an attack on the facility. Nevertheless, no Confederate guards populate Riddle's photographs. Nor did Riddle record the exterior of the stockade, where Confederate soldiers performed their guard duties, or any of the four camps where Confederate soldiers bunked. Photographs of fortifications were common in the portfolios of many other Civil War photographers, yet Riddle captured no views of the two artillery redoubts positioned to rake the stockade with cannon fire.

Equally notable is Riddle's failure to photograph any of the medical staff or primitive medical facilities associated with the prison. Given both the contemporary fascination with bodily suffering and the innovation that hospitals represented during the Civil War, the absence of any photograph of the medical facilities at Andersonville is conspicuous. Like the prison pen, the hospital was one of the most significant institutional innovations of the conflict. Just as the military officers created the modern prison camp, medical specialists responsible for the care of soldiers invented the modern American hospital. Photographers recognized the novelty and promise of these new

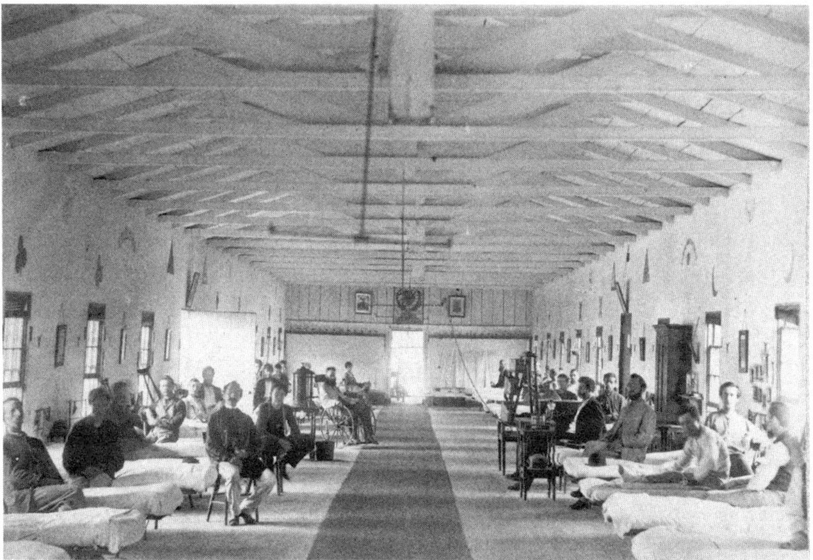

The Armory Square Hospital in Washington, D.C., exemplified the well-lighted, open design of the best military hospitals during the war. (Library of Congress)

facilities and recorded scenes of doctors at work in field hospitals, rows of convalescing soldiers in well-ordered hospital wards, and amputees modeling prosthetic limbs.

The facilities at Andersonville, however, inspired only disgust and horror. A month after Riddle's visit, Dr. Joseph Jones, a surgeon in the Confederate army, toured the camp while investigating the diseases that afflicted Union prisoners there. In his lengthy report, Jones compiled a harrowing catalog of the prison's sanitary and medical shortcomings. Each day thousands of prisoners gathered in the sick call enclosure at the South Gate of the stockade. When Riddle visited the prison, the number of sick there totaled around two thousand—roughly the same number as when Jones visited weeks later. A single harried physician attended them, making snap diagnoses before assigning the most desperate cases to any spaces in the hospital recently vacated by deaths. The so-called hospital itself was a collection of shabby and porous tent flies under which several thousand sick prisoners festered on improvised bedding and, when available, straw, or, more often, the earth itself.

Riddle elected to ignore "this gigantic mass of human misery." He recorded the somber disposal of the dead but left no images of the relentless

CROWDED HOSPITAL AT ANDERSONVILLE.

Riddle elected not to photograph the Andersonville prison hospital, its staff, or its patients, leaving the site to the imagination of later artists. (Library of Congress)

work of disease on the bodies of the Union prisoners. Like some former prisoners in their postwar memoirs, Riddle may have acceded to contemporary notions of taste and common decency to justify excluding such grim images from the historical record.

More than decorum, however, likely influenced Riddle's editorial choices. He must have anticipated the likely effects that pictures of the "helpless, hopeless misery" in the Andersonville hospital would have on viewers, especially northern viewers. Images of "dejected living skeletons crying for medical aid and food," of "millions of flies" swarming over sleeping patients, and of countless "ghastly corpses with their sick glazed eyeballs staring up into vacant space" would implicate the Confederacy directly in the human toll that filled the graveyard at Andersonville. Moreover, photographs of emaciated prisoners would have substantiated already bitter northern recriminations against Confederate cruelty.

Riddle's photographs, by design or not, were a visual apologia for the conditions at Andersonville. Photographs can stimulate sympathy or, in Sontag's words, anesthetize and miniaturize experience. By rendering invisible the mailed fist of the Confederate authorities and by eliding the most intense suffering at the camp, Riddle produced photographs consonant with the dogma Confederates parroted throughout the last year of the war. Even as Andersonville was becoming synonymous with cruelty and suffering, Confederate partisans protested that the Union, and its methods of waging war, were responsible for the plight of prisoners there. In the same article that included an appeal for someone to photograph the prison camp, the editor of the *Richmond Whig* dismissed any suggestion that Confederates were responsible for the tragedy unfolding at Andersonville. "The blame of this appalling misery," he insisted, "rests on the Abolition administration, and partly, too, on the people generally of the North."

When the Civil War erupted, neither side in the conflict had anticipated building substantial facilities for the long-term warehousing of prisoners. Instead, they looked to the swapping of prisoners on the battlefield by the contending armies to ease the burden of housing and maintaining prisoners of war. But as the war dragged on and intensified, the exchange of prisoners ground to a halt. Prisoner-of-war populations in both the Union and Confederacy exploded, ensuring that custodial imprisonment on an unprecedented scale prevailed during the final two years of the war. Confederates complained that their Union foes used any pretext to halt the swapping of prisoners, with the result that the Confederacy bore the burden of maintaining as many as sixty thousand Union prisoners at a time. Thus, "all the agonies endured by these prisoners, all the bodily deaths and all the souls sent untimely to hell," the Richmond editor raged, lay at the feet of Abraham Lincoln and his secretary of war, Edwin Stanton. The editor concluded his rant with swaggering confidence: "In the eyes of God and man we are blameless."

That Riddle avoided depicting Confederate responsibility for the conditions at Andersonville is not surprising. After all, he had married into the slaveholding gentry of Georgia and cast his lot with the insurgent nation. He also was a conscripted soldier in the Confederate army. But there were other obstacles that inhibited Riddle's capacity to acknowledge Confederate complicity in the hardships endured within the Andersonville prison pen. Living in an age that extolled individual agency, at least of white men, Riddle and his contemporaries were ill prepared to apportion culpability for collective inaction or systematic indifference to misery. Far easier it was to assign responsibility to Lincoln and other enemy villains, thereby absolving Confederates of blame while affirming their moral superiority.

Riddle's photographs freeze Andersonville at the midpoint of its existence. They capture the prison pen near its ghastly zenith, but leave unrevealed how the extraordinary facility came into being. Nor did the photographs foretell the camp's future. Within two months of Riddle's visit, the threat of General William Tecumseh Sherman's advancing army prompted Confederate authorities to disperse much of Andersonville's population across the interior of the rapidly shrinking Confederacy. Many prisoners were shunted into improvised prison pens elsewhere, while yet other prisoners suffered the indescribable misfortune of being eventually returned to Andersonville, where they lingered until the end of the war.

The narrative silence of Riddle's work at Andersonville was inherent in the limitations of photography. Photographs divide time into disassociated, discrete moments that seldom render a meaningful narrative. Riddle's Andersonville portfolio shares this deficit. It preserves an inventory of the Andersonville experience but conveys almost nothing about the prison's origins or governing logic.

From the vantage point of the twenty-first century, prisoner-of-war camps may appear to be an innate feature of war. Some system of incarceration for enemy captives has been a practical necessity in most military endeavors since the early modern era. Yet if we assume that prisoner-of-war camps are a fact of war, we overlook the innovation that the Civil War camps represented. The Civil War prison pens were not the product of a gradual evolution. Instead, they emerged abruptly and with few immediate antecedents. As the editor of the *Richmond Whig* declared, a scene like Andersonville "was never before seen on earth."

As few other historical artifacts can, Riddle's images of Andersonville prompt questions about the circumstances and beliefs that suddenly made the custodial imprisonment of huge numbers of prisoners of war acceptable. What combination of institutional authority and procedures eroded the moral inhibitions of officials, commanders, and camp staff, thereby making it easier for them to abandon the responsibility they otherwise might have felt to ease the suffering of the fellow humans who populated Riddle's photographs? Riddle's enduring achievement has been to ensure that these crucial questions about Andersonville will be pondered whenever anyone encounters his images.

Why, more than a century and a half later, should the experiences of prisoners of war during the Civil War concern us?

The fate of prisoners of war was of far greater significance to the course of the Civil War than is commonly understood. Although at the outset prisoners were an afterthought, Union and Confederate leaders soon recognized that the status of prisoners of war was bound up with the central issues of the conflict. The Lincoln administration concluded that it could not ignore the plight of prisoners of war even if negotiations with the Confederacy complicated the Union's efforts to deprive the Confederacy of international recognition as a lawful belligerent, which would have been a severe blow to the Union's prospects for victory. Within the first year of the war, prisoners glimpsed the war's grim future. As the war dragged on and intensified, both sides repeatedly targeted prisoners for collective retaliation. During the second year of the war, when the destruction of the institution of slavery became an explicit war aim for the Union, Black prisoners of war became a flashpoint that starkly divided the warring sides. The resulting impasse hastened the creation of the largest prison camps in the nation's history. By 1863, the predicament of prisoners of war was so pressing that it was a catalyst for the nation's first formal codification of the laws of war, a benchmark in international law. During the final year of the war, the Lincoln administration's policies regarding prisoners of war threatened to become a major political liability. At the same time, the conditions in Andersonville and other prison camps were milestones in dehumanization wrought in the name of military necessity.

The creation and operation of Andersonville and other prison pens underscore that neither side's conduct of the war, and least of all their prison camps, can be understood in isolation. The prison systems of the Union and Confederacy certainly had important differences. No Union camps resembled Andersonville and, by any reasonable measure, Confederate prisoners were better kept than their Union counterparts. Yet in important regards the two sides' prison policies shared important similarities. Like two warriors grappling hand to hand, the Union and Confederacy each responded to and retaliated against the other in a violent choreography. Officials on both sides offered similar rationales and justifications for the prison camps they created. Each side constantly calibrated its policies in a cycle of emulation and retaliation. The innovation of the prison camps was borne of this collaboration. To understand Andersonville, then, we must also understand such Union prisons as Point Lookout.

Prisoner-of-war camps are commonly overlooked in the tally of the most significant innovations during the Civil War. Other innovations are readily acknowledged: a national income tax, national monetary controls, national military conscription, a national welfare agency for the formerly enslaved, and a national definition of citizenship. Close students of the war have identified other milestones in modern warfare during the conflict. Nearly a century ago, the British colonel J. F. C. Fuller declared that "the civil war in America was the first of the great modern wars." The conflict, he explained, was unlike earlier wars and was a watershed in world history. The weapons employed, the scale of mass mobilization, the use of modern technologies, and the intensity of the war, so the argument goes, presaged the unprecedented destructiveness of twentieth-century warfare.

Other observers counter that the Civil War sparked no significant innovation in military technique or technology. The rifle, railways, and telegraph had already featured in the Crimean War eight years before the bombardment of Fort Sumter. Nor did the size of Civil War armies pose any new problems of scale: nearly 300,000 soldiers clashed on the battlefield at Wagram, Austria, a half century before 166,000 Americans fought at Gettysburg. To claim that Union generals, especially William Sherman and Philip Sheridan, pioneered the "total war" of the twentieth century with their scorched-earth strategies exaggerates their prescience. When Sherman led his army across Georgia on his notorious March to the Sea, he was not innovating new methods of terror. His aim "was to end the war, not to intensify it."

Whether we conclude that the Civil War was the last Napoleonic or the first "modern" war should not obscure the innovation of the prison camps, which introduced to American soil imprisonment on a scale previously unimagined. Had the great sectional contest ended in 1861 or 1862, prisoner-of-war camps would have been a footnote in its history. But thereafter, the warring sides created prisoner-of-war camps that would have successors in every major war during the next century.

The creators of Andersonville and Point Lookout almost certainly did not perceive that they were pioneering the modern prisoner-of-war camp. In subsequent decades, the innovation of custodial camps was replicated by many of the world's most powerful states to advance their interests and augment their power. Confinement on such a grand scale entailed logistical and administrative demands that hitherto armies and states had seldom been prepared or willing to undertake. Whether the task at hand was to house tens of thousands of prisoners of war, to depopulate a region plagued by anticolonial insurgents, or to corral populations displaced by war, camps concentrated internees within narrowly contained enclosures in a fixed locale. Earlier in the nineteenth century, the detention of a few hundred inmates in an asylum or penitentiary was sufficient to tax the capabilities of many state bureaucracies. The Union and Confederacy demonstrated that internment on a massive scale was now not only imaginable but also feasible.

The camps warrant attention for the role they played in the evolution of late-nineteenth- and early-twentieth-century restraints on armed conflict. The Union's codification of the laws of war in 1863 provided, in the words of one historian, "the quarry from which all subsequent codes" for the rules of war "were cut." When the Union subsequently prosecuted several Confederates for their mistreatment of prisoners of war, an important precedent in the punishment of violations of the laws of war was established.

For too long, the prison camps have been explained as products of expediency and improvisation. Let it be clear, Andersonville and the other camps were the product of design and resolve. Men, not events, made Andersonville. The creators of the Civil War prison camps were not like so much historical flotsam borne along by events that they could not control. Nor were the prison pens the spontaneous adaptation of existing institutions. To create the camps, Union and Confederate officials had to innovate and marshal prodigious quantities of manpower, technology, and resources.

The camps were also the consequence of the principles espoused by the warring sides. By the late summer of 1862 the Union was waging war in the service of both a hard-edged nationalism and a humanitarian crusade to end slavery. When the emancipation of the enslaved became a Union goal, any likelihood of a compromise peace evaporated. The subsequent recruitment of regiments of Black soldiers by the Union was deemed such an existential threat to the institution of slavery and the foundations of white southern civilization that Confederate officials refused to exchange Black union soldiers. Even after the consequences of their stance became clear, Confederates did not budge. Instead, they devoted precious manpower and resources to maintaining a sprawling complex of prisoner-of-war camps and transporting captives back and forth across the Confederacy. The Lincoln administration likewise refused to budge from its position that the abolition of slavery was irrevocable and that all prisoners of war, regardless of race, must be exchanged. With their heels dug in, the two sides became custodians for more than one hundred thousand prisoners.

Captivity in Andersonville, Point Lookout, and the other camps marked a generation of Americans in ways that we have barely recognized. The prisoners themselves understood that they were subjected to an unprecedented ordeal and left an uncommonly full and eloquent record of it. Seldom do ordinary people undergo an experience as profoundly unfamiliar and bewildering as that endured by the prisoners who marched through the stockade gate at Andersonville or boarded a boxcar bound for an unknown prison pen hundreds of miles distant. In diaries and letters, many who died in the camps and even more who survived them left poignant accounts of ordinary people under extreme duress. These prison-camp scribes were close observers of their postage-stamp-sized world, recognizing in themselves and in their comrades glaring foibles as well as quiet acts of courage, tenacity, and self-abnegation.

Just how singular were their experiences has become clear during the past century. Neither before nor since have as many Americans been captured and imprisoned during wartime. During the Civil War, an estimated 194,000 Union soldiers and 214,000 Confederate soldiers became prisoners of war. A cautious estimate is that at least half of them endured extended imprisonment. The disparity between the number of prisoners of war during the Civil War and subsequent wars is stark. The number of Union prisoners who entered the stockade gate at Andersonville during a single month in the summer of 1864 far exceeded the total number of Americans captured during the entirety of World War I. Only during World War II did the number of Americans held in captivity—124,000—begin to approach the number of prisoners during the Civil War. Even so, the odds of being captured during World War II were roughly one in a hundred; during the Civil War, they were one in five. Had the tens of thousands of former Union prisoners who returned to civilian life in 1865 after stints in Andersonville and other camps settled in one spot, they would have created a city with a population equivalent to Chicago in 1860, the nation's ninth most populous city.

Americans have been reticent to acknowledge the prison camps of the Civil War or the precedent they established. Since the war Americans have typically dwelled on feats of battlefield valor. Gettysburg and other sites of major engagements remain the focal point of the nation's commemoration of the conflict. Yet almost as many Union soldiers died in the six-acre prison in Salisbury, North Carolina, as at Gettysburg, the bloodiest battle of the war. Within the twenty-plus-acre stockade at Andersonville nearly 14,000 Union soldiers—more than three times the number of Union fatalities at Gettysburg—took their last breaths.

We understandably have sought confirmation, to borrow Abraham Lincoln's evocative phrase, that "the better angels of our nature" were at work during the Civil War. Stories of surprising acts of civility on the battlefield, of soldiers risking harm to share water with enemy wounded, and of gestures of kindness toward civilians by invading enemy armies have found a secure place in the war's lore. Equally deserving of a place in our national memory are the acts of selflessness and human dignity elicited by the conflict's prison pens. Indeed, nowhere during the Civil War was the juxtaposition between our "better angels" and our capacity for brutality and callousness starker than in the prison camps. Such was the conclusion of George R. Crosby, a Vermont infantryman who had been steeled by three years under arms before he was hustled into the Andersonville stockade. Drawing lessons from his war experiences, Crosby dwelled on his ongoing captivity at Andersonville, because "here is where I can see human nature in its true light."

CHAPTER TWO

# In Accordance with the Customs of War

## (49 BCE–1862)

Colonel John Pegram of the Twentieth Virginia Infantry surrendered to the dictates of a portrait photographer in January 1862. Careful staging presented him as unreproachable. The pillar prop and artfully draped curtain on his right replicated fine-art portraiture, bestowing a measure of grandeur to the scene. Wearing a double-breasted gray frock coat, lustrously polished boots, and buttoned black gloves, Pegram leaned with his right forearm against a shoulder-high faux marble column. His hair was meticulously parted, his mustache and beard carefully groomed. He stared into the camera lens, his stance at ease yet suggesting a latent dynamism. Together with his immaculate uniform and resolute gaze, his posture conveyed confidence and distinction. Pegram, the portrait signaled, possessed the innate authority to compel subordination. No hint of disgrace or defeat was evident. Yet the portrait captured the likeness of a prisoner of war.

Pegram had been a prisoner for six months when he posed for David Bendann, the most renowned photographer in Baltimore. Little of the confidence displayed in the portrait studio had been evident when Pegram had suffered the ignoble distinction in July 1861 of being one of the first Confederate officers to surrender.

Pegram's nine months of captivity, from July 1861 to April 1862, would have been unrecognizable to the beleaguered men whom Andrew Riddle photographed two years later at Andersonville. At no time during his captivity did Pegram endure the harsh dehumanization experienced by prisoners

Colonel John Pegram, the captive, posing in Baltimore in January 1862. (Library of Congress)

later in the war. Instead, he passed through the crucible of captivity with his pride undiminished, his appetite sated, and his dress uniform spotless.

Pegram's imprisonment was in keeping with protocols for the treatment of prisoners of war that predated the American republic. Many assumed these traditions would prevail throughout the Civil War. But the policies that made it possible for Pegram to preen before the camera while in captivity proved too irksome and too complicated. The captivity that Pegram experienced was incompatible with modern warfare.

During the weeks following the shelling of Fort Sumter, Pegram had been eager for a commission in the Confederate army. Important campaigns were under way in the crenellated depths of western Virginia, so it was there that Pegram looked to distinguish himself. He and his volunteer regiment were assigned to the command of Brigadier General Robert S. Garnett, who was highly regarded and seemingly predestined for the Confederate high command. Pegram, because of his pedigree and training, also appeared fated for a lofty station. His grandfather had been a major general during the War of 1812 and his father had been a brigadier general in the Virginia militia (as well as a prominent attorney and bank president). After attending West Point, where he graduated high in his class, Pegram received a commission in the cavalry. He served at various western outposts before returning to his alma mater as a cavalry instructor. Now, after resigning his commission and offering his services to the Confederacy, he was in command of the Twentieth Virginia Infantry preparing, with the rest of Garnett's forces, to repel Union troops led by Major General George B. McClellan.

Pegram had barely established his new command astride a road carved through an important pass on Rich Mountain when, on July 9, McClellan's army moved against his position. Displaying few of the leadership skills an officer with his experience and training was assumed to possess, Pegram allowed his troops to be flanked. Cut off from the main Confederate force, uncertain of the location of the enemy, and lost in the mountains, Pegram spurned his subordinates' proposals to escape and instead surrendered. When Garnett and his troops learned of Pegram's plight, they fled eastward. Within a day, Union troops overtook the Confederate rear guard and harried them during a running skirmish. A Union volley struck down Garnett, setting off a chaotic Confederate retreat. At the close of the three days of maneuvering in western Virginia, the fledgling Confederacy had lost a general and several hundred casualties and suffered the capture of Pegram and hundreds of his soldiers.

Surrender was a novel experience for the greenhorn soldiers and officers involved. Even Pegram and McClellan, both West Point–trained army veterans, had little familiarity with the intricacies of surrender. To navigate the unfamiliar rite, both men drew upon the military and social etiquette they had acquired as students at West Point and through their privileged station in life. Fluent in the gentlemanly manners of their age, they understood the importance of attention to the smallest details. It was those niceties that guided the two officers.

Pegram's opening gambit was an appeal to Union chivalry. The Confederate officer explained that compassion for his men, who were in a "jaded and reduced condition" after going without food for two days, compelled him to surrender. His soldiers were men of valor who warranted respect even though they could no longer wage war. Pegram next invoked the obligation of reciprocity that undergirded both the code of gentlemanly conduct and the traditions of military surrender. "I trust," he wrote, "they will only receive at your hands such treatment as has been invariably shown to the

Northern prisoners by the South." Anything less, Pegram insinuated, would besmirch the Union cause and McClellan's own reputation.

McClellan, in turn, demonstrated that he understood what the circumstances demanded of him. He affirmed that he would treat his captives with kindness. On that basis, Pegram and 555 of his men marched to Beverly, the nearest village, where they staked their arms and surrendered to a tiny force of two dozen Union soldiers. Hours later, McClellan reached the hamlet and promptly ordered the prisoners to be placed in comfortable quarters and provided with rations. He granted permission to Pegram and the other captured officers to move about freely and to domicile in private homes.

Unsure of what to do with the first substantial number of Confederate prisoners captured in the eastern theater, McClellan requested guidance from Washington. General Winfield Scott, the senior Union commander, responded that Pegram and any other captured officers who had resigned commissions in the U.S. army should be sent to Fort McHenry in Baltimore harbor. The rest were to be paroled; in other words, they should pledge to refrain from any further service in the Confederate army until they were formally released from their parole ("exchanged") for an equivalent number of Union prisoners held by the Confederacy.

In a letter to the commander of Confederate forces in western Virginia, McClellan drew attention to his punctilious treatment of his captives. He explained the parole policy for soldiers and noncommissioned officers. The paroled prisoners would be provided with wagons, draft animals, and rations for their journey to Confederate lines. "In the meantime," McClellan reassured his Confederate counterpart, "their friends may rest assured that every attention will be paid to them." Acknowledging "the unhappy fate" of the late General Garnett, McClellan reported that his body had been preserved in ice and his family could retrieve it at their convenience.

Flush with victory and keen to establish a reputation for magnanimity, McClellan closed his letter with a flourish. He vowed "to do all in my power to alleviate the miseries of the war." He continued, "It is my intention to render the condition of prisoners and wounded as little oppressive and miserable as possible." (A year later, McClellan would moralize to President Lincoln that the war "should be conducted upon the highest principles known to Christian Civilization.") Like Pegram, McClellan invoked reciprocity: "I trust that I shall be met in the same spirit, and this contest shall remain free from the usual horrible features of civil war." Having obliged his Confederate interlocutors to match his chivalry, he boasted to his wife, "The prisoners are beyond measure astonished at my humanity towards them."

Pegram experienced firsthand McClellan's solicitude. Illness delayed his transfer to Fort McHenry, so for several weeks he convalesced in a private home (which coincidentally belonged to the sister of one of McClellan's West Point classmates). While there, McClellan called on him to monitor his recovery and chat about the campaign. By the time Pegram was sufficiently recuperated to travel to Baltimore, the troops who had been captured with him had already been paroled and returned to Confederate lines.

Pegram continued to receive compassionate treatment after his transfer to Fort McHenry. His stint there was brief because the fort was wholly inadequate as a prison. Within days of his arrival he was again transferred, this time to Fort Columbus, located on Governors Island off the tip of Manhattan. There he joined seven hundred other prisoners. This fort, too, was ill suited to serve as a prison. Recognizing the facility's shortcomings, the commanding officer granted prisoners myriad privileges. For instance, they were permitted to wander Governors Island at will once they pledged to refrain from escaping. They could receive packages and money from family and friends. Some prisoners still found conditions intolerable and lobbied to hire civilians to shop for them, prepare their food, and clean their rooms.

Scrambling to find appropriate facilities to house the mounting number of prisoners sent north, Union authorities shuttled Pegram to yet another facility. On October 27 he and nearly eight hundred prisoners departed by ship for Fort Warren, a larger bastion in Boston harbor. The staff there expected approximately one hundred prisoners and were unprepared for the number that disembarked several days later. With food, bedding, and furniture in short supply, prisoners had to rough it, sleeping on the floor and eating spartan rations. Within days, a coordinated campaign by Boston donors alleviated most of these hardships.

Pegram fared well in his new prison home, where accommodations and privileges were distributed based on military rank and social standing. Along with nine other prominent prisoners, he occupied a large, well-lighted, and airy room that faced the fort's parade ground. Dissatisfied with the austere decor in their cell, they purchased beds, rugs, and other furnishings from Boston merchants. Their daily comforts were attended to by a fellow prisoner, a North Carolina private, who, according to one of Pegram's roommates, made the fire and beds, cleaned the room, polished boots, and made "himself generally useful, particularly when he is looked after and kept up to his work."

Pegram's comforts at Fort Warren included his prison fare. Three times a week, he and other prisoners received fresh beef with potatoes, salt beef, pork, or ham. Baked beans were served on Sunday. Each prisoner also received twenty-two ounces of bread per day, as well as ample tea and coffee. Pegram and his cellmates, however, deemed these rations unappealing. They contracted with a caterer in Boston to provide them with more epicurean fare. Wine, brandy, whiskey, and delicacies sent by family and friends supplemented their catered meals. Within weeks of their arrival at the fort, one of Pegram's roommates gloated in his diary, "Our mess continues to improve; fare now equal to any of the hotels; only trouble is I eat too much for so little exercise."

Aside from a periodic obligation to wait on the mess table in his quarters, Pegram devoted his days in captivity to strolling the island's twenty-eight acres, chatting with fellow prisoners, and reading newspapers. He and his cell mates feasted on elaborate dinners at six; one meal included "roast turkies [sic], roast and boiled mutton, roast beef and lobster salad, and dessert of nuts of several kinds, fresh peaches in cans, honey and coffee." Then they played backgammon, read books, wrote letters, and sang. A routine evening, according to one of his roommates, concluded with a shared pitcher of hot whiskey punch, "which we sip until eleven" while Pegram, a teetotaler, played "very fine music" on the guitar.

Prisoners in the ranks endured less elegant accommodations and refined diversions while at Fort Warren. Lacking the private means enjoyed by Pegram and his ilk, most enlisted men subsisted on prison rations and shared tight quarters. They made do with crude furniture and suffered the chill of inadequately heated rooms. Yet, whatever hardships they underwent, the conditions of their imprisonment were healthful. During the two months that Pegram spent at Fort Warren, five prisoners died. During the remainder of the war, only eight more of the two thousand prisoners captive there would die.

On New Year's Eve 1861, Pegram was paroled from Fort Warren on the condition that he not rejoin the Confederate army until he was "exchanged" for a Union officer of equivalent rank. Only then would Pegram be free to take up arms again. "Dressed as a tourist with a small leather bag over his shoulder" and without an escort, he made his way south by way of New York City. After a brief sojourn there, his next stop was Baltimore, where he took up residence at Barnum's Hotel, one of the most fashionable hotels in the country and a favorite of Charles Dickens and other celebrities. While in the city Pegram sat for his portrait. Then, after a brief trip to Washington, D.C., to iron out the details of his future exchange, he traveled by ship to Fortress Monroe, at the tip of the Virginia Peninsula. There he finally crossed Confederate lines, his journey ending in Richmond.

While awaiting exchange, Pegram threw himself into the social whirl of the Confederate capital, attending formal dances and dinners. Finally, on April 2, the Union officer for whom he was to be exchanged completed his plodding journey from captivity in Texas to Fortress Monroe. With that man restored to Union hands, Pegram's captivity—six months of imprisonment and three months of parole—came to an end.

Pegram's stint as a prisoner was a snapshot of captivity during the early months of the war. Civility was manifest at each stage of his imprisonment. After the proper display of etiquette during the surrender, his Union captors scrupulously respected his status as an officer and a gentleman even as they moved him from prison to prison. Although he was deprived of freedom of movement and provided with only a modicum of comfort, he enjoyed privileges that alleviated much of the discomfort of captivity. He took every opportunity to use his own resources to improve his circumstances.

Most important, he was the recipient of a parole, a privilege that rested on the principle that soldiers—men of honor—would abide by agreement that they affirmed by oath. He also was the beneficiary of an exchange for a prisoner held by the enemy, which ensured that his captivity did not last the length of the war. Taken together, his experiences explain how he, a prisoner of war after nearly six months of captivity, could display such confidence, even hauteur, while posing for his portrait in 1862.

Pegram's experience to the contrary, the predicament of prisoners of war is usually dire. From the moment of capture, prisoners are no longer masters of their own fate but instead are subject to the whims of others. For captors, prisoners of war almost always are an infernal inconvenience. They must be disarmed, guarded, fed, and housed, all while the captors' side continues to conduct military operations. These responsibilities weigh heavily; provisioning one's own soldiers is taxing without assuming the additional burden of prisoners.

Throughout much of recorded history, captors performed a simple calculation. Were prisoners of war best dead? Or alive and exploited in some fashion? Prior to the eighteenth century, almost no armies had any interest, let alone the capacity, to take on the responsibility of harboring prisoners of war for extended periods of time. To avoid these complications, combatants from the ancient Egyptians to medieval Europeans typically massacred, enslaved, or ransomed their prisoners.

The number of prisoners condemned to summary death during premodern conflicts was sometimes staggering. When the Romans seized the town of Uspe in the Crimea in 49 BCE, they killed all their ten thousand captives because it would have been a nuisance to guard them. Eight centuries later, Charlemagne's troops dispatched more than four thousand unarmed Saxon prisoners at Verden. In 1415, after the Battle of Agincourt, Henry V ordered the killing of thousands of prisoners. In these and countless other instances, only the comparatively small size of most premodern armies prevented butchery of prisoners on an even greater scale. Such massacres seldom elicited criticism. To the contrary, Raymond of Aguilers, a chronicler of the First Crusade, thrilled at the "wonderful sight" of an aqueduct that was choked with the corpses of Muslim prisoners. Shakespeare immortalized Henry V's slaughter.

The main incentive to preserve the lives of prisoners was their potential economic value. Soldiers readily adopted the practice endorsed by the Roman poet Horace: "Once captured don't kill him, if you can sell him." Where slavery was practiced, conquering armies avoided the expense of maintaining prisoners and instead reaped profits from their sale. This practice persisted until the late Middle Ages, when Christian clerics grew intolerant of the enslaving of Christian prisoners of war. (Church leaders displayed fewer qualms about enslaving heathens and pagans.)

The ransoming of captives thereafter provided the chief motivation to spare prisoners of war. Writing during the late seventeenth century, the English jurist Charles Molloy noted this evolution: "Prisoners taken in War do not become perfect Slaves, as of old, but only remain in the Custody of the Captor, till Ransoms are paid." The law of plunder governed the status of prisoners, who were considered spoils of war.

The motivation to spare the life of a captive was in direct proportion to his capacity to pay a lucrative ransom. A captive king like John II of France, whom the English captured during the Hundred Years War, was valued at the huge sum of three million gold crowns (roughly seven billion present-day dollars). An archer, in contrast, was worth a comparatively modest sum equivalent to about two thousand dollars. The conditions of captivity for prisoners awaiting ransom, similarly, varied according to their station in life. While captive, King John lived in a palace and maintained a lavish lifestyle, including the services of his favorite jester, an astrologer, and a court orchestra. Prisoners of lesser means scrounged for funds to buy necessities while they awaited release. The alchemy of ransoming that turned some captives into money, however, could do nothing with prisoners unable to purchase their freedom. These, who were often from the lowest ranks, had the slimmest prospects of surviving captivity. Their best option was to switch sides and join their captor's army.

While ransoming encouraged the preservation of the lives of some captives, it also animated behavior that confounded sovereigns and commanders. It incited soldiers to become incorrigibly entrepreneurial. To capture and ransom a nobleman could transform a common soldier's life. Robert Sadeler, an English archer, captured Erdrad Droyle, a French noble, at Agincourt. Droyle's subsequent ransom netted Sadeler the equivalent of twelve thousand present-day dollars. Such a sum provided a powerful spur for soldiers on the battlefield to pursue captives to the exclusion of other military priorities. Vexed by his troops' insatiable profiteering, Bertrand du Guesclin, a Breton knight during the Hundred Years War, vowed "to put an end to quarrels among his troops over the ownership of prisoners" by summarily executing all captives. Simultaneously, the prospect of being extorted for onerous ransoms led some nobles in surrendering armies to humiliate themselves. After Agincourt, Anthony of Burgundy, Duke of Brabant, made the fateful decision to hide his lofty status by donning the armor of one of his subordinates. His ruse failed dismally. He and hundreds of other prisoners who had no evident ransom value were swiftly executed.

Ransoming was one among many features of warfare that jurists and intellectuals in early modern Europe sought to reform. With increasing zeal after the seventeenth century, they contended that war should be tamed. They advocated that warfare be waged exclusively by states and professional armies, rather than as an extension of private grievances. Hugo Grotius, the seventeenth century's foremost authority on international law, urged states to abide by formal rules in international statecraft and warfare, including regarding prisoners of war. Captives, he proposed, should no longer be treated as the private property of their captors. Nor should they be punished for the actions of their sovereigns. Along with women, children, clergy, and the elderly, prisoners were to be protected from the horrors of unbounded warfare.

The Swiss jurist Emmerich von Vattel, Grotius's eighteenth-century successor as the preeminent interpreter of international law, refined the emerging precepts regarding the treatment of prisoners. Combatants, he proclaimed, were enemies only so long as they were waging war: "As soon as your enemy has laid down his arms and surrendered his body, you have no longer any right over his life." Once secured, a prisoner was to be treated humanely. While a warring state might demand compensation for the maintenance of prisoners, the old practice of ransoming individual prisoners was contrary to reason and justice. Vattel conceded that military necessity might justify the long-term retention of prisoners, but otherwise warring states should return prisoners of war to the enemy as quickly as possible.

Practical considerations encouraged the adoption of these precepts during the seventeenth and eighteenth centuries. Europe's rulers recognized that the lives of combatants were valuable during an age when states struggled to muster ever more skilled armies. With each passing decade, fractious armies of disposable hirelings motivated by booty and money gave way to permanent forces of disciplined soldiers commanded by professional officers. Warring states could ill afford to turn a blind eye to their soldiers who fell into enemy hands, especially on the scale that became common during the eighteenth century. French armies, for example, lost fourteen thousand prisoners at the Battle of Blenheim (1704). During the Second Silesian War (1744–1745) Prussia captured more than forty-five thousand Austrians and Saxons. Preventing the slaughter of surrendered soldiers and obtaining their release so that they could again wage war was imperative.

This confluence of developments in military practice and the laws of war go far to explain why the wars of the eighteenth century in Europe rank among the least horrific in the continent's history. The treatment of prisoners of war became one conspicuous measure of a nation's ascent up the ladder of civilization. By the middle of the eighteenth century, many commanders had at least a rudimentary familiarity with the ascendant laws of war, and all European powers felt a need to justify their conduct by reference to them. An army now had to be a conscientious custodian of any enemy soldiers in its hands, in order to protect its own soldiers who were prisoners of war. To treat enemy soldiers as well as or better than one's own was to secure the moral high ground while simultaneously encouraging the enemy to reciprocate humane treatment of its captives. If the enemy failed to treat its prisoners benevolently, reprisals, calibrated according to *lex talionis* (i.e., an eye for an eye), were justified.

Early modern military leaders had no more interest in tending captives than had their predecessors. Instead, triumphant armies during the eighteenth century typically either released prisoners on parole or held them until subsequent exchanges of prisoners took place. Rank-and-file prisoners awaiting exchange were consigned to ramshackle, catch-all facilities. In an era punctuated by frequent wars, states could not easily predict when hostilities might break out or how many prisoners they might have to accommodate. Hence, they repeatedly were caught by surprise and had to improvise prison facilities. Tight budgets further discouraged warring nations from investing in permanent sites to accommodate prisoners. Derelict churches, stables, barns, castles, mansions, barracks, hospitals, and decommissioned ships were impressed into service to house prisoners.

Captive officers, meanwhile, were typically granted parole in a location determined by their captor. This privilege had its origins in the earlier practice of allowing prisoners of rank to return to their own countries to raise their ransoms. The sanctity of personal oaths undergirded the entire system of parole. When a parolee gave his word of honor, he forged a solemn bond between himself and the official who accepted his oath. To violate his oath was to blacken his reputation, as well as to discredit the ruler whom he served. This system of parole, in effect, turned each prisoner into his own prison guard.

After signing a parole certificate, prisoners received a letter of protection and traveled on their own to a designated parole town. On reaching their destination, they were free to circulate within a stipulated range. Supplied with subsistence money proportional to their military rank, they were responsible for securing their own lodging and sustenance.

Once settled, paroled prisoners often blended into their host communities. French prisoners held in Britain during the Seven Years War and the Napoleonic Wars, for instance, displayed impressive habits of industry. They supplemented their parole allowances by making and selling hats, gloves, pipes, jewelry, wooden toys, and elaborate ornamental carvings. Others taught dancing, music, drawing, or languages. They opened theater companies, cafés, billiard rooms, and clubs that catered to both fellow prisoners and the wider community. Meanwhile, British prisoners paroled at Verdun in France attended horse races, joined subscription lending libraries, and patronized brothels.

Parole, in theory, was a temporary status for prisoners until they could be swapped with the enemy. Orderly prisoner exchanges, in which states took control of the process of exchanging prisoners, were a sixteenth-century innovation. Thereafter, warring states with increasing regularity entered so-called cartels that specified how prisoners of war would be treated, paroled, and exchanged. Ideally, exchanges were to be general (i.e., they would include all prisoners). To address the inevitable imbalances in the number of prisoners held by the respective sides, combatants typically agreed to quotas to redeem prisoners of differing ranks. Thus, a general might be exchanged for so many colonels, and a lieutenant for so many common soldiers. For instance, when the British general John Burgoyne was captured during the American Revolution, he was exchanged for 1047 privates.

These elaborate protocols brought a measure of order to the messy business of prisoners of war. When conflicts were brief and waged within a small area, negotiated paroles and exchanges worked comparatively well. The chaotic nature of warfare sometimes hindered accurate recordkeeping and prompt sharing of information about prisoners. Likewise, the mechanics of exchanging prisoners could be daunting. With eighteenth-century warfare taking place across Europe and far beyond, paroles and exchanges had to be conducted on a global scale. Inevitable complications slowed the exchange of prisoners, condemning some captives to lengthy imprisonment. Nevertheless, the system of cartels, paroles, and exchanges enabled European states to cope with large numbers of prisoners of war who were no longer consigned to a fate of execution, slavery, or ransom.

In these innovations, which had been widely honored for more than a century before the start of the American Civil War, can be discerned the principles that shaped the captivity experienced by John Pegram.

The formalities of war might have remained exotic curiosities to colonists in British North America had they not become swept up in imperial contests during the eighteenth century. On the far-flung fringes of European civilization and against purportedly merciless Indian foes, Europeans waged war restrained only, if at all, by their consciences. For European colonists in British North America, captivity in the hands of Indians, rather than of imperial foes, loomed largest in their fears. In the small-scale contests against Indians, Europeans did not acknowledge the customary laws of war, which applied only in conflicts between "civilized" combatants who abided by them.

Not until the Seven Years War (1756–1763) did European conventions for dealing with prisoners of war become relevant to colonial circumstances. The disposition of prisoners after the French capture of Fort Oswego in 1756 was an early application of European protocols in the North American wilderness. With sizable British and French armies facing off in North America for the first time, French and British officers pledged to wage war according to European conventions. After General Louis-Joseph de Montcalm and his troops overwhelmed the New York fort, he determined to retain the roughly fifteen hundred British and American captives as prisoners of war until they could be exchanged. He assumed responsibility to feed, clothe, and house his captives while restraining his Indian allies from enslaving or slaughtering them. Because the British had no French prisoners at that time, the captives could not be swapped promptly. With no community in French Canada having sufficient resources to house them, the prisoners were loaded on ships in Quebec and transported to Europe. Some were paroled in England, while the rest traveled to France to await exchange. Not until 1758 were the last of the prisoners returned to and freed in North America.

The widely recounted odyssey of the Oswego prisoners and other captives during the Seven Years War familiarized American colonists with some of the intricacies of the modern laws of war. Veterans of the war, including George Washington, gained firsthand knowledge of the finer points of surrender and the treatment of prisoners of war while they were both captives and captors at various times during the conflict. Washington himself commanded an Anglo-American force that surrendered to the French in July 1754. In keeping with the etiquette that prevailed in Europe, the French allowed Washington and his troops to return to Virginia without being formally taken prisoner and with their regimental flags flying. The French granted these generous terms to demonstrate to their defeated foes that "we treat them as Friends." Away from the front lines, Benjamin Franklin, Thomas Jefferson, and other well-read colonists displayed a new interest in the writings of Grotius, Vattel, and other scholars of the law of nations. Their interest only intensified when they began contemplating an independent American republic as the rightful successor to Britain's North American empire.

Acutely conscious of the need to establish the legitimacy of any republic they founded, the revolutionaries pledged that the new nation would conduct itself according to European-derived laws of nations. Citing the authority of Vattel, Americans insisted that all nations, like all men, were created equal and possessed equal rights. Only the law of nations could deter the exaggerated claims and unchecked aggression of an overweening power like the British empire. From the Declaration of Independence onward, revolutionaries tirelessly asserted the new republic's standing as a sovereign member of the community of nations. But while the rebellious colonists labored to turn a civil war within the British empire into a legitimate war between two states under the law of nations, British authorities were equally resolute to define it as an illegitimate insurrection.

This glaring discrepancy over the legitimacy of the rebellion had grim consequences for the prisoners whom both sides began collecting in 1775. Recalling practice during the Seven Years War and touting the law of nations, the American revolutionaries assumed that British authorities would consent to conventional treatment for any colonials they captured. Imperial authorities, however, looked to British civil law to determine the fate of defiant colonists.

For Ethan Allen, who was one of the earliest heroes *and* prisoners of the Revolution, the contest over prisoners translated into several years of harsh and unpredictable captivity. His plight, which he publicized in an account that went through more than twenty printings after it first appeared in 1778, highlighted the contrast between British and American policies toward prisoners of war, as well as the British disregard for civilized norms. To Allen and his compatriots, the contrast was stark. Despite being menaced by the most powerful empire of the age, Americans waged war honorably.

On May 10, 1775, less than a month after the Battles of Lexington and Concord, Allen led a small force of militia volunteers that surprised the tiny British garrison at Fort Ticonderoga on Lake Champlain. The capture of the so-called Gibraltar of America transformed Allen into a patriot hero. It also gave him unfounded confidence in his military acumen. Four months later, while accompanying a small rebel army that invaded Quebec, he hatched an audacious notion to seize Montreal. With a force numbering fewer than a hundred, Allen led an ill-conceived foray that ended with the capture of the Hero of Ticonderoga and some thirty soldiers.

Allen's subsequent treatment by his British captors offended his dignity and, he insisted, violated the laws of war. He was hurried aboard a warship and sequestered in the lowest hold in handcuffs and leg irons. While shackled for nearly a month, he railed against the injustice of his condition, which he contrasted with the humane treatment received by the British soldiers he had captured at Fort Ticonderoga. Early in November, he was taken to Quebec City and transferred to another ship, on which he received altogether different treatment. Now regarded as an officer and a gentleman, he was quartered in the officers' cabin, ate with the officers, and moved freely about the ship.

Allen's situation worsened abruptly when he was placed on a transport

Among the indignities Ethan Allen experienced as a Revolutionary War captive was being shackled. (Bridgeman Images)

ship bound for England. With some thirty other men, Allen was tossed into a dark, noxious pen about twenty feet square that contained no furniture except two waste tubs. Small allotments of food and water were periodically thrust into the cage during the forty-day voyage. In early December, the weary captives finally reached Falmouth, where they were imprisoned in a citadel overlooking the town.

In London the Cabinet was deciding what to do with Allen. The laws of war, as interpreted by the British, did not apply to Allen's circumstances. King George III had declared Americans in arms to be traitors, thereby denying them prisoner-of-war status should they be captured. Following the lead of the king, British officials in the early months of the Revolution treated the revolutionaries they captured as rebels deserving civil punishments. The same logic explained Allen's transfer to England, where presumably he was to be punished according to British civil law.

Based on precedent, Allen and the rebels had ample cause to fear British justice. Few of the "civilizing" tendencies evident in the laws of war were apparent in British civil law during the eighteenth century. To the contrary, British law grew harsher during the era, and no crime received harsher sanction than treason. British authorities demonstrated the measures they were prepared to use to suppress rebellion when they crushed the Scottish Jacobite uprising during the 1740s. They executed many of its leaders while sending thousands more into exile. Whatever penalty they applied, the British were scrupulous to avoid any suggestion that American captives were legitimate prisoners of war or to take any steps that might recognize the sovereignty of the rebellious colonies. British vengeance, however, was tempered by the necessity of suppressing an insurrection in a distant colony. Confident that the rebellion would be swiftly resolved by military victory or negotiated settlement, British officials were wary of hanging rebels for treason. To do so risked alienating colonial public sympathy that otherwise might favor the British.

In these muddled circumstances, British officials elected to return Allen to North America and thereby postpone the resolution of his case. But if Allen and the rebels were to be neither hanged nor treated as prisoners of war, how were they to be handled? The king and his advisors declined to give clear rules of conduct toward rebel captives, effectively leaving the matter up to the discretion of local British officials. Imperial officials may not have advocated mistreatment of colonial prisoners, but their failure to impose a policy granted officers in the field the widest possible latitude to do so.

In day-to-day practice, these legal complexities and ambiguous policies translated into the dizzyingly inconsistent treatment that Allen and many other prisoners experienced. At each stage of Allen's captivity, the personal whims of his captors dictated his treatment. While imprisoned in Falmouth, he was well treated. When he subsequently was placed aboard a ship bound for British North America, his treatment worsened yet again. The ship's captain scorned him as a traitor. Upon reaching North Carolina, Allen was transferred to a ship under the command of an uncommonly abusive captain, who tormented him without respite during a six-week voyage to Halifax, Nova Scotia.

Throughout his ordeal, Allen held steadfast to his belief that the British were obligated to treat him as a legitimate prisoner of war and to exchange him for a British officer of comparable rank. While in Halifax, he wrote pleading letters to the Connecticut legislature, which had awarded him his military commission, beseeching them to negotiate his release.

General George Washington and the Continental Congress likewise looked to the treatment of prisoners of the war to demonstrate the moral superiority of the nascent republic. Washington scrupulously hewed to European methods of warfare and directed that all captives should be treated humanely. In a September 1775 letter, he proclaimed that any American soldier "so base and infamous" as to injure a prisoner should suffer "severe and exemplary punishment." The Continental Congress endorsed his policy, avowing that captives should be treated "with humanity." As reports of British persecution of Allen and other prisoners proliferated, Washington warned his British counterpart that captive British officers would experience whatever treatment Allen received. The Continental Congress concurred, announcing that any "base usage of our people" would be met with retaliation.

Escalating threats against British prisoners and the ebb and flow of American military fortunes tempered British treatment of American prisoners. The British defeat at Saratoga in October 1777, and the subsequent alliance between the revolutionary republic and France, prodded the British to alter their policies. Now, the provincial uprising resembled a traditional European war between nations. British strategists recognized that they could not punish rebel prisoners without fear of reprisals against the five thousand British captured at Saratoga. Earlier American threats now gave way to actual acts of retaliation. Worn down by the expense and aggravation of imprisoning rebels and anxious to protect comrades from American vengeance, British authorities displayed a new willingness to exchange prisoners.

The evolving British policies had direct consequences for Allen. In October 1776 he was transferred to New York and paroled first in New York City and then on Long Island. With money provided by friends and family, he obtained tolerable living quarters and began to regain his health after his harsh confinement. But in August 1777 he was arrested for violating his parole and locked up in New York City, where he spent the remaining eight months of his captivity.

While in New York City, Allen witnessed what he described as the "relentless and scientific barbarity" with which the British treated those imprisoned there. After the British elected to keep most of their prisoners in North America, New York became the preferred site for holding them. At first the British fashioned prisons out of derelict churches, warehouses, and jails, but severe overcrowding persisted. Reluctant to invest in new facilities that would be redundant as soon as the rebellion was quelled, authorities converted obsolete ships into prison hulks. These maritime jails soon became synonymous with suffering and despair. The most infamous was the *Jersey*, a former man-of-war that had been stripped down to its "old, unsightly, rotten hulk," its portholes sealed, and crude iron-barred breathing holes gouged out of its sides. Prisoners on it and the twenty-odd other hulks received meager and unwholesome rations while enduring gross overcrowding, inadequate heating and ventilation, scant sanitary facilities, and apathetic medical care.

Allen's ordeal as a prisoner of war ended in May 1778. "In a transport of joy," he was exchanged for a British officer who had experienced hardships like those Allen had borne. Indeed, the harsh treatment had been in retaliation for the perceived ill treatment meted to Allen and other American officers.

The travails of Allen and other American prisoners of war during the Revolution no longer loom large in national lore. But for the republic's founders and their children the memory of Allen's torment and of the British prison hulks in New York harbor was vivid and abiding. It was a testament to both the sacrifice made to establish the republic and a devotion to the loftiest values of modern civilization, which had been displayed not only in the nation's founding documents but also in its commendable charity toward any enemy at its mercy.

The fledgling republic's professed principles were tested during the War of 1812. Memories of British treatment of prisoners during the Revolution had been revived in the years before the conflict by the British practice of seizing American sailors and coercing them into British naval service. The war had especially far-reaching significance for many of the nation's future military leaders, none more so than Lieutenant Colonel Winfield Scott. For Scott, who was then at the start of a half-century-long military career that extended to the Civil War, captivity during the War of 1812 was a formative experience.

Following the Battle of Queenston Heights in October 1812, Scott, along with more than eight hundred other regular and militia soldiers, surrendered. As the first major engagement of the conflict, it set a precedent for the future disposition of prisoners. Unlike over a quarter century earlier, British authorities from the start of the War of 1812 routinely paroled and exchanged prisoners. Already engaged in a global war with France, the British could ill afford the distraction of a no-holds-barred conflict with the United States. Thus, after their victory at Queenston, the British paroled and sent home all the captured volunteers. Only Scott and the regulars were retained and sent on to Quebec, where they were to be held until exchanged.

Decades later Scott recalled that he and his fellow prisoners had experienced "much courtesy" from the British. Indeed, Scott would maintain lifelong friendships with two of his captors. Throughout his imprisonment,

Scott was treated with meticulous dignity; he dined with British officers and suffered no intentional humiliation, degradation, or cruelty. Within five weeks of his surrender, he and the other prisoners were paroled and placed aboard a ship bound for Boston. Soon thereafter, Scott and 21 American officers were exchanged for 3 British officers, 15 noncommissioned officers, and 141 privates. Three months after his capture, Scott returned to active duty.

The exchange of the Queenston prisoners was not without controversy. While en route to Boston, British authorities seized 25 of the American prisoners, men who had been born in Ireland and therefore were traitors in the eyes of the British. To little avail, Scott vigorously protested the refusal of the British to recognize that the men were naturalized American citizens. He reassured the identified soldiers that the republic "would not fail to look to their safety" and would "retaliate amply" if they were mistreated. Upon his return to Washington, D.C., Scott filed a complaint with the War Department on behalf of the prisoners, which prompted Congress to endorse retaliation. American authorities notified their British counterparts that twenty-odd British prisoners were being held hostage to ensure the safety of the seized Irish Americans. The British in turn placed 46 American officers in close confinement and warned that their well-being depended on the treatment of the hostages held by the Americans. Threats of retaliation mounted until the summer of 1814, when American officials received confirmation that the Irish American prisoners were treated no differently than any other prisoners in British hands.

Rather than a searing ordeal, captivity had been, in Scott's eyes, a model of the humane treatment of prisoners. In subsequent decades, as Scott rose to the highest rank in the United States army, he remained committed to conducting war along the lines that he had experienced during the War of 1812. Within months of his exchange, British and American negotiators settled on a comprehensive prisoner cartel. The chronic disorganization of the American war effort and the scale of the conflict, which stretched from the Gulf of Mexico to the far reaches of the Great Lakes, complicated compliance with the cartel. Nonetheless, treatment of prisoners of war by both sides came close to fulfilling the precepts sketched out by eighteenth-century legal visionaries.

In 1821, following the war, when Scott revised army regulations, he incorporated lessons from his own experience as well as his close observation of French and British warfare. Regarding prisoners of war, Scott par-

Winfield Scott comforts Irish Americans captured by the British during the War of 1812. (From Edward D. Mansfield's *Life and Services of General Winfield Scott*, 1854)

roted Vattel, proclaiming that prisoners "are under the safeguard of the national faith and honour." They should be "treated at all times with every indulgence not inconsistent with their safe-keeping."

Scott subsequently had an opportunity to translate these principles into practice. During the war with Mexico (1846–1848) he and General Zachary Taylor commanded the invasion of the Mexican heartland. Scott and Taylor showed no pity toward Mexican guerrillas they encountered but treated Mexican regular soldiers as legitimate combatants. Confronted with the challenge of holding prisoners while occupying foreign soil, both generals elected to parole thousands of captured Mexican soldiers on the battlefield. The day after the Battle of Cerro Gordo in April 1847, for instance, Scott paroled more than three thousand prisoners. His justification was straightforward: "I have not the means of feeding them here." A small number of captured officers were held in the United States, but otherwise Americans granted paroles so promptly and uniformly that they took no pains to compile accurate tallies of their numbers. The Mexican army, meanwhile, captured comparatively few Americans, whom they treated with exemplary care. Indeed, Scott insisted the gravest threat to the propriety and orderliness of the conflict came not from Mexicans but from American volunteer soldiers.

Although Scott conducted the war against Mexico in accord with his notion of civilized warfare, he failed to persuade his subordinates that they should apply the same rules when they fought indigenous Americans. Many officers and soldiers distinguished between the "civilized" warfare they conducted and the allegedly savage warfare waged by Indians. As in the past, this rationale absolved whites of the responsibility to treat Indian captives and noncombatants humanely. Indian allies of the British had not been covered by the cartel with the British during the War of 1812. Commanders were under no obligation to accept Indian surrenders. Consequently, at the end of the Battle of Horseshoe Bend in 1814, General Andrew Jackson and his troops methodically killed roughly eight hundred of the thousand Red Stick warriors whom they had defeated in the battle. (When the slaughter subsided, troops conducted a systematic body count by cutting off the tips of the noses of the slain Indians.)

Scott briefly and unsuccessfully applied his style of warfare to the long and bitter Second Seminole War in Florida. But after Scott departed, his successors promptly adopted extreme measures, such as summarily hanging captives and stringing up their corpses as a warning to any Seminoles inclined to resist. Commanders in the West displayed no greater deference to Scott's mode of warfare. Three years before Major Robert S. Garnett was Colonel Pegram's commanding officer at Rich Mountain, he participated in a campaign in Washington Territory that concluded with the summary execution of Palouse captives.

Many white Americans easily dismissed such deviations from civilized norms as unfortunate but unavoidable consequences of the struggle to expand the dominion of "civilization" across a savage continent. Scott himself betrayed no evident qualms about his participation in the expulsion of roughly eighty thousand native peoples from their southeastern homelands during the 1830s. The scale and complexity of this operation nurtured logistical skills within the War Department that endured long after the dispossessed reached the Indian Territory. Indeed, the tragic combination of indifference, callousness, and officiousness characteristic of this coerced migration anticipated the operation of prison camps three decades later. Scott and most white Americans, however, remained confident that, when faced with "civilized" adversaries, they upheld the traditions of civilized warfare and humane treatment of prisoners. It was these traditions that both Pegram and McClellan invoked after the rout at Rich Mountain in hopes of tempering the savagery that had historically accompanied civil wars.

In an exhaustive treatise on international law published at the outbreak of the Civil War, Henry Halleck stressed the urgency of upholding the customs of war so as to "justify us at the tribunal of conscience and in the estimation of the world." Unlike George Washington, Winfield Scott, and John Pegram, Halleck had no firsthand experience with capture. But, like Scott, he revered the goal of humane, circumscribed, and orderly warfare. Months after the publication of his tome, Halleck was a Union general grappling with the daily challenge of waging war consonant with the etiquette of warfare he espoused in his book. Within a year, he succeeded Scott as the commander of all Union forces. In this lofty position, Halleck would observe the unfolding of a war that diverged sharply from the tradition of warfare he had studied.

During the summer of 1861, when Halleck's volume was just reaching booksellers, the delicate minuet between John Pegram and George McClellan after the Battle of Rich Mountain suggested that the divided nation would retain its historical fealty to the laws of war. The threads of centuries of evolving customs of war could be discerned in the captivity that Pegram experienced. It was a case study of the ideal of civilized warfare as endorsed by Washington, perpetuated by Scott, and cataloged by Halleck.

Within little more than a year, however, the treatment accorded to Pegram and his troops would seem quaint and outmoded. Indeed, one Union veteran acknowledged as much when he recalled a striking episode following Pegram's defeat at Rich Mountain. Among Pegram's captured troops was Lieutenant John S. Dorset of the Twentieth Virginia Infantry. After the surrender, he had been lent a Union ambulance so that he could escort the body of his commanding officer, Captain William Skipwith, home to Richmond. Although ineligible for parole because he had been a commissioned officer in the U.S. army, Dorset was granted this privilege with the stipulation that he thereafter return to Union lines to begin his captivity as a prisoner of war. Two weeks later, after delivering the body to the Confederate capital, Dorset completed the two-hundred-mile trek back to western Virginia under a flag of truce and surrendered himself to Union authorities. Even years later, the Union veteran remained dumbfounded that Dorset had fulfilled his pledge to return to captivity when he could easily have remained free behind Confederate lines. But, in the summer of 1861, respect for tradition and personal honor prevailed.

CHAPTER THREE

# What Is to Be Done with the Prisoners?

## (1861–1862)

Colonel Michael Corcoran's first glimpse of Richmond was unexpected and unwelcome. He had anticipated entering the Confederate capital amid a conquering Union army. Instead, his vantage point was a dingy, clattering train stuffed with prisoners of war.

On July 21, 1861, less than two weeks after Colonel John Pegram's surrender in western Virginia, Corcoran had been captured during the waning hours of the Battle of Bull Run. Wounded, he was herded into a barn along with hundreds of other prisoners. Without provisions or amenities, they sprawled on the ground overnight. The next day they trudged miles through drenching rain to a waiting train that transported them, slowly, to Richmond. Already Corcoran was discovering the "carelessness or want of system" that a fellow prisoner ascribed to railroads in the Confederacy. Corcoran's chief concern was not the train's sluggish pace but the prospect of reaching the Confederate capital. Having been told that "we would be torn to pieces by the mob," he was relieved when the train's unscheduled arrival deprived spectators of an opportunity to accost the haggard prisoners. Later caravans of captives were less fortunate. As spectacles and objects of ridicule, they were jeered, cursed, spat upon, and maltreated.

When he clambered off the train in Richmond, Corcoran cut a striking figure. He was thirty-four years old, with a long humorless face, a flinty gaze, and a mouth like the slit of an oyster shell. In the eyes of one admirer, he was "really of heroic stamp." Yet his face had "none of the conscious-

Colonel Michael Corcoran's experiences as prisoner during the first year of the war were a harbinger of the future prison experience. (Library of Congress)

ness or conceit that a small man would evince." (Not all were so smitten with him: a fellow captive privately fumed that Corcoran was "a low-bred, uneducated, selfish, cunning foreigner.") Scorning contemporary fashion, he trimmed his mustache, beard, and hair short. His eye-catching uniform sported a flamboyant sash and gaudy gold epaulets. A large badge depicting an Irish harp on a pole with the Stars and Stripes proclaimed his life's passion: Irish nationalism.

Corcoran was born in County Sligo in northwestern Ireland in 1827. While still young and serving as an officer in the revenue police, he became radicalized. Henceforth he devoted himself to expelling the English from his homeland. When in 1848 his underground activities became too risky, he departed for New York City. He flourished in his new home, becoming a force in the Democratic Party, a cofounder of the Fenian Brotherhood in America, a successful hotelier, and a colonel in the Sixty-Ninth New York Militia.

Corcoran garnered international notoriety when in October 1860 he refused to march his militia regiment in a parade honoring the visiting Prince of Wales, and instead damned the British royal for his empire's transgressions, especially during the recent Irish Famine. For his defiant protest, Corcoran was removed from his command. After the attack on Fort Sumter, his pending court-martial was dropped and he was reinstated so that he could rally Irish Americans to the Union cause. He did so with alacrity and fanfare. His regiment was one of the first units to reach Washington, D.C., where it received a rousing welcome.

Corcoran's renown won him no favors from his Confederate captors. His saga as a prisoner began less than two weeks after the start of Pegram's captivity, but he would remain in Confederate hands eight months after Pegram was paroled. While Pegram idled in genteel confinement, Corcoran underwent an ordeal that exposed the Confederacy's apathetic administration of prisoners of war and foreshadowed the misery of prisoners later in the war.

During Corcoran's extended captivity, Confederate authorities arrived at an answer to the pressing question posed by a Richmond editor, Robert Ridgeway of the *Richmond Whig*, in August 1861: "What should be done with the prisoners?" Straining to absorb trainload after trainload of captives harvested during successive campaigns, officials determined how they would be treated, who in the Confederate military command would assume responsibility for them, and what facilities would be used to hold them. While doing so, Confederates invoked the legal precedents and moral principles that had informed American policies toward prisoners of war since the Revolution. But Corcoran and other prisoners came to believe that through a combination of inept planning, bumbling administration, and cynical design, Confederates were creating prison pens that replicated the notorious British prison hulls of the American Revolution rather than the humane captivity promised by Confederate statesmen.

From the outset, Corcoran's stint pointed up the many substantial obstacles to consistent and compassionate treatment of prisoners of war. Long before the scope and intensity of the war's violence became apparent, both Union and Confederate officials began jockeying for advantage by making threats of retaliation against captives. As one of the highest-ranking Union prisoners in Confederate hands during the early months of the war, Corcoran was a celebrity who drew streams of curious southerners eager to gawk at him in his prison cell.

Corcoran inevitably became a pawn in Confederate machinations. Confederates linked his fate to that of Confederate privateers captured by the Union navy. The intertwined fate of Corcoran and the Confederate seamen set in motion escalating threats of retaliation by both sides against the prisoners they held. These calls for vengeance sharpened the anxieties of Corcoran and other captives who knew neither how long nor under what conditions they would be held.

Corcoran's plight originated with Confederate President Jefferson Davis's announcement in April 1861 that privately armed ships could apply for commissions—letters of marque—as Confederate privateers. The edict triggered a frenzy in southern ports as adventurers and profiteers rushed to provide the upstart nation with a semblance of a navy. Abraham Lincoln promptly countered Davis's directive, proclaiming that southerners who harassed American shipping under such unlawful authority would be subject to the penalties for piracy.

Lincoln's warning reflected his stance that the conflict was an internal, local insurrection rather than a war between sovereign nations. (Commentators observed that his administration's posture vis-à-vis the Confederates mirrored the British stance toward the colonial rebels during the Revolution.) Anxious to avoid alienating white southerners who might soon return to the Union, Lincoln offered mercy to those Confederates who, he believed, had been duped into secession by their leaders. At the same time, he was adamant that no overtures be made that might imply recognition of the southern insurgency. The justice of the Union cause rested on the principle that secession was illegitimate, even treasonous. To negotiate with Confederate authorities, even about prisoners of war, risked tacit recognition. The slightest concession might erode northern support for the war while increasing the likelihood that European powers would recognize the Confederacy. To promote this outcome, Confederates impatiently pressed federal officials for formal negotiations.

Early on, public opinion in the North buttressed the resolve of the Lincoln administration. Newspaper editorials urged punishing captured Confederates as traitors and freebooters. A New York businessman spoke for many when he implored, "No treating with [Confederates] as lawful enemies." With regard to captured privateers, he and others favored hanging them from the yardarm of the vessel that captured them. Prominent public figures, such as Senator Stephen Douglas, endorsed summary punishment for southern traitors. Even members of Lincoln's Cabinet reportedly clamored for executions of secessionists.

Even while denouncing these threats as bloodthirsty villainy, Confederates endorsed severe sanctions for Union captives. Two weeks after

Pegram's rout at Rich Mountain but in the afterglow of the Confederate victory at Bull Run, the *Richmond Dispatch* crowed that "the enemy has had his last Rich Mountain success." Confident of the continued triumph of Confederate armies, the newspaper predicted "we shall have it in our power to punish with inexorable rigor whatever enormities he may be guilty of in the future." By mid-September, while fretting about the expense and inconvenience of feeding Union prisoners, the *Charleston Mercury* pondered the wisdom of simply executing them. (The Atlanta *Southern Confederacy* ridiculed the suggestion as uncivilized.) Others proposed assigning prisoners to chain gangs or enslaving them. As one southern patriot explained to President Davis, "They might as well work, as they have to be fed." Another of Davis's correspondents advanced a macabre solution to the prisoner-of-war dilemma: captives should be provided nothing more than a diet of bread and water and their left legs should be systematically broken until the Union agreed to exchange prisoners.

Events on the high seas soon precipitated a showdown over Union policy. When Confederate privateers began marauding along the Atlantic coast, they threatened Union trade and extended the boundaries of the war to wherever they operated. Any semblance of a Confederate navy plying the oceans made a mockery of Lincoln's claim that the conflict was a mere insurrection. When several privateers fell prey to the tightening federal naval cordon around the Confederacy, the appropriate fate of Confederate privateers shifted from an abstract legal debate to a life-and-death issue, with direct consequences for Michael Corcoran.

The inglorious voyage of the *Savannah*, a diminutive onetime merchant vessel armed with a single antiquated cannon, brought the issue to a head. Within hours of departing from Charleston on June 2, 1861, the privateer snatched an unarmed merchant vessel as a prize of war. Exhilarated by this early success, the ship's novice crew set their sights on another vessel, which turned out to be a well-armed brig, the USS *Perry*. During the ensuing clash, the Confederate seamen cowered in their ship's hold, leaving their vessel virtually defenseless against the Union ship's barrage. Her captain prudently surrendered to his Union counterpart, and the career of the novice privateers ended after barely one day. When the captives arrived in New York City in mid-June, they were marched in shackles through streets thronged with hecklers to the Tombs, the city's jail. There, like common criminals, they remained in close confinement and squalid conditions awaiting trial in federal court for piracy.

Corcoran's fate was tied closely to that of the crew of the ill-fated Confederate privateer *Savannah*. (Library of Congress)

The fate of the crew of another privateer, the *Jefferson Davis*, soon became intertwined with that of the *Savannah*. The *Jefferson Davis* was a more substantial but equally time-worn brig that had plied the illegal slave trade before the Civil War. It was commissioned and began raiding soon after the launch of the *Savannah*. More adept than their compatriots on the *Savannah*, the *Davis*'s crew snatched ten merchant ships over a span of seven weeks. On July 6, they seized one such ship. Five of the privateers manned the captured merchant vessel and sailed for South Carolina. Before they reached their destination, however, the USS *Albatross* captured the ship and took them prisoner. When the privateers arrived in Philadelphia, they, like the *Savannah*'s crew, were jailed and charged with piracy.

The capital charges leveled against the sailors outraged Confederates, who insisted that the prisoners were legal combatants. Following the capture of the *Savannah*, President Davis sent a public letter to Lincoln pledging that if the captives were executed for piracy, he would retaliate life for life. Confederate ire intensified when the Lincoln administration ignored Davis's threat and proceeded to prosecute the privateers.

The trials, which began in October, attracted international interest. The implications of the trials extended well beyond the fate of the captive privateers to the Lincoln administration's stance on all prisoners of war. Charles P. Daly, a prominent New York jurist, pointed out as much when he addressed the difference between a soldier who took up arms against the United States on the land and the southern privateers who waged war at sea. "Practically, there is none," he explained. Both were guilty of the crime of treason or neither was. "There is not and cannot be, in this respect," he concluded, "any difference between them." A North Carolina newspaper succinctly sketched the dilemma the cases posed for Lincoln. If he treated the captured privateers as prisoners of war, "he will recognize us as belligerents," but if he treated them as pirates, Confederates would, in retaliation, "deal with prisoners in our hands precisely as he deals with his prisoners."

During the trials, the defense teams adopted similar strategies to save the two crews. They argued that the Confederacy was a de facto sovereign state and so had the right to issue letters of marque. Locked in a conflict that was an international war between two sovereign states, the Confederacy had exercised its authority to commission privateers, who were legitimate belligerents. The prosecution countered that privateers could be commissioned only by a state whose national existence was recognized and which had "diplomatic relations" with other nations. Because the Confederacy had yet to be recognized by "the family of nations," it lacked standing to issue letters of marque. Therefore, the Confederate sailors were nothing more than brigands of the sea.

The defense's arguments met with mixed success. In New York, they swayed several members of the jury. After twenty hours of deliberation, the jury deadlocked, with eight jurors pushing for conviction and four favoring acquittal. The jury in Philadelphia sided with the prosecution. After only forty-five minutes of deliberation, they returned a verdict of guilty. The privateers from the *Jefferson Davis* appeared destined for the gallows.

Infuriated by the Philadelphia verdict, President Davis on November 9 ordered an equivalent number of Union prisoners to be selected by lot from the highest-ranking prisoners held by the Confederacy. Based on an eye for an eye, these hostages were to be deprived of all comforts accorded to prisoners of war. Like "convicted felons," they would be kept in strict confinement while they awaited the fate of the condemned Confederate privateers.

Corcoran had the misfortune to be the first prisoner selected by lot when Davis's instructions were carried out. Thirteen other prisoners subsequently shared the same fate. Quickly, Corcoran and the other hostages were separated from their comrades, transferred to secluded cells, and deprived of any privileges they had enjoyed as prisoners of war. Corcoran's new quarters were an unfurnished, stone-floored cell behind an iron door. He remained in isolation even during his Christmas meal, which he purportedly ate through the bars of his cell. In Richmond, seven hostages were removed to the Henrico County jail, where they occupied a dark, dank cell that measured eleven by seventeen feet. Within these cramped quarters, they ate their rude meals and passed their days. Most oppressive was the threat of execution that hung over the prisoners. For weeks they lived each day unsure of their fate yet convinced of Confederate resolve. As one of Corcoran's fellow hostages confided, "There is I think no doubt of the determination of the [Confederate] government to carry out its expressed intention."

By the end of 1861, as the number of Union prisoners in Confederate hands swelled and the fate of the hostages hung in the balance, northern public opinion shifted in favor of negotiating with the Confederacy. When the number of prisoners had been small and the Union held as many as or more captives than the Confederacy, the Lincoln administration had preferred to defer dealing with the issue. But the administration's studied indifference became increasingly untenable as letters and petitions from embittered Union prisoners pleading for negotiations reached northern newspapers. Northern legislatures began to take up the call, and on December 11 Congress passed a joint resolution pressing the President to "inaugurate systematic measures for the exchange of prisoners in the present rebellion."

Corcoran's predicament heightened public pressure on the Lincoln administration. Many northerners anointed Corcoran a martyr. "It is a great compliment to his bravery to give him this sad preeminence," one northern patriot enthused. Prominent politicians and friends of the imprisoned colonel badgered Union officials to secure his release. So insistent was the effort that even Corcoran, sequestered as a hostage, heard "now and then of the strenuous efforts being made by my friends." The campaign reached its climax on February 5, 1862, when the Fenian Brotherhood hosted a mass meeting of more than four thousand people in Boston. Presided over by the city's mayor, the assembly demanded Corcoran's immediate release.

Fearing the corrosive effects of the colonel's continued imprisonment on northern morale, Union officials quietly inquired whether Confederates were willing to swap him for the captain of the captured Confederate privateers in Philadelphia. With a keen understanding of Corcoran's value as a hostage, Confederates dismissed the offer, countering that the only acceptable basis for Corcoran's release was a negotiated general exchange of prisoners.

Backed into a corner, the Lincoln administration seized the opportunity provided by the mistrial in New York to escape a worsening public relations fiasco. Rather than retry the *Savannah* privateers and risk a cycle of escalating retaliation, federal authorities decided to concede the rights of belligerency to the imprisoned Confederate seamen. In early February 1862, without explanation of its change of course, the Lincoln administration ordered the privateers removed from their jail cells. Thereafter, they were accorded the same treatment as Confederates who were held as conventional prisoners of war. In response, Confederate authorities released Corcoran and the other Union hostages from their hostage cells.

Corcoran remained keenly aware that his circumstances were precarious. He understood his value to his captors and recognized that at almost any moment he might again be held hostage. Only a few months later, Captain Timothy O'Meara, a fellow prisoner and a close friend of Corcoran, was selected as a hostage to discourage Union authorities from executing several captured Confederate partisans. Throughout the remainder of the war, each side would selectively deny captured enemies the protections extended to legitimate belligerents.

Most other Union and Confederate captives could, with due caution, expect to be treated as prisoners of war. The Lincoln administration in principle acknowledged that enemy captives were legitimate belligerents who should enjoy the traditional protections granted prisoners of war. Yet few had grounds to be optimistic that captivity would be brief. A full year into the conflict, the two sides had not agreed to a general exchange of prisoners.

Instead, occasional paroles took place at the discretion of officers on the battlefield, as had happened after John Pegram's surrender at Rich Mountain. The warring sides also occasionally swapped severely wounded captives, as in September 1861, when Confederates paroled fifty-seven prisoners captured along with Corcoran, most of whom were amputees. To do so was both compassionate and practical. The prisoners could no longer fight and consumed precious medical resources while they remained in Richmond. A few other prisoners, like Pegram, were the beneficiaries of individual exchanges.

From the perspective of prisoners, these exchanges were arbitrary, haphazard, and uncertain. No clear logic dictated which wounded prisoners were exchanged, and most remained in captivity regardless of the severity of their injuries. Colonel Pegram's experience illustrated the problems that beset ad hoc individual exchanges. While imprisoned, Pegram had to identify a suitable prisoner with whom he could be swapped. Consequently, he, like all captive officers, tracked the news of surrenders closely to identify an appropriate enemy candidate for exchange. Then he had to secure approval for his parole from Union authorities and persuade Confederate authorities to authorize the exchange of his Union counterpart. Even with all the advantages he possessed, Pegram still had to travel to Washington, D.C., to resolve the details of his proposed exchange and then wait months for Confederate authorities to transfer his Union counterpart to Union lines. He had the good fortune that the prerequisites for his exchange were satisfied in a relatively timely manner.

Too often, the intricacies of individual exchanges were almost insurmountable. In some instances faulty recordkeeping muddled matters. In May 1862, during the ongoing efforts to exchange Corcoran, Union officials offered to swap Colonel R. F. Baldwin, a Virginian held at Fort Warren, for Corcoran, only to discover that the Confederate officer had already been exchanged. As early as January 1862, the logistics of exchanges drove Confederate Secretary of War Judah Benjamin to his wit's end: "I am hourly assailed by propositions from different quarters for partial and individual exchanges." He sputtered, "We cannot consent to continue a system so partial in its operation, so cumbersome in detail and so difficult of execution."

Prisoners found that orchestrating exchanges added to the torment of captivity. While Corcoran studiously maintained a stoic indifference to the efforts on his behalf, some of his comrades were frantic to secure their release. Colonel Orlando B. Wilcox, one of Corcoran's fellow prisoners, had been identified as a candidate to be exchanged for Pegram. Confederate officials, however, quashed the proposal because of a seemingly trivial distinction between the two men's ranks. Throughout the remainder of his captivity, Wilcox heard rumors of his pending exchange, only to be bitterly disappointed when they fell through.

Individual exchanges further eroded prisoner morale by devolving into popularity contests. Status, reputation, and personal connections were exploited to improve the likelihood of a prisoner's exchange. Families and friends of prisoners applied whatever influence they possessed to cajole officials to approve individual exchanges. Thus, one prisoner, two months after his capture, pleaded in a December 1861 letter to his father, "I hope you are all striking hard for a speedy exchange." Captive soldiers in the ranks stood little likelihood of having the necessary influence to expedite an exchange.

Even officers, who had the greatest likelihood of organizing an exchange, were dismayed by the apparent inequities of the system. The campaign for Corcoran's release, for instance, irked Wilcox and other officers whose plights were no less dire. Wilcox sulked in private that "the Irish Lion is as near an ass [as] can be" and yet he "overshadows us at home." Wilcox groused, "His name is mentioned in Congress & everywhere before mine & every other."

Not until July 1862, when the warring governments finalized formal prisoner exchanges, could Wilcox, Corcoran, and their comrades anticipate with confidence the end of their ordeal. Until then, they lived in a melancholy limbo, unsure of their fate and whether it would be resolved before the war's end.

Soon after Corcoran entered his prison quarters in Richmond, Confederate Brigadier General John Winder paid a visit. After surveying the cramped and spartan facility, Winder vowed to Corcoran that improvements were forthcoming. Within a day, Corcoran and his fellow officers were moved into a neighboring but no less austere made-over factory. Corcoran interpreted Winder's visit to be a fitting and gratifying gesture of respect for a fellow officer, and perhaps it was. Both Winder and Corcoran shared an acute sensitivity regarding their status and personal dignity. Just as likely, however, the Confederate general intended his visit to underscore his personal authority and, above all, his power over Corcoran and the other prisoners.

No single person was the architect of the Confederacy's prisoner-of-war system, but Winder had more influence over the conditions within Confederate prison pens than anyone else. Corcoran would repeatedly experience the power that Winder wielded. While the status of prisoners was contested in the courts and debated in Cabinet meetings during the first year of the war, Winder supervised the prisons in Richmond that held the largest number of Union prisoners and translated vague policies into day-to-day practice. He granted and withdrew privileges that mitigated the grim monotony of the prisoners' existence. He oversaw the dispersal of prisoners, including Corcoran, to prison pens across the Confederacy. And he conducted the lottery that winnowed out Corcoran and other officers who became hostages.

Winder was an improbable figure to preside over the Confederacy's prisons. His flowing locks of silver white hair, doleful eyes, and deeply creased face testified both to his age—sixty-one—and to the weight of his responsibilities. He had no training that prepared him for these responsibilities; nor did he display any evident enthusiasm or capacity for them. But he was resolute and possessed a stern military bearing that was deemed fitting for the custodian of enemy captives.

Winder's overbearing demeanor had been nurtured during his four decades in the U.S. army. It also may have been a studied response to the dishonor attached to his father, William H. Winder. A prominent Maryland lawyer and politician, Winder's father had been the commander during the disastrous American defeat at Bladensburg that preceded the sacking of the nation's capital by the British during the War of 1812. Despite his father's disgrace, Winder secured admission to West Point and, upon graduation, was commissioned as a second lieutenant. Apart from a brief and unsuccessful venture as a planter, he spent the remainder of his life in uniform. During the war with Mexico, he earned two brevets for gallantry. By the start of the Civil War, he had attained the rank of colonel.

In April 1861, Winder resigned his commission and offered his services to his adopted state of North Carolina. He was appointed a colonel in the Confederate infantry and a month later was promoted to brigadier general.

GEN. JOHN H. WINDER.

FROM A PHOTOGRAPH BY REESE.

General John H. Winder.
(From *Southern Illustrated News*,
September 12, 1863)

Almost immediately thereafter he was made assistant inspector general of the camps of instruction at Richmond. Winder continued to accumulate duties, and in March 1862 President Davis appointed him provost marshal general. By then, his charge included rounding up and punishing deserters, ferreting out spies, regulating commodity prices, maintaining law and order, and overseeing the prison pens in the Confederate capital. If there was a logic to Winder's disparate responsibilities, it was that sedition, espionage, petty crime, price gouging, and prisoners of war were all deemed to be matters of military security.

Many Confederate civilians and Union captives concluded that Winder was ill suited to his duties. A few, including Corcoran, vouched for Winder's professionalism. But many more mocked him as a strutting martinet, curt in speech, with a short temper. According to Richmond editor Edward A. Pollard, "his face was a picture of cruelty." He bore a reputation for callousness that he acquired early in his career, when he taught briefly at West Point, until a confrontation with a cadet ended his appointment. The best that can be said for Winder is that he was overwhelmed by the scale and complexity of his duties and lacked the ingenuity or compassion needed to prevent the horrors to come.

Winder's imperiousness exacerbated challenges inherent in the awkward division of authority within the Confederate bureaucracy. In most regards the organization of the Confederate army mimicked that of the United States army. As on the Union side, prisoners of war were the formal responsibility of the quartermaster general. But the provost general's office assumed effective responsibility for captives because the largest concentration of prisoners was in Richmond, where Winder held sway. Eventually, in 1864, the Confederacy consolidated responsibility for prisoners of war in a single office over which Winder presided. Until then, a murky division of responsibility for prisoners bred confusion, inefficiency, and controversy.

Bureaucratic competition between Winder and the Confederate quartermaster general impeded the effectiveness of Winder's command. Winder and Quartermaster General Abraham C. Myers both jealously protected their power. Winder's relations with the Confederate Commissary General Lucius B. Northrop were worse. Northrop openly acknowledged that he had taken the position only because he had been ordered to do so. Many contemporaries struggled to identify his virtues; one observer described Northrop as "a man of no experience in business, but of great self consequence," while another christened him "the most cussed and vilified man in the Confederacy." Northrop's previous experience in military administration was a quarter century in the past and prepared him poorly for the scale of his duties procuring food for the Confederate army.

The organizational jumble and bureaucratic brawls had immediate and unpleasant consequences for Corcoran and other prisoners. From the earliest months of the war, Winder's staff had difficulty acquiring sufficient supplies and foodstuffs for prisoners. Suspicious of both Myers and Northrop and convinced they were withholding supplies, Winder began independently procuring provisions for his prisons, directly competing with Myers's and Northrop's agents. As the war dragged on, this rivalry contributed to ever escalating prices. Meanwhile, Winder's provisioning schemes enraged many Richmonders, who resented that foodstuffs were being diverted to prisoners of war.

During the early months of the war, the rations provided to captive officers fell well short of the feasts enjoyed by Pegram while he was captive in Boston. But the officers did not suffer unduly from want of food. Captives with means supplemented their meager rations with food purchased outside the prison walls. Enlisted prisoners, however, received provisions that were poor in quality and increasingly scant in quantity. One of Corcoran's fellow officers recalled many times sharing half his rations with enlisted men who clustered around the officers' quarters in desperation, looking "famished and pinched with hunger."

The efficiency of Winder's department suffered because, whether by choice or necessity, Winder surrounded himself with staff who lacked relevant experience. A week after the arrival of Corcoran and the other prisoners captured at Bull Run, when competent assistants were desperately needed to deal with the influx, Winder complained that his staff was so small and its turnover so great that his officers "do not remain long enough to acquire sufficient knowledge of the details to assist me much." This problem persisted throughout the first two years of the war.

Few of his staff had exercised command before the war. Nepotism, rather than relevant qualifications, apparently secured positions on Winder's staff for his son Captain W. S. "Sid" Winder, a lawyer, and his nephew Major Richard B. Winder, an engineer. Two other staff officers had trained as lawyers, one had struck it rich in the California Gold Rush, and another had been a homeopathic doctor and plantation overseer. A career as a book publisher apparently qualified one of Winder's officers to procure prison supplies. One staff officer was so young that Union prisoners mocked his "incipient moustache" and "foppish buffoonery." Another officer was an inexperienced twenty-year-old whose first major assignment was command of the largest prison in Richmond.

Prison guards were no more seasoned. They were not only inexperienced but also either very young or very old. One of Winder's staff recalled them as being new recruits who were woefully "awkward and inefficient." The *Richmond Dispatch* conceded that they were "lamentably deficient in the requisite knowledge" to perform the simplest tasks. A Union prisoner dismissed them as "not very formidable fellows, being many of them unfit for field duty." One, he chortled, paraded about with a bayonet on a broomstick. Some of Winder's staff were indeed assigned to prison duty because they were unfit for active duty, including the commanding officer of the Richmond prison that held Corcoran, who was recovering from a severe attack of typhoid fever.

Winder's staff compensated for their inexperience with displays of zealotry. Perhaps reflecting his Maryland origins, Winder collected staff who were born outside the Confederacy and were especially keen to flaunt their Confederate patriotism. Three of his officers were northern by birth, including one born on an Ohio River flatboat. At least seven hailed from border states, and another was Swiss. Twenty-one-year-old Marylander James W. Emack boasted the nickname "Yankee Killer," which he earned on the basis of his claims to have slain any number of Union soldiers. Lieutenant David H. Todd, a Kentuckian and the half brother of Mary Todd Lincoln, overcompensated for his family ties to the American president. Henry Wirz, the Swiss-born officer, arrived in Richmond within days of Corcoran's arrival. Assigned to guard duty at the building that held Corcoran and other officers, Wirz acquired a reputation for efficiency in the eyes of his superiors, and for malice in the eyes of prisoners. He was, a prisoner wrote in 1862, "the essence of authority at the prison." "Immensely inflated with the dignity of his position," he showed his devotion to the cause by, as a Confederate colleague put it, being "a very strict disciplinarian."

Some of Winder's staff chafed at the apparent insignificance of their role in the grand conflict. That they did so was hardly surprising. Few warriors at the start of a war seek glory by guarding prisoners of war. David Todd grumbled about his tiresome duties and pined for "the tented field and blood 'galore.'" Impatient for heroic opportunities, Captain George W. Alexander, who became the commandant of one of Richmond's prisons, resorted to flamboyant fashions and extravagant behavior. With a carefully tended mane of black hair and a large black beard, he pranced around Richmond in tight-fitting black trousers, black stockings, black shirts, and a red sash, while toting two pistols, a blackjack, and two pairs of handcuffs. Accompanied everywhere by a huge mastiff, he was a portrait of biblical wrath. No doubt, he was gratified when a Richmond newspaper dubbed him "not only one of the most gallant, but one of the handsomest men in the Confederate service." (Union prisoners, in marked contrast, reviled him as pompous, vain, and cruel.)

Some of Winder's staff displayed a penchant for brutishness and several for cruelty. Archibald C. Godwin, who served in Richmond until he was assigned to supervise the prison stockade in Salisbury, North Carolina, nursed "an intense and bitter hatred of the North" that periodically erupted during his dealings with prisoners of war. Though irksome, Godwin's occasional tantrums fell far short of the terror inspired by Alexander and Todd. Rumors of Alexander's cruelty began soon after he joined Winder's staff. By 1863 they were so rife that the Confederate congress gathered testimony from guards and prisoners confirming that Alexander had ordered inmates flogged, stuffed into "sweatboxes," and hung by their thumbs. Despite ample evidence of torture, and a stinging denunciation by one of the congressional investigators, Alexander retained his job. He lost it later in the year after another investigation revealed that he had engaged in currency speculation and taken bribes from prisoners. (He nevertheless would subsequently serve at prisons in Danville and Salisbury.) Todd's violence was so unpredictable and gratuitous that it brought his tenure as a prison commandant to an abrupt end, after only three months, in October 1861. A vainglorious and volatile drunkard, he terrorized prisoners and staff alike with "foul and scurrilous abuse." For trivial offenses he stabbed one prisoner with his saber and bashed another in the head with a musket butt. On another occasion he kicked the corpse of a dead Union prisoner onto a Richmond street.

After northern newspapers published reports of Todd's violence, Confederates strenuously reiterated their commitment to the "civilized" treatment of prisoners of war. Southern editors vouched that Union prisoners were more likely to be pampered than abused. Corcoran and other prisoners did on occasion encounter officers, guards, and civilians who displayed compassion. When a Confederate braggart heckled Corcoran while in transit, a young woman came to his defense and stopped the harassment. The jailer who fulfilled the order placing Corcoran and several other hostages in close confinement found small but much appreciated ways to lessen the hardships he imposed. When Corcoran and his comrades were eventually moved to Columbia, South Carolina, their jailer and other Freemasons feted those Union prisoners who were Masons and mitigated, to the extent possible, the discomforts of their captivity.

These instances, however, were exceptional. Beyond occasional acts of cruelty by guards and officers, prisoners during the fall of 1861 experienced tightened regulations and shrinking privileges, as the number of captives grew and anxiety about security mounted. Within a few weeks, captive Union doctors who had been granted freedom to move between prisons and hospitals to tend to wounded and sick Union captives lost that privilege. Prisoners were denied the opportunity to send representatives into the city to purchase supplies. All contact with civilians outside of the prisons was banned, and mail service was carefully regulated. Captivity became much more than the deprivation of freedom; it reduced the captives' existence to a daily struggle to keep mind and body whole.

As the prisoner-of-war policy hardened, at least one member of Winder's staff grew unsettled. When in October 1861 twenty-six-year-old Major James T. W. Hairston became superintendent of the Richmond prisons, he found his responsibility for the thirty-five hundred Union prisoners of war in the city to be "anything but congenial to a liberal and enlightened mind." The duties of a "prison keeper," he recalled years later, were "never pleasant to a man of humane inclinations." From the outset he lamented the "deplorable lack of creature comforts, or even necessaries" provided to the prisoners. The job became "intensely disagreeable when the retaliatory policy of our government" during the privateer imbroglio forced him to put the Richmond hostages in irons. Unable to reconcile his duties with his conscience, he requested and secured a transfer to the field in 1862. He preferred to risk his life for a cause he had never championed than to surrender his convictions ruling over prisoners of war.

Corcoran and his fellow prisoners understandably felt most keenly the ill treatment meted out by guards and prison officials. But their jailers bore little direct responsibility for the pervasive overcrowding, decrepit facilities, and meager provisions that defined the prison experience. These defects could be traced to Winder and his superiors, who never fully acknowledged, let alone fulfilled, their obligation to the prisoners of war accumulating in their prisons. From the outset, the watchwords of the Confederate administration of prisoners of war were expediency and extreme economy.

Corcoran most directly experienced these attributes of the Confederate war effort while shuttling among six different prisons and traveling nearly fifteen hundred miles, roughly the distance from Paris to Moscow, to do so. His journey from Bull Run to Richmond, crowded in a battered boxcar, was only the first of his treks within the rebel nation. Each transfer provoked a mixture of dread and uncertainty about the conditions he would next confront, compounded by recognition that he was "being forced by my foes further and further from my home." The erratic itineraries, dilapidated trains, and derelict prisons Union captives experienced while being shunted hither and yon were emblematic of their chaotic captivity. As one of Corcoran's comrades put it, "We are apparently destined to rival Ulysses before we get clear of this."

Corcoran's odyssey was made necessary by the failure of the Confederacy to build facilities to house prisoners of war. Only during the last year of the war did Winder and other officials finally do so. Until then, they retrofitted existing buildings to serve as improvised prison pens. As long as Confederates relied on the scattered commercial infrastructure in the region, the inventory of plausible prison sites was wholly inadequate. The result, as Corcoran learned firsthand, was a hodgepodge of ill-suited, unhealthy, impromptu prisons dictated by expediency.

Like tens of thousands of Union prisoners, Corcoran got his first taste of Confederate prison life in Richmond. When the city became the Confederate capital in May 1861, it also became, as if by happenstance, the new nation's principal prison depot. It was perhaps inevitable that the city would become, at the very least, a temporary prisoner-of-war terminus. It was close at hand to the front lines, where Confederate and Union armies battled for control of the one hundred miles that separated the warring capitals. Boasting the most extensive railroad network in the upper South, the city was an essential distribution hub for soldiers and war supplies.

In other regards, the city was ill suited to quarter captives. It had no facilities to properly incarcerate large numbers of prisoners. Before the arrival of Corcoran and the fifteen hundred other soldiers captured at Bull Run, the small number of prisoners of war already on hand had taxed the capacity of the facilities that authorities had commandeered. By August Robert Ridgeway of the *Richmond Whig* was wringing his hands in print over how the Confederacy should deal with its captives. Prisons teeming with captured enemies was an eventuality that he and others apparently had not previously considered. As recently as the year before, the state prison in Richmond, which was the oldest penitentiary in the South, had held fewer than four hundred prisoners. Now, the single train that bore Corcoran to Richmond carried many more prisoners than the city had ever harbored at one time. Not only was the city already overrun by Confederate factotums, soldiers, and wartime opportunists, but its economy and infrastructure were stretched to their limits. With lodging, food, and other essentials extravagantly expensive and in short supply, Ridgeway had ample cause to worry about the capital's capacity to absorb swelling prison populations.

In the weeks before Corcoran's arrival, General Winder began requisitioning idle commercial buildings to house prisoners. The facility in which Corcoran was initially stashed was typical of the motley assortment of factories and warehouses that came to constitute the Confederacy's prison pens. It was an austere, derelict, three-story tobacco factory in the heart of the city. Because Richmond was a major industrial center—the most important in the South—it had a scattering of vacant commercial sites that Confederate officials could usurp. Soon thereafter, three neighboring tobacco facilities were fitted out for prisoners. Eventually, almost a quarter of the city's factories and warehouses would be transformed into prison pens and military hospitals.

The tobacco warehouse in Richmond where Corcoran was first imprisoned eventually became a hospital, as it appears here in 1865. (Library of Congress)

Whatever merits the warehouses and the other improvised prisons in Richmond had possessed as commercial facilities, they were devoid of comfort. Austerity had suited their original purpose but these "sober looking" buildings provided only crude shelter. In them enslaved and free Black workers had toiled in "close confinement" and "prison-like" working conditions to convert tobacco leaf into chewing tobacco. A few commentators conceded that "the unwholesome and destructive atmosphere" in the factories had sapped the enslaved of their health and work ethic. But such concerns were ignored when the facilities were sites of bondage, just as they would be dismissed when they became sites of wartime captivity.

The filth and disarray in the buildings reinforced their grimness. Corcoran and his fellow prisoners, for instance, shared half of their living space with a jumble of dilapidated machinery used to manufacture tobacco products. Some floors in the erstwhile factories were covered with a viscous swill of licorice, flavorings, and sugar used to make chewing tobacco palatable. So sticky were the floors that prisoners had difficulty tugging their feet free while attempting to walk on them and unlucky inmates who lacked bedding stuck to them like flies on flypaper when they slept. Even after spending hours digging out and sweeping the floors at one site, a prisoner lamented it remained "a mere hog pen" with "rooms too filthy to describe."

Achieving cleanliness in these improvised prisons, which lacked adequate bathing and cooking facilities, was futile. No amenities had been provided to the enslaved who had worked on-site. Eating accommodations were rude. "Feeding a drove of swine" was one prisoner's description of mealtimes, when discarded boxes and barrel tops served as tables and fingers served as eating utensils. The toilet facilities that Confederate officials fashioned, without exception, were primitive, rancid, and inadequate for the number of prisoners. On one of the floors of the prison occupied by Corcoran, the foul discharge from the common sink pooled several inches deep in a corner of the room. In another prison, the effluvia from the upper floors leaked through the ceiling onto the floors below. Confederate newspapers noted, without evident remorse, that "the mortality among the Abolition prisoners now in Richmond is considerable."

Fear of possible prison uprisings and public health dangers associated with bulging prisons, rather than the glaring shortcomings of the facilities, motivated Confederate officials to make plans to disperse the prisoners in Richmond across the southern hinterlands. No consideration was given to building new facilities. Instead, beginning in June 1861 and continuing virtually to the end of the war, Secretary of War Leroy Pope Walker and his successors pleaded with state officials from Louisiana to North Carolina for recommendations of suitable sites that might relieve some of the city's prison population. Henceforth, the plan was for Richmond to remain a transit point for captives either en route to other prisons or awaiting exchange.

Almost any vacant building within the Confederacy seemingly was considered. In Tuscaloosa, Alabama, the Confederacy purchased an abandoned paper mill that was too broken-down to hold prisoners. Officials fared better when they came to terms with the owner of a defunct textile factory in Salisbury, North Carolina. Elsewhere, they considered slave marts in Tuscaloosa and in Macon, Georgia, an obsolete lunatic asylum in Tuscaloosa, the county jail in Atlanta, and a parish prison in New Orleans. But time after time the proffered sites proved to be too small, too insecure, too expensive, or otherwise deficient in some essential regard. The paucity of viable sites underscored how utterly unprepared the Confederacy was to assume responsibility for war prisoners.

Corcoran and about 150 other captives were among the first prisoners to be dispersed from Richmond to holding pens farther south in an ongoing transfer that would continue to the end of the war. In September 1861 he and his comrades began a grueling three-day train trip that was interrupted by long delays and periodic harassment from raucous civilians. When they reached Charleston, they were confined in regular cells in the overcrowded city jail along with "murderers, thieves, mail robbers, colored, and even the abandoned wretches of easy virtue!" Soon thereafter, hundreds of their fellow prisoners in the Confederate capital were sent to a jail in New Orleans, where they too shared quarters with common criminals. In these and other instances, Confederate authorities looked to civilian jails as convenient prison pens. They were, after all, designed to detain prisoners and required little adaptation to house Union captives.

The Charleston jail, however, was only a temporary way station for Corcoran and the other captives. Nowhere in the United States, and especially not in the South, were there enough civilian jails and prisons to hold more than a fraction of the military prisoners stockpiled during the first year of the war. The prewar southern practice of meting out private justice to slaves on plantations meant that the region's enslaved population was seldom imprisoned in jails. Consequently, carceral facilities across the region were smaller than the region's population might otherwise have warranted. To banish a meaningful number of Union prisoners to local jails would have required scattering small numbers of captives to often ramshackle jails. Had military authorities done so, they would have surrendered their control over prisoners to jailkeepers and created a logistical nightmare. The cost of compensating localities for hosting the prisoners would also have been prohibitive. Finally, local jails were often stuffed full of Confederate deserters and white men accused of evading Confederate conscription. Although Confederate authorities periodically stuffed some Union prisoners in civilian jails, they could never resolve the question posed by Ridgeway in 1861: "What should be done with the prisoners?"

Corcoran's sojourn in the Charleston jail lasted only until the completion of hurried renovations at Castle Pinckney, an aged fort in the city's harbor. Described by one of Corcoran's fellow prisoners as "a grim little place," the fort had crude accommodations that had been created by bricking up casement openings and installing heavy wooden doors on the makeshift cells. Despite their dark, dank, and dirty quarters, Corcoran and the other prisoners welcomed the move to the fort. Although they endured oppressive nights locked in their casement dungeons, they had access to the interior parade grounds during the daytime. After weeks of the fusty air in the Richmond tobacco factory and the Charleston jail, they basked in the cooling sea air that drifted through the fort.

To the prisoners' dismay, Confederate authorities quickly concluded that the fort was too small to serve as a prison. After less than six weeks the prisoners were returned to the Charleston jail. It was during his second sojourn there that Corcoran was declared a hostage and consigned to close confinement. Within weeks, a fire in the surrounding neighborhood nearly consumed the jail and compelled officials to move Corcoran and his comrades back to the fort. This stay at Castle Pinckney was considerably less pleasant; Corcoran remained a hostage while winter winds and rains chilled those prisoners who were forced by overcrowding to sleep with minimal protection on the fort's parade ground. The second stint at the fort, fortunately, was even briefer than the first.

The brevity of Corcoran's imprisonment at Castle Pinckney was a testament to the unsuitability of most forts in the South to serve as prisons. With few exceptions, the forts in the South were too small to garrison guards while housing prisoners. The largest Confederate citadel, Fort Fisher near Wilmington, North Carolina, for instance, had a garrison of nearly twenty-five hundred soldiers by the end of the war. Had it been stuffed to twice its capacity with an equal number of prisoners, Confederate prisons would still

Members of Corcoran's regiment in front of their casement cell at Castle Pinckney, September 1861. (Library of Congress)

have remained severely overcrowded. And because Fort Fisher and most forts guarded the southern coastline, they were vulnerable to attack from Union forces. Officials, consequently, looked elsewhere to house the bulk of Union captives.

The next stop on Corcoran's coerced ramblings was Columbia, South Carolina. In January 1862, after another train trip and more brushes with hostile, rock-throwing crowds, the itinerant prisoners, who now numbered more than two hundred, were crowded into the Columbia city jail and a nearby fairgrounds. Although Corcoran was crammed into a small room with eleven other men, they had an uncommonly solicitous keeper. The city's mayor, John H. Boatwright, treated the captive officers with surprising consideration. They briefly enjoyed long-denied privileges. But the compassion displayed by the mayor and the comparative liberty of the captives appalled some local citizenry. Stung by the public outcry and embarrassed by numerous escapes by prisoners, officials tightened security and rescinded most privileges. The problems in Columbia underscored again the inadequacy of jails as repositories for prisoners of war.

After less than two months in Columbia, in late March 1862 Corcoran and most of his fellow prisoners were dispatched by train back to their former prison quarters in Richmond. Their return trip removed any hope that rail service in the Confederacy had improved since their journey south six months earlier. Nor had their former prison pen been enhanced during the intervening months. In early May the prisoners were moved to Libby Prison, another nearby repurposed tobacco warehouse. Within a year this new facility would be one of the most notorious Confederate prisons. But that spring it was just "another and more dismal warehouse" among the mushrooming prison pens in the Confederate capital. It was little more than a brick-and-mortar shell with rough floors and crude walls that reeked of fish, hemp, and tobacco. Corcoran and about fifty other officers made their home in a room barren of furniture. The monotony of their captivity was interrupted by the racket of prisoners on the floor above them, their constant struggle to suppress the infestation of lice, and their attempts to dodge the "streams of filthy matter" that drained down from the floors above.

Their tenure in Libby Prison was brief. With the Union army advancing up the Virginia Peninsula near Richmond and hundreds of captives collecting in the city weekly, if not daily, General Winder dispatched Corcoran and

The spartan interior of Libby Prison. (Library of Congress)

Corcoran, seated in his uniform at the far right, observes a prison baseball game in *Union Prisoners at Salisbury, NC*, by Otto Boetticher, ca. 1863. (Library of Congress)

the rest of his prison mates by train in May 1862 to the textile mill in Salisbury, North Carolina. The facility there had been hurriedly fitted out as a prison during the previous fall. It included a large four-story brick building and six small cottages next to a busy railroad line from Charlotte to Greensboro. An eight-foot-high wooden stockade with a four-foot-high parapet encircled the facility and provided guards with an unobstructed view of the prison's interior. One officer imprisoned there described the main building as "very undesirable." The first prisoners had been transferred to the facility in December. By the time Corcoran arrived, the prison held more than fourteen hundred captives, including the prisoners who had been previously sent to New Orleans, Tuscaloosa, and South Carolina.

The Salisbury prison suggested the possibilities available to the Confederacy to adapt some of the region's cotton infrastructure to the housing of prisoners of war. Cotton warehouses, through which more than four million bales of cotton had passed every year prior to the war, might have seemed plausible improvised prisons. A derelict warehouse in Cahaba, Alabama, indeed served as an important prison beginning in June 1863. National priorities, however, precluded transforming most cotton warehouses into holding pens for captured enemies. In the first place, the warehouses were bursting with bales of cotton. With the export of cotton halted by the Union blockade of Confederate ports, many planters continued to send their cotton to warehouses because they had no practical alternative to store it. Confederate authorities, who hoped that world demand for cotton would secure their nation's recognition and future, were loath to alienate planters by displacing or destroying warehoused cotton so as to house prisoners of war. Similarly, the Confederacy could ill afford to convert operating cotton mills into prisons. (The mill in Salisbury had been idle before the start of the war.) Compounding these considerations, when New Orleans, Memphis, and Nashville fell to advancing Union armies in the spring of 1862, the Confederacy lost irreplaceable commercial facilities that might otherwise have been exploited not only to provide war matériel but also to serve as prison facilities.

Corcoran had the comparative good fortune to avoid time in any of the South's slave pens during his prison wanderings. Confederates displayed no aversion to using slave jails to house Union captives and they made plans to do so in Montgomery, Tuscaloosa, Macon, and elsewhere. Such facilities had obvious appeal to the financially strapped Confederacy. Virtually no modifications were needed to adapt them because they were already the practical equivalent of prisons. But during the first year of the war only a small number of Union prisoners were held in them and typically only for brief spells. After the fall of New Orleans, Memphis, and Nashville, only a few cities with large slave-trading facilities, such as Richmond, Charleston, Montgomery, and Mobile, remained under Confederate control. Small slave pens in remote southern towns shared the same limitations as small-town jails; they were too small and too scattered to house prisoners long-term. Consequently, while derelict depots in major Confederate cities sometimes served as temporary prisons, officials were averse to commandeering facilities that remained crucial for the flourishing wartime slave trade and were too small to hold large numbers of prisoners.

The failure of Confederate authorities to find or build enough suitable prison sites condemned Corcoran and tens of thousands of prisoners to ceaseless forced migrations from one temporary and overcrowded prison to the next. This constant churning severely taxed Confederate resources. The transfer of five hundred prisoners from Richmond to New Orleans shortly after Corcoran was sent to Charleston, for instance, took nearly six days, involved complex logistics, ten railroad companies, and the coordination of various military units that guarded the prisoners during the journey.

Each leg of Corcoran's itinerary revealed the centrality of railroads to

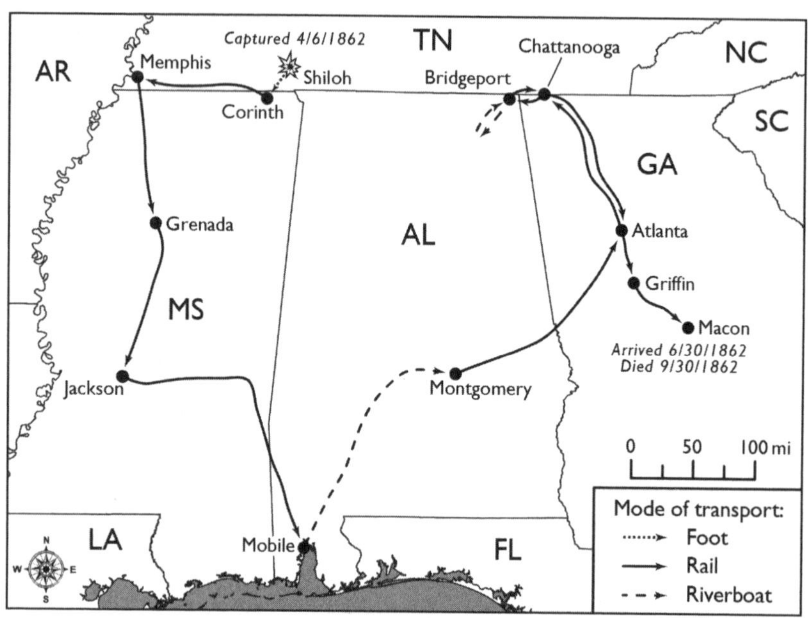


Willard Felton's Journey as a Confederate Prisoner of War, 1862.

the Confederacy's response to its swelling prison population. As the warring armies moved along paths defined by the region's railways and navigable rivers, so too did prisoners of war. With the Union navy blockading most Confederate ports, transfer of prisoners by sea was impossible. Prisoners could be marched overland under guard, but it was inconceivable that they could be marched from Richmond to Charleston, Tuscaloosa, or New Orleans. Railroads provided the only means to move large numbers of prisoners hundreds of miles relatively quickly.

The extended ordeal of Willard W. Felton reveals the hardships that prisoners endured as they were transferred willy-nilly by their Confederate captors. Felton, it would seem, was cursed. Only six weeks after he enlisted in the Eighteenth Wisconsin Regiment, he was captured during the Battle of Shiloh. The next day he and hundreds of other prisoners were marched about twenty miles to Corinth, Mississippi. There they loaded onto railroad cars, on which they spent a sleepless night. The following day they reached Memphis, one hundred miles to the west, where they were stuffed into a crude "brick house." They were next dispatched on a winding journey southeastward to Montgomery, Alabama. Absurdly roundabout, the route was the only path open after Union forces occupied much of northern Mississippi. Their train took a day to travel one hundred miles south to Grenada, Mississippi, and another day to travel an additional hundred miles to Jackson. On the fifth day of his captivity Felton arrived in Mobile. The next leg of Felton's journey began the following day. He and a boatload of prisoners spent a day and night chugging up the torpid Alabama River to Montgomery. On the tenth day of his ordeal, after a slog of seven hundred miles, Felton reached his first prison camp.

After a little more than a month, Felton's respite in Montgomery ended. He boarded another train, this time destined for Atlanta. There he and other prisoners changed rail lines and headed north to Chattanooga, where they camped for two days in rustic sheds before traveling by rail to Bridgeport, Alabama. They idled on the banks of the Tennessee River for two days awaiting a steamboat to transport them to their next destination. But when they finally reached it, the commanding officer there, for an undisclosed reason, refused to accept them. So, Felton and the other prisoners retraced their steps to Chattanooga. Two months after his capture, Felton still knew nothing of his eventual destination. On June 7, he was sent south to Atlanta and two days later to Griffin, Georgia. While there his fragile health worsened, and he spent the next three weeks convalescing in a military hospital. The physical and emotional wear and tear of the endless, soul-numbing, and seemingly pointless marches, train trips, and boat voyages colored the increasingly terse and forlorn entries that Felton scrawled in his diary. Finally, nearly three months since his capture and after a journey of more than twelve hundred miles, Felton was transferred to the Camp Oglethorpe prison in Macon. There he remained until he died three months later, at the age of eighteen, of "an abscess on the side and chronic diarrhea."

Tens of thousands of Union prisoners would follow in Felton's and Corcoran's tracks, landing temporarily in jails, abandoned factories, and other impromptu prisons that were wholly inadequate to house them.

Corcoran's *annus horribilis* finally ended in August 1862. After prisoners had spent months "living on the breath of rumor" of pending exchanges, general prisoner exchanges had begun in July. A month later Corcoran and most of his comrades at Salisbury were transferred back to Libby Prison in Richmond to await their exchange. Two weeks later, Union officials identified Colonel Roger W. Hanson, a Confederate from Kentucky who had been taken prisoner in February 1862, as an appropriate officer to exchange for Corcoran. On August 15, prison guards loaded Corcoran and several other officers onto a riverboat, which then traveled a short distance down the James River to meet a Union craft near Fortress Monroe. After thirteen months of captivity, Corcoran crossed the gangplank between the two vessels and regained his freedom.

Corcoran and the other newly freed prisoners were transported to Fortress Monroe, where they boarded a ship to Washington, D.C. There Corcoran dined with President Lincoln and gave the first of many speeches affirming his unshaken devotion to the Union cause. After receiving a hero's welcome in both Philadelphia and New York, Corcoran threw himself into recruiting more Irish volunteers to fill the ranks of what became known as the Corcoran Legion. Lionized in print and song, he was assigned command of a division guarding the nation's capital later in 1863.

Corcoran's subsequent military career was undistinguished. He did not live long enough to return to Richmond with the conquering Union army, much less to witness Irish independence. While riding alone in Fairfax, Virginia, a few days before Christmas in 1863, he was thrown from his horse and suffered a fractured skull. He died soon thereafter, at the age of thirty-six. (Corcoran's Confederate counterpart had preceded him. Four months after his exchange for Corcoran, Hanson had been mortally wounded during a charge at Murfreesboro, Tennessee.)

Corcoran's ordeal as a prisoner of war was a harbinger of the grim conditions that would prevail everywhere in the Confederacy later in the war. As Corcoran experienced firsthand, Confederate officials never fully accepted the obligation to provide for prisoners of war in the absence of exchanges. From the perspective of Confederate officials, the accumulation of Union prisoners of war was a security liability that imposed no ethical imperative. The unwillingness to build custodial facilities for prisoners of war partly reflected the Confederates' assumption that regular prisoner exchanges would mitigate the need for facilities to hold large numbers of prisoners for extended periods. Confederate authorities made a conscious decision that the long-term welfare of prisoners of war was contingent on the adoption of general prisoner exchanges. As long as no general exchange was in operation, Confederate officials were content to justify the worsening conditions in their prison facilities by invoking the imperatives of military necessity.

The failure of Confederate officialdom to meet the challenge of prisoners of war during the first year of the war was not evidence of a lack of imagination. In myriad ways, Confederates innovated. The Confederate quartermaster general, for instance, pursued an ambitious industrial policy that enabled the insurgent republic to wage war on a vast scale for four years. Likewise, from the outset of the war, General Winder and the Confederate secretaries of war exploited to the fullest the Confederacy's railroads to shift large numbers of prisoners across long distances as circumstances demanded. But Confederates devoted little ingenuity to meeting the most rudimentary needs of prisoners for adequate facilities. The consequences of this policy were already manifest by the summer of 1862. In the years to come, they would worsen catastrophically.

CHAPTER FOUR

# Where Is General Buckner?

## (1861–1862)

General George McClellan was vexed. On February 22, 1862, he implored, "Where is General Buckner?" No one in the Union army seemed to be able to locate Simon Bolivar Buckner, the highest-ranking Confederate captive. Six days earlier Buckner, along with more than twelve thousand troops amassed at Fort Donelson in Tennessee, had surrendered to an army commanded by General Ulysses S. Grant. The sudden influx of so many prisoners overwhelmed the Union army. Competing orders regarding the disposition of the prisoners further confused matters. Some officers had been pledged paroles shortly after their capture. But McClellan, now the highest-ranking field officer in the army, rescinded all paroles. At the same time, multiple commanders had issued contradictory orders sending Buckner and the other prisoners to destinations ranging from St. Louis and Chicago to Columbus, Ohio, and Boston. Amid this turmoil the Union high command lost track of Buckner and several other Confederate officers.

After a flurry of increasingly anxious telegrams over the next three days, Buckner was eventually tracked down in Indianapolis on his way to Columbus. This logistical muddle, nearly a year after the firing on Fort Sumter, underscored how unprepared the Union was to handle the prisoners of war who accumulated rapidly during the early months of 1862.

The irksome task of imposing order on this chaos fell to Colonel William Hoffman, commissary general for prisoners. He was responsible for captives held in nearly a dozen major sites, scattered from Fort Warren in

Boston harbor to the Old Capitol Prison in Washington, D.C., and as far west as Alton Prison on the banks of the Mississippi River in Illinois. The twenty thousand Confederate prisoners he oversaw during the summer of 1862 exceeded what the population of the entire U.S. army had been only two years prior. Among the numerous challenges Hoffman had to finesse was keeping track of Buckner and thousands of other prisoners as they were shuttled from distant battlefields to equally distant prison facilities.

At Camp Randall in Madison, Wisconsin, Hoffman discovered that the presiding officers and guards had plundered cots, sheets, lumber, straw, and fuel, leaving twelve hundred forlorn Confederates to sleep on bare floors in frigid barracks that were no better than crude sheds. These conditions contributed to an alarming death rate at the camp. Only the lethargy of the captives prevented their escape through the flimsy fence around the facility, which, in Hoffman's estimation, posed no obstacle to their flight.

The problems at Camp Douglas in Chicago were on a far larger scale. There, too, the perimeter fencing was grossly inadequate. Intrepid prisoners routinely fled, and visitors conversed with captives through the rickety fencing. More dire was the camp's deplorable sanitation. The pancake-flat prairie terrain, on which nearly eight thousand prisoners trod, could not absorb the human and animal waste that accumulated daily. Within weeks of the camp's opening, the site had degenerated into a malignant quagmire of "the filth and slop" from the privies, kitchens, and quarters. Visiting health inspectors recoiled in horror, declaring that "the amount of standing water, of unpoliced ground, of foul sinks, of unventilated and crowded barracks, of general disorder, of soil reeking with miasmatic accretions, of rotten bones and the emptyings of camp-kettles is enough to drive a sanitarian to despair." They urged the immediate razing of the camp.

The headaches at Camp Chase in Columbus were of a different nature but equally acute. Paroled Confederate officers were cavorting at large in the city. Irate citizens complained that the prisoners pranced about in their Confederate uniforms with sidearms, bellowed "secesh talk," camped out in the best hotels, and prowled the city's bars drinking "the mean whiskey for which Columbus is famous." They more closely resembled revelers in a bacchanal than chastened captives.

The problems Hoffman confronted were not unlike those that General John Winder wrestled with in Richmond. But the solutions adopted by Hoffman diverged in important ways. Differences in bureaucratic organization and priorities between the warring sides had lasting consequences, especially for the resources each nation committed to its war captives. Union officials, like their Confederate counterparts, had to determine where to stash prisoners. They had more and better facilities that could be transformed into prison camps but, even so, Hoffman and his superiors underestimated the ever growing number of captive Confederates who needed to be imprisoned. Just as in the Confederacy, the Union initially resorted to sending captives on forced migrations in search of secure accommodations in improvised prison camps.

In the winter of 1862 Hoffman must have felt like Hercules when he contemplated the Augean stables. Had the colonel been any less dogged, he might have surrendered to despair. Probably only someone of Hoffman's peculiar mettle could have persevered and brought a measure of order to the Union's administration of prisoners of war.

His nickname, "Old Huffy," captured many facets of his personality. Three decades in uniform left him unable to relax his ramrod stiff posture. A high forehead with a deeply furrowed brow graced his long, dour face, the lower half of which was hidden behind a plush mustache and bushy salt-and-pepper beard. Even by the standards of his era, when personal honor reigned supreme among military officers, Hoffman was acutely sensitive about his reputation and service record. Quick to perceive slights, he had a history of spats with fellow officers. Having fully internalized military protocol and hierarchy, he was irritatingly punctilious. He was also scrupulous to a fault and possessed an unflagging work ethic.

Hoffman, like Winder, was the son of a War of 1812 veteran and a graduate of West Point. Indeed, he had been a student when Winder was serving as an instructor there. After graduating and receiving a commission in the infantry, Hoffman spent the next decade and a half as a journeyman officer in Missouri, Kansas, and Florida. During the war with Mexico, he repeatedly displayed valor under enemy fire. Thereafter he returned to the life of a peripatetic frontier officer, which eventually took him in 1860 to San Antonio.

Hoffman experienced captivity firsthand before the first salvos were fired at Fort Sumter. He and twenty-six hundred other soldiers in Texas—a fifth of the U.S. army at the time—were under the command of Brigadier General David E. Twiggs. After Texas seceded, Twiggs acted on his Confederate sympathies and on February 18, 1861, surrendered all his troops to a ragtag Texas militia. Most of the captured soldiers were promptly hustled out

Colonel William Hoffman (center), ca. 1863. (Library of Congress)

of the state and sent north. But Hoffman and several other officers remained prisoners until they were offered paroles in late April. The experience of captivity left no deep impression on Hoffman. Unlike Winfield Scott nearly five decades earlier, Hoffman apparently drew no lessons from it and he subsequently displayed no heightened compassion for the legions of prisoners he oversaw.

By June, Hoffman was in New York City fretting about being sidelined from the war. Until he was formally exchanged for an enemy captive of equal rank, he was honor bound to refrain from serving in the field against the Confederacy. While Union officials struggled to find a posting for him that did not violate his parole, he lobbied for a command on the West Coast or for an expedited exchange so that he could enter the fray. (He would not be formally exchanged until more than a year later.) He was instead assigned in October to the quartermaster general's office.

For the next seven months Hoffman served under Brigadier General Montgomery C. Meigs, the quartermaster general. Like Hoffman, Meigs was meticulous and efficient. He was also hard-driving and brilliant. A Georgian by birth, he grew up in Philadelphia, where his father was a prominent doctor and educator. Meigs was sufficiently precocious to enter the University of Pennsylvania at the age of fifteen, before receiving an appointment to West Point the following year. He flourished there, graduating near the top of his class and distinguishing himself as an uncommonly able engineer. During the next two decades he oversaw the construction of forts from New York to Florida, before garnering recognition by designing an impressive aqueduct to provide water to Washington, D.C., and supervising the construction of the wings and dome of the United States Capitol.

President Lincoln appointed Meigs the quartermaster general a month after the start of the Civil War. Even while overseeing the massive task of organizing supplies for the ballooning Union army, Meigs anticipated an urgent need to prepare for the prisoners that the Union armies inevitably would capture. On the same day that Colonel Pegram surrendered after the rout at Rich Mountain in July 1861, Meigs advised Secretary of War Simon Cameron, "It is to be expected that the United States will have to take care of large numbers of prisoners of war, I respectfully call your attention to the propriety of making some arrangements in time." Drawing on the example of the War of 1812, Meigs recommended the appointment of a commissary general to keep track of Confederate prisoners and negotiate their exchange. The suitable candidate for the position, Meigs contended, should be "an accomplished gentleman" who possessed ample "knowledge of military law and custom." When his proposals were approved, Meigs nominated Hoffman, with whom he subsequently enjoyed a productive working relationship. Meigs periodically reined in Hoffman's plans but usually allowed him to conduct his office without interference.

After June 1862, Hoffman answered directly to Secretary of War Edwin Stanton. This reorganization reflected the Lincoln administration's newfound interest in prisoners of war as well as Stanton's passion for control over the sprawling wartime bureaucracy. "Mr. Stanton was fond of power and of its exercise," divulged Secretary of the Navy Gideon Welles. "It was more precious to him than pecuniary gain, to dominate over his fellow man." While a lawyer in Ohio, Stanton earned a reputation for his ruthless and rude courtroom demeanor. Observers conceded that he was exceptionally industrious and efficient. Years before the start of the Civil War, any wit and good humor he had once displayed in public had disappeared. A string of personal tragedies in his youth—the deaths of his first wife, daughter, and brother—scarred him both inwardly and outwardly. Before accepting his hand in marriage, his second wife confessed her anxiety that he was "careless

Dour but energetic, Secretary of War Edwin M. Stanton played an active role in Union prisoner-of-war policy. (Library of Congress)

and indifferent to the feelings of all." Stanton's critics, who were less forgiving than his spouse, compiled a long list of character flaws, including an "excitable and suspicious temperament," studied insincerity, narrow-mindedness, acute vindictiveness, chronic duplicity, obsequiousness, and a proclivity to embroider the truth. His appearance undoubtedly contributed to his perceived irascibility and rudeness. His stern countenance, massive head with extravagant whiskers, and heavyset frame inspired one contemporary to describe him as a "black terrier."

During the early months of the war, the Department of War had been notoriously chaotic and inefficient under Simon Cameron, Stanton's incompetent and corrupt predecessor. After replacing Cameron in January 1862, Stanton assiduously centralized authority in his office so that the army's generals no longer operated as free agents and war contractors no longer brazenly fleeced the government. Simultaneously, he oversaw the integration of transportation and communication networks across the North. Perhaps fueled by his curiosity about military law and his recognition of the political import of war captives, Stanton took an active interest in the handling of prisoners of war. (Confederates insisted that wanton vindictiveness fueled his attentiveness.) Everything from negotiations over prisoner exchanges to the captives' rations and accommodations attracted Stanton's scrutiny. He even took the trouble to make an overnight steamboat trip with President Lincoln in December 1863 to visit the Point Lookout prison camp in Maryland. If Colonel Hoffman bridled at Stanton's close oversight, he left no record of it.

The contrast between Hoffman's circumstances and those of General John Winder, his Confederate counterpart, was stark. Hoffman had no other duties to distract him from managing the imprisonment of Confederates, while overseeing prisoners was only part of Winder's portfolio. For the Union, prisoners of war were an extension of conventional military logistics. Consequently, Hoffman initially reported to the quartermaster general and worked closely with him throughout the war. While Winder engaged in bureaucratic brawls and competed for scarce resources, Hoffman was ensconced within one of the largest, most accomplished logistical operations in history. Armed with skills honed while supplying and feeding far-flung military posts scattered across the nation's continental empire, Union quartermasters were better prepared than any other arm of the military to confront the challenges of a vast civil war. Even after the quartermaster general's department swelled into a huge and complex bureaucracy, it operated with impressive efficiency. Except for rare occasions, food and supplies were plentiful. By one estimate, Union armies were better provisioned than any previous army in history.

Hoffman faced an early challenge cajoling generals in the field to acknowledge his authority over prisoners of war. The disregard displayed by some generals toward his department was another installment in the age-old jousting between front-line officers and functionaries behind lines. Early on, the problem could be traced to ignorance. In December 1861, Hoffman conceded that "the office and duties of commissary-general of prisoners are not familiar to the service." More than three months after his appointment, many officers continued to claim to be unaware of Hoffman's jurisdiction. With General Buckner's case still fresh in his mind, Hoffman complained to Meigs, "Up to this time generals whose troops have captured prisoners have exercised control over them whenever they thought proper to do so." Hoffman grumbled, "Any information I have about the movements of prisoners, I pick up from the newspapers or other chance sources." To remove any lingering confusion, in June 1862 the War Department stated unambiguously that supervision of prisoners of war "is placed, entirely under Colonel William Hoffman, Commissary General of Prisoners, who is subject only to the orders of the War Department."

To tighten his grip, Hoffman began accumulating the information needed to track and manage the equivalent of an army corps of prisoners. Decades spent conforming to military formalities prepared him well for the task. He ordered camp commanders to file lists that summarized the essential details and disposition of each prisoner. With a glance at these rolls, Hoffman could identify when and where a prisoner was captured, his rank, and whether he had died, been exchanged, or transferred to a new facility. Within a year, Hoffman's mania for data required prison staffs to submit, three times a month, nearly a dozen different rolls cataloging a wide array of information.

Hoffman was less successful at enlisting field officers in his recordkeeping. Whether from obstinacy, lethargy, or overwork, commanders submitted inaccurate, incomplete, or late returns. General Grant, for example, aroused Hoffman's ire by submitting rolls that lacked details essential for exchanging prisoners. But even laggards like Grant could not entirely hobble Hoffman's administrative machinery; once prisoners were transferred to Hoffman's domain the meticulous compilation of data began.

Hoffman coupled his data harvesting with copious regulations for the administration of prison camps. His administrative scheme was the creation of a man steeped in the methods and ethos of the army, and he took for granted that his subordinates would be versed in the army's arcane administrative procedures and regulations. He also expected them to comply promptly and meticulously with his mandates. At length and in detail, he spelled out the guidelines for camp management, from finances and rations to discipline. To ensure that his policies were uniformly applied, he initiated routine inspections. Throughout the war his periodic inspection tours would be supplemented by regular visits from his assistants. Having seen the conditions at Camp Randall and elsewhere during his first tour of the prison depots in the spring of 1862, Hoffman insisted on fastidious oversight. As he explained to an assistant, it was not enough "simply to give orders but to see them carefully executed." Ever vigilant, Hoffman commanded his aide to make sure that all regulations were enforced "minutely in daily practice under your immediate supervision."

The vagaries of his subordinates disappointed Hoffman and hampered his designs. Because of the sweep of his responsibilities, which extended from the southern battlefields where prisoners were captured to the prison camps in the North, Hoffman had to deal with distracted field officers, some professional soldiers, some clueless volunteers, and interfering politicians wherever Union prisons were located.

Some of the officers who oversaw prisoners were highly competent career soldiers. Colonel Justin E. Dimick at Fort Warren in Boston was, as John Pegram could attest, an exemplary prison commander. Considerate, diligent, and thoroughly professional, Dimick gave Hoffman no cause for anxiety over his administration of the depot that held Pegram, Buckner, and many other high-profile prisoners. Few officers of Dimick's caliber, however, remained camp commandants for long. Many, like Captain Augustus A. Gibson, an able career soldier who commanded Fort Delaware, were not keen to spend the war as wardens of makeshift prisons and stumped instead for combat assignments or more prestigious postings. Like his counterpart in Richmond, Hoffman had to contend with the constant turnover of staff, especially early in the war.

This churning of prison command created turmoil in the administration of the camps—nowhere more so than at Camp Douglas. In 1862 alone, it had six changes in command, half of which occurred during a span of less than a week in June. The dizzying parade of officers who presided over the camp manifested every shortcoming or vice that could afflict a large organization.

Such chronic turmoil impeded consistency in policies and precluded the kind of strict management that Hoffman aspired to install at all prisons. The first commandant of Camp Douglas, Colonel Joseph A. Tucker, had overseen the construction of the facility as a training camp for Illinois volunteers during the early months of the war. When Tucker was given a field command in February 1862, the camp briefly was in the hands of Colonel Arno Voss, before Colonel James A. Mulligan took over. Three months later Mulligan abruptly departed without providing any instructions to his successor, Colonel Daniel Cameron. Five days later, Colonel Tucker returned to resume command of the depot. He complained to Hoffman, "There is scarcely a record left at camp and it will be difficult to ascertain what prisoners have been at the camp or what has become of them." Tucker could not furnish names or number of prisoners who had escaped, were sick, had died, or had been discharged prior to his tenure.

None of the commandants at Camp Douglas in 1862 had the military know-how appropriate to preside over a small garrison, let alone what was then the largest military prison in the Union. With few exceptions, they were amateur soldiers who, in the opinion of Hoffman, were in well over their heads. Tucker was a commodities speculator and banker who attended to his extensive business interests even as he served as commandant of Camp Douglas. His prominence in Chicago's business circles had won him

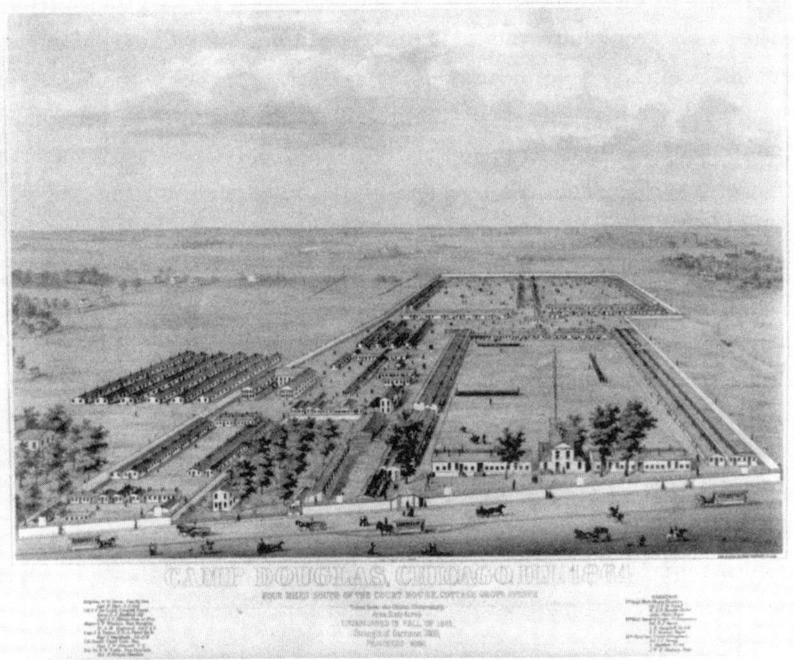

Camp Douglas appears deceptively tidy and bucolic in this 1864 lithograph. (Library of Congress)

the appointment to build and command the training camp that became Camp Douglas. Mulligan secured his place because of his stature as a well-educated lawyer and Irish American politico.

Officers' lack of familiarity with military protocol and inexperience with a complex bureaucracy like the Union army added to the administrative disarray at Camp Douglas and elsewhere. A crusty veteran like Hoffman had little patience for Tucker, Mulligan, and other warrior poseurs. Too often such volunteer officers, Hoffman rued, were "wanting in many things essential" for a prison commander. The commandant at Alton Prison was a case in point. Although a "very kind man," he seldom complied with Hoffman's orders, no matter how specific. At Camp Douglas, Mulligan displayed, in Hoffman's judgment, "the greatest carelessness and willful neglect" in his management of the camp. (Mulligan had exhibited similar ineptitude when he commanded troops in Missouri prior to his tenure as a prison commandant.) Mulligan and Tucker both maintained notoriously lax supervision of the prison garrison. Before it was a prison, security at the camp was such an embarrassment that the *Chicago Tribune* dismissed as farcical reports that the camp was to be converted into a prisoner depot: "The idea of keeping five thousand prisoners in a camp, where the strongest guard couldn't keep in a drunken corporal, is rich." The combination of "want of discipline" and lack of training among the raw recruits who staffed Camp Douglas and other prison pens in 1862, however, had consequences that were far from comical. The green and ill-supervised Wisconsin volunteers at Camp Randall, for example, proved to be trigger-happy sentinels who unjustifiably shot down several Confederates imprisoned there.

Even those officers whom Hoffman groomed for their duties disappointed him. While overseeing the construction of the Johnson's Island camp in Ohio, Hoffman identified William Seward Pierson as a plausible commander for the new depot. Although Pierson "knew nothing" about military affairs, he had served as mayor of nearby Sandusky, was an "experienced man of business," and, most important, was "particular in administrative affairs." He would, Hoffman predicted, quickly master his duties. Within a few months Hoffman conceded that he had badly misjudged. Despite copious coaching, Pierson proved to be irredeemably indecisive and inept.

The combination of lax management and incompetence at Camp Douglas gave prison staff a free hand to seize illicit opportunities that came their way. Officers, guards, and the camp sutler accepted bribes from Confederate prisoners. One guard padded his pay by selling civilian clothes to prisoners to facilitate their flight. Commandant Mulligan knew of this underground economy but did nothing to suppress it or prosecute the malefactors. Corruption surfaced at other camps as well. At Camp Chase in Ohio, the commissary and a contractor lined their pockets by inflating reports of wasted supplies and fraudulently overcharging for inferior provisions for the prisoners. The malfeasance was less crass but certainly no less conspicuous at Camp Randall, where an unexplained medical necessity required the depletion of a six-month supply of medicine—"all the liquors, 168 pint bottles"—in five days.

Hoffman acted decisively to replace unfit staff when he could. He never gained the authority to appoint or fire prison commanders, although he requested that Secretary of War Stanton grant him the power to do so. He could not even upbraid or discipline volunteer officials who had influential champions. State governors who looked upon prison positions as convenient patronage destinations for cronies, allies, and relatives routinely intruded in the management of camps in their states. Colonel Tucker at Camp Douglas was a protégé of Governor Richard Yates of Illinois, who was a close political ally of President Lincoln. Camp Chase in Columbus was administered poorly by Colonel Granville Moody, a Methodist minister who was "entirely without experience and utterly ignorant of his duties." Among the myriad problems that resulted from his ineptitude were filthy prison grounds that spread "sickness and pestilence." But Hoffman was hamstrung in his efforts to improve the situation because Governor David Tod of Ohio strenuously defended the commandant. Even when Secretary of War Stanton complained about the commander's tolerance for paroled Confederate officers cavorting in nearby hotels and bars, the governor fired back that Moody was "a strong antislavery Republican" who performed his duties "faithfully and discreetly." Moody's successor proved no better. He was "utterly ignorant of the most common requirements of the Army Regulations." But he was "a good lawyer" and, most important, the son-in-law of the lieutenant governor.

The jumble of facilities that made up the Union prison system further complicated Hoffman's duties. With the influx of Buckner and other prisoners after the capture of Fort Donelson, Union officials improvised prison facilities across the Midwest. This makeshift prison infrastructure was cobbled together with breathtaking speed. In less than a month, the twelve thousand prisoners captured at Fort Donelson were dispersed to facilities that, for the most part, had not previously held captives of any kind. Once in operation, these impromptu depots were beset by problems resulting from the haste with which they had been transformed into prisons.

The inadequacy of existing forts and federal jails to serve as wartime prisons was evident from the earliest months of the war. Old Capitol Prison in Washington, D.C., was pressed into service to hold spies and captives of various kinds. But it was small and, by common agreement, a rat trap. Similar shortcomings at Fort McHenry in Baltimore and the facilities on Governors Island in New York City were conspicuous when Colonel Pegram was briefly imprisoned at both in 1861.

The exceptions were Fort Warren and Fort Delaware. Fort Warren was large enough and sufficiently well appointed to hold five hundred prisoners, and as many as a thousand temporarily, without condemning them to a quick death. Fort Delaware, located on an island in the Delaware River just south of Wilmington, was under construction when the war began. Enough of the massive fortifications were complete in 1861 to house a small cadre of political and military prisoners. By April 1862, when facilities farther west were bursting with captives, Quartermaster General Meigs ordered the construction of shanties for two thousand prisoners on the grounds of the fort. When Hoffman visited two months later, six hundred prisoners were already in residence. Persuaded that the site was "a very suitable place," Hoffman ordered the construction of barracks for three thousand additional prisoners and announced that there would be room for yet more. This ongoing expansion would eventually transform Fort Delaware into one of the largest prison pens in the Union. But in the summer of 1862, it remained a minor depot overshadowed by other facilities in a rapidly expanding prison network.

Quartermaster General Meigs recognized the urgent need for new prison facilities to augment the meager capacity of the nation's forts. He proposed in July 1861 to build a prison on one of the small islands on the western shores of Lake Erie. The islands' chief attractions were their isolation and purportedly healthful cleansing breezes. Colonel Hoffman's first task following his appointment was to locate a site for the new facility and oversee its construction. He selected Johnson's Island; it was uninhabited, could be leased cheaply, and was close enough to the town of Sandusky for convenient resupplying. Yet it was far enough from the mainland to thwart escape by all but the most foolhardy prisoners.

The inspiration for Hoffman's design for the Union's first purpose-built prisoner-of-war camp was a military camp, not a penitentiary. There is no evidence that Hoffman was familiar with contemporary civilian prisons or the prewar debates about effective penitentiary design. But he knew a great deal about forts and military outposts. In his youth his father had overseen the construction of barracks in New York and Michigan. At West Point, Hoffman had learned about fortifications from Professor Dennis Hart Mahan, whose treatises on military engineering were canonical for Hoffman's generation. He later supervised the building of forts in Florida, the Nebraska Territory, and present-day Wyoming. This know-how almost certainly was one of the reasons Meigs selected him to be commissary general for prisoners.

The prison Hoffman designed would not have been out of place on the western frontier. It differed from the typical frontier fort in only two important regards. It was larger than any that Hoffman had served at, and its defenses were intended to keep the enemy inside rather than outside the depot. To achieve this end, Hoffman adapted the familiar tall stockade used in some frontier forts but provided a banquette along the exterior for patrolling sentries to surveil the captives inside. Otherwise, the design duplicated most of the facilities and outbuildings that normally cluttered a

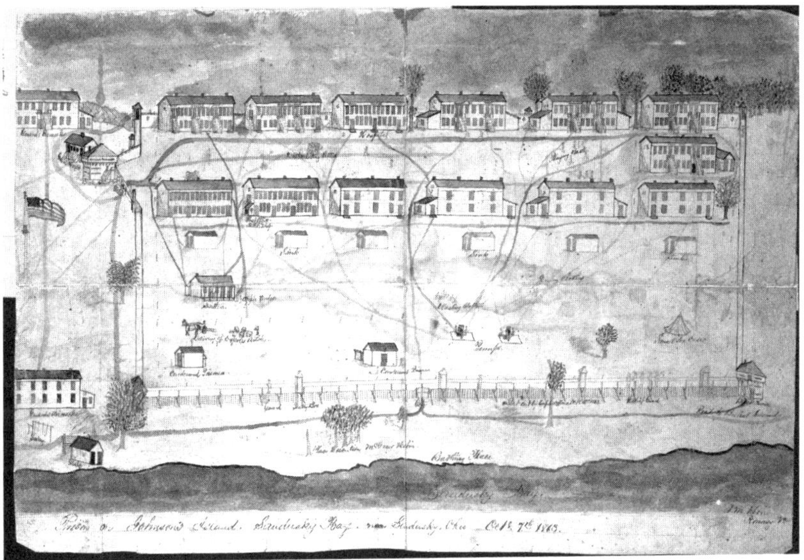

The Johnson's Island prison, as depicted by prisoner Joseph Mason Kern in October 1863, had the appearance of a well-ordered military compound. (Southern Historical Collection, University of North Carolina)

military garrison, including a hospital, storehouses, a kitchen, mess halls, and barracks for prisoners and guards. Although rustic, the quarters Hoffman designed for prisoners closely resembled the enlisted men's barracks at any military station. In subsequent years the facility would expand until more than one hundred structures dotted the island and two parallel rows of prisoner blocks housed up to three thousand captives. Even then, the prison retained the essential character of the frontier outpost that Hoffman sketched in the fall of 1861.

When Hoffman notified Meigs in late January 1862 that the depot was nearing completion, he assumed that most of the prisoners of war then in Union hands would be transferred there. But already, the facility was too small—its opening capacity was less than a thousand prisoners. Within days of Hoffman's announcement, the surrender at Fort Donelson confronted the Union with the immediate challenge of accommodating more than ten times that number. Those numbers were soon augmented by the prisoners swept up during subsequent battles. The number of Confederates captured during the Battle of Shiloh alone, for instance, substantially exceeded the capacity of Johnson's Island.

Desperation drove Union officials to house some prisoners in civilian facilities, but never to the extent of their Confederate counterparts. In St. Louis, Union officials transformed two expropriated buildings into prisons. The slave trader Bernard Lynch's two-story brick market, which was seized in September 1861, could hold only a couple of hundred prisoners, most of whom were local Confederate sympathizers. The other seized building, a medical college belonging to a doctor who had fled to the Confederacy, was substantially larger. Its classrooms became prison cells and its operating theater became a mess hall. By late 1862 the college-cum-prison held more than one thousand inmates. Because of their modest size, these two sites mainly served as transfer depots for captives who were then sent to larger prison pens farther north.

The overtaxed prisons in St. Louis prompted the conversion of the abandoned Alton Prison in Illinois into a prisoner depot. Even before the crush of Fort Donelson prisoners, General Henry Halleck, then the ranking commander in the western theater, received approval from the War Department to press the facility into service. Built in 1830 during the early prison reform movement, the state facility had been replaced by a new penitentiary in Joliet before the start of the war. The principal advantage of the empty prison was convenience. Union officials, however, refrained from housing prisoners in the prison cells, perhaps out of fear that it might prompt Con-

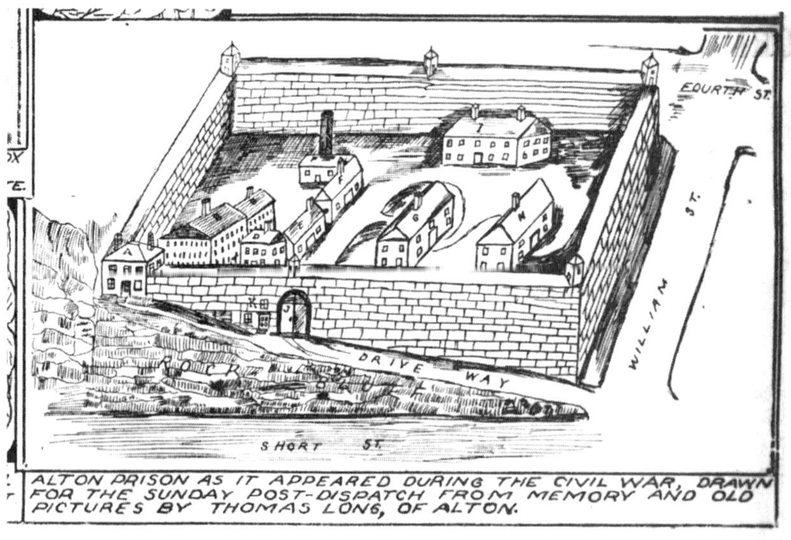


The former Alton State Prison, as recalled by a former prisoner decades after the war. (From *St. Louis Post-Dispatch*, June 15, 1902)

federate retaliation against Union prisoners. Instead, several hundred prisoners were kept in the large passageways between the cells while hundreds more occupied various outbuildings. Within weeks the Alton depot had more inmates than it had ever held as a state prison. Although considered a stopgap measure, it proved too convenient to abandon and remained in use throughout the war.

The sites that absorbed most of the Confederate prisoners in 1862 were training camps that had been used to initiate Union volunteers into the military arts after President Lincoln's call for troops in April 1861. When Union officials appealed for help housing the Fort Donelson prisoners, Midwestern governors offered training grounds in Madison, Chicago, Springfield, Indianapolis, and Columbus. Each site was accessible by rail, which greatly facilitated the speedy transfer of prisoners. And because the camps were military facilities that had already accommodated thousands of trainees, minimal construction was needed to ready them to house prisoners.

Several of the camps were purportedly garden spots. Camp Butler in Springfield, which boasted a spring-fed lake and lush forests, was pronounced an ideal place for a military camp. Camp Morton in Indianapolis had been a fairground before the war, while Camp Chase in Columbus had been both a fairground and a racetrack. At Camp Butler, fifteen barracks that had previously housed Illinois volunteers were already in place. At Camp Morton, barns and other fairground buildings had been converted into quarters for the seven thousand Indiana volunteers who trained there. Beyond constructing more barracks, little work was necessary to transform the camp into a prison pen. Meanwhile, Camp Chase had ample space for the one-story barracks and other facilities that had accommodated four thousand Ohio recruits who trained there.

The drawbacks of the repurposed training camps, however, soon became conspicuous. They had been built to serve as temporary camps, not long-term custodial facilities for prisoners. None of the camps had appropriate fencing, for not even the sternest commander had sought to treat volunteer trainees like prisoners. Most of the barracks had been outfitted for sweltering summer weather rather than harsh winter conditions. Moreover, the grounds at the camps were ill designed for the unrelenting wear and tear of large populations of milling, idle internees. None of the camps had adequate drainage.

The problems at Camp Douglas and Camp Chase were especially chronic. The byways at Camp Chase became a treacherous morass whenever it rained. A sanitarian's worst nightmare, Camp Douglas resembled

Confederate prisoners huddle at Camp Morton, Indianapolis. (Library of Congress)

an open sewer in appearance and odor. Few of the camps, moreover, had medical facilities adequate for large numbers of wounded or ill prisoners. The hospital at Camp Butler, for instance, was deemed to be in "deplorable condition" within a few weeks of the arrival of Confederate prisoners, and the facilities at Camp Randall and at the former medical college in St. Louis were arguably worse.

Given the shortcomings of the various camps, Hoffman had to conduct an ongoing triage to determine the order in which he addressed them. Establishing secure perimeters at each prison was the first priority. Equally important was amassing adequate medical staff and facilities, which proved to be a challenge because the wartime demand for trained physicians far exceeded the number of qualified practitioners. Attending to housing needs was comparatively simple. When the ongoing surge of prisoners swamped the existing housing, Hoffman mandated the use of tents on the prison grounds to handle the overflow.

Budgetary constraints curbed Hoffman's efforts to improve the prison pens. Moreover, his bred-in-the-bone deference to superiors and innate frugality made him an awkward lobbyist for the interests of Confederate prisoners of war. Any substantial renovations had to be sufficiently urgent to overcome the reluctance of the quartermaster general and the secretary of war to direct resources to prisoners rather than Union soldiers in the field. Hoffman was committed to maintaining tidy, healthful, and efficient prisons but always within the budget imposed upon him by his superiors.

Hoffman's handling of the chronic drainage problems at Camp Douglas was a telling case in point. Appalled by the "carelessness and willful neglect" at the camp, he recommended the construction of a sewage system to flush the camp's waste into nearby Lake Michigan. The need for a drastic remedy was clear to anyone who had the misfortune to be downwind of the camp. But the project required substantial labor and expense. Quartermaster General Meigs dismissed the proposal out of hand. "Ten thousand men should certainly be able to keep this camp clean," he scoffed, "and the United States had other uses for its money." In the face of General Meigs's veto, Hoffman ordered new latrines dug. But they only added to the problem.

Hoffman had considerably more success bringing order to the chaotic distribution of prisoners among the various camps. He set out to consolidate officers, enlisted men, and civilian prisoners at specific facilities. His underlying assumption reflected the long-standing tradition of separating officers from the ranks, over whom the officers might exert a corrupting influence, such as organizing prison escapes or discouraging prisoners from joining the Union ranks. Segregating officers and the ranks in theory also eased efficient exchanges of captives. Thus, some officers were sent, as were Colonel Pegram and General Buckner, to Fort Warren in Boston harbor. The rest were sent to Johnson's Island. Confederate irregulars—partisans and bushwhackers—were sent to St. Louis, Alton, and Columbus, while enlisted men were shunted to Camps Douglas, Butler, Morton, and Chase. (Later in the war, enlisted prisoners would be sent to Fort Delaware and newly constructed camps in Maryland, Illinois, and New York).

The mix-up regarding General Buckner's whereabouts, while embarrassing, proved to be atypical. The confusion that hampered the dispersal of prisoners in February 1862 soon dissipated, and thereafter Confederate prisoners were moved with impressive speed across the breadth of the Union. Still, moving captives long distances securely and efficiently remained challenging. In the western theater, where Union armies penetrated deep into the Confederacy by the summer of 1862, most Confederate prisoners had to be transported at least five hundred miles from the front lines to prison depots in the North.

Even in the East, where much of the war was waged within a hundred miles of Washington, D.C., captive Confederates could anticipate a journey to their prison pen of at least three hundred miles. Confederate officers destined for Johnson's Island or Fort Warren traveled even farther.

Transporting prisoners from the southern hinterlands to northern prisons involved elaborate logistical choreography. Hundreds and sometimes thousands of prisoners were moved at a time. Sufficient railcars and boats were needed to transport the prisoners, rail and boat schedules had to be synchronized, guard units had to be assigned to each leg of the trip, rations had to be available while in transit, and authorities at the end of the journey had to be prepared for their new charges. Actual practice fell short of precise plans, and prisoners endured delays, discomfort, and other annoyances. Nevertheless, many Confederate prisoners during 1862 experienced the impressive wartime integration of the North's transportation network.

Colonel Randal William McGavock gained a firsthand view of the initial disarray and subsequent efficiency of Union logistics. He brought to the experience the keen eye of a world traveler. He had been raised in genteel comfort in Nashville before graduating from Harvard Law School in 1849 and spending the following two years touring Europe, Asia, and Africa. While commanding the Tenth Tennessee Infantry, he was captured at Fort Donelson.

On February 18, the day after his capture, McGavock and eight hundred other prisoners squeezed aboard a steamboat bound for Paducah, where Confederate captives were clustered before being sent elsewhere. By the following evening, they reached their destination but remained on the squalid boat because there was no suitable place ashore to corral them. The following day, they steamed up the Mississippi toward St. Louis, which they reached on February 20. They briefly anchored beside a flotilla of other boats bursting with Confederate prisoners before starting upriver toward the newly repurposed state prison at Alton, Illinois. But two days later they were redirected back to St. Louis, where their boat and its human cargo festered for three days. "The crowd, the filth, and the stench made it exceedingly disagreeable," McGavock grumbled in his diary. Finally, on February 27, McGavock and the other officers were dispatched by rail to Camp Chase in Columbus.

For a man who prided himself on his refinement, the beginning of McGavock's train trip to Ohio was excruciating. He was packed in a box car with fifty men in the ranks, "without any stove and nothing to eat or drink." Unable to endure the conditions, he accosted the officer in charge and demanded a seat in one of the passenger cars. Because he was a field

Colonel Randal William McGavock experienced both the inefficiency and efficiency of the Union's transport of prisoners. (Library of Congress)

officer (and knew the commanding Union officer) he traveled the remainder of the day-and-a-half-long trip in relative comfort. On arriving at Camp Chase he was appalled: "The more I see of this dirty and loathsome prison, the more outraged I feel." He vouched that "no farmer in ten" would hazard his hogs or cattle to live in such wretched conditions. Three days later, to his great relief, he and several other officers were sent on to Fort Warren.

McGavock's journey of eight hundred miles from Fort Donelson to Columbus took eleven days. He traveled the remaining eight hundred miles to Boston in a day and a half. The pace of the first half of his journey had been dictated by the slow progress of riverboats traveling upriver as well as inchoate Union plans for the prisoners. Lacking any clear arrangements, Union officials had kept them in motion. But once authorities determined their final destinations, McGavock and other prisoners were transferred with impressive speed.

The contrast between McGavock's and Corcoran's experiences on the railroads of the two warring nations was telling. Recall, for instance, that the first leg of Corcoran's trek from Richmond to Wilmington, a distance of about two hundred fifty miles, took three days and three different rail lines. McGavock, on his trip to Boston, covered three times the distance in half the time and with a measure of comfort. As Corcoran could attest, the southern railway system was a disparate collection of relatively small lines. More than one hundred different companies operated the region's nine thousand miles of rails. Most lines were short and local, few extending as many as a couple of hundred miles, and they had been built to carry agricultural products to ports. The absence of trunk lines and the prevalence of different rail gauges (track widths) impeded through traffic. Even southern railroads that used the same gauge were often not connected so that passengers and freight had to be unloaded and transferred from one line to the next. Corcoran and his fellow prisoners experienced these inconveniences time and time again during their migration among the Confederacy's prisons.

Although seldom acknowledged, the relative ease with which the Union could move McGavock and other captives around its expanding network of prisons figured prominently in the Union's long-term handling of prisoners. The coordination of the Union's transportation and communications network allowed the Union to shift Confederate prisoners without interfering with military or civilian transportation. The North's extensive web of railroads also gave Hoffman license to look for possible prison sites without undue concern for their distance from the front lines of the conflict. Ease of transit did not relieve the burdens associated with prisoners of war, but it made it possible to transfer prisoners quickly from war zones to places where their maintenance was less challenging. After February 1862, logistics imposed few constraints on the Union's capacity to accommodate ever more prisoners of war.

In July 1861 Quartermaster General Meigs had anticipated the need for a prison camp that could hold only hundreds. Nevertheless, within a year Hoffman had made great strides toward building a prison system that could organize and accommodate tens of thousands of prisoners with unprecedented efficiency. By the fall of 1862, northern newspapers boasted that the Union treated prisoners of war more humanely than had any previous nation.

That Hoffman, who was so rule and tradition bound, had such a central role in fashioning the modern prisoner-of-war camp is one of the unrecognized ironies of the Civil War. He was an innovator neither by nature nor intent. Despite the unprecedented scale of the war, Hoffman relied on the methods and traditions he had internalized during his long military career to tackle the task at hand. He demonstrated that by harnessing the century's technological innovations and applying ample resources, a robust system of custodial prison pens not only was feasible but also held out the promise that long-term imprisonment might be tolerable, even merciful.

Unfortunately Hoffman's accomplishment had a grim underside. Hoffman displayed no enmity toward the prisoners he oversaw and he endeavored to mitigate the capriciousness of ill-trained, undisciplined, and apathetic prison staff by instilling professionalism throughout his command. His official correspondence is free of commonplace invective against "rebels," "traitors," or "slavers." He never advocated punitive measures or harsh punishments against the captives, and few Union prisons in 1862 displayed the flagrant dehumanization that already prevailed in Confederate prisons.

Yet neither did Hoffman dwell on the humanity of the captives filling the North's prison pens. Through his words and actions, he demarcated clear boundaries for the treatment of prisoners. He repeatedly calibrated what could or should be done on their behalf in accordance with his devotion to prudent, practical, and economical administration. As he attested to General Meigs, his "great desire has been to be governed by the strictest economy in all cases." Prisoners were to have just enough food, clothing, and protection against the elements to remain healthy. As Hoffman periodically intoned, "It is not expected that anything more will be done to provide for the welfare of the rebel prisoners than is absolutely necessary."

Hoffman's subalterns calibrated conditions in the camps accordingly. Buildings to house prisoners were to be of "a temporary and cheap character, though suitable to give protection against inclement weather." He cautioned one of his assistants that any renovations at a camp had to be made with due regard for economy: "At best it must fall far short of perfection." With regard to clothing for the inmates, Hoffman declared that prison commanders should requisition only "such clothing as may be absolutely necessary." During spring and summer months he mandated that "neither drawers nor socks will be allowed except to the sick [prisoners]." Hoffman presumed that "contributions by their friends" would clothe the prisoners so camp staff should supply clothing "only in extreme cases."

Hoffman also fostered exaggerated economy. In March 1862, he deemed the daily ration for prisoners excessive for "men living quietly in camp." By "judiciously withholding" rations and selling them back to the commissary, camp commandants could create a fund "with which many articles needful to the prisoners may be purchased and thus save expense to the Government." Thereafter, his proposal became policy. Simultaneously, Hoffman instituted another cost-saving and fund-raising scheme. Instead of purchasing bread for rations, camp administrators were enjoined to establish camp bakeries and to practice economies of scale. Rather than allotting each prisoner twenty-two ounces of flour per day, the prison bakery should issue each prisoner twenty-two ounces of bread. Because less than twenty-two ounces of flour was used to bake twenty-two ounces of bread, the surplus flour could be resold to the commissary, and the resulting money could augment the prison fund.

Both practices had been commonplace in the antebellum army. Funds gathered in this manner had provided garrisons with luxuries that parsimonious politicians and army administrators had otherwise been loath to fund. While commanding Newport Barracks in Kentucky from 1852 to 1854, Hoffman himself had tapped the post's fund to build an icehouse and a bowling alley, support a post band, purchase lumber for school desks, spruce up the camp chapel, and improve camp cuisine. The objective of such funds, he explained, was "to make the prisoners as comfortable as circumstances will admit and at the same time relieve the Government as far as possible of the expense of their keeping."

Most Union prison-camp commandants, however, showed little interest in tapping prison funds to ameliorate conditions in the camps. Some commanders purchased brooms, buckets, pumps, cooking and eating utensils, and bedding with the funds. But elsewhere they bought items of little if any benefit to prisoners. At one camp, for instance, officials used the fund to buy leg irons, padlocks, and handcuffs. Worse yet, many prison-camp commandants, whether through indolence or malice, left untapped funds to accumulate in camp coffers. By the end of the war, nearly two million dollars that could have been used to improve Union prison pens remained stashed away.

Hoffman's unstinting emphasis on protocols, efficiency, and economy encouraged insouciance about the hardships endured by Confederate prisoners of war. When Hoffman inspected a "deplorable" prison hospital or observed filthy prison barracks, he was most appalled and embarrassed by evidence of slipshod management, inefficiency, and waste. While he did not condone cruelty or license gratuitous mistreatment, he wasted no words on the suffering of prisoners. Like the model bureaucrat described generations later by the sociologist Max Weber, Hoffman obsessed about precision, speed, conformity, efficiency, and frugality without regard to persons. Hoffman almost certainly would have agreed with Weber's enduring dictum that "bureaucracy develops the more perfectly, the more it is 'dehumanized' the more completely it succeeds in eliminating from official business love, hatred, and all purely personal, irrational, and emotional elements which escape calculation."

CHAPTER FIVE

# Upon Terms of Perfect Equality

## (1862–1863)

The men's desperation leapt off the page. Among the torrent of administrative dross that crossed the desk of Navy Secretary Gideon Welles during the summer of 1863 was a singular petition from Orin H. Brown, William H. Johnson, and William Wilson, three Union sailors and prisoners of war. When Welles forwarded the petition to a colleague, he attested that "from the walls of their prison they make themselves heard."

After months moldering in the same Charleston jail that had previously held Michael Corcoran, the captives fretted: "We suppose the Government has forgotten us altogether." They complained that "being shut up so close all the time, we are in a very bad situation, indeed." They entreated, "Are we to be exchanged, or are we to be left here to perish?"

Their ordeal had begun in January, when their ship, the USS *Isaac Smith*, had been raked by Confederate batteries on the Stono River in South Carolina. Rather than risk the lives of wounded crew strewn on the deck, the ship's captain surrendered. Brown, Johnson, and Wilson, along with more than one hundred other crew and officers, were hustled to Charleston, where they were taunted by civilians before being packed into the jail.

The prisoners had reason to hope that their captivity would be brief. General exchanges of prisoners between the warring sides had begun six months earlier and had emptied the prison pens and dramatically reduced the length of time captives spent in enemy hands. Within weeks the enlisted sailors from the *Isaac Smith*, excepting Brown, Johnson, and Wilson, were

The fate of three Black sailors hung in the balance after the capture of the USS *Isaac Smith* in 1863. (Library of Congress)

dispatched to Virginia and by the end of February had been returned to Union lines. The ship's officers were less fortunate. They remained captives for three months until they too were exchanged. By the time Brown, Johnson, and Wilson's plea reached Welles in July 1863, the rest of their shipmates had been back in the safety of the Union for several months.

Brown, Johnson, and Wilson, mere minions in the huge Union war machine, were targets of a single-minded persecution. Anathema in the eyes of Confederate authorities, they embodied one of the paramount issues of the war. From the standpoint of their captors, the sailors' most important characteristic was the color of their skin.

The fragile principle of reciprocity upon which prisoner exchanges rested shattered when Black men donned the Union uniform. The status of the three captives otherwise was straightforward. They had duly enlisted in New York City in September 1862, served honorably, and been captured in uniform during combat while performing their duties. On that basis, they were entitled to the same treatment as the other crew members of the *Isaac Smith*. Yet, Confederates could not accept any measure that suggested the equality of white and Black men while waging a war to defend the righteousness of the institution of slavery. Unwilling to exchange the Black sailors, Confederates instead misled Union officials by reporting that all surviving crew of the *Isaac Smith*, including Brown, Johnson, and Wilson, had been exchanged. Confederates left their fates unresolved, dooming the men to an oppressive limbo in their Charleston cell, wondering if they would be enslaved, executed, or forgotten.

Brown, Johnson, and Wilson displayed uncommon pluck in bringing their plight to the attention of the Lincoln administration. Through undisclosed means, they got their appeal into the hands of the U.S. consul in the Bahamas. Perhaps a Black employee smuggled their plea out of the jail. Maybe a good Samaritan in Charleston, moved by their plight, aided them by dispatching their petition. Maybe they bribed someone to carry their letter on a blockade runner. Whatever the subterfuge, their letter escaped the attention of Confederate censors and wended its way from Charleston to the Bahamas and then to Washington.

Once prisoner exchanges began, both sides consoled themselves that subsequent captives would escape the hardships of extended imprisonment. No one anticipated that the prospects for ongoing exchanges would hinge on the treatment of obscure Black servicemen like Brown, Johnson, and Wilson. Yet, within months the warring sides had staked out irreconcilable positions, which subsequently choked off the exchange of prisoners. In short order, the number of captives began mounting in lockstep with the escalating intensity of the war. Thereafter, tens of thousands of prisoners on both sides faced the likelihood that they, along with Brown, Johnson, and Wilson, would regain their freedom only if they survived until the war's end.

The prisoner exchanges that Brown, Johnson, and Wilson awaited so desperately started only after months of halting negotiations during the spring and summer of 1862. The negotiations, which took place without fanfare near Richmond, were the most important bilateral negotiations that the warring sides conducted during the conflict. Both sides recognized the import of the meetings and sent negotiators of the first rank. During the first round of talks Major General John E. Wool represented the Union, and Brigadier General Howell Cobb the Confederacy. Wool was a spry career military officer with striking violet eyes and a patrician face befitting a senator in Cicero's Rome. He began his career during the War of 1812 and distinguished himself as a field commander during the war with Mexico. A national hero, he was repeatedly mentioned as a possible Democratic presidential candidate. At the start of the Civil War he was, at seventy-eight, the oldest general on either side. Wool's Confederate counterpart, Howell Cobb, was a Georgia lawyer and planter, a Unionist turned secessionist, and, above all, a career politician. Despite his watery eyes and downcast mien, he was an affable raconteur who entertained extravagantly. He had been a steadfast prewar Democrat who had served in the U.S. House and in President James Buchanan's Cabinet, and been elected governor of Georgia.

Wool and Cobb met on February 23 and again on March 1, 1862. Neither man was versed in the laws of war; nor were they inclined to innovate. They agreed that the arrangement between the United States and Great Britain during the War of 1812 should serve as a template for their negotiations. But they clashed over details, and they broke off negotiations in hopes that the other side would make concessions when the burden of prisoners mounted during the pending campaign season.

Intense fighting around Richmond had just that effect, amplifying the problems the Confederates faced accommodating more prisoners and arousing heightened desperation in the Union to secure the release of prisoners of war. During a lull in the fighting in June 1862, the two sides initiated another round of talks on exchanges. This time, General Cobb parlayed with Colonel Thomas M. Key, an aide to Major General George McClellan.

Cobb must have been pleased to negotiate with Key rather than Wool. Whereas Wool was an ardent Unionist, Key was a Kentucky-born lawyer who had "a binding love for the South." Trained at Yale, he moved to Cincinnati, where he rose to prominence in the Democratic Party. When his friend McClellan was given command of Ohio's militia at the start of the war, Key joined his staff. Like McClellan, Key dismissed President Lincoln as inept and obtuse, was opposed to federal interference with slavery, and advocated waging a war that imposed as little hardship as possible on southern civilians. When Key met with Cobb, he deliberately turned the discussions from prisoner exchanges to the conduct of the war and the prospects for a negotiated peace.

This impromptu peace overture, which Cobb spurned, confirmed the suspicion among the ranks of Republican congressmen that McClellan and his staff were deliberately subverting Union war policy. Enraged by Key's gambit, Secretary of War Stanton assumed direct oversight of the negotiations. He appointed Major General John A. Dix to conduct new talks. By then, Cobb was ill, prompting General Robert E. Lee to name Major General Daniel Harvey Hill to negotiate for the Confederacy.

Dix and Hill were mirror opposites. A political rival of Dix recalled him as "firm, but temperate" and his career as "even and smooth." After serving in the Army from 1813 until 1828, Dix resigned his commission and returned to civilian life. He then practiced law, dabbled in the literary arts, edited a respected journal, and served as the president of three different railroads. He achieved national prominence in the Democratic Party and served in the Buchanan administration. When the war erupted, Dix's political prominence as an ardent Unionist assured him good standing with the Lincoln administration, which was eager to enlist Democratic support for its policies. Lincoln, who was frugal with accolades, dubbed Dix "a very, very wise man."

Hill, in contrast, was notorious for his pugnacity, sarcasm, and intemperate language. Sympathetic observers attributed his irascibility and stiffness in manner and carriage to a nagging spinal affliction, while his critics detected incurable stubbornness and arrogance. Hill had graduated from West Point in 1842 and served with distinction during the war with Mexico. In 1849 he resigned his commission and spent the next decade as a college professor and administrator in Virginia and North Carolina. By 1859 he anticipated war with the North and turned his attention to training future

Union General John A. Dix (left) and Confederate General Daniel Harvey Hill negotiated a prisoner exchange that briefly emptied the warring nation's prisons. (Library of Congress)

warriors at a military academy in Charlotte. When war erupted, he proved to be a skilled battlefield commander and quickly rose to the rank of major general. Presumably, Lee appointed him to tilt with Dix because Hill's innate truculence would make him a hard-nosed negotiator. One of Hill's subalterns recalled, "For that portion of our Northern brethren who came to the South to drive hard bargains with our people and cheat them by false pretenses, he felt and expressed the most sovereign contempt."

Dix met Hill for a preliminary conference on July 17. A few days prior, Stanton had ordered Dix not to stray in the negotiations the way his predecessor had or make any gestures that implied recognition of the Confederate government. He was not even to refer directly to the War of 1812 agreement, which might be misconstrued as tacit recognition of the Confederate nation as a sovereign state. After the meeting, Dix dutifully traveled to Washington to brief Stanton, before conferring with Hill again on July 23. After six months of intermittent dickering, the two sides were so keen to settle the issue that the negotiations concluded swiftly.

Drawing on established traditions of handling prisoners of war, the so-called Dix-Hill cartel resolved the problems that had thwarted previous negotiations. Prisoners of war and privateers were to be exchanged according to rank, in line with the War of 1812 precedent. Personnel of equal ranks could be exchanged man for man, while prisoners of differing ranks could be exchanged according to an equation of so many seamen or soldiers in exchange for an officer. Each side could exchange noncombatants, such as citizens accused of disloyalty, and civilian employees of the military, such as teamsters and sutlers. Exchange of captives could take place on the battlefield, but all other prisoner swaps were to occur either on the James River near Richmond or at Vicksburg, Mississippi. Any prisoners not formally exchanged within ten days of their capture were to be paroled. Until formally exchanged, paroled prisoners were forbidden from returning to military duty in any capacity.

In a gesture that proved both naïve and empty, the cartel included provisions to ensure that it was fairly and speedily enforced. Each side agreed to appoint agents to oversee the parole and exchange process. They were to resolve any "misunderstandings" that arose and guarantee that the release of prisoners was not interrupted. With a flourish of principled optimism, the pact concluded with the pledge that "the object of this agreement may neither be defeated nor postponed."

The first prisoner exchange took place on August 3 at Aiken's Landing, a plantation wharf about ten miles south of Richmond. Confederate Commissioner of Exchange Robert Ould and Union Brigadier General Lorenzo Thomas, the newly appointed exchange agents, oversaw the release of three thousand prisoners by each army. While the Confederate prisoners traveled by ship, the Union prisoners marched from Richmond. Once at the exchange site, where there were no facilities for them, the freed Confederates set off on foot for Richmond while the freed Union men bunked down overnight on scattered straw in the open air while they awaited transport north. Despite the haphazard process and crude preparations, the exchanged prisoners were jubilant and the prospects for ongoing exchanges seemed auspicious. Within weeks the exchanges accelerated, and thousands of prisoners were on the move to the eastern and western exchange stations.

One aim of the cartel was to make exchanges predictable and orderly. It only partially succeeded. The logistics of large-scale prisoner transfers now replaced the minutiae of individual prisoner exchanges that had previously afflicted the leaders of both armies. Whereas Colonel Pegram, for instance, had been sent on his way unescorted from Fort Warren when he was paroled in early 1862, the thousands of Confederate prisoners sent south from Johnson's Island in September had to be guarded while being

Released Union prisoners boarding steamboats at Aiken's Landing, on the James River near Richmond, 1865. (Library of Congress)

transported one thousand miles by train and steamboat to Vicksburg. And whereas Pegram had sojourned in luxury during his return southward, the prisoners exchanged en masse endured conditions in transit that were as bad as or worse than those in the camps they had departed.

The absence of all comforts defined the journey south for Andrew Jackson Campbell. Captured at Fort Donelson in February 1862, Campbell had been held at Camp Chase and Johnson's Island. On September 1, he and the rest of the prisoners on Johnson's Island boarded trains and departed for Indianapolis. Campbell groused in his diary that "we are so cramped up that our blood has almost ceased to circulate." Two and a half days later, he and the other prisoners reached Cairo, Illinois, where they idled aboard the *Universe*, a "crazy old" riverboat. It was far too small for its cargo of hundreds, forcing the men to jostle for space in every nook on the boat. They received scant rations of "gunwadding bread" and raw meat, which they had no means to cook. After five sweltering days, a convoy of teeming prison boats set off for Vicksburg. After two weeks exposed to the elements on the deck of the riverboat, Campbell was exultant to reach Vicksburg and to be "relieved of the presence of the hated Yankee." By then, like many of his fellow prisoners, he was sick, hungry, and exhausted. "The boys were nearly worn out," another passenger reported, "but very glad that they were alive."

The hardships endured by Campbell foreshadowed intractable shortcomings in the exchange process. The priority of both Confederate and Union authorities was to move prisoners to the exchange sites as expeditiously and cheaply as possible. Neither side invested effort or expense into adequately provisioning prisoners en route to exchange. Men already weakened by captivity had to endure even more intense privation. Nor was adequate medical care provided. Dozens of sick Confederates died for want of medical attention while on the boats in the flotilla that carried Campbell to Vicksburg.

Prisoners endured perilous overcrowding throughout the extended exchange process. Conditions in Richmond were especially grim. Having worked to disperse prisoners from Richmond's overwhelmed prisons, Confederate officials now had to funnel all the prisoners held in the eastern theater back into the city's prisons before their exchange just south of the Confederate capital. It was this process of consolidation that had returned Colonel Corcoran to Libby Prison in July 1862. Richmond prisons, already stretched to the breaking point with captives from both the failed Peninsula campaign and the Second Battle of Bull Run, now had to absorb an equal or greater number that had been shifted from elsewhere. Out of necessity, General John Winder deposited five thousand prisoners on four acres of Belle Isle, an island in the James River off the shores of Richmond, where they lived desperately while awaiting exchange.

To the relief of the prisoners in the vortex of the exchange, conditions improved as the number of prisoners held by both sides shrank. When the cartel was signed, the Union held approximately twenty thousand prisoners, scattered mainly from Ohio to Illinois. Confederate prison pens, primarily in Virginia, held just under twelve thousand. By the end of August, Ould and Thomas had effected the release of more than seven thousand prisoners in the eastern theater. Prisoner exchanges in the West followed a similar schedule. By late September, most prisoners in the western theater had also been released, leaving the Union camps in the Midwest nearly empty.

Although the exchange agreement achieved the repatriation of the bulk of prisoners, its long-term prospects were tenuous. No issue was more problematic or contentious than parole. The cartel specified that paroles would happen by mutual consent, either on the battlefield or at the designated exchange sites. But unresolved was how to handle unilateral battlefield paroles. Victorious commanders who secured mass surrenders of the enemy were often desperate to escape the burden of providing for them. Confederate officers began to unilaterally parole captured soldiers without making any attempt to forward them to a designated exchange site.

These problems were especially vexing to Union General William Rosecrans's army in Tennessee. When Confederate forces in the area summarily paroled captives, Union officials had no opportunity to prepare to receive them. These sudden impositions of parolees were not only inconvenient but also deleterious to combat readiness. Ad hoc paroles also contributed to pitched disputes over the numbers of prisoners held by each side. Discrepancies invariably arose between the number of prisoners paroled and the number of paroled prisoners who reached their army's lines. The paroling side had strong incentives to inflate the numbers of parolees so as to increase the number of its own captured soldiers who would be eligible for exchange. When a Union commander protested that such paroles abrogated the terms of the exchange agreement, Confederate General Braxton Bragg batted away the rebuke and ordered his officers to "pay no respect to that [challenge]."

Battlefield paroles, moreover, allegedly encouraged Union soldiers to surrender at the first opportunity. For those soldiers who found the martial life oppressive or who were overwhelmed by the battlefield experience, surrender with a subsequent parole had obvious appeal. Some soldiers purportedly looked upon capture as an excuse, as the saying went, "to take a vacation by falling into the hands of the enemy." After the cartel was established, captivity (in theory) was limited to ten days before a prisoner was paroled. While the parolee waited to be officially "exchanged" for an enemy prisoner, which might take months, he was precluded by the terms of the cartel from most military duty.

The problems created by paroled soldiers awaiting exchange were so legion that the Union army began imprisoning its own paroled soldiers in some of the same facilities that had previously held Confederate prisoners. Paroled men bitterly resented their continued de facto incarceration, while Union officials were vigilant to ensure that parole was not mistaken for a vacation. At Camp Chase, where the parolees were deemed to be lazy, dirty, louse-ridden, and demoralized, Secretary of War Stanton ordered them to drill incessantly. Everywhere, paroled soldiers were tasked with repairing barracks and performing onerous camp chores, which parolees vigorously, sometimes violently, protested. The men at Camp Douglas, for example, set

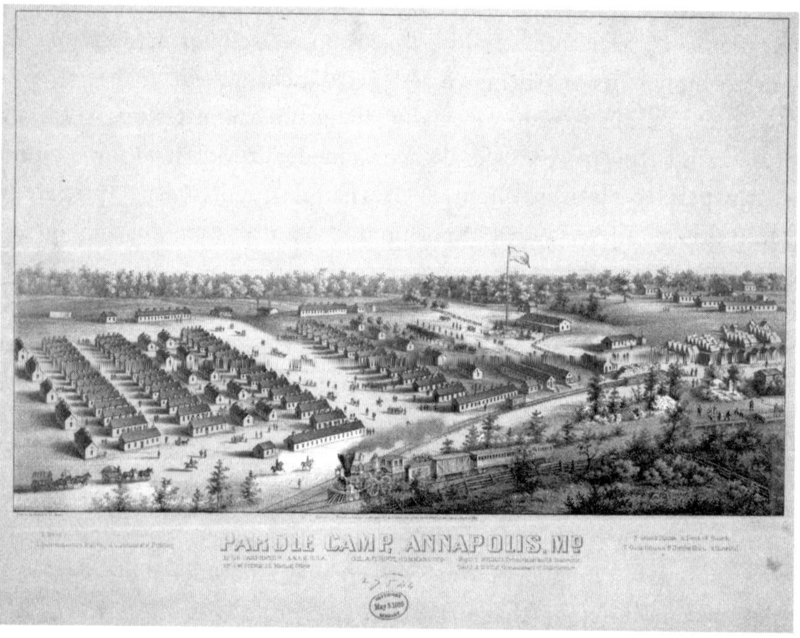


Paroled Union prisoners of war waited impatiently to be "exchanged" at a camp at Annapolis. (Library of Congress)

fire to their barracks and destroyed fences and a guardhouse. Only stern discipline overcame their resistance.

By December 1862, Confederates were contending with growing numbers of their own disgruntled paroled soldiers. General Martin L. Smith, who was responsible for paroled Confederates near Richmond, complained that they had given "more annoyance and trouble than any other of the many charges upon the command in Richmond." He fretted that the men arrived "full of the idea of deserving unusual privileges because of their capture" and were "exceedingly unruly, mutinous and difficult to manage."

The Confederacy relieved the headache of dealing with its paroled soldiers by unilaterally declaring them exchanged and sending them back to the front lines. This problem became especially acute in July 1863, when a Union army under the command of General Ulysses S. Grant captured thirty thousand Confederates at Vicksburg. Averse to the logistical complexities of feeding and guarding a captive army while shipping it north to camps, Grant paroled his captives. Because the Confederates did not have enough Union prisoners on hand to exchange for the Vicksburg parolees, Grant assumed that the Confederates he paroled were unlikely to see combat soon (or perhaps ever). But a month later Confederate officials declared the Vicksburg parolees to have been formally exchanged. In September, Union troops in the field encountered the paroled Confederates during battle at Chickamauga. When Union officials protested this high-handed violation of the cartel, Confederate authorities shrugged off the accusations and cited technicalities to justify their action.

With compliance in the eyes of the beholder, both sides resorted to using exchanges as a lever to influence the behavior of the wayward enemy. In December 1862, Confederate President Jefferson Davis suspended the parole of Union officers to protest the execution of a New Orleans citizen during the previous April by order of Union General Benjamin F. Butler. Confederate officials had demanded an explanation for the severity of the punishment but were unable to elicit a Union response. President Davis replied on December 24 by pronouncing General Butler a felon and an outlaw, adding that no commissioned Union officer would be paroled until "Butler shall have met with due punishment for his crime." His "due punishment": hanging.

Nothing in the cartel condoned Davis's retaliation against Union officers. There was no legal relationship whatsoever between the civilian's execution and the status of Union prisoners of war. But Union officers were at hand and so became convenient targets for retaliation. In reaction, Union

Secretary of War Stanton matched Davis's order to halt all exchanges of commissioned officers.

By then each side harbored an understandable mistrust of and rancor toward the other. The constant jockeying and sparring created a toxic atmosphere that impeded any resolution of disputes. The terms of the cartel required that the commissioners of prisoners and their staffs display "good faith" and offer "friendly explanations" to settle any controversies. Instead, disagreements over technicalities became entangled with larger grievances and frustrations over the enemy's conduct of the war. In the absence of any impartial observer, each side vouched that the enemy flouted both the cartel agreement and civilized behavior.

To operate efficiently and without acrimony, the exchange process required administrators with the wisdom of Solomon and the patience of Job. None of the men responsible for overseeing the exchanges qualified. Exacerbating the discord was the complete absence of civility between the officials involved in prisoner exchanges. Among the only representatives of the warring states who were in routine contact, the agents tested one another daily while withholding the mutual respect and commitment to reciprocity upon which the exchange agreement rested.

Robert Ould, during his tenure as the Confederate commissioner of prisoners from 1862 to 1865, got under the skin of every Union exchange agent with whom he dealt. A plump, thick-shouldered "bull of a man," he had been a lawyer of note in his hometown, the nation's capital. Following Lincoln's election, Ould moved with his family to Richmond, where he was appointed assistant secretary of war and then commissioner of prisoners. Having briefly trained to be a minister before earning his law degree, Ould retained a dull "clerical air" but leavened it with sybaritic tastes. He and his wife, who had been a famed Richmond belle, entertained lavishly in Washington and then in Richmond.

When Ould sought a pardon after the war, he presented himself as a reluctant Confederate who had been tireless in his concern for Union prisoners of war. During the war, however, he insinuated himself among the highest ranks of Confederate leadership by currying favor with President Jefferson Davis. Ould made the most of his position. During his frequent trips to Fortress Monroe, where he met with his Union counterparts, he stocked up on food and luxuries that were virtually unobtainable behind Confederate lines. His house boasted some of the best fare in the Confederate capital.

COLONEL ROBERT OULD
CONFEDERATE AGENT FOR THE EXCHANGE OF PRISONERS

The most important person in the exchange of prisoners in the South was Colonel Robert Ould. His appointment as Confederate agent for exchange came immediately after the signing of the agreement to exchange prisoners, July 22, 1862. When Virginia left the Union, Colonel Ould followed his State. He served for a short time as Assistant Secretary of War. His relations with Colonel William H. Ludlow, the Federal agent of exchange, were always pleasant. Though they frequently clashed, it was as lawyers seeking to gain advantages for their clients, and without personal animosity. With General S. A. Meredith, who succeeded Colonel Ludlow, Colonel Ould was at odds; he preferred to deal with Major Mulford, the assistant agent. He refused to treat with General Butler at first, but finally opened negotiations with him. Colonel Ould had one advantage over the Federal agents in that he was seldom hampered by interference by other officials of the War Department. He remained in charge of all questions relating to exchange to the end of the war.

Robert L. Ould, the Confederate commissioner of prisoners, resolutely defended his government's refusal to exchange Black prisoners. (From Francis Trevelyan Miller, *The Photographic History of the Civil War*, 1911)

Whatever social skills Ould possessed were seldom displayed in his relations with Union officials. He was confrontational, self-righteous, and arrogant. During one flare-up with a Union exchange agent, he erupted, "Let God judge between us. . . . I have no self-reproaches." He was constantly aggrieved by the purported disrespect and duplicity of his enemy counterparts. He regularly complained to Davis and others that Union officials were "taxing their ingenuity to find out the most available methods of deceit and fraud." He dismissed Brigadier General Sullivan Armory Meredith, one of the Union agents, as incompetent, forgetful, untruthful, and "an ass."

Ould's contempt was returned in full by the Union agents with whom he dealt. The first was Major William H. Ludlow, who had been a member of General Dix's staff before he was appointed exchange agent. During one contretemps, Ludlow upbraided Ould for acting stupidly and without the facts. In another exchange, after Ould invoked God as his witness, Ludlow fired back, "Were I in your place, I should hardly dare to invoke the judgment of the Great ruler of nations." Compounding the breach with the Confederate agent, Ludlow rebuked Ould for being "all wrong in [your] premises, arguments, and conclusions." Ludlow was succeeded by Brigadier General

Meredith, who laced his communications with Ould with sarcasm and recrimination. At the close of a string of testy exchanges, Meredith assailed the Confederate agent for deceitful recordkeeping, confessing that he would have been surprised had he not already been familiar with Ould's habit of "perverting the truth." While sparring over another issue, he informed Ould that he had no objection to the Confederate's acting in accord with his conscience so long as his conscience was guided by justice. But, Meredith lamented, he had seen no evidence that Ould possessed a conscience.

Both Ludlow and Meredith answered to Major General Ethan Allen Hitchcock. He was the grandson of Ethan Allen, whom he closely resembled. He graduated from West Point and served for four decades in the army in Florida, Mexico, and the Pacific Northwest. Past sixty at the outbreak of the Civil War, Hitchcock was appointed commissioner for the exchange of prisoners in November 1862. Conspicuous with his furrowed eyebrows, piercing yet vaguely haunted gaze, and an expansive bald pate, Hitchcock had little patience for the obfuscation, parsing of words, and massaging of numbers that accompanied his assignment. He would have preferred to devote his time to the study of philosophy, theology, mysticism, and alchemy. He groused in his diary that "I am not in my proper vocation—that is, I have

General Ethan Allen Hitchcock, the Union commissioner for prisoner-of-war exchange, concluded that only Union victory would free Black prisoners of war. (Library of Congress)

read and studied myself out of it." Having lost any tolerance for military hubris, he concluded that "generals and great men are pygmies."

Hitchcock assigned Ould to that same ignominious category. He did not rebuke Ludlow or Meredith for their tactless exchanges with the Confederate agent. To the contrary, he periodically displayed his own contempt for Ould, whom he described as "so utterly reckless of integrity and fairness and so full of finesse" that he doubted the value of negotiating with him.

The disrespect that colored the exchange process was not just an expression of fleeting pique. The Union's refusal to acknowledge the Confederacy as a sovereign state was a constant irritant. Virtually all official communications from Union agents included circumlocutions that denied the legitimacy of the enemy. Confederates, for instance, were referred to as "rebels," their insurgent nation as "the so-called Confederacy." Confederate officials, in turn, assailed their Union interlocutors for exhibiting the very imperiousness that had purportedly driven the South to secede.

In other circumstances, the recriminations and insults exchanged by these men would have culminated in fisticuffs and duels. As highly educated men from privileged backgrounds, they were conversant in the etiquette that gentlemen were expected to observe. While the agents conformed superficially to this etiquette, they violated it in spirit in almost every exchange. Ludlow and Ould were political veterans versed in the nineteenth-century art of rhetorical parrying and thrusting, during which blows were delivered with a carefully measured mix of wit, panache, and decorum. Instead, the agents traded insults. If any of the agents treated their adversary with courtesy, they did so as a concession to form rather than as a sincere gesture.

For all these reasons, the exchange cartel was already fragile before the controversy regarding Brown, Johnson, Wilson, and other Black prisoners of war arose. The exchange was cumbersome to carry out, complicated to adjudicate, and premised upon trust and reciprocity that were seldom in evidence. The Lincoln administration's aim, after all, was the destruction of the Confederacy. Even before the issue of Black prisoners of war arose, the limits of Confederates' commitment to reciprocity drove both sides to clarify what they were fighting for and to demonstrate the sacrifices they were willing to make to uphold their principles.

In the spring of 1862 the institution of slavery gained a foothold in Ohio, hitherto a "free" state ever since it had been carved out of the Northwest

Territory in 1803. Even more incongruous was that the enslaved Black men were in Union prisoner-of-war camps.

Following the Union victory at Fort Donelson one hundred Black "servants" accompanied the captured Confederates sent to Camp Chase. While their white owners arraigned Union camp officials for reducing prisoners to the condition of slaves, the enslaved Black men cooked meals, washed clothes, polished boots, and tidied the quarters of their owners. No Union official protested when additional enslaved Black men accompanied their captive owners from New Orleans to the Johnson's Island depot. General Nathaniel Banks, the commander in Union-occupied Louisiana, even issued special orders permitting the slaves to travel with the Confederate officers at the expense of the federal government.

Ohio Republicans and abolitionists were appalled that enemy captives extracting service from their human chattel were violating the state's constitutional prohibition of slavery. State legislators demanded the immediate emancipation of the imprisoned slaves. The issue festered until Colonel Hoffman ordered their gradual release. This and other instances of punctilious respect for Confederate property fueled surging Republican support for the confiscation of the property—human and otherwise—of Confederates.

The incarceration and subsequent emancipation of the enslaved Black men at Camp Chase anticipated the evolution of Union war aims. During the pivotal year of 1862, northerners engaged in fierce debate over the emancipation of the enslaved. At issue were not only the future of slavery but also the role of Black men in the war. That this debate absorbed the nation's attention underscored how rapidly Union objectives had evolved during the first year of the war.

The lack of a national law of citizenship rights and the deference shown the property rights of slave owners had long rendered the status of all Black Americans murky and precarious. Freeborn Black Americans tenaciously affirmed that they were citizens and comported themselves accordingly. But even in states where Black citizenship was acknowledged, it guaranteed few rights or privileges. Black men, for instance, were excluded from militia service, suffrage, and office holding. During the decades before the war, several northern states disenfranchised free Black men who since the Revolution had exercised the right to vote.

To the frustration of abolitionists and some Republicans, President Lincoln was reluctant to advocate for citizenship for Blacks. He rejected the Supreme Court's 1857 Dred Scott decision that persons of African ancestry had no "rights which the white man was bound to respect." But he held that the power to grant citizenship lay with the states, not the nation. He neither proposed nor supported legislation to grant legal citizenship to African Americans who lived under federal jurisdiction in Washington, D.C., or the federal territories. He also was inordinately deferential to white northern opposition to emancipation. In December 1861 he justified his caution, explaining that he was "anxious and careful" lest the conflict "degenerate into a violent and remorseless revolutionary struggle." He later conceded that during the first eighteen months of the war he had sought "to get along without touching the 'institution'" because he believed the Constitution protected slavery where it existed.

By early 1862, many Republicans in Congress displayed growing impatience with the Lincoln administration's perceived dithering. Thaddeus Stevens, a Republican leader in the House, called for total war against the rebellion, including the emancipation of slaves. Abolitionists and allies of Stevens endorsed his appeal, arguing that the loss of enslaved labor would cripple the southern economy and doom the Confederacy. Congressional Republicans also condemned the policy enforced by some Union commanders of returning fugitive slaves who had reached Union lines to their owners. The appearance, and reality, of the Union army functioning as slave catchers for rebellious slave owners was abhorrent. Congress forbade the policy in March 1862 and thereby began to deliver ever more serious blows against the long sacrosanct institution of slavery. It passed the Confiscation Act of 1862, which authorized the seizure of property of Confederates, including slaves. The act also established that confiscated slaves were thereafter free and provided special authority for the President "to employ as many persons of African descent as he may deem necessary and proper for the suppression of this rebellion." (Based on this congressional act, Hoffman liberated the enslaved men in Camp Chase.) If the intent of Congress was not already clear, the Militia Act, passed on the same day as the Confiscation Act, authorized the recruitment of Black men to build fortifications, tend camps, and perform any other labor "for which they may be found competent." The elastic language of the act provided ample leeway for the Union army to bolster its ranks by recruiting Black men.

Before Lincoln would countenance Black soldiers, however, he first had to accept that military necessity compelled him to strike at slavery. On September 22, five days after the Union victory at Antietam, he issued a provisional proclamation that permanently freed all slaves in all areas of the

Confederacy which did not return to Union control by January 1863. If the rebellion continued until then, Lincoln vowed to issue a second proclamation on January 1, 1863, formalizing emancipation in the Confederacy.

Cynics and critics of the Lincoln administration swiftly pointed out that the proclamation immediately freed only a small percentage of the enslaved, because most slaves remained behind Confederate lines or in Union-occupied areas and therefore were exempt from its effect. Detractors, however, underestimated the momentous import of the edict. Wherever the Union armies advanced into the Confederacy the institution of slavery was destroyed. A Union colonel from Indiana confessed no doubts about the consequences of Lincoln's edict, declaring: "This army will sustain the emancipation proclamation and enforce it with the bayonet." General Grant agreed, hailing the effects of the promised emancipation as "the heaviest blow yet given the Confederacy."

In response to congressional passage of the Confiscation Act, Lincoln declared that Union military commanders should employ "as many persons of African descent as can be used to advantage." Northern public opinion shifted as well. While many white northerners opposed Black soldiers, they endorsed using Black laborers to augment the war effort. Even soldiers unsympathetic to the plight of the enslaved tolerated their presence because they relieved soldiers of the chores that were the bane of camp life. As a Wisconsin private joked in August 1862, if escaping slaves continued to come into Union camps, "we will soon have a waiter for every man in the Regt."

Lincoln and others understood that when Black men donned the Union uniform the conflict would be transformed into a war of liberation. Black abolitionists touted Black participation in the Union war effort, invoking the principle that bearing arms and citizenship went together. Once a Black man got "an eagle on his button, and a musket on his shoulder and bullets in his pocket," the abolitionist Frederick Douglass predicted, "there is no power on earth which can deny that he has earned the right to citizenship in the United States." It was this eventuality that made Lincoln reluctant to arm Black men and place them on the battlefield. To do so, the President acknowledged to Colonel Daniel Ullman, "would drive many of our friends from us," especially slave owners in border states. He cautioned: "The people," including Union officers who would command Black soldiers, "were not ready for it."

By January 1863, when Lincoln issued the Emancipation Proclamation, he had overcome his earlier opposition to mustering Black soldiers. During the following months he encouraged governors and generals to enlist freedmen. Simultaneously, Union recruiters led a surprisingly effective campaign to enlist Black men across the Mississippi River valley.

The evolving policies on the enslaved and on the exchange of prisoners followed independent paths until Lincoln issued the provisional Emancipation Proclamation. But in September 1862, when the first general prisoner exchanges were wrapping up and when Lincoln made the decision to commit the Union to the destruction of slavery in the Confederacy, the fates of the enslaved and prisoners of war became knotted together. The announcement of the Emancipation Proclamation and mustering of Black troops ensured they would remain so throughout the war.

The advent of Black soldiers gave rise to issues on which the Dix-Hill exchange agreement was silent. Were Black soldiers on the battlefield entitled to the same protections extended to other soldiers by the customary laws of war? Were Black men in arms subject to the same captivity as their white comrades? Were Black captives eligible for exchanges? Debates provoked by these questions were an important catalyst for the acknowledgment of the nation's obligation to African Americans, including to extend protections that had previously been enjoyed exclusively by whites. That the two warring sides reached discordant conclusions to these questions is less surprising than the ardor with which they clung to their stances. The positions they staked out had tangible consequences for not only Brown, Johnson, Wilson, and other Black prisoners, but also every other prisoner of war.

Even before Lincoln issued his provisional proclamation, northern commentators speculated about likely Confederate responses to any recruitment of Black soldiers into Union ranks. Prisoners of war had repeatedly provided a convenient means to retaliate for any measure one side deemed intolerable. With the treatment of Michael Corcoran and other victims of Confederate retaliation in mind, the *Boston Journal* predicted that any Black men who were captured "would be treated worse than our white prisoners of war." Lincoln shared similar concerns. He pondered limiting the employment of Black military laborers to places far behind the front lines to lessen any likelihood of their capture.

The furious Confederate response to emancipation confirmed that these fears were warranted. For many Confederates, Lincoln's proclamation vindicated their rebellion and affirmed their suspicions of Republicans' long-standing designs against slavery. President Jefferson Davis reviled Lincoln's action as "the most execrable measure recorded in the history of

"Contrabands," like these Black men working on a Union railroad in Virginia in 1863, contributed mightily to the Union war effort. (Library of Congress)

guilty man." Confederate Secretary of War James A. Seddon warned that the Lincoln administration was inciting a "servile insurrection" that would culminate in the "abandonment of all rules, conventions, mitigating influences, and humanizing usages." The *Charleston Daily Courier* howled that the decree was "an invitation to murder, rape, and spoliation." Lincoln's "savage and brutal policy," General Robert E. Lee regretted, left white southerners with "no alternative but success or degradation worse than death."

Beyond denouncing Lincoln's proclamation, Confederates began considering measures to punish enslaved southerners who joined the Union cause. Recognizing the need for a swift response, the Confederate Congress on September 29, 1862, urged "severe retaliatory measures." Confederate General P. G. T. Beauregard proposed prompt summary justice against the "abolition prisoners" already in Confederate hands. "Let the execution be made with the garrote," he suggested.

Confederates were in accord that Black men in uniform should be punished like rebellious slaves. Confederate military and civilian officials made a point of referring to Black soldiers as "slaves in arms" or "slaves in armed rebellion." Southern whites had never been overly punctilious about how they punished slave revolts before the Civil War. Alleged participants in slave uprisings had often been summarily executed by white vigilantes in gruesome spectacles intended to intimidate local enslaved communities. When the exodus of enslaved Black men to Union lines accelerated after Lincoln's provisional proclamation, for instance, whites in northwestern Mississippi executed recaptured fugitive slaves and left their dangling corpses to terrorize remaining slaves. On other occasions, local and state officials formally tried and executed alleged slave insurrectionists.

President Jefferson Davis preferred letting Confederate states settle the fate of captured Black soldiers. His policy relieved both the Confederate army and the national government of responsibility, while affirming that existing state laws could meet any wartime exigencies. In December 1862 Davis decreed that any slave captured in a Union uniform would be turned over to state authorities and dealt with according to state laws regarding slave insurrections. Under those various laws, a Black soldier who fell into Confederate hands might be executed, returned to his former master, or auctioned off to a new one. Four months later, the Confederate Congress endorsed Davis's directive, legislating that any Black men who were "taken in arms against the Confederate States," or who gave aid to the enemy, should be punished according to the laws of the state where they were seized.

Confederates had little time to contemplate their responses to Black soldiers in the abstract before they began encountering "slaves in arms." Although only a few regiments of Black soldiers had been mustered by the end of 1862, many more Black men were already serving as camp hands and teamsters. Black men such as Brown, Johnson, and Wilson (who had enlisted in September 1862) also were serving in similar capacities in the Union navy.

Unsure of evolving policy regarding captured Black soldiers, Confederate commanders in the field peppered Confederate leaders with questions and suggestions about how best to handle them. In November 1862 the commanding general at Savannah reported the capture of four Black men "wearing the abolition uniform" on nearby St. Catherine's Island. He proposed a "swift and terrible punishment" to dissuade slaves in the area from following their example. Summary execution, the Confederate secretary of war Seddon agreed, was an appropriate sanction, and Seddon encouraged the general to "exercise [his] discretion" in punishing the prisoners, as well as "any others hereafter captured."

Confederates dismissed out of hand any exchange of Black men for Confederates held by the Union. In Confederate eyes, an enslaved man who absconded and joined the Union army remained a slave; his identity as a soldier was ephemeral and secondary to his innate status as property. But much more was at stake in an exchange of former slaves for white soldiers than the incommensurability of property and white human beings. Confederate Major Thomas R. Livingston made this point crudely following one of the earliest encounters between Confederates and Black Union troops, in May 1863. When a Union commander proposed to swap Confederate captives for Black soldiers, the Confederate officer bristled, vowing that he would not demean "white men and jentalmen to eaquallize them Selves" with "eatheuoppieons commanded by a lot of low down thieving white men." Or, as a Virginia daily explained with more polish, "If we were insane enough to yield this point, to treat black men as the equals of white, and insurgent slaves as equivalent to our brave soldiers, the very foundation of slavery would be fatally wounded."

However varied were the possible fates of Black captives, Confederates demonstrated their resolve to target Black soldiers for singular persecution. While conducting raids in Missouri and Kansas during early 1863, Major Livingston and his guerrillas encountered Black soldiers. On May 18 in Jasper County, Missouri, they surprised a white artillery battery and a foraging party of forty-five Black soldiers from the First Kansas Colored Infantry. The marauders killed more than a dozen foragers, leaving "their bodies most horribly mutilated." They took five prisoners, including two Black soldiers. Livingston immediately secured a swap of the three white prisoners for some of his men who were in Union hands. But he adamantly refused Union requests to exchange "the colored prisoners." What happened to the Black prisoners is not clear, but they almost certainly were re-enslaved.

Reports of Confederate armies acting like legions of slave catchers had previously reached Union lines. Following the Confederate invasion of Maryland in September 1862, newspapers published reports of Black men and women who were abducted and carried off by Confederates. Union officials took the reports seriously. When the Confederates failed to return Brown, Johnson, and Wilson with the rest of the crew of the *Isaac Smith* in February 1863, Assistant Secretary of the Navy Gustavus V. Fox wrung his hands: "We are trying to find out what has been done with the colored persons in the crew." He was aghast that "they have proposed in Richmond to sell our cooks &c into slavery."

During the protracted Union campaign to capture Vicksburg, more accounts of Confederates re-enslaving Black soldiers accumulated. At

Milliken's Bend, Louisiana, on June 7, 1863, Confederate Captain George T. Marold and his troops captured nineteen black soldiers. His commanding officer, General Henry E. McCulloch, subsequently advocated to his superiors that "I would regard it nothing but fair to give to Captain Marold one or two of the best of them." Eight members of the Eleventh Louisiana (African Descent) who were captured during the battle were subsequently taken to east Texas, put "under guard," and forced to work. Several weeks later, eighty enlisted men of the First Arkansas (African Descent) who were captured by Confederate raiders in east Arkansas became war booty. They were transported to Texas and enslaved.

Accounts of Confederates killing wounded and captured Black soldiers on the battlefield gave added weight to oft-repeated Confederate threats to show no mercy to Black men in uniform. In the spring of 1863 Confederate officers openly regretted the taking of Black prisoners. After the fighting at Milliken's Bend, General Richard Taylor exalted that a "very large number of negroes" had been killed or wounded, but, deplored that "unfortunately, some 50, with 2 of their white officers, [were] captured." News of these inadvertent captures dismayed General Edmund Kirby-Smith, Taylor's superior, who stressed that Confederates should avoid taking Black prisoners in the first place: "I have been unofficially informed that some of your troops have captured negroes in arms. I hope this may not be so, and that your subordinates who may have been in command of capturing parties may have recognized the propriety of giving no quarter to armed negroes and their officers. In this way we may be relieved from a disagreeable dilemma." Weeks later, after the fighting near Goodrich's Landing, Louisiana, General John G. Walker lamented, "I consider it an unfortunate circumstance that any armed negroes were captured."

Just as "free negroes" before the Civil War had confounded white southerners, so too Black captives who had been free before the war posed a special "dilemma" for Confederates. They could not be condemned as "slaves in armed insurrection." They could not be returned to a previous owner because there was none. Like Brown, Johnson, and Wilson, the three sailors in the Charleston jail, they were distinguished from their white compatriots only by their skin color. With no clear plan for them, Confederate officials consigned them to the same terrifying uncertainty that Brown, Johnson, and Wilson experienced. Neither enslaved nor executed, they were instead held at the sufferance of their captors and were subject to whatever captivity Confederates elected to impose.

The threat of Confederate retribution also hung over white officers of Black troops. Jefferson Davis's December 1862 proclamation denied prisoner-of-war status to captured Union officers commanding black troops. They, too, were to be delivered to state authorities, who could prosecute them for inciting slave insurrections. In practice, however, Confederate officials recognized that persecution of Union officers would likely provoke severe Union reprisals and so they acted with caution. The exchange of the white officers captured on the *Isaac Smith*, for example, was delayed until Confederate officials decided not to prosecute them for fomenting slave insurrections. Even so, Union officers of Black soldiers could not take Confederate mercy for granted.

The combination of Confederate threats of retaliation against white officers and reports of the enslavement of Black soldiers fueled demands that the Lincoln administration guarantee protection and equal treatment for Black soldiers. Early enthusiasm to enlist among free Black men waned as they considered the risks. Adding to their reluctance was blatant discrimination against them in the Union army. After more than a year of urging the recruitment of Black men into the Union army, Frederick Douglass stopped his recruiting efforts and denounced Lincoln for failing to declare the nation's commitment to the unequivocal protection of Black soldiers and prisoners of war.

The Lincoln administration was hesitant to retaliate against the Confederacy for its treatment of Black soldiers for fear of sparking an escalating cycle of tit-for-tat retaliation. Instead, with the aim of justifying and calibrating Union responses to Confederate policies, Major General Henry Halleck requested that Francis Lieber, the nation's foremost expert on international law, draft a summary of contemporary laws of war. Lieber enthusiastically tackled the assignment in early 1863, producing a short tract that the War Department subsequently issued, under Lincoln's signature, as General Orders No. 100.

The order served as a legal brief for the Union's conduct of the war. It was another instance of Lincoln's careful explanation of the Union's principles and incremental policymaking. Lieber sought to establish rules that restrained warfare and limited its destructiveness, to the extent possible, to combatants. At the heart of the code was an emphasis on military necessity and the presumption that it was compatible with legal principles that restricted the violence of war. Men at war, the order underscored, "do not cease on this account to be moral beings, responsible to one another, and to God."

The largest number of the articles in the code addressed the treatment, parole, and exchange of prisoners of war. The code prohibited "intentional infliction of any suffering" and expressly forbade giving "no quarter" to the enemy (i.e., killing prisoners of war). It declared that "no belligerent has a right to declare that enemies of a certain class, color, or condition" would not be treated as prisoners of war. The order repudiated crude revenge but condoned retaliation when an enemy violated the laws of war and military necessity warranted a response. This calculus of retaliation was directly relevant to the treatment of prisoners of war. The code addressed the Confederacy's policy of re-enslaving Black prisoners of war; it warned that if "an enemy of the United States should enslave and sell any captured persons of their army, it would be a case for the severest retaliation." In response, the Union army could condemn to hard labor or execute Confederate prisoners of war.

The practical effect of the code on the conduct of the war is hard to measure. The order had little influence on the Union army's behavior in the field; most Union generals ignored it and soldiers hardly knew of it. Confederate commentators immediately denounced it as a charade intended to legitimize Union atrocities, including fomenting slave insurrection. More important, Confederates made it clear that they would not be bound by any of the Code's injunctions and would conduct the war as they saw fit.

The code's significance, however, was not in its efficacy but its symbolism. It provided Lincoln with a set of codified principles to justify his eventual pledge of reprisals against Confederates. Invoking the principle of commensurate retaliation, the President proclaimed on July 30, 1863, that for every Union soldier killed in violation of the laws of war (as codified in his General Orders No. 100) a Confederate soldier would be put to death. For every Union soldier enslaved or sold into slavery, a Confederate soldier would be assigned to hard labor. The July 30 order reaffirmed the principles already laid out in General Orders No. 100, but the new order left no ambiguity that it was prompted by Confederate treatment of Black soldiers. "It is the duty of every government," Lincoln vowed, "to give protection to its citizens, of whatever class, color, or condition, and especially to those who are duly organized as soldiers in the public service." To distinguish the treatment of prisoners of war based on "color," he affirmed, made a travesty of

*Harper's Weekly* found humor in President Lincoln's July 30, 1863, order to retaliate against Confederate mistreatment of Black prisoners. (Library of Congress)

the customs of war. The enslavement of prisoners on account of their color was "a relapse into barbarism and a crime against the civilization of the age."

Amid the swirl of events during the summer of 1863, the import of Lincoln's July 30 order is easily underestimated. Recall that the President had been loath to acknowledge the explicit citizenship of freed people, preferring instead to grant them specific rights. His July 30 order did not establish legal citizenship for Black soldiers, but it acknowledged the government's obligation to protect Black soldiers as it did white soldiers.

Others in his administration were less grudging in their recognition of Black citizenship and pointed to Lincoln's July 30 order as confirmation of it. In April 1863, William Whiting, an ardent abolitionist and the solicitor general for the War Department, began publicly declaring that Black soldiers were citizens. To a curious commander in the field who wondered about the citizenship status of Black men in the ranks, Whiting answered, "If they [Blacks] are in the army, then they are citizens." On the day after Lincoln's July 30 order, Whiting sought to remove any confusion over the matter in a letter to a convention of Blacks in Poughkeepsie, New York. "Now while colored men are admitted to be citizens of several of the

Northern States and of the United States" he explained, "there seems to be no reason why such citizens should not be placed upon the same footing with other soldiers." Lincoln, he underscored, "wishes every citizen to share the perils of the contest, and to reap the fruits of victory." Only a year earlier, enslaved Blacks had been transported along with their Confederate owners at Union expense to prison camps in the North; now, the same government was pledging "to give protection to its citizens, of whatever class, color, or condition."

The Lincoln administration understood that the Confederacy would not recognize Black men as soldiers unless compelled to do so. Short of victory, retaliation offered the only method to influence Confederate behavior and policy. Lincoln's order clarified what was at stake in the treatment of prisoners of war. Confederates might recoil at the proposition that a Black soldier was the equal of a white soldier, but it was now official Union policy. Moreover, the order ensured that the Confederacy's refusal to exchange Black prisoners would not be overlooked. Bolstered by the principles outlined in General Orders No. 100 and refined yet further in the July 30 order, the Lincoln administration boxed the Confederacy into an unenviable position. As long as the Confederacy held that only some prisoners could be exchanged, the Union would exchange no prisoners.

William Ludlow, the Union exchange agent, expressed bafflement at the Confederacy's intransigence regarding Black soldiers. The Confederate government had negotiated and agreed to the Dix-Hill cartel without any mention of the race of prisoners of war. Ludlow denounced the refusal to exchange Black soldiers as a violation of the cartel and scolded Robert Ould, the Confederate agent of exchange, "You have not a foot of ground to stand upon . . . passing events will clearly show the impracticability of refusing to exchange blacks." Ludlow closed by pledging that the United States would protect its officers and men without regard to color and would "promptly retaliate" for violations of the cartel or the laws of war.

On August 27, Ould made clear that the Confederacy would not budge. They would, he vowed, "die in the last ditch before giving up their right to send slaves back to slavery as property recaptured." He left open the possibility that his government would make an exception for free Black soldiers but offered no explanation to Sullivan Meredith, Ludlow's successor as Ould's Union counterpart, as to the basis upon which free Blacks and former slaves would be distinguished. Meredith predicted that differentiating them would be impossible and consequently the whim of

Confederates would determine which, if any, Black captives were eligible for exchange.

The two sides were at an impasse. Confederate Secretary of War Seddon concluded on November 15, 1863, that "all exchanges have now ceased with little apparent prospect of renewal." On November 28, Ethan Allen Hitchcock, Meredith's superior, wrote a statement to the editor of the *New York Times*, with the approval of the secretary of war, explaining the exchange standoff. Hitchcock blamed the suspension on Confederate subterfuge and quibbling, but the main purpose of the letter was to publicize the Confederates' refusal to exchange Black prisoners. Only Union threats of retaliation, he explained, constrained Confederate fury.

Some effects of the halting of routine exchanges were apparent almost immediately. Others became so only during the following year. Whether from steadfast principle or a misreading of Union resolve, the Confederacy spurned exchanges and faced the challenge of replenishing its military ranks. By the spring of 1864, nearly all the white men in the insurgent nation who could serve were already in uniform or had absconded to avoid service. Few remained to take the place of those prisoners trapped in Union prisons. The Union, in contrast, still had an untapped population of men of military age. Many of those men were not keen to serve, as a violent draft riot in New York City in July 1863 demonstrated. But, whether through appeals to patriotism or at the point of a bayonet, Union ranks could be filled. Indeed, in July 1864, President Lincoln issued a call for an additional five hundred thousand recruits, a number that was wholly inconceivable in the Confederacy.

The most significant consequence of the halting of general exchanges was that the United States and the Confederacy began experiments in custodial imprisonment on a scale beyond anyone's worst prewar premonitions. The prison pens of the first year of the war would be restocked with captives and would expand manifold as the number of prisoners held by both sides ballooned. The origins of the sprawling prison at Andersonville, built during the winter of 1864, as well as the vastly expanded camps in the North, lay in the cessation of exchanges a year earlier. The tightening of the screw was beginning.

As momentous as the Lincoln administration's evolving policy on Black soldiers and prisoner exchanges proved to be, it was powerless to improve the circumstances of Brown, Johnson, Wilson, or any other Black prisoners.

Brown, Johnson, and Wilson's appeal had one immediate consequence of which they were almost certainly unaware. In accordance with the policy of retaliation outlined in the July 30 order, Secretary of War Stanton ordered that three Confederate prisoners be held in close custody as hostages until the three Black sailors were exchanged. Promptly, three captive South Carolina cavalry men were assigned to hard labor on public works in Washington, D.C., and Confederate authorities were notified of their assignment.

Union officials recognized the gravity of the Black sailors' plight. When General Hitchcock forwarded their petition to Navy Secretary Welles, he pinpointed the crux of their predicament. "The rebellion exists on a question connected with the right or power of the South to hold the colored race in slavery," he observed, "and the South will only yield this right under military compulsion." Regrettably, Hitchcock predicted, the Charleston prisoners and other Black captives would remain imperiled until the Union achieved victory.

Brown, Johnson, and Wilson did not perish, as they had feared they would in 1863. After the war they left few traces, other than in the federal census. Brown settled in Westfield, New York, while Johnson and Wilson returned to New York City. How and when they regained their freedom is unclear. They may have been included in a special prisoner exchange near Charleston in October 1864. If so, their exchange did not mark a formal change in Confederate policy regarding Black prisoners. However, high-ranking Union officials were unaware if they had been exchanged and continued to press for their release in January 1865. Or perhaps the three sailors languished in Confederate hands until Union troops occupied Charleston in February 1865.

CHAPTER SIX

# THE ACCUMULATION

## (1863–1864)

On July 23, 1863, Newell Burch scratched "dilapidated by hard usage" in his pocket diary. Although in the prime of his youth—he was twenty-one—he had ample cause for his fatigue and melancholy. During his previous ten months in uniform, Corporal Burch had little experience under enemy fire. Then, three weeks earlier, at Gettysburg, he and his regiment, the 154th New York Infantry, had been ordered to cover the retreat of the XIth Corps on the first day of the battle. They were overrun by Confederates attacking the Union's eastern flank. With no path of escape, Burch and nearly two hundred men of his regiment surrendered on July 1. As one recalled, "The few that did get away were the best runners."

Burch quickly experienced the hardship and privation of captivity. While the battle raged, Confederates corralled him and hundreds of other prisoners behind lines. Not until July 4 did Burch receive rations—a half pint of flour. Although he and many prisoners had not eaten in days, they left their paltry provisions untouched because inclement weather made cooking them impossible. When Union General George Meade rebuffed General Robert E. Lee's proposal to exchange captives on the battlefield, Burch and his comrades were destined for the prison pens of the Confederacy.

On the afternoon of July 5, Burch and more than four thousand Union captives began their slog southward alongside Lee's retreating army. They marched until two a.m., covering twenty miles. A day later they reached the banks of the rain-swollen Potomac River, where they spent two days waiting to be ferried to the Virginia shore. Another two days of trudging brought the miserable procession to Winchester. From there they tramped up the Shenandoah Valley to Staunton, where their two-hundred-mile, fourteen-day ordeal ended and a new one began.

Scrambling aboard dirty flatbeds and boxcars, Burch and the other prisoners became human freight. Although worn down by the journey, Burch found humor in his arrival in the Confederate capital. For a year, he and his comrades had whooped, "On to Richmond." Now, on July 24, he noted wryly, "a few of us have reached the goal." He and his companions were no more conquerors than Michael Corcoran had been when he preceded them the year before. Instead, they were a motley mélange of "dirty, ragged, and ravenously hungry" prisoners destined for the prison pen on Belle Isle.

Burch's captivity lasted another 638 days. After the war he insisted that he, of all Union prisoners, had endured the longest captivity. His claim almost certainly was exaggerated. When Burch was captured, Orin Brown, William Johnson, and William Wilson had already spent five anxious months in the Charleston jail, where they remained until virtually the end of the war. Yet perhaps Burch's grim boast should be excused; he survived twenty-two months of exceptionally harsh captivity, including seven months at Belle Isle and a year at Andersonville.

His extended imprisonment was a direct consequence of the impasse over prisoner exchanges. With both sides digging in their heels on the resumption of exchanges even as the 1863 campaign season quickened, long-term incarceration became Burch's fate and that of tens of thousands of

Captured at Gettysburg, Newell Burch spent the remainder of the war in Confederate prisons. (From Hal E. McWethy, "'Conclude It My Duty to Enlist and Therefore Enlisted': Diary of a Union Soldier," *Ramsey County History*, Spring 1964)

other prisoners. By the fall of 1863, Burch and his compatriots in the camps recognized the diminishing prospects for their release before the war's resolution. In his diary, like countless of his fellow prisoners, Burch dismissed the likelihood of his exchange even while he impatiently awaited it.

During his drawn-out captivity, Burch witnessed and endured many of the tragic and predictable consequences of the cessation of exchanges. Most pronounced was the rapid growth of prison populations. Confederate prison pens that held a few hundred captives at the beginning of 1863 would house more than 35,000 by the end of the year and more than 60,000 a year later. Union prisons contended with a corresponding explosion in their populations.

Neither Union nor Confederate authorities made adequate preparations for this influx. Based on the experience of the previous year and a half, they could have projected the number of prisoners they were likely to have to accommodate after exchanges slowed. Both sides could have anticipated substantially larger numbers of prisoners as a consequence of their ambitious military operations planned for 1863. To be prudent, each side should have braced to handle at least twice as many prisoners as in the past.

Instead, unprepared officials futilely scrambled to absorb the swelling numbers of prisoners while presiding over a repetition of the problems of the first year of the war, but on an even larger scale. Prison facilities that had been hard used and inadequate in 1862 were now a year older and confined many, many more prisoners than in the past. Both sides continued to cobble together hastily built and shabby facilities that were inadequate even before the first prisoners crossed their thresholds.

Unfounded confidence and managerial indifference were at the root of these conditions. They could not be excused as a result of inexperience. Nor as a product of ineptitude. Perhaps nowhere was the combination of hubris and indifference more evident than in the new mammoth prisons erected by the Union and the Confederacy. Both sides recognized the urgent need for purpose-built prisons on a previously unimaginable scale to complement the existing array of improvised facilities. At Point Lookout, Maryland, the Union created a gigantic prison pen while the Confederacy undertook its most drastic experiment in mass imprisonment at Andersonville. Neither Union nor Confederate authorities acknowledged any likelihood that these enormous camps, which were little more than storage dumps for prisoners, would concentrate and magnify the manifold traumas of captivity. As Burch and other prisoners experienced firsthand during 1863 and 1864, the warring nations began exploring the boundaries of what they deemed permissible in the treatment of prisoners.

As the number of prisoners mounted in 1863, the defining characteristics of captivity became oppressive overcrowding and appalling squalor. Motivated by expediency, both sides stuffed as many captives as possible into existing facilities. By the end of the year many prisons held double, even triple their intended populations. Everywhere, the resulting overcrowding produced a rapid and seemingly irreversible degradation of prison conditions.

Wherever possible, Confederates resorted to packing captives into existing sites. The population at Salisbury prison in North Carolina, for instance, mushroomed from negligible in early 1863 to more than ten thousand, or four times its planned capacity, by the following year. Simultaneously, Richmond's prisons absorbed previously unimagined numbers of inmates. Libby Prison, after having been emptied by exchanges in late 1862, quickly filled during the summer of 1863. It remained filthy and putrid, little changed from the previous year, when Michael Corcoran had been confined there. But now, with the prison population topping four thousand, it was virtually impossible to shoehorn more inmates within its walls. So extreme was overcrowding that the *Richmond Enquirer* reported, "Everywhere there is a wrangling, jostling crowd." At night, the newspaper disclosed, the floors of the pen were "covered, every square inch of it by uneasy slumberers" who were as tightly packed as "a huge, improbable box of nocturnal sardines."

Belle Isle, which was the destination for Newell Burch and most rank-and-file prisoners, was similarly overcrowded. It had been opened in 1862 as a temporary holding pen for Union prisoners destined to be exchanged. At the start of 1863, the island camp stood virtually empty. But the capture of thousands of Union prisoners in May during the Battle of Chancellorsville prompted the facility's revival. Two months later Burch and the other prisoners captured at Gettysburg entered the camp. By November, after the addition of prisoners taken at the Battle of Chickamauga, the prison's population exceeded six thousand, double its intended capacity. Eventually, nine thousand captives would be confined there.

Richmond newspapers enthused about Belle Isle's bucolic setting. On one side the turbulent James River bounded the camp. On the other three sides an eight foot-deep ditch with a three-foot-high embankment marked the prison's extent. One paper described it as a "very pleasant spot" where prisoners would "pass a pleasant summer." Another account announced that Union inmates were "better satisfied than they would be if placed in houses, as they have good tents, plenty of water, and a large space to ramble about."

Nary a prisoner described the site in such rosy terms. William Dolphin, a private in the First New York Calvary who entered Belle Isle two months after Burch, deemed it "a dirty lousy hole." He protested in his diary, "Hell was a palace to it." Another prisoner who entered the camp just a few weeks before Burch recoiled at the sight of his new prison home: "Not a spear of grass growing. It is nothing but sand full of lice and vermin." As described by *Harper's Weekly*, the prison site was a damp sandy "desert" swept by "winds and wrapped in fogs."

No barracks graced the four-acre prison. To the extent that Burch and other prisoners had shelter, it was the tents admired by Confederate journalists. A contemporary of Burch at Belle Isle dismissed the shelters as an "irregular mass of old dilapidated, worn out, rotten, weather beaten tents." With the gallows humor common among prisoners, he cautioned that many of the tents were so threadbare "that in order to get out of the rain you have to go outside." As many as twenty prisoners stuffed themselves into tents designed to house ten or fewer men. When Burch reached the camp, "we found about

Burch spent his first year of captivity at Belle Isle prison, here rendered by *Harper's Weekly* in December 1863. (Library of Congress)

3000 ahead of us" in the scramble for tents and space to hunker on the lice-infested ground. Some, like Burch, eventually finagled spots in tents. Hundreds of others remained without any shelter for months, burrowing into the ground and sleeping wrapped in whatever blankets they had been able to retain after their capture. Because "the rebs have taken everything from us," Dolphin complained, he and others had no blankets to shield against either the damp or the cold. Over and over, he recorded in his diary, "slept cold last night" and somber predictions that "men will freeze tonight."

Burch looked on with pity as new prisoners arrived at Belle Isle during the fall of 1863. As the daylight hours shortened and temperatures dropped, half-naked prisoners weathered cold nights by huddling together "like pigs just as close as they could get." Others, in a fog of their own spent breath, formed restless coveys of prisoners slapping warmth into their limbs and pacing to keep warm. "The silent hours of night," one Belle Isle denizen explained, "are always broken by the dismal tread of a hundred shivering forms as they pass to and fro." Burch coped by sleeping as little as possible during daytime so that exhaustion overwhelmed him by nightfall, allowing him to "sleep more [at] nights [and] to make them as short as possible."

The James River was the Belle Isle's sole amenity. A 10-foot upstream section of the river shore provided access to drinking water, while a 30-foot section below it was reserved for bathing. Another 150-foot section of shoreline served as the latrine. Because of the prison's porous perimeter, Confederate guards placed tight restrictions on prisoners' movement. Inmates were allowed access to the river only under strict guard and were denied it altogether at night. Prisoners had no alternative to defecating around their tents. They were expected to clean the effluent every morning, but they did so listlessly. Consequently, one inmate estimated, "one fourth of the filth is never touched at all," leaving the camp "filthy beyond description."

Confederate officials were fully aware of Belle Isle's glaring shortcomings. With the prison located less than two miles from General Winder's headquarters and President Jefferson Davis's home, a visit to the pen required little time and no expense. Proximity, however, did not spur attentiveness. In November 1863, William Allen Carrington, a Confederate physician, provided Winder with a sobering appraisal of the facility. The inmates were "too much crowded," lacked blankets and firewood, slept on bare ground, and were exposed to "the vicissitudes" of Richmond's climate, especially chilly and damp winds blowing off the river. Four months later, the prison's on-site surgeon amplified Carrington's assessment, again noting the intolerable overcrowding that had only grown worse since his predecessor surveyed the facility.

Despite the damning reports, the site remained unimproved. General Winder contemplated erecting barracks with lumber from a government mill, but nothing came of the plan. Winder groused about the scarcity of essential resources for Belle Isle, but neither he nor his superiors were intent on improving the camp. Not until October 1864, when the Union siege of Petersburg threatened supply lines to Richmond as well as the Confederate capital's security, was Belle Isle largely emptied of prisoners.

Union authorities displayed a similarly cavalier attitude regarding the appropriate capacity of their existing camps. Camps Chase and Douglas, for example, which had both been transformed into camps for paroled Union prisoners, were reconverted into prisoner-of-war facilities. In June 1863 the two sites held a combined total of fewer than 500 prisoners. By the end of summer their populations had ballooned to more than 2000 and 6000, respectively. Especially marked was the expansion of the prison at Fort Delaware. In July 1862, Fort Delaware's population peaked at over 3000 and overwhelmed the existing facilities. Exchanges rapidly shrank the prison's population until only 17 inmates remained by the year's end. To Colonel William Hoffman's credit, he anticipated the need to expand the prison. During a visit at the fort in April 1863, the Union commissary general for prisoners ordered the fort's commander to begin construction on facilities to house 10,000 Confederates. Still incurably penurious, Hoffman forbade the addition of any amenities beyond the barest minimum when the facility was expanded. Little progress was made on the additions until just before the deluge of new prisoners began in May 1863. Then, with construction barely keeping pace, the number of prisoners shot up to more than 9000. By fall, the facility was a veritable city with nearly 16,000 residents, approaching the population of nearby Wilmington.

The newly constructed barracks at Fort Delaware, in accordance with Hoffman's orders, were primitive and shoddy. Nevertheless, they provided a degree of protection from the elements that Burch and his compatriots at Belle Isle could only dream of. Yet, just as Belle Isle had too few tents, Fort Delaware had too few barracks. And like Belle Isle, the space allocated to prisoners at the fort was woefully inadequate. Prisoners devised various stratagems to mitigate the near perpetual crush of fellow inmates. Private Thomas Jenkins of the Fourth Georgia Infantry, who was one of the earliest inmates at the expanded Fort Delaware, planned his days with care.

"I find," he noted in his diary, "that (in such a crowded place as this is) if a person wishes to be enabled to move about, to wash and to bathe himself, the best plan is to rise early."

The site's setting magnified the prisoners' discomfort. The stench from the river and wetlands intensified the malodor inside the barracks and fort. Authorities recognized the harmful qualities of the fort's brackish environs but took inadequate measures to address them. A system of dikes and drains was intended to remove standing water and filth generated by the prisoners, but it had not been designed to handle the waste disposal of a community of nearly sixteen thousand. The prison privy compounded the problem. Located along the shores of the island, the river in theory flushed waste away. Yet, too often it accumulated rather than dispersed waste.

Medical inspections of the prison described conditions strikingly like those that prevailed at Belle Isle. Prisoners, one inspector reported, "were much crowded together," rendering the barracks "impossible to keep clean" and resulting in "many deaths at this place." The number of inmate deaths jumped sharply as soon as the prison filled in the fall of 1863. On some days smallpox, dysentery, measles, and chronic diarrhea claimed the lives of as many as twenty prisoners. With an apparent mixture of enthusiasm and anxiety, Dr. Washington G. Nugent, one of the surgeons at the post, wrote to his wife, "It is a first rate place to see every type of disease."

The unmet need for prison capacity urged on searches by Union and Confederate authorities for yet more facilities that could become improvised prisons. Especially intrepid were Confederates, who were even more pressed for resources and funds than they had been during the first year of the war. The makeshift facilities they cobbled together offered at best primitive accommodations. But several fell short of even that modest accomplishment.

Such was true of the Confederate prison at Cahaba, Alabama. Before the war, no one entertained the notion that the brick skeleton of a cotton warehouse in the fading Alabama town might become a prison pen. Conveniently located where the Cahaba River joined the larger Alabama River, the facility was a relic of the community's unfulfilled ambitions. In 1860, a local planter began expanding a cotton warehouse nestled beside the river. But only the exterior walls and part of the warehouse's roof had been erected when the war started. No matter its unfinished state, the warehouse did not long remain vacant. As early as 1862 Confederates imprisoned a small number of alleged

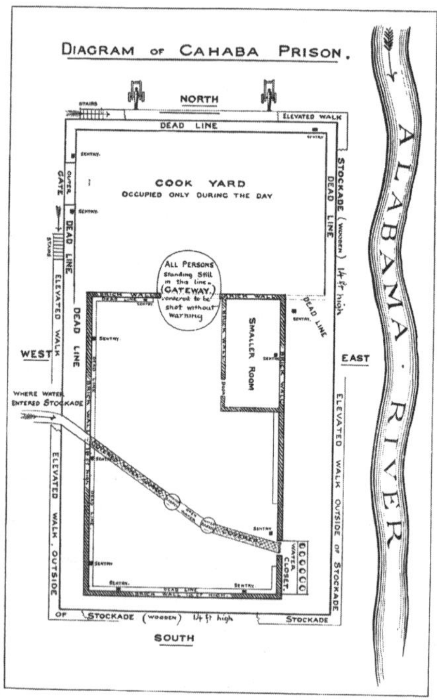


Cahaba in Alabama eventually became one of the most overcrowded prisons in the Confederacy. (From Jesse Hawes, *Cahaba: A Story of Captive Boys in Blue*, 1888)

spies and political prisoners there. By June 1863 it was a full-blown prison for captured soldiers, and would remain one until the last month of the war.

Aside from the ease of transporting prisoners to the facility, little else recommended the Cahaba site. Potable water was scarce there. The prison's doctor observed that the open ditch that channeled water into the prison compound was garnished with the "washings of the hands, feet, faces, and heads of soldiers, citizens, and negroes, buckets, tubs, and spittoons of groceries, offices and hospital, hogs, dogs, cows, and horses, and filth of all kinds from the streets and other sources." The structure itself provided merely the most makeshift accommodations. Its unfinished roof leaked and only partially covered the impromptu prison. It had a bare earth floor and a single modest fireplace that heated only the immediate vicinity around the hearth. A small, uncovered prison yard, enclosed by a stockade fence and beyond the warehouse walls, was available to prisoners during the daytime. There they built fires to cook and to warm themselves, creating an inferno-like landscape of flames and smoke. Bunks, five high, clung to the interior walls. They lacked bedding or straw and could accommodate four-hundred-odd prisoners, leaving the rest of the more than three thousand prisoners to bed down where they could. So congested was the warehouse that by late 1864 each prisoner could lay claim to space equivalent to an economy-class seat on a modern airliner.

Conditions at other newly repurposed facilities in the Confederacy were even worse. In October 1863, General Robert E. Lee urged Secretary of War James Seddon to shrink the prison population in Richmond by shifting Union captives to the southwestern Virginia city of Danville. Military necessity, rather than concern for the prisoners' well-being, prompted Lee's plea. The nearly thirteen thousand prisoners in the Confederate capital consumed foodstuffs and firewood in a city already haunted by scarcity. The *Richmond Dispatch* complained bitterly that "it costs the Confederacy $1.50 per day to support each one of the vandals in idleness." In March 1863 General Winder exacerbated popular anger by requisitioning large amounts of flour, which otherwise might have been sold to the city's civilians, to feed prisoners. The combination of unchecked inflation and scarce foodstuffs fed mounting outrage among city residents, who erupted in periodic civil unrest, including a full-blown food riot in April. Equally alarming to Lee was the threat of Union raids to liberate captives in the Confederate capital.

With little evident forethought, Seddon ordered the establishment of military prisons in Danville three days after receiving Lee's request. From the vantage point of the overtaxed Confederate capital, Danville appeared a convenient locale for stashing enemy captives. Remote from the front lines, it was served by an important railroad, and foodstuffs and other supplies were (mistakenly) assumed to be more plentiful there. Tobacco factories left vacant by wartime disruptions provided plausible prison facilities. Seddon promptly secured six such factories to host prisoners of war.

Little more than two weeks after Lee broached his proposal, seven hundred prisoners arrived in Danville by train from Richmond and began populating the new prison complex. Day after day, trains deposited hundreds of prisoners from the Confederate capital. By November 25, less than two weeks after the prisons opened, more than four thousand prisoners were sequestered there.

The facilities that welcomed the prisoners were grim, filthy, vacant shells. Bergun Brown, a twenty-four-year-old private in the Twenty-Ninth Indiana Infantry captured at Chickamauga, recorded his first impressions: "Looks about as usual only dreadful dirty & very closely crowded." Confederate authorities had made no improvements to the buildings other than to remove all furnishings, bar the windows, and strengthen the doors. No arrangements had been made to heat the prisons. Weeks—and, in at least one case, months—passed before stoves were installed. Even so, the pens remained frigid because of a shortage of fuel. Compounding the prisoners' discomfort, the ground-floor windows in the buildings were only partially boarded up, so cold air raced through the buildings. Even prisoners crowded into the upper floors experienced winter winds that filtered through the floors "so freely as to make it seem as though we were sleeping in ice."

Yet again, prisoners endured chronic overcrowding. To impede escape attempts, prison guards emptied the ground floors at night, forcing all the prisoners into the upper floors of the buildings. Prisoners who had endured overcrowding in Libby Prison complained that they had even less space in the Danville pens. One inmate calculated that each prisoner had less than eleven square feet of space. Another objected that his captors presumed that a prison "could always take in a few more."

An outbreak of smallpox and the steady toll of disease, rather than any official intervention, began easing the overcrowding. By April 1864 one prisoner estimated that five hundred of his compatriots had died since arriving in Danville, while another, who had previously complained that he "could scarcely find room to lie down," noted with relief "less crowding." Prisoner

Four tobacco warehouses that served as prisons are in the foreground of this 1865 view of Danville, Virginia. (Library of Congress)

George Putnam explained, "There were enough vacancies through death to give space on the floor."

Prison protocols and facilities in Danville deterred good hygiene. The prisons lacked any running water so prisoners relied instead on the nearby Dan River. Small squads of prisoners filled buckets in the river and lugged them back to the prisons. Under any circumstances the task of bearing water for thousands was onerous. By late 1864 many prisoners were so malnourished and weak that two men often struggled to carry a bucket the short distance from the riverbank to the prisons. At times, the object of so much toil must have seemed unworthy of the effort; sometimes clear, the water turned muddy, gritty, and unpalatable whenever it rained.

The prison buildings themselves were filthy, caked with tobacco juice and dirt. As had been true in Richmond prisons, the number of prisoners far exceeded the capacity of the sinks (latrines). With hundreds of prisoners suffering from chronic diarrhea, dysentery, and other ailments, prisoners waited in long lines to visit the sinks. Unable to endure the wait, many "were obliged to make their evacuations right on the floor."

So overpowering was the foul odor and so plentiful the filth from the prisons that residents of Danville avoided their environs. Within ten days of the opening of the prisons, the local newspaper editorialized against the "most wretched conditions" in the prisons. In January 1864, city officials and residents petitioned Confederate authorities, complaining that the stench of the prison facilities was "offensive at the distance of several hundred yards" and caused "the greatest annoyance." Their plea for the immediate closure of the prisons went unfulfilled, and the prisons remained in operation until the war's end.

Union authorities were more deliberate when transforming existing facilities into prisons—but only by degree. Rock Island, a three-mile-long and half-mile-wide island in the Mississippi River between Davenport, Iowa, and Moline, Illinois, was a case in point. The site had several selling points. The government already owned it, the neighboring cities were railheads and river ports, and a major arsenal was already under construction there. With plans furnished by Colonel Hoffman, local contractors expanded the island's facilities between July and November 1863.

Frugality, yet again, prevailed. The prison's construction was slapdash in keeping with Quartermaster General Montgomery Meigs's orders that the barracks "should be put up in the roughest and cheapest manner, mere shanties, with no fine work about them." When rumors of extravagance reached Washington, he grew anxious: "It is reported here that there is much finer work intended than necessary." Only "very rough work," he barked. By all accounts, the eventual facilities were fittingly primitive.

Despite the months of preparation, the facility was still incomplete on December 3, when the first Confederate prisoners arrived by train. The captain charged with overseeing the camp's construction had previously warned Hoffman by telegraph, "no water yet in prison yard" and no "clothing, blankets, etc., etc., on hand." Nor were there provisions or straw for bedding. Nevertheless, two days after the commandant's frantic warnings, more than 800 exhausted captives arrived. Consignments of prisoners flooded the facility and within a week another 2300 "dirty, ragged, care-worn looking objects of pity" had crossed the prison's threshold.

Although surrounded by the continent's most prodigious river, prisoners at Rock Island lacked a dependable source of water. An antiquated and unreliable steam pump drew water from the river to supply the prisoners' water needs. And like so many other prisons, the Rock Island site drained poorly. But improving drainage was not a simple matter because any feasible system would foul the prison's water supply, which had been carelessly located beneath the prison on the shores of the Mississippi River. In the near term, prison authorities used portable privies to improve waste disposal. Each day hundreds of barrels of collected offal, along with waste from the prison hospital, were dumped into the river. When the camp's quartermaster officer proposed a system to flush the prison's open sewers, Hoffman balked at its expense. Only after the budget was severely pared did he approve it. But after the delays, the scaled-down sewer system did not go into service until the war's end.

Worse yet, the prison staff was ill prepared to deal with prisoners worn down by arduous rail travel from the Deep South in bitter cold. While one of the severest winters on record lashed the region, underdressed inmates had no choice but to venture outside into the near lethal cold to collect their rations and to visit the privies. They returned to dangerously cold barracks that woodstoves failed to warm adequately. Stunned prisoners who hailed from the Deep South reported that water froze five feet from barrack stoves.

A new and grim severity distinguished the mammoth prison camps that the Union and Confederacy erected in 1863 and 1864. Hitherto, most prisoners had been stuffed in repurposed training camps, unfinished warehouses, derelict factories, and dilapidated forts. The exception was the Johnson's Island prison in Ohio, which resembled a frontier outpost. In contrast, the new purpose-built facilities at Point Lookout and Andersonville could not be mistaken for anything but prison pens. Their design revealed the evolution of attitudes toward prisoners of war after two years of intensifying war. With exchanges halted, the new prisons were conceived as sites of long-term captivity rather than temporary holding pens. Despite the likelihood that camp inhabitants were destined for long stretches, the new prisons were, by design, mercilessly primitive.

Contemporary lithographs portrayed the Union prison camp at Point Lookout as a spick-and-span facility in a setting more appropriate for a vacation idyll than the long-term domicile of twenty thousand prisoners. Indeed, before the war the site, which occupied a Maryland sandspit separating the Potomac River and the Chesapeake Bay, had been a pleasure ground for well-heeled Washingtonians. Even after the prison was built, the site remained alluring. During daylight hours in good weather, thousands of prisoners gathered on the shoreline that served as the eastern boundary

This 1864 lithograph reveals the clutter of tents that housed Confederate prisoners at Point Lookout in Maryland. (Library of Congress)

of the camp. There they mingled, gambled, bathed, washed clothes, fished, and rummaged for seafood until guards herded them back into the prison stockade for the night.

The peninsula had first caught the eye of Union officials early in the war as a convenient location for a massive, fourteen-hundred-bed hospital for wounded soldiers. Three weeks after the Battle of Gettysburg, Quartermaster General Meigs announced that a prisoner-of-war camp would be erected a short distance from the existing hospital. The site was poised at a marine crossroads where ships from Washington, Baltimore, and points farther afield could easily offload prisoners and supplies. Additionally, the landscape of sandy, low-lying, and flat shorelines offered no obstructions to complicate the erection of an expansive prison compound.

Within a month of Meigs's announcement and even before the stockade around the camp's perimeter was complete, the new prison held more than 1800 prisoners. By year's end a proper twelve-foot-high fence confined more than 9000 prisoners. The forty-acre site housed 15,500 by mid-1864, and more than 20,000 during the last months of the war.

The overabundance of water at Point Lookout, as at Rock Island, did not translate into plentiful drinking water. Six shallow wells supplied the camp with water, but four of them produced brackish water laced with iron and alkaline salts. In December 1863, a medical inspector warned that water from these wells provoked "digestive and intestinal derangements." Prisoners confirmed the inspector's findings. Prisoner George M. Neese drank camp water the day after he arrived at Point Lookout and suffered a violent bout of diarrhea "that clung to me like a leech for several days." Thereafter, he drank as little well water as possible. Eventually, even the good wells became so fouled that Union authorities had to import barrels of drinking water from Baltimore.

Bare-bones amenities were erected at minimal cost. Latrines were built at the end of piers that extended out into the bay, where the relentless motion of the coastal waters scattered the waste. On the presumption that barracks were a needless luxury in a locale blessed with a balmy summer climate and healthful breezes, the prisoners were housed in tents. In the fall of 1863, with damp and colder weather looming, the prison commander proposed that barracks be erected. Secretary of War Stanton, however, nixed the proposal.

Many observers, especially Confederates, saw in Stanton's hard-line stance on Point Lookout evidence of the secretary of war's twisted personality and sinister ambitions. Perhaps indifference to suffering, vindictiveness, and a compulsion to exercise power all played a role in Stanton's veto. The most benign explanation for his stance was that barracks were an unnecessary expense. Soldiers in the field endured inclement weather in tents, so surely prisoners of war could as well. Using surplus tents to lodge prisoners reduced the cost of building and operating the prison. Thrift, however, was at most only a partial explanation for Stanton's stance. Even the ever frugal Hoffman endorsed the proposal to build barracks. The costs of the barracks would have been modest, especially because Hoffman proposed using the prison fund generated by the sale of surplus prison supplies to purchase building materials. Labor costs would have been small because Hoffman intended to enlist prisoners to build the barracks.

Stanton's decision likely was an expression of his resolve to retaliate for the shoddy (or wholly absent) housing provided to Union prisoners at Belle Isle and elsewhere. If Confederates built a tent-city prison along the shores of the James River, the Union would build an equivalent on the shores of the Chesapeake. To do so was consonant with the logic of retaliation that the Union had formally endorsed in General Orders No. 100. Stanton's decision was one more instance in the cycle of calibrated retaliation that became more and more pronounced as the war continued. Whatever his motivation, no Union official, from President Lincoln and General Henry Halleck down to the prison commander at Point Lookout, took exception to his decision.

Point Lookout became a veritable open-air museum of almost every type of tent used by the United States military during the several preceding decades. Some were simple shelter tents, which could accommodate three prisoners. Others were tepeelike Sibley tents, which could hold twelve, and yet others were large hospital tents that had space for eighteen. While the grounds of the prison were spacious enough to accommodate as many as fifteen thousand prisoners without undue congestion, there were too few tents, especially of good quality. Prisoners jostled for the best available tents. The site's climate, which varied from withering heat in the summer to bone-chilling cold in the winter, exposed all the failings of the tents. Prisoner James T. Wells blasted them as "miserable affairs, . . . full of holes and very rotten." During dry and warm spells, the "old rickety" tents were an annoyance; during storms and winter months, they were virtually impotent against swirling winds and rains. B. T. Holliday, who entered the camp soon after it opened, recalled that the tents had "seen so much service that they would leak and we spent a very uncomfortable time . . . packed like sardines in a box." When heavy rains and high tides inundated the camp, one former prisoner complained, "our situation became truly deplorable." The prisoners' assessments of their accommodations were confirmed by one of Hoffman's inspectors, who declared at least a third of the tents in the camp utterly unfit for use. Desperate to elevate themselves above the damp, cold, lice-ridden ground, prisoners scavenged anything that could improve their living spaces. Prison guards engaged in a robust and lucrative trade in discarded wooden supply boxes, which prisoners coveted and used to build precarious box shanties.

When Newell Burch reflected on his ordeal in Andersonville, he recognized that in many regards, the camp was just another Civil War prison pen, only more so. Like most, it was overcrowded, squalid, and inadequate for its purposes. But as he came to understand during the year he spent there, everything about Andersonville was on an epic scale. The overcrowding defied description; the lack of sanitation was uniquely execrable; the unhealthfulness was acutely lethal.

Burch entered the Andersonville stockade around March 1, 1864, in the arms of a fellow prisoner. His stint at Belle Isle had left him so weak that he had to be carried from the rail station to the Andersonville stockade, a distance of about one mile. With the stockade still incomplete and only a few thousand prisoners tenanting the site, the prison was yet uncrowded and comparatively clean. Burch spent his first night sleeping without shelter on an improvised mattress made of pine boughs. The next day, his friend rigged a primitive lean-to from the detritus left from the clearing of the prison grounds. Initially, Burch was heartened that rations at Andersonville were better than those he had received at Belle Isle. But, to his profound disappointment, "it soon got to be the same old story," leaving him to complain that the rations were "no food that a dog would hardly eat."

Andersonville was the apotheosis of the Confederacy's haphazard handling of prisoners. The managerial smugness that informed prison planning on both sides was extravagantly on display at Andersonville, where Confederate authorities seemingly vowed that if it had to be done, it could be done, and if it could be done, it would be done: damn the consequences. The ruthless logic of military necessity gave license to imagine, build, and operate an otherwise unconscionably wretched site.

As envisioned in official Confederate correspondence, Andersonville was the solution to the Confederacy's prisoner crisis. On November 24, 1863, a month after General Lee's plea to remove prisoners from Richmond, Secretary of War Seddon ordered Captain W. S. "Sid" Winder, General Winder's son and aide-de-camp, to identify an appropriate site for a military prison in southwestern Georgia. Advised by Howell Cobb, now general of the reserve forces in the state, and Governor Joseph E. Brown, Captain Winder considered several locales before selecting the site near the tiny village of Anderson Station. The spot was sufficiently large to allow for the prison's expansion at minimal cost. Jefferson Davis claimed after the war that the location was deemed suitable because of its purported "salubrity" and abundance of water and timber. It was served by a rail line, distant from advancing Union armies, and in a "productive farming community" still untouched directly by the war. There, according to the *Richmond Sentinel*, "no difficulty will be encountered in supplying" the prisoners' needs. Prisoners also would pose no threat to any important centers of population if they staged an uprising.

Confederate officials devoted more attention to the planning of this camp than to any other prison pen. Although Andersonville subsequently became a byword for mismanagement and disorder, experienced officers oversaw the construction of the facility. Sid Winder, who selected the site, had served on his father's staff since 1861. So too had Captain Richard Winder, General Winder's nephew and a longtime assistant quartermaster, who supervised the construction of the camp. Captain Henry Wirz, the superintendent of the interior of the post, was yet another member of General Winder's staff. When assigning Wirz to Andersonville, Winder described him as "an old prison officer, a very reliable man and capable of governing prisons." Since November 1861, Wirz had been dealing with prisoners in one manner or another. His earliest posting was as the assistant to the prison commandant at Tuscaloosa, Alabama. In 1862 he joined General Winder's staff and commanded both Belle Isle and Libby prisons.

Mustering officers to preside over Andersonville proved easier than amassing the materials to build it. In his role as quartermaster, Richard Winder had to scrounge for literally everything to build and stock the prison, from salt to nails and tents to lumber. His first challenge was securing labor to construct the prison itself. With no troops initially assigned to the site, the only available labor force was enslaved Blacks from neighboring plantations. Local slaveholders refused to rent their slaves for the task, forcing Winder to impress more than two hundred slaves for sixty days to erect the stockade that would imprison their erstwhile liberators. Pressed by the impending arrival of the first prisoners, harried slaves furiously felled hundreds of towering pines, hewed them into posts, and stood them upright in trenches to form the prison's imposing stockade.

Because the stockade was an urgent priority, no attention was devoted to building any sanitation system for the camp. Out of necessity, the earliest prisoners to enter the stockade improvised their own latrine adjacent to the creek in the southern portion of the camp. By the time Richard Winder secured shovels and other tools to construct proper latrines, the stockade was so overcrowded that no other location for the latrines was feasible. Thus, the impromptu latrines became permanent. To the whims of nature, particularly periodic drenching rains, fell the responsibility for flushing away the accumulated filth of tens of thousands of prisoners that collected in the creek bed. The same creek was the source of water for drinking and bathing. When the creek inevitably became unpalatable, desperate prisoners used their hands, spoons, sticks, and any available tools to dig exploratory wells in often futile searches for fresh water. Like many of his compatriots, Newell Burch either held his nose and drank from the creek or begged water from those few prisoners lucky enough to have working wells.

Amid this scarcity, Confederate officials nevertheless assembled the resources—firewood, manpower, and rolling stock—to transport prisoners south to Andersonville. Moving three thousand prisoners a week to the camp, as General Winder planned, severely tested the organizational capacities of the Confederacy. By the time the transfer of prisoners to the camp was completed, it ranked among the most ambitious logistical operations undertaken by the rebel nation.

No precise record of prisoner transfers to Andersonville is extant, but we can estimate the scale of the task. Based on prisoners' accounts, as many as 75 prisoners were stuffed cheek by jowl in boxcars that measured twenty-eight feet long, eight feet wide, and a little over six feet high. Between 75 and 90 trainloads of prisoners would have been needed to transport the 45,000 prisoners who were sent to Andersonville. The scale of this undertaking becomes clear when the number of railcars needed for the task is calculated. Roughly one thousand boxcars, or one fifth of the entire inventory of boxcars in the Confederacy, were required to transport prisoners to Andersonville. A similar commitment of resources was needed later in 1864, when Sherman's army seemed poised to liberate the camp. The equivalent of another sixty trains, comprised of a total of 750 to 800 cars, dispersed prisoners from Andersonville across Georgia and South Carolina.

Confederate officials evidently gave no consideration to the hardship imposed on the tens of thousands of prisoners transported over the rickety Confederate rail system. The massive and continuing transfer of prisoners to Andersonville obligated a substantial commitment of troops to serve as guards. Loath to use more than the barest minimum of troops, Confederates purposefully concentrated prisoners in stuffed boxcars so as to minimize the force needed to surveil and control them. Wary and outnumbered, guards were little inclined to gestures of compassion toward their charges.

Beginning when the first train left Richmond on February 19, 1864, and continuing throughout the summer, hundreds of prisoners boarded trains in the upper South every week and undertook the grinding journey to Andersonville. During the ordeal of transit, prisoners were constantly reminded of their degradation. The earliest prisoners who were sent south that February and March traveled in unheated boxcars. To lessen the risk of frostbite, prisoners resorted to desperate measures. Private William Hawkins of the 154th New York greased his limbs with lard and wrapped himself in his blanket. Prisoners could not presume that they would regularly receive either rations or water during the trip, which usually took at least five days. With the trains seldom reaching speeds more than twenty-five miles an hour, and more often traveling little faster than a walking pace, anxious guards kept the car doors partially or fully closed. For the thousands of prisoners who suffered from chronic diarrhea and other forms of digestive distress, spending days (and nights) in closed and crowded cars with only buckets to serve as latrines was excruciating. Along with the struggle for light and water, prisoners in transit gasped for air free of fermenting odors of sweat, vomit, urine, and excrement.

Charles Smedley endured the deprivation, tedium, and dislocation that made the trek to Andersonville so punishing and, for some prisoners, deadly. Although Smedley was a battle-hardened veteran who had survived a serious battle wound and brief captivity, nothing in his previous experience prepared him for his passage to Andersonville. From the Wilderness battlefield he was hustled to a prison in Danville, where he remained for two weeks. On May 18, he and hundreds of other prisoners were woken at daybreak, loaded onto boxcars, and sent south. By noon they had traveled to the end of the rail line that was under construction between Danville and Greensboro, North Carolina. They then marched six miles to another railhead, where they waited until after dark for another train. When it arrived, the prisoners scrambled aboard, filling the cars so tightly that both standing and sitting were disagreeable. Worse yet, Smedley's car leaked badly during a heavy rain. The train took all night to crawl thirteen miles to Greensboro. After further delays there, the prisoners departed for Charlotte, which they reached twelve hours later (averaging less than eight miles an hour). While Smedley and the other prisoners huddled without shelter beside the tracks, another overnight rain drenched them. At noon on the following day, they boarded a train that aimlessly shuttled back and forth within the environs of Charlotte for hours before they were unloaded on the outskirts of the city to spend another night. At sunrise on the fourth day, the prisoners jostled for space on yet another train that took until sunset to deposit them in Columbia, South Carolina. By then, Smedley and his fellow prisoners had traveled only about two hundred fifty miles and were less than halfway to their destination. In Columbia they were stuffed into another train, with the loading door partially closed, "which nearly smothered us." While the train dawdled toward Augusta, Georgia, Smedley was tormented by a guard who slept with his head on Smedley's chest and by other prisoners who piled their legs on top of him. "Could not sleep," he noted drily in his diary. The train arrived in Augusta at noon on the following day, and yet again the prisoners changed trains. Fortune seemingly smiled on Smedley when he secured a seat at the car's door. But, to his dismay, it was closed throughout the night so he had to sleep while pressed against it. Finally, late on May 23, after six arduous days in transit, he arrived at Andersonville.

As ponderous as was the transfer of tens of thousands of prisoners hundreds of miles to Andersonville, it was businesslike compared to the provisioning of the camp. General Winder and his staff failed to assemble the essentials to complete anything but the crudest skeleton of a prison. Had the consequences been less tragic, the scarcity of almost everything needed to outfit the camps might have been comical.

Despite vast pine forests that surrounded the prison environs, even green lumber was unavailable, because Georgia sawmen refused to sell their stock for the paltry sums offered by the Confederacy. Attempts to requisition lumber from recalcitrant lumbermen failed as well. Thus, no barracks were built to house the prisoners. Nor could tents be procured. Prisoners were left to their own ingenuity to secure shelter. Newell Burch and his friend, for instance, teamed up with a few other prisoners and dug out a hovel that they covered with pine limbs. Charles Smedley spent the last fifteen cents in his possession when he entered Andersonville to purchase two split pieces of pine which he and his friend used to construct their shebang. Not even

Among the Andersonville relics displayed in 1866 were eating and cooking utensils improvised by prisoners. (Library of Congress)

straw was available in sufficient quantity to provide rudimentary bedding, so Branch, Smedley, and others slept on whatever they could find to cushion the ground. So scarce were cooking and eating utensils that camp denizens either did without or improvised their own fork, spoon, or plate out of anything that would suffice.

The presumption that foodstuffs for the Andersonville prisoners could be secured locally was quickly exposed as daft. Confederate authorities had already been alerted two years earlier to the challenge of provisioning prisoners in nearby Macon, the small city sixty miles to the north. In early May 1862, prisoners captured during the Battle of Shiloh had been sent to Macon, where a prison was opened. Within days, the local newspaper labeled the new prison "an elephant of immense magnitude." The paper complained, "At a time when it is difficult to feed our own population, we are now to be *blessed* with the presence and custody of 900 prisoners of war." Subsequent events justified the anxiety. Prisoners were soon complaining about scanty rations and their "foul and unwholesome diet." Maconites continued to harp on the scarcity of supplies during the following year. By then, the want of food and other necessities in central Georgia was so severe that at least one prominent local wrote to President Jefferson Davis pleading that he take measures to address the scarcity.

Even before the prison opened, Richard Winder warned General Winder that, aside from coarse cornmeal, most foodstuffs were unavailable. If ample supplies were extant in the region surrounding Andersonville before the spring of 1864, no one had figured out how to extract them for the prisoners' benefit. Nor did anyone explain how a reliable and adequate food supply for an artificial city was to be established in an isolated and undeveloped region. In a matter of months, Andersonville doubled, tripled, and then quadrupled the county's population. The supply chains that served the civilian population were wholly inadequate, so the prison remained dependent on fragile military supply chains. To meet the most basic needs of the prison, the equivalent of a train of approximately thirteen cars filled with provisions was required weekly. But when the supply trains were delayed, as happened periodically, prisoners had to make do with meager rations of cornmeal, bacon, occasionally rice, and less often beans or potatoes.

Confederate officials, including Secretary of War Seddon, were fully apprised of the chronic problems at Andersonville. From the outset Winder's own son and his nephew had vented their frustrations in reports to their superiors in Richmond. General Winder himself added his voice to the chorus of complaints immediately after his arrival at the camp. By then prison inspectors dispatched from Richmond had already attested to the dire conditions at Andersonville.

On May 25, only three months after the camp opened, Major Thomas P. Turner inspected the prison. Although seasoned by his long experience overseeing the wretched prison pens in Richmond, Turner was shocked by conditions at Andersonville. So filthy and poorly drained was the camp that he declared it virtually uninhabitable. The best solution, he contended, was to abandon the current site and build another stockade nearby.

Two months later, on August 1 (and two weeks before Andrew Riddle photographed the camp), Captain Daniel T. Chandler inspected the camp. In a stinging report, he confirmed Turner's dire assessment of Andersonville. He cataloged the lack of supplies, the wretched condition of the prisoners, the urgent need for shelter, the inadequacies of the stockade, the unhealthfulness of the rations (which contributed to Newell Burch's worsening scurvy), and the demoralized condition of the guards. Chandler urged that no more prisoners be sent to Andersonville and that several new prison sites be quickly prepared.

No significant palliative measures, however, were undertaken to improve the conditions in the camp. Distracted by other concerns, Secretary of War Seddon washed his hands of Andersonville by authorizing General Winder to use his best judgment and to act on his own responsibility without consultation with Richmond. Winder could establish new prisons, procure guards, and take whatever steps he deemed necessary to establish secure prisons. Winder pointedly ignored the order's import. Instead of wielding the authority he was granted, he continued to fire off pleading missives for resources and troops and to request approval for every action he undertook. No one in the Confederate high command displayed any interest in providing the decisive leadership that the deteriorating prison situation demanded.

Not until Union General William Sherman's advancing armies posed a threat to the camp did Confederate officials finally revise their plans for Andersonville. Horrified by the prospect of Sherman liberating the camp's thirty-thousand-odd prisoners, who might then join his marauding columns as they carved a path of destruction across Georgia, Confederate officials in September 1864 ordered the dispersal of most of Andersonville's inmates. Along with other prisoners who were too sick to be transported, Newell Burch remained at Andersonville, where he would be joined by thousands of unfortunate prisoners who returned to the camp after having been hustled across the state for weeks eluding Sherman's advance. The camp would never again be as overcrowded as it had been during the summer of 1864. But the festering filth of the stockade, the rancid rations, and the omnipresence of misery continued to define life at Andersonville.

The captivity that Newell Burch experienced at Belle Isle and Andersonville bore no resemblance to the imprisonment that John Pegram had undergone two years prior. The principle of reciprocity, which was to serve as an incentive for humane treatment of prisoners, now encouraged a downward spiral. No candid observer of the conditions at Point Lookout could defend the claim that Confederate prisoners there received the same resources as Union soldiers in the field. And certainly no one could make a convincing case that prisoners in Andersonville fared as well as even the most beleaguered Confederate soldiers.

As the stalemate over prisoner exchanges continued and conditions in the prison camps deteriorated, Union and Confederate officials hurled accusations that the other side displayed unconscionable indifference to the suffering of prisoners. Supplementing these charges were plaintive letters from prisoners themselves and a spate of early prison chronicles published by Michael Corcoran and other former prisoners of war. Additional fodder was provided by the appalling condition of seriously ill prisoners periodically exchanged by the two sides. Newspapers carried grim reports on prison conditions and editorialized about the perfidy of the opposing side's prison officials.

With recriminations swirling, officials began refining their excuses for violations of previous pledges of humane treatment. Each side dismissed claims that inhumane conditions were prevalent. When Confederates carped about the deficiencies of Point Lookout, the *Baltimore American* thundered that "rebel prisoners are treated as well as our own men, both in camp and hospital." Another editor countered, without any apparent evidence, that prisoners at Point Lookout "have more to eat here than they had before they were captured." He quipped, "If this is harsh treatment, we hope the rebel authorities will retaliate upon our men in like manner."

Officials complemented their dismissal of wretched prison conditions with denials of responsibility for the conditions that prevailed in the prisons. Such was the case at Rock Island after a series of articles in a local Democratic newspaper compared the prison with the worst Confederate camps. Intended to discredit the Republican conduct of the war, the charges outraged Colonel Adolphus J. Johnson, the camp commandant. While denying charges that prisoners were deliberately mistreated, Johnson placed responsibility for conditions at Rock Island on his superiors. Johnson confessed that if he had the "discretionary power" to treat his Confederate charges as he thought appropriate, "strict retaliation would be practiced by me." Instead of the purportedly well-heated barracks, "I would place them in a pen with no shelter but the heavens, as our poor men were at Andersonville." Plentiful rations would be replaced with "the same quantity and quality of provisions that the fiendish rebels give our men." And rather than provide clothing, "I would let them wear their rags, as our poor men do in the hands of the rebel authorities."

Confederate apologists diligently turned claims of cruel treatment of prisoners back on their Union foes. The *Richmond Dispatch*, for instance, cackled at reports of the "imaginary sufferings" of Union prisoners in Confederate hands. The much maligned Libby Prison was, according to the newspaper, "scrupulously clean and neat," and prisoners were rendered "comfortable" in the "capacious building." Moreover, prisoners "get full rations, and the best that can be gotten." Confederate officials accused their

Union counterparts of hurling baseless charges to distract from the Union's own policy of intentional cruelty to prisoners. Exchange agent Robert Ould raged to his Union counterpart, "You yourself see the living wrecks that come from Fort Delaware—men who went into the cruel keep hale and robust, men inured to almost every form of hardship and proof against everything except the regimen of that horrible prison."

Even while dismissing lurid Union accounts of prison conditions, Confederates were at pains to deflect responsibility for the actual conditions in the prison camps. Everyone in the chain of command at Andersonville, from Captain Wirz to General Winder, denied responsibility for the conditions there. Each protested that he was a victim of circumstance and did his best to mitigate the consequences of actions beyond his control. Wirz complained that he lacked the requisite authority to redress the camp's problems; Richard Winder railed against uncooperative local planters and dilatory commissary agents; camp physicians deplored chronic shortages of medicine; and General Winder griped about everything.

Winder and other Confederate officials charged that the suffering of Union prisoners was largely the responsibility of the Lincoln administration, which countenanced the blockade of the Confederacy and refused to exchange prisoners. Early on, Confederates dismissed the Union efforts to strangle the Confederacy's sea trade as a "paper blockade"; Jefferson Davis mocked it as a "monstrous pretension." But as Union forces captured more and more Confederate ports and the blockade tightened, Confederates increasingly complained that the blockade inflicted hardship on civilians by depriving them of medicines, foodstuffs, and other necessities. Over and over, Confederate apologists insisted that in the absence of the blockade, Union prisoners of war would want for nothing.

Even some Confederates found these denials of responsibility unconvincing, as did Colonel Chandler when he inspected Andersonville in August 1864. In his report he identified General Winder's intentional inaction as contributing to the prisoners' plight. The general, Chandler reported, advocated deliberately leaving the prisoners in the inhumane stockade until the number had been "sufficiently reduced by death to make the present arrangements suffice for their accommodation." So acute was Winder's disregard for the welfare of prisoners that Chandler recommended that Winder be replaced by someone more efficient, competent, and conscientious.

Winder's response to Chandler's report was telling. He dismissed it as "false" and impugned Chandler for his "unbecoming" conduct during the inspection. Winder had foreseen the tenor of Chandler's report because of "the very great sympathy expressed by the inspectors for the prisoners." Winder found such sympathy misplaced and "unbecoming."

Winder's denials of responsibility were both exaggerated and disingenuous. He was, after all, the officer in command of the Confederacy's prisons east of the Mississippi, and after August 1864, of all prisons. He failed to remedy chronic problems that were within his purview. He did nothing, for instance, to correct the byzantine command structure at Andersonville. Wirz was frustrated by unclear lines of responsibility throughout his tenure at the prison. He was assigned the daily operations inside the prison, including taking roll of the prisoners, maintaining security, and issuing rations. However, a separate officer was in command of the overall Confederate post. The quartermaster's office and hospital both operated independently of Wirz's command. This command structure meant that Wirz, who was the officer responsible for the welfare of prisoners, was dependent on others for the manpower and resources to manage the prison. Despite the recurring conflicts generated by the confusing dispersal of authority, Winder did nothing to unravel this gordian knot.

Winder similarly was as responsible as anyone in the Confederacy for the overcrowding at Andersonville. He had repeatedly condoned the crowding of prisoners while dismissing suggestions that overcrowding contributed to the unhealthfulness of the camps. His only anxiety about overcrowding at Andersonville and elsewhere, as Chandler's report underscored, was that prisoners might overwhelm outnumbered prison guards. Winder's complacency about overcrowding explains his failure to act on the authority granted him by the Confederate secretary of war to establish new prisons as he saw fit during the summer of 1864. If Winder did not intend to kill prisoners, he displayed little resolve to protect them.

By the summer of 1864, then, both Union and Confederate officials had settled on their excuses for the conditions in the prisoner-of-war camps. They not only dodged personal responsibility but also denied any broader collective responsibility for the prisoners' suffering. This toxic mixture of complacency and evasion reduced the swirl of public recriminations over the treatment of prisoners into theater that had little bearing on the daily struggles in the prison pens. By then, Newell Burch's principal concern was survival. Increasingly "drawn out of shape by scurvy and gangrene," he understood the hard truth that to him and his fellow prisoners fell the life-and-death challenge of figuring out how to outlast their captivity.

CHAPTER SEVEN

# A Mixture of Indifference and Half-Witted Cruelty

## (1864–1865)

Among the hardships that Frederic Augustus James endured while imprisoned first in Salisbury and then in Andersonville was erratic mail service. For a captive, living by his wits, beset by hunger, and sapped by worsening health, his angst about personal correspondence may seem curious. Yet for James the problem was singularly demoralizing. When he enlisted in the Union navy in August 1862, he was a thirty-year-old ship joiner from Massachusetts with a wife and two young daughters. In September 1863, while serving as a landsman aboard the USS *Housatonic*, he was captured during an ill-conceived naval attack on Fort Sumter. For five months thereafter he wrote to his wife often and anxiously awaited word from her. Not until late March 1864 did he receive a letter, in which she recounted the death of Mary, his beloved eight-year-old daughter, five months earlier. His wife had shared the heartrending news in four previous letters, none of which had reached James. When he condensed his grief and reflections on God's "chastening providence" into a letter that conformed to the strict dictates for prison correspondence, he had no assurance that it would survive the scrutiny of an anonymous censor. Nor could he know whether it would ever reach its destination. In June 1864, any realistic hope of communicating with his wife ended with his transfer to Andersonville. From then until his death from dysentery four months later, he received no word from her.

James's experience with the vagaries of prison mail was one measure of the isolation that he and other prisoners endured during the final year and a half of the war. With the end of general exchanges, captivity became a test of their will and resilience. Both warring sides institutionalized, to borrow the sociologist Erving Goffman's evocative phrase, violations of the "territories of the self." Neither Union nor Confederate officials ever articulated an intention to create total institutions—the phrase would not be popularized for another century—yet they did just that.

The prison camps of the late Civil War were not the first total institutions in the United States. During the half century before the war, Americans demonstrated an eagerness to build laboratories of coerced rehabilitation to regulate, tame, and transform human souls. They condoned civilian prisons and asylums that imposed servility and dependence with methods ranging from water torture to solitary confinement. But by the end of the war, the prison camps had evolved into some of the most extreme total institutions of the nineteenth century.

The intentions of the creators and supervisors of Civil War prisons were at times more modest and more ambitious than those of civilian prison keepers. Aside from exceptional cases, prison commandants during the Civil War did not seek to control the totality of a captive's existence. No

In the sketch *A New Batch at Andersonville*, artist William Waud captured the moment when a group of arriving prisoners first glimpsed their new prison home. (Library of Congress)

one expected wartime prison camps to transform combatants' souls or allegiance. The objective was to deprive the enemy of the services of the captive soldiers, not produce contrite prisoners.

Yet the scale of the prison camps and the vulnerability of the inmates inside them was breathtaking. Even the smallest wartime prison camps held many more inmates than had the largest prewar penitentiaries. The control that prison-camp staff exerted over inmates was less invasive than that exercised by staff at antebellum penitentiaries, but it was unconstrained by any conscientious regard for the welfare of the prisoners of war. Antebellum penitentiaries had been subject to public scrutiny and legislative oversight. No legislature in the prewar republic would have remained silent while conditions at a penitentiary deteriorated to the level of those at Andersonville.

The evolution of the prison camps was consonant with the intensification of the war. Impatient with the course of the war and appalled by the mounting toll of death and destruction, both civilians and soldiers voiced fantasies of retribution. Within Union military circles, recognition that nothing short of military victory would restore the Union led to growing acceptance of harsher modes of warfare. Simultaneously, both civilian observers and career military leaders demanded a new emphasis on authority, hierarchy, and discipline—not only within military ranks but more gen-

These Confederate prisoners captured in Tennessee in 1863 appear surprisingly chipper and well clad at Rock Island prison. (Library of Congress)

erally across northern society. Sentimentality and compassion had no place in this increasingly grim and hard-nosed conception of war.

Even in those camps where the captors' mailed fist pressed down comparatively lightly, prisoners underwent the profoundly disorienting experience of living within total institutions. Prison authorities found reasons to increase the isolation and deprivations borne by prisoners. For Frederic James and other prisoners, the known world shrank to the grim confines of the prison stockade and what they could glimpse just beyond it.

Few prisoners were as forgiving as Frederic James. Preternaturally optimistic, he found evidence each day of God's beneficence. Like most prison diarists, he decried the wretched rations and horrid conditions in the camps, but otherwise he refrained from censuring his guards or their superiors. Other prisoners, abiding the truism that no man loves his jailer, were not circumspect about their contempt for their keepers. Prison diaries and memoirs are stuffed with stories of brutal guards and ruthless prison officers. Prisoners denounced their keepers as villains and brutes whose personal defects were compounded by the moral bankruptcy of the civilization that had nurtured them. According to Union prisoners, their guards were the spawn of a barbaric slave-ridden society. For Confederate prisoners, their keepers were, as one prisoner put it, the "scum" of the North's mongrel and mercenary society.

By 1864 most prison officers had enough command experience to manage the fractious, enclosed worlds of the camps with the skeleton staffs at their disposal. Many were experienced administrators, and some even had experience with prisoners. Most of the prison officers at Andersonville, for instance, had dealt with prisoners as members of General Winder's staff since the early months of the war. Gone were most of the prison officials who were political hacks or military poseurs.

Conscientiousness to official duties, however, did not necessarily benefit prisoners. Despite deteriorating conditions at Andersonville, Captain Wirz's superiors universally praised his dedication and competence. Lieutenant Colonel Sam Jones, who was responsible for camp security at Cahaba, was lauded for his energy and efficiency. When prisoners carried out a well-planned prison revolt in early 1865, Jones decisively suppressed it. Yet he displayed no compassion for prisoners. He complained to a Union prisoner assigned to bury a deceased inmate that "I'm only sorry that the damned blue-bellies are so tough—they don't die fast enough." He supplemented his verbal abuse with physical violence, kicking those who strayed too close to the dead line and, allegedly, ordering the summary execution of one of the ringleaders of the prison uprising. Years after the war, Jesse Hawes, who served in the Ninth Illinois Cavalry and spent a year at Cahaba, recalled Jones as "a sickening blotch upon humanity."

To prison guards fell the humdrum tasks necessary to confine thousands against their wills. In the Confederacy, where almost all able-bodied white men of military age (between eighteen and fifty) were sent to the front, prison guards typically were men who were deemed too young, old, disabled, or incorrigible for any other service. They received little if any training to prepare them for their duties. And because guard duty was neither heroic nor memorable, they seldom enjoyed prestige.

Andersonville was typical of Confederate prisons in the competence of its guard units. In July 1864, when the camp was bursting with prisoners, most guards were members of the Georgia Reserves. An appalled Confederate inspector dismissed them as "without discipline" and their officers as "incapable" and "ignorant." One unit was, in the opinion of the same inspector, "thoroughly demoralized" and "mutinous." Only a small fraction of the guards were battle tested and confidence inspiring.

Few Union units were as green as the Confederate reserves assigned to Andersonville. Recovering wounded soldiers made up much of the Union guard force. These veterans were, in the opinion of the commandant of Rock Island, "good, steady, obedient & willing men." The Union army had fewer superannuated soldiers than the Confederacy, yet its most ballyhooed guard unit was the Thirty-Seventh Iowa Infantry Regiment. Organized to demonstrate the patriotic fervor of Iowa men who were past the conventional age of military service, many of its officers and soldiers were more than fifty years old, and some were over seventy. The so-called Graybeards spent the war migrating between several prisons, including Rock Island, where the prison surgeon described them as "the most unpromising subjects for soldiers I ever saw." Although desertion and disability thinned their ranks, they guarded prison camps until the close of the war.

Beginning in early 1864, units of United States Colored Troops (USCT) bolstered the ranks of the guards at Rock Island, Point Lookout, and Elmira, New York, prisons. The task of guarding white slave masters, including in a few instances their former owners, was a heady experience for the formerly enslaved Black men who made up a substantial portion of these units. They generally won the respect of prison commanders, and some officers hailed them as uncommonly good guards. No one, least of all prisoners, had any cause to question their resolve.

Regulations in Union and Confederate prisons inhibited intimacy between guards and prisoners. Guards were required to keep prisoners at a distance. The only authorized pretext for conversing with prisoners was official camp business. These rules, along with the frequent churning of the units assigned to guard duty, ensured that prisoners and guards remained strangers to one another.

Swelling prison populations further impeded familiarity between prisoners and guards. By the summer of 1863, Confederate prisoners at Fort Delaware outnumbered their guards ten to one. A year later, Union prisoners at Andersonville eclipsed the camp's Confederate forces twelve to one. On any given day in August 1864, when the Andersonville stockade held thirty thousand prisoners, the force that patrolled the stockade numbered only about two hundred, with another three hundred at the ready nearby.

Outnumbered by masses of prisoners, guards had no incentive to sympathize with them. Bored and fatigued by daily prison routines, guards enacted casual cruelty. Most guards treated prisoners with what a Confederate prisoner named Anthony Keiley described as "slip-shod indifference" and what George Putnam, a Union prisoner, labeled "a rather curious mixture of good-natured indifference and a kind of half-witted cruelty." Nowhere was cruelty prescribed, and every cruelty was officially frowned upon. Guards were not taught to abuse prisoners, but neither were they encouraged to see captives as deserving sympathy and respect.

Although they are full of solecisms, the letters that David O. McRaven, a Confederate soldier, wrote to his wife provide a glimpse of the perspective of a prison guard on his duties. He had mustered into service in July 1864, leaving behind his pregnant wife and three children. Soon after arriving at Salisbury prison that October, he allowed that "I culd stay here contented for it is a stirring place and suits me." But the tedium and loneliness of his duties began to wear and he soon complained that "guard duty is severe."

Any sympathy McRaven felt for the prisoners he guarded quickly evaporated. He confessed to "feeal a touch of sorrow" as he watched "the Amount of suffering and wretchedness in the space allotted to the yanky prisoners." But he dismissed the sentiment, countering that "at other times I feeal that if I had the power they would suffer more." He denounced the captives as "the wickedest people On Earth." Yet he also found them entertaining: "I often see things to amuse me among the yankees they steal from Each Other and it is very common to see them fight Each other like Dogs." McRaven later shared that the guards relished thwarting escape attempts "so that they Can get to kill more" prisoners. After reporting the cavalier treatment accorded the bodies of dead prisoners, McRaven acknowledged some disquiet; "it looks bad to see humanity so carelessly delt with." But, he added, "we see it every day and it has lost its effect on us."

In exceptional circumstances, guards and prisoners discovered they shared common affiliations. With most of the nation's important institutions, including most Protestant denominations, sundered before the war, few institutions retained the allegiance of both Confederate and Union soldiers. One notable exception was Freemasonry. Captured Masons were on the lookout for any "brothers" among their captors to whom they could appeal for concessions. Lieutenant Colonel Homer Sprague of the Thirteenth Connecticut Volunteer Infantry exploited his membership in the brotherhood within hours of his capture in September 1864. While in an ambulance, he "commenced my free-masonry on the driver." Confirming that he indeed was a member of the order, the enemy driver provided Sprague with food. The Masonic spirit prevailed even within the camps. With a mixture of envy and respect, John McElroy of the Sixteenth Illinois Cavalry, concluded that "the only interest manifested by any Rebel in the welfare of any prisoner was by the Masonic brotherhood." At Andersonville, Masons on the prison staff donated food, including vegetables, "which were literally beyond price," to captive Masons. They awarded preferred work assignments to their imprisoned Union "brothers" and supplied them with building materials for their rude hovels.

These acts of compassion were so uncommon, however, that they drew the notice of prison diarists. Tellingly, in the vast library of prison-camp diaries, correspondence, and memoirs, the names of few guards are recorded. Instead, guards were apparently as faceless and indistinguishable to prisoners as they themselves were to their guards. Together, the anonymity in the prison pens and the severity of prison regulations left wary guards and prisoners viewing one another, at a distance, with a volatile mixture of indifference, contempt, fear, and suspicion.

Guards labored to maintain distance while prisoners endeavored to overcome it. Isolating prisoners was the paramount concern of prison commanders and their staffs. Conversely, the abiding resolve of most prisoners was to erase the prison expanse that separated them from the world beyond the stockade. Boundaries became the focal point of an ongoing contest between prisoners and prison staff.

Through a combination of soul-numbing isolation and oppressive surveillance, Civil War prisoners experienced an especially onerous invasion of the "territory of the self." Some degree of isolation is inherent to captivity. But the experience of continuous surveillance within a stockade, endured by thousands simultaneously, was an innovation of the nineteenth century.

Prison-camp authorities made choices about the degree of isolation they enforced in the pens. Had they drawn inspiration from contemporary American jails, that isolation would have been modest. Many local jails resembled rustic boardinghouses in which jailers served as landlords. If a jailed prisoner had the means, he could order meals from restaurants, and loyal friends and family could supply him with clothing and company. Such lackadaisical captivity was ill suited to wartime needs. Alternatively, prison authorities might have drawn inspiration from civilian penitentiaries, where, for a half century, some inmates had undergone extreme isolation, including solitary confinement.

The Civil War prisoner-of-war camp required a different kind of isolation. Authorities strove to seclude prisoners of war not as individuals but en masse. Other than separating officers from soldiers in the ranks, prison officials took no steps to isolate prisoners from one another. Neither side had the resources to house prisoners in separate cells. Solitary confinement for prisoners of war made sense only in exceptional circumstances as an act of retaliation against specific prisoners. Even the most oppressive Civil War prisons afforded prisoners freedom of movement *within* the prison confines during daylight hours. The challenge for prison staffs was to confine and regulate that movement.

Boundaries at Civil War prison pens were often imprecise. Decades later, barbed wire would become a ubiquitous feature of both prison and concentration camps. But, only some borders of prison camps were clearly etched onto the landscape. Many were invisible to the eye and required assiduous surveillance to maintain.

At Andersonville, the crucial boundary was not the stockade wall, but the stakes driven into the ground, with pieces of scantling nailed to the top, that snaked parallel to the stockade wall. To straddle, duck under, or touch this so-called dead line was to court death. At Libby Prison in Richmond, the boundary was cruelly imprecise. Prisoners made life-and-death calculations about how close to get to the barred windows. The allure was strong; these windows offered the freshest air and the only cooling breezes a prisoner was likely to experience. If so inclined, prisoners could extend their arms through the bars into the space beyond the prison walls. But those who did so risked death at the hands of the Confederate sentinels.

The cessation of prisoner exchanges magnified the challenge of compelling prisoners to observe prison boundaries. Prison staff deliberately fostered rumors of impending exchanges in hopes of rendering prisoners more tractable. As long as general exchanges continued, they discouraged captives from reckless escape attempts. Why risk death or harm while escaping if captivity was likely to be brief? But as more prisoners were destined for long stints in the camps, tunneling under, climbing over, and breaking through prison walls took on a new urgency. Escape, Andersonville prisoner John Ransom, a quartermaster sergeant for the Ninth Michigan Cavalry, recalled, became the idée fixe of countless prisoners.

Coordinated prisoner escapes posed the greatest threat to the maintenance of prison security. Prison diarists recorded countless plans for

Private Robert Sneden illustrated his diary with this depiction of a Confederate guard shooting a prisoner who crossed the Andersonville dead line. (Museum of Virginia History)

mass escapes. That so few took place is a testament to the obstacles prisoners faced. They had few tools or resources at their disposal, and were unarmed, ignorant of their immediate environs, and ill equipped to survive as fugitives. Nevertheless, they schemed, prepared, and awaited any opportunity. At Libby Prison dogged prisoners spent nearly six weeks tunneling from the prison basement to a neighboring lot. On the night of February 9, 1864, they staged their break. More than one hundred prisoners scrambled through the tunnel before Confederates discovered the breach. Half of the escapees reached Union lines while the rest were returned to their familiar prison confines. Even more audacious was the escape plan of Confederates on Johnson's Island. They plotted to rush the guards, pile aboard the fort's steamship, and sail across Lake Erie to freedom in Canada. The logistics required to carry out the scheme proved too complicated and the prisoners accomplished little beyond panicking the prison commandant.

Escape attempts were certain to trigger tightened security and deeper isolation. At Fort Delaware in August 1863, a prisoner named Thomas Jenkins observed, "they are becoming more strict on us owing to the fact that several of our men have succeeded in making their escape from this place." Prison officials in Danville responded to a flurry of escape attempts in 1863 by cramming Union prisoners into the prison's upper floors so as to inhibit tunneling under the ground-level floor. When prisoners at Camp Douglas dug under their barracks, the commandant, Colonel Charles De Land, ordered the removal of the barrack floors, thereby exposing any tunnels beneath them. According to his crude cost-benefit calculation, "This will undoubtedly increase the sickness and mortality, but it will save much trouble and add security."

During the fall of 1864 and the ensuing winter, desperation prompted mass uprisings at several Confederate prisons. On November 25, 1864, prisoners at Salisbury came close to busting out. During the changing of the guard, several hundred prisoners rushed a camp gate. They overpowered guards, grabbed their weapons, and fired at soldiers stationed along the stockade parapet. In the ensuing melee, two guards were killed and several more were wounded. Any promise of success evaporated when guards fired rounds of canister into the swarming prisoners. The prisoners retreated into the prison grounds, leaving behind sixteen dead and more than sixty wounded. In a letter written a few days later, guard David McRaven described his comrades as both chastened and emboldened by the uprising. They no longer had "any confidence" in the prisoners, leaving the guards disposed to shoot them "on every occasion." Two months later, on January 20, Union prisoners at Cahaba overwhelmed and imprisoned several guards while breaking out of the stockade. But they quickly retreated into the prison when guards obstructed their path with loaded cannons.

In addition to keeping prisoners in the stockades, prison commandants and their staffs had to defend against military operations to liberate the inmates. Some plans to rescue prisoners were too outlandish to warrant concern. Confederate plans to liberate prison camps in Ohio, Illinois, and Indiana were thwarted before they posed a serious threat. But the nightmarish prospect of Confederates opening the prison gates at Point Lookout or of Union forces liberating thousands of prisoners in Richmond was too terrifying to ignore.

Both sides launched raids on prison camps. In late 1863, General Robert E. Lee schemed to storm Point Lookout from both the land and the sea. Freed prisoners would either join in an attack on Washington, D.C., or be ferried across the Potomac to Confederate lines. Concluding that the conditions were not then favorable, Lee shelved his plans until the following summer. In June 1864, Lieutenant General Jubal Early led an invading army into Maryland, and by early July had reached the outskirts of Washington, D.C. Confederate cavalry was dispatched to ride around the fringes of the capital and then dash down to the Point Lookout peninsula. Meanwhile, preparations were completed in North Carolina to launch an amphibious force that would rendezvous with the Confederate cavalry at the prison on July 12. But on July 10, just before the naval force was to depart, President Jefferson Davis halted the mission. Rumors of the attack had circulated so widely in Richmond that Union officials were alerted. They quickly strengthened the stockade at the prison and stationed gunboats to thwart any Confederate maritime attack. Any threat to Point Lookout ended on the thirteenth, when Early and his army withdrew across the Potomac.

Prisons in Richmond, because of their proximity to Union lines, were especially vulnerable to attack. After Union forces had advanced within ten miles of the prisons in the Confederate capital during the summer of 1862, officials worried about future Union forays to rescue prisoners. Those fears were realized on February 28, 1864, when Brigadier General Hugh Judson Kilpatrick led a cavalry raid targeting Belle Isle, Libby Prison, and other prison depots. In an operation that Union General George Meade called "desperate," Kilpatrick and his troops reached the outskirts of the city on

March 1. By then, they had lost any element of surprise and were met with stiff resistance. Kilpatrick's force scurried to safety within Union lines.

The unsuccessful raid had severe consequences for prisoners in Richmond. While it was unfolding, Confederate authorities took extraordinary steps to intimidate Union prisoners at Libby Prison. With General Winder's approval, two hundred pounds of gunpowder were placed under the cellar floor in the prison. If ignited, the mine would have obliterated the building and incinerated anything that withstood the explosion. After placing the explosives, Major Thomas Turner, the prison commandant, warned prisoners that "they would all be blown to Hell" if they attempted an uprising. Winder justified this desperate measure by insisting that the mine was intended merely to intimidate the prisoners.

Security in Richmond's prison pens became markedly tighter following the aborted raid. In subsequent weeks at least four prisoners were shot by sentries for standing in windows at Libby Prison. General Winder also accelerated his campaign to move prisoners as quickly as possible out of Richmond and to more secure sites farther south, particularly Andersonville.

As potentially catastrophic as prison uprisings and attacks were, prison officials recognized that unregulated contact between civilians and prisoners posed a serious, if more routine, threat. No camp, not even the most geographically isolated, was hermetically sealed off from its surrounding community. Both the prison pen on Belle Isle and the nearby Libby Prison were within easy walking distance of the Confederate president's office. The camp in Salisbury was a stone's throw from the town center and abutted one of the busiest rail lines in the Confederacy. Camp Douglas was within four miles of Chicago's downtown. Even Fort Delaware, situated on an island in the Delaware River, attracted revelers from nearby Philadelphia and Wilmington, Delaware.

Civilians took an unwelcome interest in the prisons in their communities. Citing concerns about safety and disease, residents of Salisbury, Danville, and Richmond raised a ruckus about the Union prisoners in their midst. Equally vexing to camp administrators were civilians who displayed solicitude for prisoners. Some civilians, moved by compassion, periodically provided prisoners with food, books, or clothing. By 1864 such acts of charity were deemed a threat to camp security and no humanitarian gesture was above suspicion. When a group of local white women, including a minister's wife and the wife of a prison doctor, arrived at the Andersonville depot with a wagon of donated provisions for the prisoners, General Winder and other officers erupted in rage, denouncing them as traitors who deserved to be hanged. Prison officials were understandably anxious about collaboration between sympathetic civilians and prisoners planning escapes or uprisings. Authorities in Richmond knew that local Unionists helped fugitive prisoners flee the city. Confederate sympathizers were similarly active helping inmates escape Camp Chase in Columbus, Ohio, and Camp Douglas in Chicago.

Enterprising civilians created yet more headaches for prison staffs by seizing any opportunity to profit from prisoners. Unless prevented by authorities, civilians hawked foodstuffs and other goods to prisoners. Prison officials looked askance at these impromptu transactions, which encouraged the mingling of civilians and prisoners while undercutting the tight control that prison staff sought over prisoners.

Just as antebellum penitentiaries had attracted sightseers, so too did Civil War prisons. Visitors gathered at prison gates, sought out promontories with views into the stockades, and craned to peek into the camps from passing trains. With more equanimity than most prisoners displayed, Michael Dougherty took this ogling in stride. He noted in his diary on May 24, 1863: "Quite a number of visitors here to-day to see a real live Yankee; he is quite a curiosity, especially in this predicament." Prisoners were less tolerant of being reduced to objects of spectacle by civilian women. In January 1864, John Ransom seethed after several young women visited Belle Isle and dismissed conditions there as "comical and ludicrous" while mocking the inmates as "wild men and hungry dogs." In the opinion of Robert Bingham, the brazenness of "she Yankee brutes" who gawked at bathing Confederates at Fort Delaware was an intolerable violation of common decency. When, several days later, he again experienced the appraising gaze of Union women who used opera glasses to observe him and his comrades while they cavorted naked in the water, he could only marvel at the women's depravity.

Recognizing the curiosity harbored by civilian voyeurs, some prison authorities accommodated them. Soon after the Elmira prison camp opened in 1864, savvy entrepreneurs erected two observatories, as well as food and beverage stands, near the prison stockade. Curious onlookers paid up to fifteen cents (nearly three present-day dollars) to observe prisoners and their daily activities inside the camp. Although impressed by the cynical profiteering of the platform owners, prisoner Anthony Keiley took offense that he and his fellow inmates had been turned into "a menagerie" for the edification of "the refined and valorous people" of Elmira.

The commercial observation tower overlooking the Elmira prison camp testified to the civilian interest in scrutinizing the prisoners. (Chemung County Historical Society)

The prying eyes that offended Keiley were one form of the surveillance that complemented the isolation of the prison-camp regime. Prisoners were familiar with surveillance because it was an inescapable element of military service. Recruits in both armies experienced the oversight of superiors that infringed on their notions of personal dignity and independence. The experience of being an object of scrutiny in the prison pens, however, was a far greater violation of the self.

Prisoners could not escape conducting their lives in public. According to camp protocols, prisoners were to spend all their waking hours under surveillance. At Point Lookout, Belle Isle, and Andersonville, tents and improvised lean-tos provided only modest shelter from the scrutiny of guards pacing the stockade parapets. At Elmira, during the night, forty-one locomotive lights bathed the prison area while sentries at half-hour intervals broke the stillness by announcing that all was well. Above the din of the Andersonville camp, prisoners were reminded with clocklike precision of their captor's gaze. "Every hour of the day and of the night one could hear the pacing of the sentries, and at each recurring hour of the night, the call, 'Post No. 1, eight o'clock and all's well.'" Even erstwhile private activities— such as excreting and urinating—were public acts in the pens. At Andersonville, the creek where men both bathed and visited the sinks was in full view of the sentries. At Fort Delaware, guards peered down into roofless latrines.

The invasion of privacy, as Frederic James could attest, extended to prisoners' private correspondence. Prison staff exercised absolute power over the mail. On grounds of security, as well as to limit the work of censors, prison officials on both sides restricted the length of prisoners' letters to a half page. Only matters "strictly of a private nature" were appropriate subjects for prisoners' letters. Authorities displayed no tolerance for letters complaining about prison conditions. Years later, prisoner John R. King recalled that Union censors at Point Lookout refused to send letters that revealed "how much we suffered."

With inventiveness borne of desperation, prisoners looked for ways to subvert the censorship. After his capture in 1864, Major Charles P. Mattocks, who was a verbose letter writer, never forgot that his readers included prison censors. In one letter, as though winking at an unknown censor, Mattocks included an apology for trespassing "on the good nature of the examining officer" by exceeding the half-page limit. Other prisoners took to writing multipage letters and then mailing them, page by page, in separate envelopes. Others, according to Anthony Keiley, "cultivated a microscopic penmanship" and crammed as much as possible onto a single page. One canny Fort Delaware prisoner used lemon juice to write a letter in invisible ink and then drafted another innocuous letter atop the hidden message.

Prisoners generated huge volumes of correspondence that overwhelmed prison staffs. During the summer of 1864, the chore of wading through as many as two thousand letters a day posted by prisoners at Fort Delaware became so time-consuming that the mail service there ground to a halt. Recognizing that the four censors assigned to the task were swamped, the commandant imposed severe restrictions on letter writing. Eventually, he hired a battery of new censors and restored regular mail service.

The prison staff at Andersonville gave outgoing mail little attention. Letters from Frederic James and other prisoners were collected and occasionally sent north. But few prison accounts, including James's diary, mention mail from the North reaching the men in the stockade. More than Confederate disorganization explains the breakdown of the mail service at the prison. According to Lewis Dyer, a member of the Twelfth USCT imprisoned in the camp, thousands of letters for the prisoners collected at the depot, where they were pilfered and destroyed by prison staff.

Packages sent to prisoners received similar scrutiny from prison staff.

Early in the war, prison administrators tolerated prisoners receiving packages from family and friends. (Recall that thanks to such packages, Colonel Pegram and his messmates at Fort Warren in 1861 had a well-stocked larder and library.) Family and loved ones stuffed packages with photographs and other items invested with incalculable sentimental value for men desperate to preserve home ties. Foodstuffs sent by friends and family provided a break from the monotony of camp rations. Often, fruit, potatoes, and clothing were lifesaving for prisoners suffering from scurvy or exposure to the elements. Few events in the daily life of prisoners surpassed the joy of receiving a package. When the prison staff at Libby Prison in December 1863 read off the list of package recipients, Michael Dougherty reported, "you could have heard a pin drop." When he heard his own name, "Oh! how glad I was."

As the war continued, prison authorities recognized that the packages threatened the isolation that they strove so hard to create. Infuriated that Confederate prisoners were receiving bursting packages from friends, Colonel Hoffman increasingly restricted which packages prisoners could receive. In November 1863 he informed the commanding officer at Point Lookout that because "prisoners are bountifully supplied with provisions" they were not to be allowed to receive boxes of "eatables." He instructed the commander of Camp Douglas that the inmates could receive clothing only from their immediate families and were restricted to one "suit" (i.e., set of clothes) at a time. Any excess clothing sent in packages was to be seized as contraband. He left the responsibility for policing the other contents of packages to prison staff, with the injunction that "nothing shall be allowed which can be looked upon as a luxury or improper indulgence." In August 1864 Hoffman reiterated the prohibitions of supplies from prisoners' friends and relatives.

Confederate authorities did not tighten their policies regarding packages so much as they simply failed to distribute the items. During April and May 1864, boxes for Union prisoners continued to arrive sporadically at Andersonville. A few purportedly even reached the prison in early June. But thereafter packages sent to the thirty thousand men in the camp went undelivered or were pilfered in transit.

The thrill a prisoner experienced after receiving a package was dampened by anxiety about the larcenous ways of prison staff. Seldom did a package's contents survive intact inspection by prison officers. On almost any pretext, prison staff seized items that caught their fancy. Union guards, Henry C. Dickinson complained, routinely absconded with hats, shirts, and pants on the grounds that they exceeded the prisoner's clothing quota and therefore were deemed contraband. Prudent prisoners refrained from complaining about such thefts. Michael Dougherty understood these conventions when he opened a box, observed by an officer and two guards. The officer examined every item, before seizing one: *The Collegians*, a novel by the Irish writer Gerald Griffin. "I said nothing," Dougherty explained, "for if I did, he would not let me have it [the rest of the package] at all."

Reports of the pilfering of packages and mail for prisoners became so commonplace that some families became reluctant to send packages of any kind to the camps. Charles Mattocks, to his mounting frustration, could not coax his mother to send him a package. In letter after letter, he pleaded for a litany of items he coveted. Week after week he waited in vain. Eventually, his mother wrote explaining that she had been advised that sending boxes to a prison camp was like "throwing a feather into the wind."

Control of food and clothing was another important tool used by prison staff to establish their mastery over prisoners. By the end of the war, rations had become one of the most glaring symbols of the systematic dehumanization of prisoners. Grievances about food are rife in the letters and diaries of prisoners.

The prevailing laws of war obligated captors to provide prisoners with the same quantity and quality of rations distributed to soldiers in the field. Both sides adopted the same standard rations, consisting of either twelve ounces of pork (or bacon) or twenty ounces of fresh or salt beef, supplemented with twenty-two ounces of soft bread or a roughly equivalent amount of corn bread or hardtack. In addition, rations included portions of beans and rice. The total caloric value of daily rations was about four thousand calories. After 1863 neither side consistently supplied such rations to prisoners.

Food became an obsession of prisoners. Many, with near laboratory precision, tallied in their diaries everything they ate. Chester Berry recorded the exact amount and kind of rations he received each day while he was a prisoner in Andersonville. So too, Confederate prisoner John Allen and Union prisoner Henry H. Stone scrupulously tabulated their meager diets. Few noted their motivation for their meticulous recordkeeping. The tallies of tablespoons, ounces, and cups of food were a stark measure of their abject dependency on their captives.

Prior to 1864, Confederate prisoners typically received similar rations, although in smaller quantities, to those provided to Union soldiers. While

Confederate diarists complained about the monotony of prison rations, they acknowledged that their rations were as good as or better than those distributed within the rebel army. A careful analysis of the rations provided at Fort Delaware in January 1864 reveals that guards received more beef and flour, prisoners more bacon and cornmeal. These differences aside, the caloric value of their rations was almost identical.

Conscious design was at the root of the mounting complaints of Confederate prisoners about their rations. In April 1864, in retaliation for the treatment of Union prisoners, the Union began withholding rations from Confederate prisoners. Secretary of War Edwin Stanton first proposed the measure during the fall of 1863 but did not implement it until the following spring. Then, Hoffman issued regulations reducing prisoners' rations to fourteen ounces of hard bread or eighteen ounces of soft bread or cornmeal and fourteen ounces of beef or ten ounces of bacon or pork. On May 19, 1864, Hoffman clarified that the prison ration should be "considerably reduced." General Halleck concurred and proposed that tea, coffee, and sugar also be omitted from prisoners' rations. With Stanton's approval on June 1, 1864, Hoffman issued the new restrictions.

How rigorously prison staff followed Hoffman's directive to reduce rations is unclear. Some staff apparently reduced rations even more than Hoffman had directed. After visiting Point Lookout, an inspector reported that the prisoners there received "half the amount of meat they were entitled to." The commissary accounts at Fort Delaware in January 1865 confirm that the prisoners there received half as much pork, fresh beef, beans, rice, and potatoes as they once had, a quarter less flour, and no sugar whatsoever. They received more salt beef, which was a dubious blessing. According to prisoner George Neese, it was "salty enough to make a hound yell." Salt beef aside, Neese's main complaint with the rations at Fort Delaware was that they were "much too diminutive in quantity."

In Confederate prisons, inefficiency, indifference, and policy ensured that prison rations were criminally inadequate. In August 1863 Commissary General Lucius Northrop, with the approval of Secretary of War Seddon, decided that Confederate soldiers in the field would receive preference for rations over both Confederate soldiers behind lines and prisoners of war. While supplies remained scarce, all Confederate soldiers were given priority over prisoners of war. Northrop advocated going further, recommending that prisoners receive rations of oat gruel, cornmeal gruel, and pea soup, but no meat. His drastic proposal, which would have condemned prisoners to life-threatening malnutrition, was not formally adopted. Nevertheless, haphazard Confederate provisioning resulted in much the same outcome, with most prisoners subsisting on meager and innutritious rations.

Hunger became the Union prisoner's constant and unwelcome companion. Within days of being imprisoned at Libby Prison, William Dolphin, a Union cavalryman, complained of being "hungry as Satan." So acute was the hunger of George Hegeman, an eighteen-year-old New Yorker captive at Belle Isle, that he began eating his cornmeal ration raw because he "could not wait to cook it."

Confederates dismissed claims that they scrimped on prison rations by countering that their army subsisted on the same rations. In most instances, this claim is impossible to confirm. Almost certainly at Belle Isle and definitely at Andersonville, guards received more generous and better rations than did prisoners. John C. Bates, a doctor stationed at Andersonville, judged his rations to have been better than those offered to prisoners. Even so, he acknowledged that "I did not presume to live upon [them]." Ashley V. Barrows of the Twenty-Seventh Massachusetts Infantry complained that while he and other prisoners at Andersonville received almost no vegetables, their captors had plenty. John H. Goldsmith of the Fourteenth Illinois Infantry, the Union soldier responsible for distributing rations at Andersonville, later testified that prisoners there received rations about half the size of those provided to their Confederate guards.

Confederate staff seldom survived solely on their rations. David McRaven at Salisbury prison relied on packages from home to supplement his rations. Nazareth Allen, who served as a guard at Andersonville, recalled with evident regret that sometimes "I had to live upon the rebel rations." But during most of his service he received frequent packages from home. Even better, when he was on picket duty outside the prison, he "fared very well" by living "a good deal off the citizens." When citizens were less than forthcoming, Confederate soldiers could requisition supplies. Prisoners had no such recourse. The relevant fact, then, was not that Confederate guards and Union prisoners received the same rations, but that Confederates got them and more besides.

Rations in Confederate prisons were dangerously unwholesome. Prisoners subsisted on coarse ground corn, molasses, and tiny portions of pork or beef. Frederic James's diet during a week in June 1864 was typical of the fare at Andersonville. He received "a small bit" of ham and a half cup of rice on the twelfth and the following day. On the subsequent days he ate

Rations were the basis of robust barter economies in Andersonville and other camps. (From Century Magazine, 1890)

small servings of boiled rice or beans. Rations of beef were so uncommon that they merited mention whenever he received them. For several weeks in August he noted daily distributions of a "scant measure" of fresh beef. But by that point his dysentery was so advanced that he subsisted increasingly on a paste of boiled rice and flour.

Desperate to stave off scurvy and other ailments, prisoners in Confederate camps clamored for vegetables. Other than an occasional ration of field peas, commonplace vegetables—onions, turnips, potatoes, and carrots—were a rarity. Prisoners traded with guards and locals for them whenever possible. These occasional small-scale transactions were of undoubted benefit for the prisoners who made them, but they did nothing to alleviate the plight of those prisoners who had to survive on the standard-issue rations.

The deprivation in the Confederate camps extended to cutlery, cookware, and crockery. At those prisons where prisoners received uncooked rations, they had to use whatever was at hand to improvise cooking techniques and recipes. Even at prisons that had cookhouses in which rations were cooked before their distribution, industrious prisoners who rustled up vegetables or meat on their own had to find a way to cook them. Under such conditions the simplest preparations often required extensive planning. To make a crude corn cake in Andersonville, Charles Smedley first systematically saved some of his rations while trading with fellow prisoners for other ingredients. Even then he had no oil with which to grease his frying pan, which was made from half of a battered canteen. Having no alternative, he spent precious money to buy a postage-stamp-sized piece of bacon, with which he oiled his pan. In these circumstances every meal had to be a rudimentary one-pan dish. Adding to the rustic character of prison fare was the chronic scarcity of firewood at most Confederate camps and the inevitable bouts of inclement weather, which prevented prisoners from cooking over open fires. Prisoners often had to choke down undercooked or wholly uncooked bacon, rice, and other foods.

Food that in other circumstances would have been deemed inedible was eaten with relish. An Andersonville guard recalled a revealing encounter with a drayman delivering a wagonload of rancid peas into the stockade. "Hell," the guard protested, "no man can eat them; they stink too bad." The wagon driver nevertheless proceeded, replying that "perishing men will eat anything." As the drayman understood, Confederate and Union prisoners were driven to eat whatever they could by the dull, permanent greed of hunger. At Point Lookout, a prisoner named Charles Loehr recalled that his comrades became so hungry they would rummage in the camp sewers for "potato peelings, cabbage stalks, or most any kind of refuse that hardly the cattle would eat." It seems plausible, as prison lore recorded, that both Union and Confederate prisoners stalked stray dogs and cats that wandered into the stockades and harvested rats that thrived in the prison pens. Multiple accounts from both Union and Confederate prisons report such foraging.

Clothing was another life-sustaining necessity that prison officials lorded over prisoners. That many prisoners were reduced to wearing rags was not happenstance. By 1864 the Confederacy made no pretense of supplying prisoners with clothing. To the extent that Union prisoners got clothes they did so by trading among themselves or receiving them in packages. When fewer and fewer packages reached them, prisoners lost their most reliable source of clothing and shoes. At the same time, the wear and tear of living in the same clothes month after month resulted in few prisoners having any surplus clothing to trade.

Accounts of ill-clad and ill-fed Union prisoners in 1863 prompted the Sanitary Commission, a philanthropy established in 1861 to aid Union soldiers, to undertake a gargantuan relief effort on their behalf. Thousands of uniforms, shoes, and blankets were shipped south to be dispersed in the prison camps. Some of the clothes and blankets eventually reached prisoners at Belle Isle and a few other camps. But Union prisoners complained bitterly that clothing intended for them ended up adorning Confederate soldiers. Such was apparently the case at Andersonville. Bales of clothing and blankets provided by the commission, as well as shoes and foodstuffs, were hoarded by prison staff. So widespread and plausible were the allegations of Confederate pilfering that the commission suspended its relief efforts in early 1864.

The Union calculus of calibrated retaliation, rather than pilfering, dictated that Confederate prisoners received only the barest minimum of clothing. Often poorly dressed when they were captured, Confederates were seldom attired to survive winter on the shores of the Chesapeake Bay, let alone in Chicago or Elmira. Colonel Hoffman was unmoved by their plight. He spelled out the prerequisite for issuing clothes to a prison official who displayed unwelcome solicitude for his prisoners: "As long as a prisoner has clothing upon him, however much torn, you must issue nothing to him." On another occasion, he informed a prison official to provide clothing only to those truly sick prisoners who needed them: "There are very many sick who can do very well without them."

A similar calculus of parsimony and retaliation dictated the provision of blankets to prisoners. When and where they could, Union and Confederate prison staff limited each prisoner to no more than two blankets. Any excess blankets were seized and redistributed to prisoners without blankets or to guards. For prisoners who slept on the ground in derelict tents or worse at Andersonville, Belle Isle, Cahaba, and Point Lookout, two blankets were seldom adequate to protect against the cold, and one blanket was never sufficient to protect against the wet.

Guards recognized that fear, not deference, provided them with their mantle of authority. Lest prisoners conclude they were tentative or fainthearted, guards demonstrated their power through periodic acts of discipline and intimidation. Prison staff enjoyed wide latitude in exercising their power. They had the leeway to rifle the belongings of prisoners, to harass refractory inmates, and to enforce the dead line as rigorously as they deemed proper.

Guards seldom missed the opportunity to seize the property of prisoners. The thoroughness of searches varied, but no prisoner could have any confidence that his possessions would be spared. When Amos Stearns, a private in the Twenty-Fifth Massachusetts Infantry, entered Libby Prison, he was warned that he had best turn over his money and other valuables because "if we find them on you we will take them and you will lose them anyhow." At Belle Isle, Private William Hawkins resorted to desperate measures to protect his cache of money from predatory Confederate guards. He left a small amount of money in his wallet as a diversion, but secreted the rest of his money in his foreskin. During a search, a Confederate sergeant quickly snagged the money in the wallet but failed to find the rest of Hawkins's stash. William Dolphin was not so fortunate; on September 27, 1863, he recorded in his diary that "the rebs have taken everything from us D——D robbers." Guards pledged to return all items they seized when the prisoners were transferred or exchanged. As James Wells of the Second South Carolina Infantry attested, Union guards at Point Lookout had a handy excuse at the ready when they failed to do so: "Valuables were never returned, as they could not be found."

The most feared and resented power possessed by guards was the authority to shoot to kill. Contrary to rumor, guards did not receive plum furloughs as reward for shooting prisoners. But guards seldom suffered any punishment for shooting prisoners. The frequency with which guards targeted prisoners varied widely from camp to camp. At Point Lookout, vague boundaries and aggressive guards bred violence. On John Robinson's first night there, the Union guards "shot into the prison all around." The lengthy fusillade was "a custom" to welcome each "new lot of prisoners." A different danger haunted prisoners in Richmond warehouse prisons, where zealous guards reportedly fired as many as fourteen times a day at prisoners who strayed too close to windows. In a few instances, prisoners provoked guards by taunting them or hurling objects at them. But such provocations were exceptional. Indeed, few of the recorded shootings at Union or Confederate prisons were of prisoners who directly menaced guards.

Contests over authority and deference were especially volatile wherever Black Union soldiers guarded Confederate prisoners. The indignities of captivity ate at all prisoners but to a Confederate soldier "the greatest insult" possible was to be compelled to defer to Black guards. "It galls them terribly," a Union officer observed. B. T. Holliday, a prisoner at Point Lookout, agreed, noting that "we felt the insult keenly." Prisoner William H. Haigh branded his Black prison keepers "imperious" while fellow prisoner Anthony Keiley complained of their intolerable "insolence and brutality." Black soldiers responded in kind, taunting inmates by singing "John Brown's Body," a song especially loathed by white southerners for its glorification of the executed white abolitionist.

Hostilities between imprisoned Confederates and their Black guards flared into running skirmishes at Rock Island, Elmira, and Point Look-

A Confederate's nightmare: a Black guard at Point Lookout boasts, "De bottom rail on top now." (Naval History Society Collection, series 37, Point Lookout sketches, 1864; New York Historical)

out. When prisoners pelted guards with rocks and other projectiles, guards retaliated by firing into the prison yards. These dangerous confrontations seldom resulted in death or serious injury at Rock Island and Elmira. Not so at Point Lookout. If prisoners' diaries and memoirs are accurate, Black guards shot more than thirty prisoners at the camp, or more than 70 percent of the total number of prisoner shootings at the camp.

Shootings of prisoners, whether premeditated or not, were exemplary killings intended to terrorize prisoners into acquiescence. Prison authorities acknowledged as much in their official reports. After guards shot and killed five prisoners at Camp Chase in late 1863, the prison commandant explained the killings to Colonel Hoffman. One prisoner had been killed during a fracas in the prison yard that purportedly was a diversion while other prisoners attempted to escape. Two prisoners were shot for straying across the prison dead line. Although not threatening, they had been intolerably defiant. The other two casualties had the misfortune to be in barracks that violated the nightly curfew. In both instances, night guards shouted out warnings to extinguish lights in barracks, and then fired into the buildings. In neither instance were the guards certain they had shot the prisoners responsible for defying the curfew. The assistant commandant for the camp conceded that it was regrettable that "a perhaps innocent man" had died. But, he attested, "it has proved to be a most excellent lesson." Previously, prisoners had shown a disposition to ignore orders. "They have since changed their minds and obey," he gloated.

Prison staff drew upon extensive inventories of formal punishments to compel obedience in the camps. Prison commandants usually reserved the severest methods of physical discipline to punish unsuccessful escapes. At Andersonville, absconding prisoners were chained together with neck collars and forced to wear heavy balls attached to their ankles. Sometimes as many as twelve prisoners at a time were shackled together for days on end. Failure to report an escape condemned E. Kellogg, a prisoner and a hospital steward at Andersonville, to being restrained and gagged. On other occasions, offending prisoners were locked in stocks outside the stockade without food or drink for hours, even days. At Camp Chase, escape attempts that went awry usually concluded with the offenders being suspended by their thumbs, wearing a ball and chain while performing hard labor, or being restrained and gagged for hours in a solitary cell. At the officers' prison in Columbia, South Carolina, recaptured fugitives were put in irons and placed on a bread and water diet for ten days.

Hanging Prisoners by the Thumbs.

Prison discipline incorporated military punishments such as hanging prisoners by their thumbs. (From Joseph Barbie, *Scraps from the Prison Table, at Camp Chase and Johnson's Island*, 1868)

Both Confederate and Union prison officials also used incentives to encourage compliance. Their motivation was entirely practical. There was not enough manpower at most prisons to operate them without exploiting the labor of prisoners. By any measure, prisoners were cheap labor. Indeed, the more desperate conditions became in the prison pens, the greater the likelihood that prisoners' labor could be marshaled with trivial incentives.

The inducements for prisoners to work varied. Prisoners typically received more generous rations for erecting camp facilities, digging camp latrines, and cleaning barracks. Work duties offered other benefits valuable to inmates. For instance, prisoners at Andersonville who harvested firewood in the forests surrounding the prison had first claims on the wood they collected. Joining a work detail also provided prisoners with opportunities to escape the claustrophobic and fetid confines of the stockade.

Any reservations prisoners may have had about their labor benefiting their captors were assuaged by the compensation they received. When Samuel Melvin volunteered to make shoes at Andersonville, he explained his decision in his diary: "I must try and do something for myself." Andrew J. Spring of the Sixteenth Connecticut Volunteers had no difficulty justifying his work in the bakery at Andersonville, which offered opportunities to filch extra rations. "I procured all that I needed," he explained, "and also sent quantities in to our boys by smuggling them by the guards."

Most prisoners distinguished between working to survive and to cooperate with the enemy. Following Kilpatrick's raid on Richmond in February 1864, Confederate authorities recruited Union prisoners to build fortifications to protect the Confederate capital. But prisoner John Ransom reported that most prisoners spurned the work because "it is considered a great crime among us to work for them." When Confederates enlarged the Andersonville stockade in May 1864, they offered prisoners extra rations to perform the work. Some inmates volunteered, prompting James Burton of the 122nd New York to complain: "Hope they will have a good time working for the Confeds in the hot sun, rather aiding and abetting the Confed Govt."

Of all the prisoners who cooperated with their captors, none were more reviled than informers. Informers remain the most obscure inhabitants of the camps. Their existence is lamented in almost every prison diary and memoir. But no one subsequently admitted in print to having been an informer, and prison records are mute on the subject. It is unclear whether inducements or threats inspired prisoners to inform on their comrades within the pens. Whatever their motivation, informers sabotaged countless planned escapes and uprisings by alerting prison staff. Informers must have concluded that the benefits of complicity outweighed the very real risks of retaliation by fellow prisoners. At Salisbury in November 1864, prison authorities had to remove from the pen a prisoner whose life was in danger after he betrayed an escape plan. Four months earlier at Andersonville, Frederic James noted the fate of one "blower" (aka informer) there. After he "blew" the cover of a planned escape in July 1864, he was tracked down by irate prisoners and "roughly handled."

Union and Confederate officials made few allowances for the spiritual life of prisoners. Frederic James felt keenly the privation of church services at Belle Isle and Andersonville. As a result, the camps were profane spaces, or, as prison guard David McRaven put it, places of "wickedness."

The contrast with the world beyond the stockade was stark. A captive who crossed the prison threshold entered the unfamiliar domain of the unchurched. If city boosters and state gazetteers of the era are trustworthy, an important measure of any community's welfare was the number of houses of worship it supported. A community the size of Point Lookout prison in 1864, for instance, would have boasted a score of churches. Utica, New York, with a population roughly equivalent in population to Point Lookout, was home to twenty-three churches. Nashville, with an equivalent population, had twenty-one. Yet, no churches embellished the prison landscape at Point Lookout.

Even profane prisoners found it unsettling to pass through unvarying days without the familiar punctuation of a sabbath. A pious man like James found it galling that Sunday at Andersonville was "observed as a play day." Samuel Melvin was among those prisoners whose sabbath behavior disturbed James. On a Sunday in July 1864, Melvin confided that "there is no difference here, one day from another, and I played a game of cards, not thinking it was the day it is." At home and even in military camps, card playing that might be tolerated on other days was discouraged on Sunday. Army commanders continually reaffirmed the importance of attending services and observing the sabbath. No such mandate prevailed in the camps, leaving James to yearn "to live once more in a land of sabbaths."

Pious prisoners had to perform their religious devotions where they also slept, ate, and lived their circumscribed lives. Not until the war's end did the commandant at Camp Douglas allow prisoners to construct a rustic chapel that could seat six hundred. The prison commandant at Fort Delaware granted permission only to stretch a tarp over a portion of the prison grounds to create an impromptu arbor chapel.

Early in the war, captive chaplains provided some religious succor to their comrades. But in 1862, both sides agreed that chaplains should be treated as noncombatants and, if captured, paroled immediately. Thereafter, captured chaplains usually were imprisoned only for brief spells.

Camp authorities made no provisions for their own chaplains to minister to inmates. A shortage of chaplains in both armies discouraged either side from assigning chaplains to serve imprisoned enemies. Confederates managed to muster sufficient chaplains to staff about half of all Confederate regiments, while the Union chaplaincy was only marginally better organized and staffed. Both sides also assumed that prisoners would be innately suspicious of clerics appointed by their captors. When a group of Confederate prisoners at Fort Delaware invited a Union chaplain to preach to them in March 1864, they provoked a backlash from their comrades. One who took offense seethed, "I want no advice on religious matters from any one who at the same time is urging yankees to join in the attempt to subjugate us." Other prisoners demonstrated their contempt for the unwelcome cleric, treating him "very disrespectfully, by both language & action."

Prisoners displayed no more tolerance for civilian clerics who preached to them. Union officers at Libby Prison took umbrage at "Rebel ministers" conducting services there. Although northern missionaries provided tracts and Bibles to outfit libraries at several northern prisons, they prudently refrained from proselytizing in the camps. When several ministers took it upon themselves to deliver occasional sermons to Confederates in the Elmira camp, they faced hostile audiences. Reverend Thomas Beecher, the brother of Harriet Beecher Stowe of *Uncle Tom's Cabin* fame and the son of Lyman Beecher, a noted antislavery minister, was grudgingly tolerated by his captive audience because he was a gifted orator. But services conducted by a local Baptist pastor were roundly shunned. He was, complained prisoner Anthony Keiley, "a freedom shrieker" whose sermons were "one long insult to the prisoners." Fellow captive James Huffman recalled that he and his comrades "had no time to waste on old political hypocrites" and boycotted sermons that offended their sensibilities.

In most prisons, prisoners relied on comrades who had previously been ministers or who were lay preachers to conduct improvised services. At Fort

Delaware, Reverend Isaac Handy, who was imprisoned for disloyalty, conducted daily services for those in his portion of the prison. At Camp Chase, furtive prayer groups and "religious associations" were held most evenings. To attend them prisoners had to ignore regulations against mingling after dark and risk being shot.

Prison commandants kept a close eye on religious observances in the camps. At Point Lookout, the commandant refused a request by prisoners to congregate for services on the ground that they "prayed treason." At the officers' prison in Macon, Captain W. Kemper Tabb, the commandant, bridled at reports of prisoners praying for God to bless Abraham Lincoln and "to give victory to the loyal armies of the nation." Prison authorities made it known that such prayers were forbidden. When subsequently similar prayers were offered, the commandant stepped in and halted the service. In this instance, after an impassioned argument in front of the gathered prisoners between the imprisoned chaplain who was preaching and the commandant, the service continued. But the message of the commandant's intervention was clear; religious devotion, like all other activities, was at the discretion of the prison authorities.

Virtually unique in the annals of Civil War prisons were the labors of Catholic priests. Their presence in the camps reflected the distinctive circumstances of their church during the war. The Civil War strained but did not splinter the Catholic Church. The Diocese of Savannah, for instance, included both Union and Confederate soldiers within its jurisdiction. In March and April 1864, Bishop Augustin Verot of the diocese visited Confederate units from the Tennessee border to the Florida border. Then, in April, he traveled south to Florida, crossed Union lines near Jacksonville, and ministered to Catholics in the Union army.

Andersonville's large number of Catholic prisoners was brought to the bishop's attention by Reverend William Hamilton, a pastor in Macon, who urged him to appoint a priest to serve the camp. That May, Hamilton visited Andersonville while engaging in missionary work in southwestern Georgia. He discovered that perhaps 10 percent of the prisoners there were Catholic, making the prison by far the largest Catholic community in Georgia. Moved by Hamilton's appeal, Bishop Verot in June sent Father Peter Whelan to Andersonville. A few weeks later, Father Henry Clavreul arrived at the prison. In July, Verot himself visited the camps and spent two days tending to the "spiritual wants" of dying prisoners. He returned to Savannah, while Whelan and Clavreul remained at the prison.

Father Peter Whelan ministered to Catholics prisoners in Andersonville. This was exceptional in the annals of Civil War prisons. (Andersonville Prison, Camp Sumter, Ga., as it appeared August 1st 1864 when it contained 35,000 prisoners of war / drawn from memory by Thomas O'Dea, late private Co. E. 16th Regt. Maine Infi. Vols.; on stone by T. J. S. Landis, 1884)

That Captain Wirz, the Andersonville commandant, tolerated the priests' presence in the prison may seem puzzling. Wirz, by all accounts, was irreverent and vulgar. But he also was a Catholic. Wirz had no reason to doubt either Whelan's or Verot's loyalty to the Confederacy. Although Whelan had been born in Ireland and Verot in France, both had endorsed secession and denounced abolitionism. Whelan had volunteered to be chaplain of the Montgomery Guards, an Irish unit raised in Savannah. Wirz also must have recognized the urgent need for a Catholic ministry in the camp. In the absence of a priest, Catholic prisoners on death's door could not receive the sacraments and forgiveness of their sins, jeopardizing their salvation.

The task undertaken by the Catholic priests at Andersonville was crushing. They ministered to the sick, depressed, and dying from nine in the morning until sundown. Afterward, Father Whelan bedded down in a crude hut about a mile from the stockade, where he fell asleep "full of sorrow for what he had seen all day." The diary of Father Clavreul conveys some sense of the "sorrow" that he and Whelan encountered. During the thirty-three days that Clavreul spent in the camp, he administered the sacraments to 340 prisoners, performing them as many as twenty times during a single day. For Bishop Verot, the prison work was "a new genre of ministry" that required priests "to receive, in the middle of the crowd, the confession of the sick lying on the ground." He explained, "The imminence of death did not leave room for human respect."

The cumulative toll of the degradation, deprivation, and isolation in the camps on Frederic James and his fellow prisoners was profound. Yet it never rendered James and his comrades as abjectly compliant as prison officers and staff planned or hoped. Prison officials had ambitions to create tightly regulated and enclosed realms but lacked the means to do so. Within the stockades, prisoners retained a degree of agency in the conduct of their lives. They worked out among themselves the degree to which cooperation, competition, compliance, and contrariness defined their prison lives. When they did so, they preserved a measure of their creativity and purpose that was otherwise relentlessly corroded by the degradations of captivity. At the very least, the communities they built prevented the camps from claiming an even greater toll of death and misery.

CHAPTER EIGHT

# To Be Content in Narrow Limits

## (1863–1865)

When Private William Haigh staggered ashore at Point Lookout, he made what he described as his "'grand entrée' upon the theatre of prison life." A successful lawyer in Fayetteville, North Carolina, the son-in-law of a United States senator, a proud graduate of the University of North Carolina, and a father of two children, he had enlisted in August 1864. By then the war-weary Confederate army had begun filling its ranks with men senior even to forty-one-year-old Haigh. On January 15, 1865, he and others in his regiment had defended Fort Fisher, near Wilmington, against an amphibious Union assault. Eventually overwhelmed, they were marched about four miles north, where the grim procession halted and Haigh and the other exhausted Confederates collapsed on the frozen beach. When sentinels took up posts surrounding them, Haigh experienced "that first *conscious* knowledge of being a prisoner." He and six hundred other prisoners were then crammed into the holds of a reeking cattle transport, which tossed and heaved on its northward voyage. Its memory, he confessed to his sister, "sickens me."

Haigh searched for analogies that would render legible the unfamiliar world of the prison camp. He settled on the self-contained realm of a playhouse stage as an apt metaphor. The prison pen was wholly separate from the world of everyday life; normal human relations were seemingly absent from it. Like members of a grotesque theatrical troupe, each inmate assumed a camp role by either choice or necessity. Some were comical, others colorful, many irksome, and a few malevolent. The jester, the peacemaker, the stoic, the curmudgeon, the bully—every personality type was represented.

Haigh struggled to identify his own place in the ensemble. Like an onstage actor subject to the scrutiny of an audience, he felt keenly the constant surveillance of his captors. Yet, despite the intrusive influence that guards and prison staff had over his life in the stockade, they remained offstage and faceless, making their presence felt more as spectators than as members of the dramatis personae. Some prisoners, he noted, appeased their captors by displaying sullen compliance, while in private they professed their Confederate fervor. Others, he grumbled, played up to their custodians, including the Black guards, seeking "to bask in the sunshine of a negro sentinel's smile."

William Haigh's foray into amateur ethnography was one among countless examples of prisoners seeking to find a role, an identity, a place, in the prison communities into which they were thrust. The scale of the camps and the disorder within them tested the social aptitude of every prisoner. With some social boundaries that had prevailed outside of prison rendered porous and others hardened by prison conditions, prisoners fashioned a singular society suited to the demands of captivity.

As Haigh had quickly grasped, prisoners had to negotiate among themselves the degree to which cooperation, competition, compliance, and contrariness defined their prison lives. Prison officers and staff never created the tightly regulated and enclosed realms they envisioned. Especially at the largest prisons, once prisoners passed through the prison gates, they might as well have become feral. Within the prison stockade, prisoners confronted the challenge of preserving a measure of their humanity, creativity, and purpose that was otherwise relentlessly eroded by the degradations of captivity.

Upon entering the disorienting world of the prison camp, new prisoners scanned the stockade crowds for familiar faces. When Corporal Henry Devillez of the Ninety-Third Indiana Volunteers entered Andersonville in June 1864, he shook off his fatigue and set about searching for soldiers from Indiana among the press of prisoners that seemed to block every path. A few weeks earlier, George Crosby, a private in the First Vermont Cavalry, had done likewise when he passed through the camp gates. After weeks of diligent hunting, he located more than sixty members of his regiment. So meaningful did he deem his findings that he devoted precious

The morning assembly of sick prisoners at Andersonville overwhelmed the prison's medical staff and facilities. (From John McElroy, *Andersonville: A Story of Rebel Military Prisons*, 1879)

space in his pocket diary to listing the numbers he had tracked down from each company.

For a disoriented new prisoner, the pleasure of seeing a remembered face or encountering someone from home held out the promise that familiar forms of sociability could be restored within the prison stockade. Most mid-nineteenth-century Americans, after all, hailed from small rural communities where face-to-face personal interactions prevailed. Few had any experience with large anonymous institutions. Their churches were small and typically served fewer than one hundred worshippers drawn from the church's immediate environs. Only a handful of urban churches, the megachurches of the day, had as many as a few thousand members. In an era when only a minority of the nation's children regularly attended schools, those who did so attended small, often one-room schools. Colleges, which only a tiny minority of Americans attended, were similarly small. The University of North Carolina, William Haigh's alma mater, was one of the largest universities in the nation yet it enrolled fewer than four hundred students in 1860. Most colleges of the era had a quarter as many students. Workplaces were intimate as well. Even in industries that boomed during the war, a labor force of five hundred was uncommon. For instance, the foundry in Pittsburgh that cast the largest guns in the world had fewer than three hundred hands. Only the largest northern textile mills, which employed as many as three thousand, were on the threshold of becoming the anonymous industrial worksites of the future.

The intimate localism that characterized American life was conspicuous even within the mammoth armies that waged the Civil War. Unlike modern armies, which strip recruits of their civilian identities, Civil War armies were an aggregation of local militias stuffed with volunteers drawn from a single county or a few neighboring counties. Haigh's unit, for instance, had been filled with men from his home county of Cumberland, North Carolina.

Given their provincial origins, most prisoners of war were understandably disoriented when they found themselves thrown amid a chaotic mass of prisoners from unfamiliar locales. New prisoners marveled at the exotic diversity within the camps. Invoking Revelation, Private G. W. Jones of the Twenty-Fourth Virginia Cavalry recalled that he "was thrown in company with prisoners of every nationality, kindred and tongue" in Point Lookout in December 1863. Within the improvised lean-to at Andersonville that sheltered John Ransom, a quartermaster sergeant for the Ninth Michigan Cavalry, were prisoners hailing from six states. Samuel Melvin, as he lay dying in the Andersonville hospital, thought it noteworthy that to his left lay a "Dutchman" (i.e., German) and to his right an Irishman.

Captors recognized no obligation to keep prisoners from the same units together and captured officers were routinely separated from their troops. These practices added to the bewilderment and vulnerability of prisoners. In September 1864, when the rank and file of the 111th United States Colored Infantry were sent to Andersonville while their officers were transferred elsewhere, Lyle G. Adair, an orderly sergeant in the unit, openly wept. "Sad indeed was the parting," he confided in his diary. At any moment and without explanation, prison authorities might select seemingly random prisoners and dispatch them to parts unknown. Thomas Sharpe could do nothing but record his dismay and unease when eight of his comrades were removed from Camp Chase and sent away. George A. Hitchcock of the Twenty-First Massachusetts Volunteer Infantry experienced a similar mixture of anxiety, grief, and loneliness when members of his unit were transferred from Andersonville to the prison camp in Florence, South Carolina, while he remained behind. Especially heartrending was the splitting of family members imprisoned together. At Andersonville, Michael Dougherty witnessed the separation of two brothers, one who was "almost dead" and the other who had nursed him. Confederate authorities ignored their pleas to be transferred together. "What agony," Dougherty mused, "when comrades must part in this way, knowing full well that we will never see each other again."

It is perhaps tempting to assume that as prisoners became acclimated to the prison pen they acquired a sense of shared identity with their fellow prisoners. Together they were subject to the same hardships and insults to their dignity. Together they experienced the whims of their captors. And together they endured the anguish of their uncertain fates. Even so, their common circumstances fostered among many prisoners the conviction that they were in a competition for survival with those who surrounded them in the prison pens.

Newcomers often experienced the hostility of existing cliques in the camps, who had to decide whether to share whatever advantages or resources they had already secured for themselves. When Charles E. Tibbles first entered Andersonville, he and some fellow "new fish," as prison newcomers were known, sought to join a group of prisoners who were clustered around a fire. "They ordered us away," he recalled. "They would not let us stay close to the fire." After a similar experience, John McElroy concluded that prisoners at Andersonville became "strangers to each other and distrustful of all outside their own little circles." Amos Stearns regretted that Andersonville was a crucible of competition and suspicion. He had assumed that "amid such privation and suffering, all would do what good they could,

The scarcity of food at Andersonville and some other prisons set prisoner against prisoner. (From *Harper's Weekly*, September 16, 1865)

with what means they had, and be, as it were, members of one family." He regretted that "I was not long in finding out my mistake."

Divisions that predated captivity widened within the stockade. The pens herded together men of diverse nationalities, social backgrounds, religious affiliations, and levels of education who would otherwise never have lived, literally, within a few feet of one another. In the larger camps, prisoners segregated themselves by language and nationality into discernible neighborhoods. At Andersonville could be found large clusters of Germans, Irish, Russians, and other Slavs, as well as pockets of Italian-, French-, and Spanish-speaking prisoners. Inherited prejudices reinforced these linguistic and ethnic boundaries. Ever present was a current of the anti-Irish bigotry that had been evident when Michael Corcoran was imprisoned in Richmond in 1862. Prisoners at Belle Isle and Andersonville, for instance, routinely tagged their Irish comrades as responsible for the crime and disorder in the camps. Even service affiliation divided camp denizens. Frederic James, a navy man, complained that the army prisoners who surrounded him at Belle Isle and Andersonville were not "neat in their habits & persons."

Class and cultural distinctions festered in the stuffed, hothouse milieu of the prison pens. Thomas Gibbes Morgan, a captain in the Seventh Louisiana Regiment, reassured his mother that at Johnson's Island, "the society" included "the very best," but conceded that it also extended to "the lowest." How prisoners segregated the prison community into these categories varied according to their prejudices. Reflecting their studied gentility, Confederate officers were especially appalled by their vulgar and uncouth compatriots. At Johnson's Island, Robert Bingham complained that "really many of the officers are the veriest rabble I ever saw." On other occasions, he skewered his fellow prisoners as "positively hoggish." William Haigh groused about the "unwashed" with whom he had to mingle at Camp Lookout.

While some prisoners grew to tolerate the surrounding babel of languages and diversity of human fauna, few reconciled to the oppressive overcrowding in the prison pens. Exhausted by the daily competition for space, prisoners hungered for privacy. Henry White, a major in the Sixty-Seventh Pennsylvania Volunteer Regiment, lamented that at Libby Prison "men are thicker hear then [sic] hair on a *dog*." He concluded "it is much more preferable to be alone" than to endure forced "society" with his prison comrades. Edmund DeWitt Patterson felt similarly during his imprisonment at Johnson's Island. He protested that "from morning until night it is the same, talking, reading, walking, playing all kinds of games, in doors and out, and there is not a spot within the walls of this prison to which one can go for quiet reflection and meditation."

Overwhelmed by the inescapable press of people, some prisoners adopted a strategy of studied indifference and predatory selfishness. Rare was the prison diarist or camp memoirist who did not deplore comrades for their wanton pursuit of self-interest. A few days of captivity was sufficient to leave George Crosby dismayed by the behavior of his comrades. With regret, he wrote, "Here is where I can see human nature in its true light." From his vantage point in Camp Butler, Illinois, Josephus C. Moore drew a similar lesson: "One thing which makes us all feel so lonesome is the knowledge of the fact that in a place like this it is every man for himself and I might add the devil for all."

Brazen selfishness was displayed when prisoners played up fake wounds and illnesses to qualify for special exchanges otherwise restricted to seriously wounded or ill prisoners. In November 1864 Joseph E. Hodgkins of the Nineteenth Massachusetts Infantry observed a Confederate surgeon separating ill prisoners from the rest of the prison inmates. He joined the sick prisoners, although he conceded he was "as well as most of the men who are sick enough of Rebel prisons and empty stomachs." When he was examined by the surgeon, he complained of rheumatism and an old wound, which in fact only "ached once in a while." Although skeptical, the surgeon ordered Hodgkins to join the other sick who were destined for special exchange. William James McKell of the Eighty-Ninth Ohio Volunteer Infantry noted similar subterfuges by prisoners "playing off, sick and going out to the hospital every morning" hoping to dupe Confederates into placing them on the medical exchange lists. Some healthy prisoners increased their odds by bribing guards to get preferential placement, thereby taking spots that should have been filled by prisoners on death's doorstep.

The conditions at Andersonville elicited habitual acts of selfishness. Writing home weeks after his release from the Georgia prison camp, John England of the Second New York Cavalry struggled for words to describe "the utmost heartlessness, the most cold-blooded inhumanity" that he witnessed daily. To illustrate the callousness, he appended a litany of examples: "the weak were robbed and kicked about by the strong; the sick could not get a drink of water from the convalescent or well; gangs of thieves and rowdies roamed and plundered with impunity."

Within the prison stockade, even the smallest dispute or offense could, and often did, provide the pretext for melees. So routine were brawls at

Andersonville that George Hitchcock deemed them worthy of only passing notice in his diary, appending "usual number of fights" to his account of the day. Another prisoner reported, "A fight every day sure, and sometimes 2 or 3."

Nothing illustrated the limits of prison comity as did the chronic problem of theft. Stealing from the enemy was admirable; stealing from fellow prisoners was a grave breach in the eyes of prisoners. Prisoners, many of whom had been relieved upon capture of most of their possessions, were fiercely protective of any items they retained in the camps. As if to compensate for the devaluation of their lives, prisoners clung tenaciously to personal items. Some articles—a blanket, shoes, a coat—were prerequisites for survival. Others were objects of incalculable sentimental value, such as an heirloom watch, a hairbrush gifted by a loved one, or a cherished pen.

No camp was reprieved from the curse of widespread pilfering. At Point Lookout, Bartlett Malone lamented that he and his tentmates had fallen victim to "some men in camp who had been going about of nits [nights] and cuting tents and sliping mens Knapsacks Hats Boots." In this instance the thief made off with clothing and one hundred dollars that had been sequestered in their tent. Theft was especially prevalent in Confederate prisons because Union prisoners experienced acute shortages of every necessity.

Literally anything in a shebang at Andersonville was valuable, and thus nothing—not an improvised lean-to frame, a cooking pan fashioned from a broken canteen, or a comb whittled from wood—could be left unattended. As countless victims could attest, the lean-tos and derelict tents that housed prisoners posed no challenge to thieves, who easily cut holes into tents or reached into hovels and absconded with items. Not even death dissuaded thieves, who pounced on and robbed the bodies of the deceased. So bold was one thief at Andersonville that he snatched the pants from under the head of another prisoner who was using them as a pillow. Some camp malefactors abandoned subterfuge altogether and instead resorted to brute force. The "roughs" who terrorized the Richmond prison that held Robert Knox Sneden would "prowl about at night like hyenas, three or four in a gang," attacking those weakened by illness, and if a victim resisted "they club him into a state of insensibility."

Of the hooligans who preyed on prisoners, none achieved greater notoriety than the so-called Raiders at Andersonville. On June 29, 1864, Ransom Chadwick scrawled in his diary that each day he witnessed "the most horible Barberism Amongst our owne Men I ever red [read] of or hurd [heard] of." By then, the Raiders were, as prisoner George Crosby put it, "very bold." Numbering perhaps as many as one hundred, they openly assaulted and robbed new prisoners, even murdering some. The gang apparently was well organized under the leadership of six so-called chieftains. Amid the tens of thousands of unarmed prisoners at the camp, the Raiders brandished weapons, ranging from axes to bowie knives. Their campaign of plunder and intimidation kept them well fed and well housed compared with other prisoners in the camp. Using mostly stolen materials, they built an imposing tent that was large enough to shelter virtually the gang's entire membership.

By mid-June 1864, the Raiders' crimes aroused the other prisoners to action. Initially, they organized small, informal groups to defend one another from the Raiders. But these ad hoc measures proved ineffective, and victims of the Raiders appealed to Confederate authorities to bring them to heel. Mindful of the practical limits of his authority and his inability to police within the stockade, Captain Wirz announced that he would cut off all rations within the stockade until the prisoners apprehended and turned over the Raiders. In effect, the Confederate commandant gave the prisoners license to organize a vigilante force to arrest the Raiders. A quasi-organized police force made up of prisoners harried the Raiders for several days and eventually rounded up dozens of alleged gang members. With Wirz's approval, the vigilantes set up a court and put the offenders on trial. (Had Confederate authorities executed the Raiders, there was a risk that Union officials might have deemed retaliation warranted against Confederate prisoners.) Many of the prisoners convicted by the kangaroo court were given light sentences commensurate with traditional military justice, such as a stint in the stocks or being strung up by the thumbs. Others were forced to run a gauntlet of inmates who battered them with clubs. The court reserved death by hanging for the six alleged leaders. On July 11, 1864, the vigilantes executed them on a hastily erected gallows within the stockade. Unchastened, Patrick Delaney, one of the chieftains, defended his lawlessness, proclaiming with the noose around his neck that he would "rather be hanged than live here [in Andersonville]." With his and the other executions, the fevered looting and intimidation of prisoners at Andersonville came to an end. Even so, few prisoners dared to leave their possessions unattended or to wander the stockade alone in the dark.

The cumulative toll of daily acts of thievery and selfishness could be overwhelming. Any sentiments of fraternity had to withstand the inexorable impoverishment that only the wealthiest or most predatory prisoners

In this painting by J. E. Taylor, prisoners resort to vigilante justice to punish comrades who engage in thievery. (Library of Congress)

escaped. Trapped in communities seemingly on the verge of devolving into atavistic savagery, some prisoners resolved that civilized conduct was ill suited to the Hobbesian state of nature they confronted in the prison pen. Within six weeks of his arrival at Andersonville, Samuel Melvin retained little of the spunk and optimism that had carried him through nearly three years of military service. Compassionate, eloquent, and observant, Melvin was distressed by the devolution that he had already witnessed in himself and those around him: "Here all is bestial, just like a hog pen, & hogs we must be, for like hogs we live, like hogs we act."

Not even William Haigh, who resolutely sought to keep above the camp fray, could escape its undertow. On the brink of regaining his freedom in July 1865, he worried about the impact of captivity on his capacity for empathy and congeniality. He reflected on the ordeals of Jean Valjean, the tortured protagonist of Victor Hugo's recently published *Les Misérables*. After surviving a harsh prison sentence for stealing bread to feed his sister's famished children, Valjean had struggled to lead a normal life. Perceiving a kindred spirit in Valjean, Haigh conceded in a letter to his sister that he might no longer be capable of embracing "good will," "gentleness," or "peace." He wondered whether he had succumbed during his imprisonment, as Valjean had, to "hate" and "anger against men."

Even aloof prisoners like Haigh sought relief for their acute loneliness and soul-numbing boredom in any engrossing pursuit that would interrupt, in the words of prisoner Robert Bingham, the "semi-living state" and "ripple days" that defined their daily lives. Haigh puzzled over the apparent paradox of his severe loneliness even while he was jostled on all sides by the multitudes at Point Lookout. Josephus Moore observed similarly that "one not acquainted with prison life would suppose this was anything but a Solitary life." Instead, "it is one of the most solitary and loathsome lives a man can live."

Beyond the pleasure of fellowship, communal camp activities eased the anxieties of many prisoners about their enforced idleness. Time in captivity was at once time lost and time stolen. Instilled with a deep-rooted cultural and religious aversion to indolence, inmates searched for productive uses of their time. Henry W. Tisdale, a twenty-six-year-old sergeant in the Thirty-Fifth Regiment of the Massachusetts Volunteer Infantry, observed that "those who keep busy stand it best." Tisdale and like-minded prisoners looked to the acquisition of new skills as "devices to keep from idleness." They took up the study of science, mathematics, or languages, while others, especially officers trained at West Point, refreshed their command of engineering principles. Inevitably these programs of self-improvement reflected the books that were handy in the various camps. When appropriate texts were unavailable, would-be students enlisted their prison comrades to serve as tutors in languages, the law, dance, and myriad other areas. Charles Mattocks, for instance, took up the study of German and sought out his German comrades to practice his new skill. Whatever the subject, these undertakings redirected attention from the here and now—the prisoner's current plight—to a longed-for future when the prisoner's life would no longer be defined by the prison walls.

Prisoners read voraciously. In their letters and diaries, many prisoners methodically recorded the books they read along with their reflections on them. Reading, of course, could be a solitary endeavor, but in prison it often also was an important social activity. Prisoners read aloud to each other. And they turned camps into circulating libraries; books, manuals, newspapers, religious tracts, and any other reading material passed from hand to hand until worn out by use.

Early in the war, prisoners in comparatively coddled circumstances, like those enjoyed by John Pegram, ordered books from booksellers or received them from family and friends. Officers, both because of their comparative wealth and the generally better prison conditions they experienced, were more likely than men in the ranks to have access to diverse reading material. Lieutenant John M. Porter of the Ninth Kentucky Cavalry, a prisoner on Johnson's Island, boasted, after receiving a box of reading material from a friend, "Our supply of books is now very respectable. Historical, Religious, Dramatic and Poetical."

By 1864 few prisoners were boasting about the wealth or variety of reading material within the stockade. When both Union and Confederate prison authorities began limiting access to newspapers and packages, the range and quantity of reading material in the prisons shrank markedly. Only in exceptional circumstances, as prevailed at the Cahaba prison in Alabama, were the reading habits of prisoners satisfied. When Melvin Grigsby, a nineteen-year-old from Wisconsin, arrived at Cahaba in April 1864, he was amazed to encounter prisoners reading both "new and nicely bound" books as well as some "much the worse for prison use." The books, he learned, were the property of Amanda Gardner, whose house abutted the prison stockade. Despite losing one son at the Battle of Seven Pines and having another son in Union hands, she was moved by the plight of the prisoners amassed less than ten yards from her back porch. Possessing a large private library, she began lending books to them. Improbably, captives who otherwise were in desperate need of clothing and medicine had access to "all the standard poets," the novels of Sir Walter Scott and Dickens, as well as handsomely bound "histories, biographies, travel accounts, philosophy, and religion." Grigsby and his comrades appreciated their remarkable fortune. Before being exchanged in late March 1865, prisoner C. W. Hayes of the Third Illinois Volunteer Cavalry expressed his gratitude to the prison's benefactor. "The kind dispensation of your books," he wrote in a letter to Gardner, allowed prisoners "to while away the tedious hours of captivity both pleasantly and instructively." (Unknown to the prisoners, Gardner's generosity came at a cost. She was publicly denounced as "a Union woman" and "for furnishing aid and comfort to the enemy.")

Reflecting the prestige accorded book learning, prison readers at Libby Prison and other sites established literary societies modeled on the genteel clubs that had proliferated during the prewar era. Michael Corcoran and the other prisoners captured at the Battle of Manassas in 1861 had established the first literary society at the Richmond prison. Subsequent cohorts of prisoners there perpetuated the tradition until 1864. Johnson's Island similarly hosted the "Island Prison Debating Society," which deliberated on a slate of varied topics during the summer and fall of 1863. The Jeff Davis Literary Association at Camp Chase, which was founded by the prison's "literary gentlemen," did likewise. Prisoners elsewhere held informal lyceums to examine subjects ranging from alchemy and spiritualism to geology and history. These gestures at cultural appreciation within the prison pens, however modest in scale and sophistication, manifested the prisoners' stubborn refusal to surrender to the "hoggish" ways that had so alarmed Samuel Melvin.

Music making provided another popular communal diversion. It could evoke pleasant memories of life before the camps. A prisoner at Camp Douglas was heartened that "some nights they will get an old violin & fiddle & dance until lights out." Music also was one of the few public expressions of collective solidarity available to prisoners, who seized pretexts to stage brief gestures of mass defiance. They, for instance, annoyed their captors by striking up national anthems and patriotic songs. At Libby Prison, inmates periodically hollered out the prison windows "The Star-Spangled Banner," "Hang Jeff Davis on a Sour Apple Tree," "John Brown's Body," and other tunes offensive to Confederate ears. When Jefferson Davis and General Howell Cobb passed by the prison, accompanied by a marching band performing "Bonnie Blue Flag," prisoners answered by lustily singing "Yankee Doodle Dandy." Although miffed by the performance, guards had no easy way to suppress it without, as prisoner William Wilkins put it, "gagging every man."

In impressive displays of ingenuity and energy, prisoners in several instances overcame the severe constraints of their captivity to stage elaborate musical and theatrical performances. A production at Libby Prison in 1863 replicated the contemporary minstrel shows that were popular with both northern and southern audiences. Prisoners there managed to wheedle "apparel for the performers who took the ladies' parts," as well as "materials for costumes, stage curtains, and other purposes," from prison guards and officials. Inmates purchased instruments from beyond the prison walls and even printed a program to advertise the show. Prison officials attended and were duly impressed; "evening entertainment by Bogus darkeys good," one observer reported. Almost simultaneously, amateur minstrels were active at Johnson's Island. Later in 1864 the Island Minstrels, "an operatic troupe" accompanied

As this handbill illustrates, at Camp Douglas, Libby Prison, and elsewhere, Confederate and Union prisoners staged minstrel shows. (Special Collections, University of Virginia)

by flute and guitar, delivered a series of performances, which prisoner Joseph Kern deemed "quite creditable." Yet another company, the Rebelonians, subsequently performed "a combination of negro minstrels & Thespian performance" at the camp. Despite their primitive performing space, which was a prison cookhouse that reeked of bacon, their production was, one prisoner deemed, worth the ten-cent admission fee.

Games and sports were another welcome interruption to the tedium of prison life. Baseball became a routine diversion at Salisbury during 1862. Weather permitting, prisoners played nearly every day. On July 4, 1862, prisoners celebrated the republic's founding with a reading of the Declaration of Independence and music, followed by sack and foot races, a greased-pig-catching contest, and a baseball game. Union officers imprisoned at Camp Oglethorpe in Macon regularly played cricket and baseball, until overcrowding overwhelmed the playing field. Confederate prisoners at Johnson's Island also took up baseball. Colonel Daniel Hundley, perhaps best known as the author of the widely read *Social Relations in Our Southern States*, recounted in his diary in June 1864 a baseball game between "the Southron [sic] and Confederate clubs." He marveled that during the game nearly all the prisoners "looked on with eager interest," while the Union soldiers outside the prison yard evidenced "as much interest almost as did the rebels themselves."

By 1864 such pleasant diversions ceased at most Confederate prisons. Conditions in the prisons rendered lectures, sporting events, theater performances, and minstrel shows practically inconceivable. Prisoners at Andersonville and Danville, for example, had neither the physical space to devote to baseball nor the physical conditioning to play it. And no Andersonville inmate consumed by hunger was inclined to devote time and effort to gathering materials for a theatrical performance. By then, life within the stockade had indeed been reduced to the "hoggish" existence that Samuel Melvin had prophesied.

In these dire conditions only card games and gambling thrived. The ubiquity of gambling was yet another manifestation of the topsy-turvy world in the camps. Before their capture, soldiers had been prohibited from gambling, which purportedly undermined morale, discipline, and good order. Enough officers vigorously enforced the proscriptions that gamblers in uniform had to be careful and vigilant. No such discretion was needed in the camps. Prison diarists everywhere remarked on the boldness of gamblers in the stockades. Most primly lamented it. Robert Bingham carped that the prisoners at Johnson's Island "amuse themselves mostly by gambling."

At Andersonville, such scruples seemed to many to be misplaced or irrelevant. After a morning spent playing cards in 1864, Charles D. Lee almost certainly expressed a common view within the Andersonville stockade: "Some think it is a sin to play cards but I do not, especially in this place where a man can find nothing else to do." More than a diversion, gambling was for some a strategy to secure necessities without resorting to theft or violence in the cash-deprived milieu of the prison pens. After carefully weighing the benefits of playing poker, George Albee of the Thirty Sixth Wisconsin Infantry concluded that he should try his hand at cards. If he was a prudent bettor, he averred, "I will be no worse off & I may win enough to buy a loaf or two of bread."

In prison settings in which almost everyone had chronic and unmet needs, acts of indiscriminate charity were exercises in futility. Even so, acts of charity were not wholly absent in the camps. Instead, most prisoners directed their selfless acts to friends, messmates, or individuals with whom they felt some attachment. When facing the vicissitudes of camp life, prisoners had compelling reasons to collaborate with comrades. By pooling resources and sharing know-how, prisoners increased their likelihood of surviving captivity. At a bare minimum, new prisoners had an immediate need to learn the nuances of camp protocols and culture.

New prisoners discovered how dangerously inadequate were the perfunctory summaries of camp rules provided by overworked and apathetic prison officials. With lives at risk when the norms were violated, prudent prisoners sought out prison mentors. After Confederate guards deposited Amos Stearns and others from his company in Libby Prison, "we were not long in finding out what we could *not* do," Stearns recalled. Sweltering in the summer heat and searching for any hint of a breeze, one of Stearns's comrades sat on a windowsill in the prison. Without warning, a guard shot him for violating the stricture against getting too close to prison windows. The neophyte prisoner survived, with a shattered bone in his arm, while Stearns drew an important lesson that served him well when later he was transferred to Andersonville. Upon entering the stockade there, he met a prisoner who previously had been a member of his company. From him, Stearns learned

In a sketch made in Danville, prisoner Henry Van der Weyde depicted a prisoner's meticulous search for lice in his clothes. (Danville Museum of Art and History)

"what the 'dead line' was." New arrivals without similar good fortune paid the consequences for their ignorance. George Hitchcock noted that a parched newcomer to Andersonville, "not knowing the rules," had stretched across the dead line to reach a pool of clear drinking water. Without a word, a guard immediately shot him and "his brains were blown into the water."

Beset by the pandemonium of the camps and pressed together in barracks, tents, and lean-tos, savvy prisoners appreciated the importance of collective standards of conduct and hygiene. To share space in the most overcrowded camps was to live in unhealthy intimacy with one's mates. A prisoner who ignored his personal hygiene, who failed to vigilantly delouse himself, or who was indiscriminate with his human waste threatened the well-being of his comrades.

Peer pressure was often crucial in overcoming prisoners' apathy about maintaining cleanliness, especially in Andersonville and other massive camps where proper hygiene was well nigh impossible. Everything there conspired to prevent prisoners from staying clean; clean water was scarce, the latrines were filthy, the living conditions were primitive, and the climate was often severe. Within days of arriving at Andersonville, John Ransom and his tentmates drafted a set of rules and pledged to abide by them or face expulsion from their tent. In addition to vowing to drink only boiled water and to keep clean and "free as circumstances will permit" of vermin, they promised to maintain good cheer by making "as light of our affairs as possible." As quaint as the pledge may appear, it was a vow to resist, individually and collectively, the degradation of captivity.

The scourge of thievery in the camps encouraged prisoners to collaborate for self-protection. Tentmates worked together to guard their possessions and defend their shared space. David Whitenack of the Fifth Indiana Calvary and five other prisoners at Andersonville "agreed to stand by each other until death." He recalled, "We slept together, ate together, and watched over each other as best we could." Special precautions were necessary when prisoners received boxes of provisions in the mail. Michael Dougherty was a wizened prison veteran by the time he received a box. First, he savored the sublime pleasure of drinking tea: "How good it tasted." Then, he shared his new treasure with several of "the sick boys who are close to me" while remaining vigilant for thieves, who had already pillaged boxes received by other prisoners. He and several others agreed to alternate watching over his box. "Of course I have to pony up [share] with them," he noted. Otherwise, "it will be all stolen from me in one night."

The most practical inducement for prisoners to join with comrades was the method of distributing rations at most prison camps. Prisoners were obligated to participate in collective "messes," which either they chose for themselves or were assigned to by their captors. Membership in a mess was, in most instances, the most elemental identity that a prisoner possessed in the stockade. George Crosby succinctly outlined the allocation of prisoners into messes at Andersonville. "We are divided into detachments of two hundred and fifty, each detachment divided into three messes, ninety in each with a sergeant in charge of each to draw rations and call the roll." In Crosby's case he was a member of the fifty-first detachment, second mess.

Being a member of a mess imposed both duties and obligations. At camps with regular rations, including most Union camps, one member of each mess had the task of retrieving its daily allowance of food and wood. A prerequisite for receipt of the rations was the mustering of all the mess members at the morning roll call. Once the daily rations were in hand, the mess officer divided them between the smaller groups within the mess, who then cooked their portion of the rations. Within these smaller groups, cooking duties typically rotated from man to man. Canny prisoners were attentive to see that these obligations were scrupulously fulfilled. Anyone who "shorted" the rations by withholding or dividing them unfairly risked ostracism or worse. A messmate who wasted or spoiled rations during his cooking rotation might face similar penalties. And a prisoner who was tardy or missed a roll call usually suffered immediate punishment, because his minor transgression often led to the withholding of rations for an entire mess. On February 17, 1864, Michael Dougherty noted that his messmates had tormented a comrade by riding him on "a rail about the camp." Their victim had been absent during roll, resulting in the delay of the distribution of the entire company's rations for hours. In this and similar instances, neither patience nor clemency came easily to famished men.

No prisoner, no matter how self-sufficient, could refrain from participating in the trading bazaars that emerged in most prison camps, especially the larger pens. The inadequacies of camp rations and the prisoners' desperation for even the most rustic comforts created moneymaking opportunities for anyone who could satisfy these cravings. The prison markets that arose to meet these needs were, in important regards, the crucial sinews of the prison community.

Prisoners themselves became avid traders, wheeling and dealing goods and services with equal measures of hucksterism, ingenuity, and desperation. But their needs and desires could not be satisfied by the paltry goods they possessed within the camp confines. Recognizing the opportunity for lucrative arbitrage, guards and outside vendors made available to prisoners a cornucopia of goods from beyond the stockade walls.

Licensed sutlers operated within the stockades of many camps. Prisoners were already familiar with the intrepid merchants who trailed behind even the smallest military units during the war. For the privilege of selling to the troops, sutlers typically paid a modest tax in proportion to the volume of their trade. At Johnson's Island, L. B. Johnson, who was the owner of the island on which the prison was situated, also profited as the prison sutler. At Andersonville James W. Selman Jr., a Confederate quartermaster clerk, erected a shanty in the middle of the northern half of the prison and stuffed it with merchandise. Three prisoners, who worked on commission, hawked meal, peas, salt, sweet potatoes, tobacco, and anything that might "draw hidden money from the 'Yanks.'" At other prisons, such as Danville, itinerant sutlers periodically visited and sold rice, flour, beans, vegetables, and fruit to prisoners with the wherewithal to buy them.

In the eyes of prisoners, sutlers were necessary evils. Within the closed world of the stockade, there was no alternative source for most of the goods they sold. Johnson, the sutler at Johnson's Island, was reviled as "a most infamous lying, cheating scoundrel," but his trade thrived. Prisoners complained bitterly but futilely about the exorbitant prices charged by sutlers. At Libby Prison three onions sold for $1.00 (roughly equivalent to about $36 in 2025) and a dozen eggs for $6.00 (about $200 in 2025). At Andersonville, Michael Dougherty recorded similarly exorbitant prices: "a teaspoonful of salt, 25 cents; a small biscuit, 50 cents; turnips, 25 cents each; sweet potatoes, 25 cents each; and other things in proportion."

Prison guards played an essential role in the prison economy by trading in goods that sutlers could not or did not sell. For a commission, a willing guard could usually be recruited to supply prisoners' diverse requests, such as musical instruments, items of clothing, and assorted luxuries. Both Union and Confederate prison officials prohibited trade between guards and prisoners, fearing that it would erode their control over prisoners and promote unwelcome intimacy between guards and prisoners. But entrepreneurial guards ignored the statutory prohibitions and sometimes even resisted attempts to curtail their illicit trading. At Andersonville, sutler

Selman chastised a Confederate soldier for trading with a prisoner and threatened prosecution, but the alleged culprit's friends waylaid the sutler, bound him, and paraded him through the camp while he "rode the rail."

Confederate guards were especially energetic currency traders. Because Confederate money was not backed by hard assets, its value fluctuated with the prospects for Confederate victory. As the likelihood of victory waned after 1863, the value of the currency plummeted. In response, the Confederate government printed ever increasing quantities of notes, setting off crippling inflation. Across the Confederacy, Union "greenbacks" (paper bills) and gold became the preferred currency. Recognizing an opportunity for arbitrage, Confederate guards and officers offered Union prisoners favorable exchange rates and vacuumed up as much of the prisoners' money as possible. Especially at Andersonville, any money a prisoner retained after capture was certain to be sucked into the prison exchange, whereupon it inevitably passed into the hands of either the guards or the sutler.

Guards also entered commercial partnerships with prisoners. The sutlers at Libby Prison in 1864, for instance, were three Union prisoners who worked out an arrangement with the prison staff to purchase vegetables, meat, and bread to be sold inside the prison. In return, the prisoners ceded a portion of their profits to their captors. More common were arrangements to trade carved bone and wood objets d'art produced by both Union and Confederate prisoners. Guards secured the raw materials that prison yard artisans used to produce their wares. Guards then sold the finished products on a commission basis to eager customers on the outside. In some instances, the trade proved impressively lucrative for all parties concerned. A guard at Elmira prison, for instance, earned five hundred dollars in four months by serving as a middleman between a prisoner there and a sales agent in Baltimore who marketed the prisoner's handicrafts.

The prison markets unleashed the entrepreneurial spirit of prisoners who traded anything they could. Would-be realtors at Andersonville occupied desirable spaces within the stockade and then "sold" them to newcomers in need of a spot to bed down. Samuel Melvin and two friends, for instance, paid $4.50 for "a little lot" there. Prison yard chefs peddled corn pones and other rustic edibles that they cooked in earthen stoves and on makeshift cookware. Where everything was scarce, almost anything could be hawked. Shrewd prisoners at Andersonville sold water from their private wells, bunches of straw they had hoarded, and firewood scraps they had gathered. Bradford Sparrow, a Vermont infantryman, noted that a friend had swapped a knife for a share in a makeshift well. Other entrepreneurs rented scarce items, such as axes and saws that prisoners used to build their accommodations or to hack firewood. New Yorker John Hoster displayed the creative entrepreneurship that Andersonville inspired by purchasing a bucket, outfitting it, and then allowing owners of a nearby well to use the bucket in return for water for himself and three friends.

Impromptu commercial districts emerged in many of the largest camps, expediting and concentrating prison yard wheeling and dealing. These dreamworlds of consumable pleasures and services were strikingly incongruous against the backdrop of the surrounding prison-scapes. Like a metropolitan flaneur, Joseph Kern of the Thirteenth Virginia strolled through Johnson's Island's business district on a July afternoon in 1863:

> Passing up the street we see different signs displayed—Tailor Shop—Shoe Repairing—Beer & Cakes—Barber Shop—Pies—Green & Dried Apple Pies. One "Rebel" has opened a "Restaurant" with a regular "Bill of Fare." While passing along you can but note the apple vendors who stationed at regular intervals offer their apples to you. You will also meet boys with "Ice Cream & Lemonade." At nearly every kitchen biscuits [can] be had at 1 cent a piece. Apple Dumplings & sauce at 5 cents apiece.

Even Andersonville boasted a commercial area along the thoroughfare appropriately known as Market Street. "We have stores oppen in every direction," one prisoner wrote. George Fechnor, who conducted a bustling trade in vegetables and foodstuffs there (along with participating in much of the camp's gambling activities), described Andersonville as "a city—a marketplace." He supposed, "All it lacked of being a bazaar was the women."

Prisoners without marketable goods participated in the prison economy by selling their skills and labor. A crude wood sign, a small patch of ground in the camp marketplace, a pair of scissors, and a razor were enough to establish a barber shop. Washing clothes was perhaps the most accessible foothold in the prison economy; a sign and stamina sufficed to enter the laundry trade. Andersonville even boasted an inmate dentist who pulled teeth for barter or cash.

Because these prison yard marketplaces existed at the sufferance of prison authorities, they were always vulnerable to shifting policies. Both Union and Confederate officials tolerated trading and bartering within the camps, because they could not wholly prevent it and there was money to be made off the prisoners. But Union officials, responding to intensifying demands for retaliation, began tightening regulations on prison economies beginning in December 1863. Then, Secretary of War Edwin Stanton took the drastic step of prohibiting all trade between sutlers and Confederate prisoners held in Union prison camps. Almost immediately camp commandants appealed for exceptions to the policy, above all the ending of tobacco sales to prisoners. Colonel William Hoffman cautioned Stanton that depriving imprisoned Confederates of tobacco "would be a greater inducement to endeavor to escape than any other course which is likely to influence them." Robert Ould, the Confederate agent of exchange, protested the hardship caused by the abrupt closure of the sutlers' shops.

Three months later, in March 1864, Stanton relented, but with conditions. He enumerated a list of items that the sutlers could sell and emphasized that their inventories should be modest in size. That August, Stanton again tightened regulations, restricting prison sutlers' merchandise to tobacco, writing supplies, and personal hygiene equipment (e.g., combs, razors). While rations in Union prisons were being systematically reduced, Confederate prisoners lost the opportunity to purchase foodstuffs from sutlers. Underground trade between guards and prisoners persisted, but it could not compensate for the closure of the sutlers.

In Confederate camps the gradual pauperization of Union prisoners during 1864 had a similar effect of severely curtailing prison markets. By late 1864 at Andersonville, after the cash had been siphoned off by the sutler and guards, there was too little left for sutler Selman to turn a profit. He departed for richer pastures, as did his successor, after only a brief spell. Confederate authorities simultaneously continued to inveigh against guards trading with prisoners. Those that did so were threatened with court-martials while civilians risked civil prosecution. The aim of Confederate authorities was not to shut down prison markets, but to redirect the flow of Union currency from the sutlers to government coffers. However, the policies that the Confederate government introduced in its last months, when the prison system was in complete shambles and Union prisoners were insolvent, failed to generate any meaningful revenue.

Conspicuous and inescapable, the prison markets evoked conflicting emotions in prisoners. Prison yard trading kept some prisoners busy and enabled some to supplement their meager rations or enjoy an occasional luxury. With money, prisoners could tame the endless cravings for food, delay the advance of scurvy and its debilitating effects, savor water uncontaminated by human or camp waste, shod bare feet, adorn an improvised lean-to with a blanket roof, purchase writing paper, and post letters to loved ones. With money, the accoutrements of normal life were within grasp, even at Andersonville.

But trading also accentuated the extraordinary disparity between the deprivation endured by most prisoners and the comparative affluence enjoyed by a few inmates. In the prison milieu, prisoners learned that money was no less precious than it was beyond the stockade walls. In early August 1864, George Hitchcock recorded the angst that the juxtaposition of plenty and scarcity provoked: "We are continually tormented and tantalized with the sight of peaches, apples, chicken and soda water offered for sale at fabulous prices." His anguish persisted, and three months later he described his craving for the roast chicken, boiled sweet potatoes, biscuits, pumpkin pies, soda cakes that were for sale "in abundance." But, to his dismay, "the Ancient Mariner's experience is our own. 'Water, water everywhere, but not a drop to drink.'" Gripped by a similar anguish, Michael Dougherty sympathized with the "famished skeletons" who "would stand around and look in on the good things."

While the prison markets fostered relationships of convenience, the ever present threat of disease and illness encouraged cooperation. Despite the obstacles to compassion in the camps, friendships within the stockades could become uniquely close. Such was the case for George Clarkson and Corwin Kenney, two members of Fifth Michigan Cavalry who shared blankets at Andersonville. On the night of January 11, 1865, Kenney roused his friend, complaining of illness. Within hours, he died, leaving Clarkson disconsolate. Like many other prison diarists, he felt acutely inadequate in the face of his friend's illness. In a terse sentence in his diary, Clarkson memorialized an intimacy with Kenney that was practically familial: "I shall feel lonesome now for we slept together for most of seven months."

As much as prisoners valued their friendships, most had only a vague understanding of the degree to which their prospects for surviving captivity correlated with the strength of their friendships. Indeed, the worse the conditions that prisoners experienced, the more important their friendships were to their fortunes. A careful analysis of the survival rates of prisoners at Andersonville concluded that partnerships, especially between prisoners who were kin or shared the same ethnicity or hometown, increased the likelihood of survival by more than 10 percent.

Many of the benefits of prison friendships were buried in the mundane daily activities recorded in diaries or recalled in postwar memoirs. When sickness struck down prisoners in camps, they often had only friends to rely upon for care. Friends offered moral support to keep depression at bay, scrounged up extra food or clothing for the bedridden, protected against the predations of other prisoners, and tackled the daily chores that were beyond the capacity of the sick.

Robert S. Brown tended William James McKell with touching devotion during the latter's protracted illness at Andersonville. Despite serving together in the Eighty-Ninth Ohio Volunteer Infantry for three years, the two men had not become friends until their imprisonment at Danville. There, McKell had joined a "squad" of nine prisoners organized by Brown, who recalled, "We all bunked in the same corner of the building and shared with each other what little conveniences we had." Both were sick when in May 1864 they were transferred to Andersonville. Brown recovered, while McKell's health worsened. Recognizing that the rations at Andersonville were likely to hasten McKell's death, Brown and another messmate began selling their meat rations and using the proceeds to buy small amounts of vegetables to feed to their sick friend. When the camp switched to cooked rations in June, they found few customers for their rations. By then McKell "had no desire for the food the rebels issued." To Brown's dismay, it was "an impossibility to trade his rations off for any thing that he could eat." And because so much of the prisoners' cash had been drained out of the prison by then, rations could not be sold for cash. Undaunted, Brown returned daily to Andersonville's marketplace in search of anyone willing to exchange fruit or a biscuit that might be toothsome to McKell. "Often," Brown reported, "all attempts would be fruitless."

After concluding that McKell had no prospects for recovery in the stockade, Brown and another friend carried him to the prison gate, where prison doctors determined which prisoners to admit to the camp hospital. Once there, the trio became subsumed in the vast crowd of desperately sick prisoners that had already assembled, awaiting the doctors' triage. They waited several hours, during which McKell became delirious. Eventually a Confederate guard announced that no more prisoners would be admitted to the hospital that day. Despairing of getting McKell into the hospital, Brown

The grim daily task of interring the dead at Andersonville, as rendered by former prisoner Thomas O'Dea in 1885. (Library of Congress)

and his messmate lugged him back to their lean-to. Brown, who himself was suffering from scurvy and malnutrition, waited on McKell, periodically pressing a cup of water to his lips, changing and washing his clothes every day, and "by all means that were available" making him comfortable. Brown's ministrations relieved some of McKell's agony until July 28, when, in Brown's words, he made the "transition from that place of misery to one of perfect felicity."

Death and burial in most of the camps had none of the attributes of the "good death" that nineteenth-century Americans craved. Men died in agony, distant from family and, in most instances, without the attentions of a minister or priest. They received no funeral. Their corpses were not embalmed. Not only were their grave sites not consecrated, but they also were crude trenches that held scores of other dead prisoners. Such a burial made no allowance for the dignity of the individual. As a final insult to the dead at Andersonville, their individual identity was erased. Rather than their names, numbers adorned the crude wooden stakes on their graves and recorded their place in the prison's catalog of abbreviated lives. Their interment was as much the erasure as disposal of their bodies.

Henry Dickinson observed the callous disregard for the captive dead in March 1865, while under sail near Fort Delaware. During four years of hard service in the Second Virginia Calvary and ten months in Union prison camps, Dickinson had witnessed many examples of the war's savagery. But he was appalled by the cavalier disposal of the corpse of Lieutenant

A. W. Edwards, who had died in his bunk as the ship neared its destination. Edwards's Union captors had previously refused to put the dying man ashore. Once he was dead, they prepared to dump him overboard. Dickinson and other prisoners implored them to take the corpse ashore so that Edwards could have a proper grave and his family might be able to retrieve his body. "The Yankees," Dickinson regretted, "were inexorable." A heavy bar of iron was placed between the legs of the corpse and a heavy blanket was sewed tightly around it. Then, the two Union sailors who were preparing the body lopped off the ears of the corpse and tossed them overboard. Finally, while Yankee officers were smoking, joking, and "swaggering around," Dickinson and two other Confederate prisoners "committed our friend's remains to the deep." By the time that Edwards's weighted body hit the water, the ship was almost within sight of its anchorage at Fort Delaware. "May God pardon our wicked persecutors for this hasty and unnecessary burial," Dickinson confided in his diary.

Military necessity, of course, dictated cursory burials in many wartime circumstances. By 1863 combat-weary soldiers were all too familiar with the hurried disposal of corpses on the battlefield. Because death en masse was commonplace, so too were mass burials. Armies in the field, after all, had to inter their dead while in motion.

No such exigencies applied to burials in the prison pens. The only practical imperative in the camps was to dispose of the dead in a timely manner. Prison officials need not have been clairvoyant to anticipate that death rates at prisons would surge when prison populations swelled in 1863. Death, especially by disease and sickness, was a routine occurrence wherever soldiers were clustered, including soldiers who lived in substantially better conditions than those in the prison pens. Experience during the first year of the war had already revealed a clear correlation: the longer captives remained in the prison camps, the greater the proportion who would die.

The banality of death in the camps, combined with war fatigue, almost certainly contributed to the general indifference toward the dead in the camps. Clerics, journalists, and soldiers alike commented on a pervasive aloofness to suffering. "We see it every day," prison guard McRaven had written his wife, "and it has lost its effect on us." After only a brief sojourn at Andersonville, Bishop Augustin Verot of Savannah confessed to a flagging of his empathy. "The continuous sight of death" and suffering in the camp, he lamented, "finally dulled all human feeling."

Not all prison dead were treated like so much rubbish. Burials at Elmira lacked solemnity, but at least their corpses were treated with a modicum of respect. The man responsible was John W. Jones, a fugitive enslaved Virginian who had escaped to Elmira in 1844. Fifteen years later he was appointed the sexton of Elmira's new Woodlawn graveyard. When the prisoner-of-war camp opened in 1864, Lieutenant Colonel Seth Eastman, the post commander, leased land in the cemetery to inter Confederates who died while imprisoned. Jones received $2.50 to perform each burial. Squads of prisoners placed the bodies inside pine coffins and loaded them, nine at a time, into a wagon for transport to the cemetery. Each coffin, on the inside and outside, bore the name of the deceased. At the cemetery Jones supervised the placing of the coffins in trenches, marking each grave with a wooden headstone that included the deceased's name, rank, regiment, state, and date of death. To expedite subsequent identification of the buried remains, Jones tucked a glass bottle containing the dead prisoner's vital information in the armpit of each body.

Jones left no explanation of his attentiveness. Perhaps dedication to his position motivated his uncommon behavior. Perhaps his deep personal piety, which had informed his abolitionism and had inspired decades of good works, prompted him to prepare all dead, even dead Confederates, for the Day of Judgment. Perhaps his experience of bondage engendered an especially keen measure of sympathy for captives. Whatever the case, his respectful handling of prison dead stood in marked contrast to practices at other prison camps.

Frederic James had to go to extraordinary lengths to ensure that his friend Victor Bartlett was buried with as much dignity as the prison milieu made possible. Captured together, the two men were imprisoned at Salisbury when Bartlett developed various symptoms with no discernible cause. Within a few days, he was off his food and required constant nursing. When his deteriorating eyesight prevented him from writing letters, James stepped in and penned lines to Bartlett's family. When Bartlett suffered from severe pains in his chest and abdomen, James rubbed his body with cold water. Throughout Bartlett's illness, James kept him as clean as possible and washed his clothes. After several weeks without any improvement in Bartlett's condition, James and another friend carried him to the prison hospital. There he lingered for several days, during which James visited him whenever possible. Summoned to his bedside, James was present to pray when the combination of pneumonia and measles killed Bartlett.

James knew that at Salisbury the dead were piled up like sacks of grain before being tossed in long trenches. Earlier in the war a few prisoners had been buried in coffins but by 1864 they were entombed in soil as they had been born—naked. A cleric in Salisbury recoiled at the memory of the "sickening and heart-rending spectacle."

Bartlett's passing deeply moved James, who only days before had learned of the death of his young daughter. With three other prisoners, James provided the young sailor with a formal funeral. The men carved a wooden headboard and somehow secured a coffin. They buried Bartlett in a grave near the prison building that housed them. During an improvised graveside service, they read from 1st Corinthians 15:20 ("But now is Christ risen from the dead and become the first fruits of them that slept") before closing with a hymn. It was, James judged, "a very solemn and impressive occasion."

The ceremony was a poignant testament of both loyalty to a deceased comrade and the sanctity of each human life. For James and other prisoners, the anonymous and apathetic interment of their deceased comrades was as profound an affront as any they endured in the camps. Like most Americans of the age, James believed that how one died had consequences for one's fate in the afterlife. His care of Bartlett during his prolonged decline was motivated as much by his concern for his friend's salvation as for his physical discomfort. Too few other prisoners who died at Salisbury or elsewhere after 1863 were tended with comparable benevolence or interred with comparable reverence.

The abject anonymity of death in the camps weighed heavily on William Haigh. Despite his efforts to remain aloof from the "theater" of prison life at Point Lookout, he dwelled on the deaths of fellow prisoners. He blessed the miracle of death that liberated some from Camp Lookout and confessed to his sister that he envied their release. But he grieved that there was "no friend to stand by their grave or know their resting place—not even is their death known to men in Camp." Death in camps, Haigh perceived, exposed the limits of the fragile communities that prisoners fashioned within the camps. Not even extraordinary acts of generosity and compassion, like those made by Frederic James, could relieve Haigh's despair that he had been exiled from civilization and the human family.

CHAPTER NINE

# On Account of My Color

## (1864–1865)

In July 1864 Isaac Gaskins was free and eighteen years old. For the first seventeen years of his life, he had been enslaved in Yazoo County, Mississippi. The advancing Union army and Emancipation Proclamation had liberated him the year before. He then became a servant of a Union officer and followed him north to Chicago, where he enlisted in the Twenty-Ninth United States Colored Infantry. His regiment was accepted for service in April 1864 and sent east, first to Maryland and then to the outskirts of Richmond. Because General George Meade, the commander of the Army of the Potomac, harbored doubts about the battle worthiness of Black soldiers, he consigned them to dig earthen fortifications and guard wagon trains. By late July an exhausted member of Gaskins's regiment mused that they had "built two forts and about three miles of breastworks." He acknowledged, "We are learning to make fortifications, whether we learn to fight or not."

Days later, the greenhorn regiment was tested in combat for the first time. On July 30, Union forces exploded a massive mine, obliterating more than one hundred feet of the Confederate defenses around Petersburg, Virginia. White soldiers from the IXth Corps, with Gaskins's regiment and other Black units in their wake, streamed into the breach. Given their scant training, Gaskins and his comrades must have been gripped by a volatile mixture of excitement, bewilderment, and dread.

Any engagement with Confederates carried perils for Black soldiers beyond those faced by white soldiers. No Black soldier could have any

Hundreds of Black Union troops, like these near Petersburg, were captured in the summer of 1864. (Library of Congress)

confidence that he would be treated as a prisoner of war if he was captured. A year after the capture of the Black crewmen of the USS *Isaac Smith*, the Confederacy still had no consistent policy regarding Black prisoners. Instead, a range of possible fates, all grim, awaited.

Gaskins and the other men in the Twenty-Ninth understood the dangers they faced when they marched into battle on July 30. They knew that Black captives had been deliberately massacred after engagements at Olustee, Florida, that February, and at Fort Pillow, Tennessee, in April. The memory of those massacres had become a rallying cry for Black soldiers and the white officers who led them. Before departing Chicago, the commander of Gaskins's regiment, Colonel John A. Bross, had publicly proclaimed, "When I lead these men into battle, we shall remember Fort Pillow and shall not ask for quarter." When Gaskins and the Black units pressed forward into the clouds of smoke and falling debris after the explosion of the Petersburg mine, they repeated that pledge, yelling, "Remember Fort Pillow!"

Unfortunately for Gaskins and the white and other Black soldiers who filtered into the massive crater, the Confederates quickly recovered after the explosion. They repulsed the Union thrust and then pinned down the disorganized attacking soldiers in the gaping pit itself. Within hours, Confederates had routed the Union forces and restored their lines. Union losses were heavy, especially in the Black regiments. At least five hundred Union soldiers died and nearly two thousand were wounded. More than fourteen hundred were captured. In Gaskins's unit, eleven officers were killed or wounded and thirty-eight enlisted men were killed; Gaskins and thirty-one other soldiers were taken prisoner.

Gaskins was fortunate to survive the fiasco. The treatment that he experienced quickly confirmed his suspicion that he was being "punished severely on account of my color." He and the other Black prisoners experienced the isolation, deprivation, and degradation that all prisoners of war endured. But in important regards their circumstances were distinct, and markedly worse. While Confederate officials insisted that their policies regarding Black captives were consistent with long-established laws of war, their treatment of Black captives differed little from the now scorned practices of the premodern era, when prisoners of war were slaughtered, enslaved, or held prisoner at the whim of their captors.

Confederate officials remained adamant that no Black soldier who had once been enslaved would be recognized as a prisoner of war. Union policymakers in turn continued to fret over how to respond to the severe, if inconsistent sanctions that Confederates imposed on Black captives. Simultaneously, fierce debate raged in the Union over responsibility for cessation of prisoner exchanges. The controversy became increasingly heated during the months leading up to that year's presidential election. At issue was whether the Union should concern itself principally with the fate of white prisoners of war. Or, as the Lincoln administration contended, should the Union consider the fates of Black and white Union soldiers to be inseparable?

At no time during the first few days after his capture was Gaskins's survival assured. During the chaos of the battle, Gaskins's captor had not realized that his prisoner was Black. Gaskins had so much blood and grime on his face that the Confederate "couldn't tell what I was." When he discovered Gaskins's race, he became enraged. "If he had knowed I was a nigger," Gaskins recalled, "he would have never taken me prisoner." The rebel soldier refused to acknowledge "any damn Negro" as a prisoner of war and vowed that Gaskins would never get back to his "brother Yankees" alive. Intent on hastening that outcome, the soldier shot Gaskins but failed to fatally wound him.

Cold-blooded shootings of unarmed and wounded Black soldiers like

Gaskins were tragically commonplace after the battle. South Carolina quartermaster Hall T. McGee recorded in his diary that Black soldiers were slaughtered without mercy because "we were not allowing them to surrender." A private in the Twelfth Virginia Infantry confirmed, without evident discomfort, that Confederates had bayoneted wounded Black soldiers as they lay on the battlefield. Black prisoners like Gaskins who were not immediately executed were not free of danger. According to a soldier in the Sixteenth Mississippi, "Most of the negroes were killed after they surrendered." By one estimate, between 1863 and the war's end, more than seven hundred Black captives were summarily executed by Confederates.

Confederates evinced no regrets about their slaughter of Blacks during and after the Battle of the Crater, as the engagement is known. Colonel William Pegram, a Confederate artillerist and a younger brother of the erstwhile prisoner John Pegram, was unapologetic. The summary execution of Blacks, he insisted, "was perfectly right as a matter of policy." Newspapers in the Confederate capital endorsed the massacre, lamenting only that "some negroes were captured instead of being shot." The *Richmond Enquirer* urged Confederate soldiers not to "soil their hands with the capture of one negro." Addressing the commanders in the field, the paper beseeched, "Let the work which God has entrusted to you and your brave men, go forward to its full completion; that is until every negro has been slaughtered."

Practical considerations and the Confederacy's raison d'être, however, discouraged the extermination of all Black prisoners. Most white southerners were loath to endorse the wholesale destruction of valuable human chattel that, in their eyes, still belonged to slaveholders. The Confederacy, after all, had been established to defend slavery. In August 1863, Confederate Secretary of War James Seddon stated his opposition to executing Black prisoners except when absolutely necessary. Instead, they should be "returned to their owners." He held this line through 1864, but added an exception for "free" Black captives who had been born in the North. Those "free born" prisoners were to be "held in strict confinement," during which they were to be "treated very much in the same manner as our other captives," except "in some trivial particulars indicative of inferior consideration." And, like all Black prisoners, they were not to be formally recognized as prisoners of war in any official dealings with the enemy.

Gaskins and the other Black prisoners, who numbered at least a hundred and possibly as many as two hundred fifty, were amply reminded of their "degraded status" after their capture. Herded into an open field, they were robbed of their possessions and stripped of most of their clothes. Their guards held them overnight without food, water, or cover. The wounded, who were "shrieking, praying, and cursing in their agony and delirium," eventually received rudimentary care from captured Union surgeons. Gaskins suffered with his untended wounds, but at least was spared the ignominy endured by healthy Black prisoners who were forced to bury the Confederate dead and to rebuild earthworks destroyed by the mine explosion.

The deliberate degradation of the captives continued the next day, when Black and white prisoners, at the behest of Confederate General A. P. Hill, were paraded through Petersburg. A long line of white officers and enlisted prisoners, interspersed with their Black comrades, circulated through the streets of the town. As Hill had anticipated, crowds of white civilians greeted them with scorn, shouting, "See the white and nigger equality soldiers!," "Yanks and niggers sleep in the same bed!," and "That is the way to treat the Yankees, mix them up with the niggers." One spectator taunted that they were bound for Andersonville and "you will never live to see home again."

Two days after the battle, Gaskins and most of the enlisted white prisoners were loaded into boxcars and began an achingly slow trip to Danville. Gaskins somehow avoided the fate of most of his fellow Black prisoners, who were detained in Richmond and Petersburg, where they were put to work building military fortifications or held until their former owners reclaimed them.

Unlike their white comrades, "reclaimed" (i.e., re-enslaved) Black prisoners viewed captivity as literal slavery. The isolation they experienced extended to the erasure of whatever legal personhood they had enjoyed while free and in the Union uniform. Once they were claimed by their purported owner or bought by an enslaver, they no longer were under the umbrella of Confederate authority. With their retransformation into property, they disappeared, often without a trace, into the vast ranks of the South's enslaved.

That Gaskins escaped this fate is suggestive of the challenges that Confederate officials faced when applying Secretary of War Seddon's directive. Authorities first had to identify and then locate the prisoners' owners. In a few instances, Black captives were known by their captors, so identifying their owners was simple. Otherwise, separating formerly enslaved from freeborn prisoners was not a straightforward undertaking. More than 50,000 Black men born in the North served in the Union's Black units alongside more than 130,000 former slaves. Some Black units consisted solely of freedmen, but many units organized in northern states recruited both freeborn men and fugitives from slavery. In addition, there were soldiers like Gaskins who were free by virtue of the Emancipation Proclamation. According to the Confederacy, men like Gaskins were fugitive slaves, not free men.

To untangle the status of Black prisoners, Confederates had to rely on the prisoners themselves to divulge whether they had previously been enslaved. After contemplating the prospects of captivity in Andersonville or the other prison pens, some Black captives perhaps concluded they had a better chance of surviving re-enslavement than a stint in the camps. Whatever their reason, some provided the name of their former owners. But others, who deemed re-enslavement an unendurable fate, dissembled and claimed to have been free from birth. Gaskins, who was "unusually well educated" and apparently confounded conventional white conceptions of a slave, may have done so.

Confederate authorities faced the added challenge of reuniting slave owners with their captive property. In Gaskins's case, his captors may have determined he was a slave but concluded that returning him to Mississippi was impractical. They lacked the resources to trace slave owners scattered across the hinterlands of the South, especially when so many white southerners had taken flight to avoid the advancing Union army. Authorities on occasion dispersed small numbers of captured Black prisoners to slave depots that the Confederacy had established to house recaptured enslaved people. But these facilities were never intended to hold Black soldiers. Stymied by these practicalities, Confederate authorities settled for advertising the names of captured Black soldiers who were presumed to have been slaves and encouraging owners to reclaim them at Confederate depots. After the Battle of the Crater, for instance, Richmond newspapers carried notices alerting readers that nearly ninety captives awaited reclamation by their owners. Gaskins's name, for whatever reason, was absent from it.

Confederate officials resolved that if they could not return former slaves to their owners, then someone else should benefit from their exploitation. We may never know how many Black captives became war booty, but it is clear that Confederate leaders sought to harness the pecuniary self-interest of Confederate soldiers to the ongoing project of re-enslaving Black soldiers. On three occasions in 1863, the Confederate Congress endorsed the proposition that Black captives, including freeborn Black soldiers, should "become the property of their captors, and shall thereafter be held and considered as slaves." Some officers ignored such legal niceties and simply claimed Black prisoners as their private property, either using them as personal servants or sending them to work behind lines. In a few instances Black captives were sold to slave traders and planters. Whether the money from the sales went to their captors or into government coffers is unknown. A brisk trade in Black prisoners might well have developed had the Confederate nation not vacuumed up the largest number of Black captives.

Perhaps two thousand or more Black prisoners, for all intents and purposes, became property of the Confederacy. If the Confederacy had been victorious, it presumably would have divested its slaveholdings. But while the war continued, the national government was the largest slaveholder in the rebel nation. Confederate officials coerced formerly enslaved Black prisoners, just as they had in Petersburg, to build fortifications, repair railroad tracks, and perform other grueling tasks. Such was the fate of the Black prisoners captured at Fort Pillow in 1864. They were sent to Mobile, where they joined the largest cluster of Black captives in the Confederacy. Eventually, nearly six hundred Black prisoners toiled there as carpenters, blacksmiths, draymen, and common laborers.

To be a military slave was perhaps the worst outcome, short of death, for a Black prisoner. This permutation of bondage made a mockery of the paternalistic slavery that defenders of the institution had lauded before the war. Unlike slaves impressed by the Confederacy, whose owners often continued to take a keen interest in their treatment by the Confederate army, no one had a vested interest in the survival of re-enslaved prisoners. They were wholly at the mercy of their Confederate overseers and endured working and living conditions that combined the worst of slavery and captivity.

The smallest group of Black prisoners, perhaps numbering several hundred, were treated, in a fashion, as prisoners of war. Presumably these Black captives had been identified as "free" Blacks and, in accordance with Seddon's orders, were separated from formerly enslaved Black prisoners. Reflecting white prejudices and the war secretary's wishes, they received different, and usually harsher treatment than their white comrades. The worst spaces in the pens were typically assigned to Black prisoners. In Danville, Gaskins recalled that the Confederates deliberately segregated him and other Black prisoners from their white comrades. At Libby Prison, Black captives were shunted into cellars that were "dark and horrible beyond description."

Imprisoned Blacks were compelled to "do the drudgery of the prison." White prisoners could rebuff Confederate efforts to recruit them to work, but Gaskins and other Black prisoners in Danville "were marched out every morning about 8 o'clock to build breastworks." At Andersonville a variety of onerous tasks, including unloading lumber, gathering firewood, and working on earthworks, were imposed on Black prisoners. Private Frank Mattocks of the Thirty-Fifth United States Colored Infantry recalled that he and other Black prisoners were eventually removed from the prison altogether. They worked at the train depot half a mile from the stockade beginning in September 1864, loading railcars with rations for prisoners being transported elsewhere. At the same time, Confederates assigned to Black prisoners the camp's grimmest job—burying the dead.

Whether Black prisoners received extra rations for their work, as white prisoners did, is unclear. They may have, but it is also altogether plausible that they did not. As bad as rations were for white prisoners, they apparently were even worse for Black ones. Gaskins complained that he never received "anything respectable to eat while in prison," and what he did get was so scant that he was consumed by hunger and crippled by scurvy. Conditions were no better at the Charleston jail, where imprisoned white officer Charles Mattocks observed Black prisoners, "who look like death," root for scraps of discarded food in the prison trash "like a hog in a farmer's yard."

Confederates, a white prisoner at Andersonville observed, "seemed to have a particular spite toward the colored soldiers." On the day after Gaskins arrived in Danville, a guard beat him so severely that he suffered internal injuries that plagued him for the remainder of his life. His infraction? He was Black, a soldier, and a prisoner. Thereafter, whenever he passed the guards they were certain to "give me a blow with whatever was most convenient."

Confederate guards at Andersonville left little doubt of their contempt for Black prisoners. John McElroy, a white Illinois cavalryman, claimed Black men in the camp were "treated as badly as possible." The earliest Black prisoners to reach the camp were stuffed indiscriminately into the stockade. They clustered near the South Gate, eventually establishing a small settlement that numbered about one hundred. Keeping to themselves, they attracted as little attention from their white comrades and their jailers as possible. Guards were so abusive that Black prisoners "had to go without rations several days at a time on account of not daring to go forward" to collect them. They "were treated worse than dumb brutes," another white prisoner remarked, "and the language used toward them by the rebels was of the most opprobrious character."

Confederates conserved their harshest punishments for Black prisoners. There are credible accounts of floggings of Black prisoners at every prison where they were confined. Two diarists reported the whipping of a

Black prisoner at Libby Prison in July 1863. At Mobile, a Black prisoner who escaped to Union lines after three months of captivity testified that Black prisoners were kept at hard labor on fortifications. "If we lagged or faltered or misunderstood an order," he reported, "we were whipped and abused," sometimes by fellow prisoners who were detailed with the task.

At least four prisoners were whipped at Andersonville, although some prisoners claimed that many more felt the lash. Two of the three Black men who were flogged were deemed to be laggards. In March 1864, William Henry Jennings, a Black soldier in the Eighth United States Colored Troops (USCT), refused, on account of sickness, to perform his assigned work. After being whipped on the orders of Captain Wirz, Jennings was placed in the camp stocks, where he remained without food and water for a day. John Fisher, another soldier in the Eighth USCT, was whipped that October after he refused work. He also was restrained and gagged. A third Black prisoner, Isaac Haskins of the Fifty-Fourth Regiment of Massachusetts Volunteer Infantry, was beaten for either stealing potatoes while on a labor detail or passing contraband food to prisoners in the camp hospital. Vincenzo Bardo apparently was the only white prisoner who was flogged. He aroused Wirz's ire by blackening his face and joining a squad of enslaved Black men who had been working at the camp. His desperate bid to escape failed when a Confederate officer saw through his disguise. Bardo was placed in the stocks and later whipped. The irony of a white prisoner of war assuming the identity of an enslaved Black man in pursuit of freedom went unremarked.

It was not coincidental that these instances of whipping evoked symbolic connotations of slavery. Black prisoners were reminded that their uniforms did not protect them from the traditional punishment inflicted on slaves while Bardo, the would-be blackface fugitive, was symbolically reduced to the status of a slave and suffered accordingly. As Wirz put it, "he had tried to make a nigger of himself, [so] he should be treated as a nigger."

We may never know with any certainty how many Black prisoners died in Confederate hands. Because Confederate authorities treated most Black captives as property and were intentionally duplicitous about the status of the remainder in their negotiations with the Union, most Black prisoners were effectively "disappeared." They only reemerge in the historical record if they survived captivity and eventually returned to their military units or applied for a veteran's pension. Any estimate of the mortality of Black prisoners is necessarily speculative.

At Andersonville, Black prisoners apparently had a substantially lower mortality rate than did white prisoners. Only twelve Black prisoners at Andersonville, out of approximately one hundred, are known to have been buried there. If this total is accurate, their mortality rate was half that of white prisoners. But at Danville their prospects for survival were far worse. Isaac Gaskins claimed that the conditions he and the other Black prisoners endured there killed most of them. Out of one hundred eighty Black prisoners, he reported, only seven survived. Although this toll may be inflated, a white prisoner confined in Danville made similar claims about the mortality of Black prisoners there. Acknowledging that "the negroes suffered most," Lieutenant Colonel Homer Sprague of the Thirteenth Connecticut Volunteer Infantry reported that the prison had previously held about two hundred Black prisoners. But "some had died, [and] others had been delivered to their masters or set at work on fortifications." Only sixty-four remained at the prison in October 1864 and by the following February, only seven of those men remained alive. Although unknown to Sprague, Gaskins was one of those seven.

The predicament of Black prisoners compounded the severe challenges that the Lincoln administration confronted in 1864. The human toll of General Ulysses S. Grant's campaigns in Virginia and the sluggish pace of Sherman's offensive against Atlanta fed mounting anxiety in the North about the war's course. Nearly continuous combat during the spring and summer produced new captives by the thousands who had to be squeezed into already bursting camps. Sensing deepening fatigue and weakening resolve across the Union, northern Democrats urged the immediate restoration of prisoner exchanges while furiously attacking Republicans for waging a brutal and inept war.

Whatever course the Lincoln administration pursued regarding prisoners of war was certain to be severely criticized. The administration had no more leverage in 1864 than it had the previous year to compel the Confederacy to treat Black captives as prisoners of war. The most expedient course regarding prisoner exchanges after 1863 would have been to negotiate a restoration of exchanges for white prisoners. Had the Lincoln administration accepted such terms and had the Confederates honored them, the populations in the prison pens might have shrunk back to the levels that prevailed in the spring of 1863. Such a concession would have been applauded by the families and friends of many white prisoners. But it would have surrendered any meaningful influence over the fate of Gaskins and other Black captives, while leaving Black soldiers in the field at risk of re-enslavement. Administration allies, including prominent Black activists, were certain to excoriate any abdication of the pledge to protect Black soldiers.

Lincoln's growing appreciation of Black soldiers made repellent any policy that conceded the re-enslavement of any Black soldiers. In his annual message to Congress in December 1863, he lingered on the contributions of former slaves now in the Union army. To date, they had proven to be "as good soldiers as any." The President went further in April 1864 after Black soldiers distinguished themselves during the Battle of Port Hudson in Louisiana, declaring his opposition to abandoning Black prisoners to their fate. "There have been men who have proposed to me to return to slavery the black warriors of Port Hudson & Olustee to their masters to conciliate the South." Lincoln predicted, "I should be damned in time & eternity for doing so."

The other course available to the administration was to hold to the tenet that either all prisoners—white *and* Black—would be exchanged or none would. But this stance left the administration open to accusations of callousness for ignoring the heartrending pleas of white northerners desperate to hasten the return of sons and husbands from Confederate prisons. The perception of callousness was compounded in the summer of

Confederates sometimes retaliated against, and more often enslaved, Black soldiers like these in battle at Port Hudson, Mississippi, in 1863. (National Archives)

1864, when General Grant voiced his opposition to reestablishing prisoner exchanges. Grant conceded that Union prisoners suffered in Confederate prison pens, but countered, "It is hard on our men held in Southern prisons not to exchange them, but it is humanity to those left in the ranks to fight our battles." With the example of the Confederates' hurried return of the paroled Vicksburg prisoners in mind, Grant explained that every prisoner the Union released became "an active soldier against us at once." Better to not exchange any prisoners, he contended, lest his armies "have to fight on until the whole South is exterminated."

However uncaring Grant's justification may have appeared, nothing in his stance contradicted the administration's insistence that Black prisoners would not be abandoned to Confederate whim. That Grant justified the administration's policy on grounds of military necessity revealed his understanding of the politics swirling around the issue of prisoners of war. He offered the most pragmatic defense available at a time when Democrats were bellowing that the war's aims had been distorted by Republicans' obsessive commitment to Black equality.

Lincoln's stand was indeed a significant political liability as the Republican Party prepared for the 1864 elections. By July of that year, the party had united behind a commitment to abolish slavery everywhere by law, preferably by a constitutional amendment. The party subsequently never wavered in its stance. But the longer the impasse over exchanges continued, the greater the import of the Union insistence on the exchange of all prisoners, regardless of race. It was not an abstract debate at a time when reports of rising death rates in the Confederate prisons were being tracked in both Confederate and Union newspapers.

The controversy surrounding the policy played out along deep fault lines in northern society over the war's course. Even within Lincoln's Cabinet, it provoked sharp disagreement. Gideon Welles, the secretary of the navy, assumed the issue of Black prisoners was a pretext to prevent general exchanges. Despite his earnest antislavery convictions, Welles confessed sympathy for the slave owners who reclaimed fugitive slaves who had donned Union uniforms and then fell captive. He huffed in his diary: "to absolutely stop exchanges because owners held on to their slaves when they got them was an atrocious wrong."

The Democrats, meanwhile, were badly divided, with one faction supporting the war to restore the union and another faction advocating immediate negotiations to end the war. Debate over the future of slavery also roiled the party. Some Democrats encouraged the party to abandon its opposition to emancipation and its defense of the property rights of slaveholders. Others remained steadfast that emancipation by decree was an intolerable subversion of the Constitution by the Republicans. One issue that Democrats could agree upon was that the President and his allies stood in the way of ending the suffering of prisoners of war.

When the Democrats met in convention in Chicago, their otherwise brief platform voiced "the severest reprobation" for the Lincoln administration and its "shameful disregard" of prisoners. The attention devoted to the plight of prisoners allowed Democrats to highlight the alleged extremism of the Republican Party. The party was willing, Democrats charged, to sacrifice white Union prisoners in the name of protecting a trivial number of Black prisoners. Couched in both humanitarian and starkly racist terms, this indictment placed the onus on Republicans, not Confederates, for the needless suffering and deaths of tens of thousands of white prisoners.

Democratic newspapers seized every opportunity to highlight Lincoln's responsibility for the unconscionable deaths of soldiers and prisoners alike. The *Cincinnati Daily Enquirer* declared that "every soldier . . . that is killed, will lose his life not for the Union, the Stars and Stripes, but for the negro." According to the *Chicago Times*, perhaps the most strident of all the Democratic papers, the radicalism of the Lincoln administration, rather than Confederate perfidy, was solely responsible for the exchange impasse. Secretary of War Edwin Stanton had stopped exchanges when the administration "ascertained definitely that the Confederate government did not recognize our niggers in uniform (or, rather, *their niggers* [sic], stolen from them) as soldiers, would not treat them, or their officers, on a perfect equality with our white officers and soldiers." Appalled at the notion that Black soldiers were accorded "perfect equality in all things with white men," the newspaper concluded that the Lincoln administration was "determined in its pet measure of making a negro as good as a white man." The anguish of white prisoners and their families was inconsequential because "this is a war for the negro."

The administration was backed into a tight corner, much as it had been in 1862 before prisoner exchanges were negotiated. Neither the President nor his most trusted advisors were willing to surrender on the principle of equal treatment of Black prisoners of war. And there was little Lincoln could say to assuage critics of his policy. He flirted with addressing the topic in a letter he drafted to a convention in Buffalo, New York. He rejected any notion of keeping Black men in military service without assuring they

The toll of war casualties including prisoners of war, prompts Columbia to scold President Abraham Lincoln for his insatiable appetite for new recruits in this 1864 political cartoon. (Library of Congress)

would be accorded proper treatment by the enemy. Otherwise, the Union would be yielding to the Confederacy's immoral policies, "with the express or implied understanding that upon the first convenient occasion, they are to be reenslaved." Lincoln decided not to send his letter, perhaps because he had already made his views clear and any further statements would only roil his critics.

Adding to the awkwardness of the issue for Republicans was the pressure brought to bear by Union prisoners and their families. Many white soldiers and officers remained unenthusiastic about, even vocally opposed to, the Lincoln administration's embrace of emancipation and enlistment of Black men, let alone any guarantee of their protection by the federal government. A lieutenant colonel from New York caterwauled, "I did not come out to fight for the nigger or the abolition of Slavery." Another New Yorker proclaimed, "I don't want to fire another shot for the negroes and I wish that all the abolitionists were in hell." Sergeant Olney Andrus of Illinois vented his disgust, "I consider my life & the Happiness of my family of more value than any Nigger."

Prisoners who were tormented by every rumor about the prospects for the resumption of exchanges understandably became embittered. When the Lincoln administration halted exchanges in July 1863, at most a few hundred Black soldiers and perhaps 15,000 white prisoners were in Confederate hands. A year later, the number of Black prisoners was probably about 2000 but the number of white prisoners then totaled more than 50,000. David Kennedy, a sergeant in the Fourth Vermont held at Andersonville, professed no sympathy for the Lincoln administration's stand while complaining in his diary that "we must stay here because they can't agree on some nigger question." When prisoners at Andersonville began discussing a petition to the Lincoln administration urging a resumption of exchanges, John Ransom of the Ninth Michigan Cavalry vented that it was "rough that it should be necessary for us to beg to be protected by our government." With a mixture of disgust and resignation, Samuel J. Gibson conceded, "I hardly know which to blame most, the relentless cruelty of the Rebels or the perfidy of the government of [the] U.S. for deserting its soldiers in the hour of trial and keeping back the exchange of prisoners."

Sensing the vulnerability of the Lincoln administration, Confederate officials in Richmond actively sought to aid the Democrats in 1864. Commissioner of Exchange Robert Ould released correspondence with his Union counterparts that highlighted his apparent willingness to agree to the exchange of all but a small number of Black prisoners. The clear intent of the disclosure was to rattle the Lincoln administration and to heighten the popular clamor against it. Democratic newspapers quickly republished the correspondence and scolded the Republicans for their obstinacy.

At Andersonville Captain Wirz and General Winder exploited the prisoners' discontent to embarrass Union policymakers. On July 14, Wirz had the mess sergeants (the prisoners who collected rations for each mess) marched to his headquarters outside the prison stockade. He informed them that the Confederacy was eager to release them, but the Union refused to resume exchanges. He encouraged the prisoners to petition the Lincoln administration to revive exchanges.

On stationary supplied by Wirz, a committee of prisoners began drafting an appeal to President Lincoln. While composing the petition, prisoners wrestled to square their loyalty to the Union with their desperate yearning for release from the prison pens. Samuel Melvin decided the petition "cannot do harm, & if it will do good, for the sake of humanity send it along." The day after the petition was broached, Samuel Gibson affirmed in his diary: "I love my country & government & I believe I am as loyal as a man can be." But, he protested, "I do not like an administration that will not protect its citizen soldiers." And then he drew an invidious distinction between the Black and white prisoners: "The everlasting niggers must be protected and the soldier may take care of himself." In contrast, Eugene Forbes, a corporal in the Fourth New Jersey Infantry, scoffed at the petitioners because they initially threatened to take an oath of allegiance to the Confederacy if the Lincoln administration ignored their demands. "The government should punish any man who would sign such a document," he seethed. Albert Shatzel agreed, grousing, "What the hell did they enlist for onley to serve their country & protect her rights & suffer the consequence."

On July 19 the drafting committee submitted a revised petition, which had been shorn of the threat to enlist in the Confederate army, to the prisoners for their approval. Advocates of the petition harangued crowds of prisoners and, to the dismay of Forbes, mustered "considerable favor." After polling prisoners, the petition committee announced that the revised appeal had received overwhelming support.

The petition would have amounted to little more than stockade theatrics had Wirz and Winder not actively aided it. They paroled a delegation of prisoners to carry the appeal through enemy lines to President Lincoln himself. On August 9, the envoys departed Andersonville and began a roundabout journey to Beaufort, South Carolina, where they entered Union lines. From there they traveled by ship to New York City, where they tarried until their envisioned rendezvous with Lincoln.

By late August, newspapers across the North and the South were reporting on the delegation and its petition. As some of the first prisoners to return north from Andersonville, they attracted the interest of everyone anxious for a firsthand report about the conditions there. The men also ventured north just as the Democratic Party was meeting in convention in Chicago and declaring its commitment to the immediate resumption of prisoner exchanges. The published petition, which dwelled on the horrendous conditions at Andersonville while affirming the Confederacy's eagerness to be freed of the burden of prisoners, coincided with the Democrats' orchestrated denunciation of administration policies. The *Charleston Mercury* thrilled at the prospect that the mission would reveal to Lincoln "the actual state of that hell on earth to which his love of the nigger" had condemned Union prisoners. The paper predicted the petition would provoke "a frenzied howl" across the North, but "the Democrats will not be slow to fix the blame where it belongs."

The prisoners' petition posed a rhetorical question that no defender of the administration's stance was keen to answer: "Is it not consistent with the national honor, without waving the claim that the negro soldiers shall be treated as prisoners of war, to effect an exchange of the white soldiers?" To hammer the point, the petitioners drew a marked contrast between the purported circumstances of Black and white prisoners. "The whites are confined in such prisons as Libby and Andersonville, starved and treated with a barbarism unknown to civilized nations." Black prisoners, however, were seldom imprisoned but instead were "distributed among the citizens or employed on government works." The petitioners affirmed (on the basis of no evidence) that these Black prisoners received ample food and "worked no harder than they have been accustomed." The crux of the petition was stated baldly: "True, they are slaves again, but their slavery is freedom and happiness compared with the cruel existence imposed upon our gallant men."

The frustration, bitterness, desperation, and cynicism evident in the petition were undoubtedly accurate reflections of the sentiments in the Andersonville stockade. But the rhetorical sophistication of the petition also suggests the authors' savvy grasp of the political moment. It is not clear who wrote the petition. No one claimed authorship. Most of the members of the delegation of paroled prisoners, who had lived lives of quiet obscurity before the war and did so after their exchange, seem to have been unlikely authors.

Edward Wellington Boate, the chairman of the delegation, was probably the lead author of the petition and architect of the subsequent machinations to draw it to the attention of President Lincoln. Boate was one of those outsized personalities who enjoyed ephemeral prominence during the tumult of the Civil War. He had been born in 1822 into a well-to-do family in Waterford, Ireland. He pursued a career as a journalist working locally until he moved to England, where he acted first as a foreign correspondent and then as a political correspondent for *The Times* of London. Sometime around 1861, he and his family moved to New York City, where he again worked as a journalist. He quickly earned an unsavory reputation as a "bohemian" bon vivant and as a less-than-trustworthy husband. In the summer of 1863, he joined the Forty-Second New York Volunteers, a strongly Democratic and Irish regiment organized by Tammany Hall, the city's powerful Democratic machine. For unexplained reasons, he had enlisted under the alias of Edward W. Bates and was so identified throughout his captivity and during the petition campaign. His military career was altogether brief; he was captured during his first engagement, the Battle of Bristoe Station in

October 1863. He began his imprisonment at Belle Isle, where he remained until his transfer in March 1864 to Andersonville.

Boate's journalistic flair, connections with New York newspapers, and affiliation with the city's Democratic Party presumably were crucial to the petition's notoriety. When the Andersonville envoys reached New York, Boate used his connections to publicize the petition. He simultaneously began honing his own expansive denunciation of Union policy. In the coming months, he assailed the legitimacy of the Union's blockade, which prevented Confederates from acquiring medical supplies to ameliorate the suffering of prisoners. Most provocatively, he drew a sharp contrast between Confederate authorities, who he insisted were conscientious and sincere in their solicitude for prisoners of war, and the heartless Lincoln administration.

Despite, or perhaps because of, the publicity surrounding the petitioners' activities, the Lincoln administration gave the delegation the cold shoulder. Had the delegation not been advocating an abrupt policy reversal by the administration, they probably would have been feted in the capital. As exchanged prisoners, they had been conveyed at government expense from South Carolina to New York City. But once there, Union officials denied any obligation to pay for the delegation's expedition to Washington, D.C. Representatives of the Sanitary Commission in New York City eventually stepped in and subsidized their journey. Having finally reached Washington, the committee members idled for three days awaiting an invitation from the President. But Lincoln ignored them. Instead, they had a cursory and unsatisfying meeting with Secretary of War Stanton and departed Washington empty-handed.

The mission inflamed the debate about the administration's stance on exchanges. Democratic newspapers pointed to Lincoln's refusal to meet the envoys as evidence of his callous attitude toward white prisoners. Under the provocative headline "Thirty-Five Thousand White Men vs. a Few Negroes," the *Coshocton Democrat*, an Ohio newspaper, described the administration's opposition to exchanges as "this last dreadful sacrifice on the altar of negro equality." The paper predicted that it would "prove too much of a strain upon the patience of the North" and would bring an end to "the Lincoln dynasty." The *Quad City Times* in Davenport, Iowa, similarly blistered the Lincoln administration for letting white men "rot in unheard of misery" on account of "the negro who is a thousand times better off than they." The *Daily Register* in Wheeling, West Virginia, mocked the administration's professed concern for Black prisoners: "Oh, the humanity that weeps over

Pompey's and Sambo's condition" yet failed to display any concern over the white prisoners trapped at Andersonville.

The corrosive effect of the petition campaign on morale was soon evident both inside and outside the prison pens. Perhaps inspired by the debate at Andersonville, Union prisoners in Savannah drafted their own petition to the Lincoln administration on September 28. At the officers' prison camp in Macon, support for the Union policy on prisoners also faltered. Charles Mattocks and his comrades were aware of the extreme suffering sixty miles away at Andersonville. Three weeks before the petition campaign began at Andersonville, Mattocks and the other officers debated a similar course on behalf of the men imprisoned there. Camp officials in Macon, like their counterparts at Andersonville, quickly endorsed the proposal to send a delegation to Washington. But the officers were so divided that the proposal stalled. Mattocks himself initially worried that they risked being made "cat's paws" by Confederates. At that moment in late June, Mattocks was certain that Union authorities were blameless. "The U.S. only asks the exchange of all soldiers," he reasoned. By September, his confidence in his government's policy had weakened. The grounds for the administration's refusal to exchange prisoners, he concluded, was "but a poor excuse for murdering by inches" soldiers who had the misfortune to fall into the hands of the enemy. A few weeks later, he speculated that by "yielding a comparatively unimportant point"—namely, agreeing to exchange white prisoners while leaving the status of Black prisoners to be resolved—the Union could alleviate the hardship of thousands of prisoners. By then, he had lost all patience with the government's "clinging with such tenacity to the 'Negro question.'"

Walt Whitman, the celebrated poet, followed a similar path to his eventual censure of the Union position. Despite his long-standing Democratic proclivities, Whitman had voted for Lincoln in 1860 and had rallied to the Union cause the following year. But after witnessing the war's slaughter while serving as a nurse in Washington, D.C., Whitman lost much of his war fever. Then on September 30, 1864, following the peak of the rancor over the Andersonville petition, Whitman's brother George was captured in Virginia. George had joined the Fifty-First New York Infantry Regiment in 1861 and until his capture had escaped misfortune. He was first sent to Libby Prison and then to Danville. Anxious about his captive brother, Whitman waded into the debate over prisoner exchanges in December 1864.

Writing to the *New York Times* and the *Brooklyn Eagle*, Whitman made no mention of his brother's circumstances while professing to speak on behalf of the "public mind." It was, he observed, "deeply excited, and most righteously so, at the starvation of the United States prisoners of war in the hands of the Secessionists." He posed a question for which both the Democrats and Lincoln's critics had a ready answer: "Whose fault is it at bottom that our men have not been exchanged?" Whitman's own answer was unambiguous: Secretary of War Stanton and his henchmen. The secretary's refusal to exchange soldiers unless all Black soldiers were included was, Whitman declared, "more cruel than anything done by the Secessionists." Dismissing the Black prisoners as "a drop in the bucket," Whitman went on to blame the Union prisoners' "anguish and death" upon "members of our own Government." He closed his screed with a warning that unless the administration changed its course it would be responsible for the death of the remainder of the Union prisoners.

Whitman's tirade and Mattocks's waning support are suggestive of how far in advance of white opinion was the Lincoln administration's position. Both Mattocks and Whitman remained staunch advocates of the preservation of the Union and stout opponents of slavery. But their opposition to slavery did not entail a belief in racial equality. For all the sympathy that Whitman had expressed for the enslaved in *Leaves of Grass*, his magnum opus, he never entertained the notion that Black people were his equals. Before the war he had supported the Free Soil movement, which the abolitionist William Lloyd Garrison had aptly dismissed as "white manism." After the war Whitman would infamously compare immigrant and Black voters to "so many baboons." In other postwar musings, he confessed that "the blacks can never be to me what the whites are." He explained, "Below all political relations are still deeper personal, physiological, and emotional ones, the whites are my brothers."

Freedom, Mattocks and Whitman presumed, was the innate and sacrosanct natural state of white men. The officer and the poet supported the war because of the threat that slavery and its grasping defenders posed to the liberty of all white men of the North. For Mattocks, who was himself a prisoner, and Whitman, whose beloved brother was a prisoner, captivity was a state worse than bondage. In sharp contrast, Whitman and Mattocks looked on Black freedom as contingent and negotiable. Both men took for granted that Blacks, with their long experience in bondage, would not suffer inordinately by re-enslavement. Mattocks acknowledged the bravery and resolve of Black soldiers, yet he did not perceive them to be true brothers in arms. Whitman gave even less consideration to the ordeal of Black prisoners. These prejudices and presumptions predisposed Mattocks and Whitman to rationalize the re-enslavement of a few thousand Black men as regrettable but tolerable if it freed thousands of white men from captivity.

Such sentiments justified elevating the service of white soldiers above that of Black soldiers. When Samuel Gibson protested that the Lincoln administration failed to protect "its citizen soldiers," he drew a pointed distinction made by many white Union prisoners. They were "citizen soldiers" who had risked captivity and death to defend the Union, whereas Black soldiers fought in their own self-interest. From the vantage point of Gibson and others, the administration withheld recognition of the sacrifice made by selfless white citizen soldiers while obsessing about the plight of Black captives.

That almost no one posed the question of why the Confederacy refused to exchange all prisoners is a telling measure of how successfully the Confederates, Democrats, and critics of the Lincoln administration framed the public discussion of prisoner exchanges. The Confederacy's intransigence, at least as much as Union policy, condemned all white prisoners—Union and Confederate—to captivity without exchange. After all, the Confederates stood to regain tens of thousands of their soldiers if they exchanged the few thousand Black prisoners they held.

Not even Confederate prisoners in Union pens voiced any public criticism of their government's stand. In September 1864, against the backdrop of the Andersonville delegation's mission, Confederate prisoners at Camp Chase pondered the appropriate course for their government. According to diarist Thomas Sharpe, he and his fellow prisoners debated the propriety of "exchanging the negro for a white prisoner." Some argued that the Confederacy should remain steadfast; no Black man should ever be accorded recognition as the equal of a white, so no Confederates should be exchanged for Black prisoners. Others countered that Confederates should "do that or almost any thing for independence." Military necessity perhaps justified surrendering the commitment to re-enslaving captured Black soldiers. Apparently, no consensus emerged among Sharpe's interlocutors.

The Camp Chase debate anticipated by four months the deliberation within the highest levels of the Confederacy over the recruitment of enslaved Black men to serve in the Confederate army. Only then did Confederate leadership decide that the rebel nation's transcendent goal—the continued independence of the white South—warranted wavering on its hitherto rigid defense of slavery.

The bitter and highly partisan argument over prisoner exchanges in 1864 had lasting consequences for how white Americans viewed the Black and white experiences of captivity. The assumptions that framed the debate discouraged whites from acknowledging the unique ordeals that Black soldiers endured during captivity. White men who came of age in a culture awash with blackface minstrelsy and proslavery texts had long been habituated to the notion of American slavery as an exotic frolic. Confederate prisoners and many Union prisoners accordingly drained all pathos from the term "slave" and instead channeled it to the term "prisoner."

In the minds of many white prisoners, especially Union prisoners, the prospect of seemingly endless captivity reduced them to a state indistinguishable from the harshest imaginable enslavement. White prisoners of war, northerners and southerners alike, sprinkled references to enslavement in their descriptions of their prison experiences. William Farrand Keys, a Pennsylvanian embittered by the Lincoln administration's concern for Black prisoners of war, voiced a common refrain when he described his captivity at Andersonville as "bondage." The abysmal conditions that prisoners endured while in transit elicited repeated comparisons to the Atlantic slave trade. When Confederate George Bell was transferred from a prison in New York to Fort Delaware, he protested in his diary, "such a Stowing away of human beings i Never Saw or do i believe it Ever was Resorted to in the african Slave trade." Appalled by crowded conditions in Libby Prison, a Union prisoner objected that he and other inmates had to cluster "like slaves in the middle passage."

White prisoners intent on conveying the squalor in the prison pens often employed the simile of blackness. Michael Dougherty surveyed his Andersonville acquaintances and remarked, "We look like a lot of colored persons." White prisoners in Andersonville, Sergeant Edward Beach observed, were "so black that we can hardly tell them from the Negroes in here." According to John E. Warren, an artillerist from Wisconsin, the cumulative effects of exposure to the sun and campfire smoke rendered white prisoners' hair "kinky" and their skin so dark that they "could hardly be told from Mulattos." The tattered rags that they wore, prisoners complained, were worse than the rustic clothes that adorned slaves. The prison diet of cornmeal and bits of rancid bacon at Andersonville and other Confederate pens, they insisted, was inferior in quality and quantity to foods consumed by slaves. Even the most heartless slave masters provided their bondspeople with shelter while Union prisoners fashioned hovels out of mud and debris.

Confederate guards were as likely as Union prisoners to conflate captivity and slavery. Guards commonly insulted white prisoners by referring to them as "white niggers." Some prisoners, like Michael Dougherty, claimed to find humor in pronouncements of Andersonville guards who periodically yelled, "Make Georgia's soil rich with the black abolitionists!" and "Free the nigger and enslave the whites!" Others considered the verbal abuse an extension of their systematic degradation. Although white prisoners escaped the worst punishments that Black prisoners suffered, Samuel Boggs, a sergeant in the Twenty-First Illinois Infantry, nevertheless believed that Confederates selected slave drivers to serve as prison guards so that they could exercise their "barbarous appetites on helpless captives."

After witnessing comrades manacled and chased down by bloodhounds, Union prisoners understandably saw themselves as victims of the slave master's tyranny. Confederate policies reinforced the perception of white prisoners that they were being deliberately reduced to the status of their Black comrades. In March 1864, officials at Libby Prison ignored the convention of separating officers from men in the ranks when they partitioned off a small space, fourteen by twenty feet, in one of the large prison rooms. Into this cramped cell were crammed four Black privates, along with ten white officers. They had neither a stove nor facilities for washing. A bucket, emptied once a day, served as their toilet. "This was done for mere spite," a fellow prisoner asserted. The *Richmond Whig* agreed. "This is a taste of negro equality," the paper gloated, "we fancy, the said Yankee officers will not fancy overmuch."

Invocations of enslavement by Confederate prisoners bore only a superficial resemblance to those of Union prisoners. More often, prison diarists instead complained that their prison accommodations, food, and medical care were unfit for livestock. Confederates used slavery as a metaphor for captivity, with no implied comparison with slavery as it existed in the South. To the extent that they referred to slavery, it was to assail the looming "Yankee rule" and enslavement of white southerners. To acknowledge the wretchedness of Black slaves in any comparisons they drew was virtually inconceivable; in the slaveholders' republic for which they fought, slavery was a humane and productive institution that retained a legitimate place in the modern world.

Confederate prisoners were more likely to rail against their subordination by formerly enslaved Black soldiers. When a Black Union guard stood sentinel over his imprisoned and now former slave master, "nature's law," as white southerners understood it, was reduced to tatters. Confederate Vice President Alexander Stephens had said in March 1861 that "subordination is his [the Black slave's] place." But at Point Lookout, Fort Delaware, Rock Island, and other Union prisons, the subjugators and subjugated had changed places. The formerly enslaved had transcended their subordinate place in the world, acquired literal (military) rank, and now wielded influence over whites. The words of Black people, which white southerners hitherto had treated with contempt, now had to be obeyed. White prisoners, not the enslaved, had to don a mask of obedience and comply with commands. Now, they had to calculate the risks of face-to-face verbal and physical confrontations with Black men who exercised the power of life and death.

Witnessing fellow white prisoners surrender to fear and submission, rather than demonstrate the mastery and control that was a white southerner's birthright, deeply offended many Confederate prisoners. William

In *On a Cold Night in January*, by prisoner Jacob Omenhausser, a Black guard commands Confederate prisoners at Point Lookout to do his bidding. (Naval History Society Collection, series 37, Point Lookout sketches, 1864; New York Historical)

Haigh, it may be recalled, was appalled that fellow white prisoners played up to Black guards, seeking "to bask in the sunshine of a negro sentinel's smile." Haigh had never imagined that he would witness not just submission but supplication by white men. Charles Warren Hutt, a private in the Fortieth Virginia Infantry imprisoned at Point Lookout in 1864, was beside himself when Black soldiers took up guard duty at the camp. "Was there ever such a thing in civilized warfare?" he sputtered.

However unwarranted, these invocations of bondage by white prisoners were nonetheless of enduring importance for the memory of Civil War captivity. The experiences of prisoners of war were so far outside the experience of most contemporaries that prisoners labored to find appropriate language, metaphors, and analogies to describe their ordeal. In subsequent wars, war captives could tap an extensive catalog of increasingly familiar tropes—barbed-wire enclosures, guard towers, snarling dogs, and sadistic guards—to portray their captivity. Civil War prisoners had no comparable stock of imagery at their disposal. They understandably were disinclined to compare themselves with imprisoned criminals during peacetime. To do so would have implied that they were in some manner dishonored or guilty of some offense, whereas they stressed that they were wholly innocent victims.

Few Civil War–era Americans, moreover, had any familiarity with prisons. The most common depictions of captivity in popular culture before the Civil War were tales of whites held captive by Indians, not by law officers. Even Victor Hugo's *Les Misérables*, which was published in 1862 and avidly read in translation by those prisoners who were able to secure copies, did not provide an apt template to portray wartime captivity. Some prisoners, like William Haigh, identified with Hugo's remarkable creation, the tormented former convict Jean Valjean. Yet Valjean's anguish, borne of guilt and persecution, had little in common with the misery that most prisoners of war struggled to describe and understand.

The language of the nation's Founders, with its emphasis on stark dichotomies between freedom and servitude, liberty and dependence, encouraged both white Union and Confederate prisoners to employ slavery as a convenient simile for wartime captivity. The binary of liberty and bondage permeated American cultural discourse of the time. Participants in contemporary debates over "wage slavery" invoked it. So too did those who raised the alarm about the "Slave Power," a coalition of resolute defenders of slavery and their sycophants that purportedly threatened the liberty of citizens in the free states. At the same time, white southerners who championed secession warned of the impending bondage of the southern states by avaricious and unhinged Yankees.

After more than a generation of fevered controversy over the institution of slavery, white Union prisoners of war predictably grasped for parallels between the dehumanization and objectification evident in two of the age's extreme institutions—slavery and prisoner-of-war camps. Beyond translating the experience of captivity into something comprehensible, the comparison established the prisoners' sacrifice in the context of a titanic struggle over the future of slavery in the United States. In the two decades before the war, a surfeit of firsthand travel accounts, antislavery novels, and slave autobiographies had prodded white Americans to reflect on the existential state of enslavement. For Union prisoners who had been exposed to sentimental renderings of the pathos of enslavement in these writings, comparisons with slavery offered a storehouse of potent language and images. In such renderings, the slave and the prisoner together were poised on the threshold between the world of humans and the world of brutes.

The experience of captivity did awaken a measure of empathy for enslaved Black people among some Union prisoners. Camaraderie of a sort even developed in some instances. Union prisoners seldom had any opportunity to do more than observe the impressed slaves who toiled under Confederate oversight. But momentary impressions gathered during fleeting encounters convinced some prisoners that together they and the enslaved, as one Union prisoner put it, were "the same victims of Rebel hate." Sometimes the sense of shared suffering was manifest in mere glances. Ezra Hoyt Ripple recalled the faces of enslaved Black people in the crowds that gawked at the trainloads of Union prisoners bound for Andersonville. Amid the sea of glowering white faces would be scattered Black faces, in whose eyes "was always that look which said to us plainly as words 'we pity you.'"

Prisoners at Andersonville had more frequent interactions with the enslaved Black men who built the stockades and surrounding earthworks. In his memoir, John McElroy recalled an epiphany that he experienced while observing "the workings of the 'peculiar institution'" at the camp. The enslaved Blacks he met gave the appearance of being "dull" and "oxlike." But whenever they were unobserved by their Confederate overseers, their vacant faces lighted up and all resemblance to "credulous yokels" disappeared. The spectacle of white men suffering intense hardship at the hands of white southerners and in a cause that promised to end the thralldom of slavery apparently was revelatory to these enslaved Black people. Taking their masters' enemies to be their friends, they and countless other slaves attached themselves to the Union cause.

Scores of escaping Union prisoners in late 1864 reached similar conclusions about the enslaved. While fleeing helter-skelter from the prison pen in Columbia, South Carolina, Charles Mattocks and two other officers appealed to a Black slave they encountered on a byway. Despite the potentially deadly repercussions if his white neighbors discovered his generosity, the Black man welcomed the escapees into his cabin, where they warmed themselves and ate a hastily assembled but ample dinner of chicken, corn bread, and potatoes.

John Hadley of the Seventh Indiana Infantry and a small group of fellow fugitives also experienced the extraordinary courage of Black slaves they encountered while fleeing captivity in Columbia. In a postwar memoir, Hadley recalled the stealth and shrewdness displayed by the Black people who fed his party of escapees on a moment's notice and led them through Confederate territory. Especially surprising to Hadley was the extent of the slaves' knowledge of political and military affairs. Hadley and other escap-

Guard dogs at Confederate prisons, here overwhelming an escaped prisoner from the Florence camp, loomed large in the diaries and memoirs of prisoners. (Library of Congress)

ing prisoners quickly developed, as John Ransom put it, "perfect confidence" in the willingness and sincerity of Black southerners to give aid, whether as "a guide to escape, as sentinel to signal danger, or a purveyor of food."

Some comparisons of captivity and slavery, then, were more than another example of cavalier white appropriation of Black experience. If sometimes hyperbolic and insensitive to the peculiar hardships experienced by the enslaved, the analogies between captivity and enslavement drawn by some Union prisoners were not intended to deny or extenuate the horrors of bondage. White soldiers who advanced with Union armies farther and farther into the Confederacy saw enough of slavery and of the enslaved to disabuse them of any notion that either minstrelsy or proslavery tracts accurately depicted slavery. Sitting on the banks of the James River on Belle Isle or in their earthen hovels in Andersonville, prisoners sensed that they and the enslaved shared the same experience of deprivation of almost everything that made human life precious.

The ordeal of Isaac Gaskins and the several thousand other Black prisoners garnered only fleeting acknowledgment in white accounts of captivity. The common saga of captivity was principally, indeed almost exclusively, of white men suffering extreme hardships. Nevertheless, Gaskins and the other Black captives had an impact on the conduct of the war out of proportion to their numbers. They made up only a small fraction of the total number of Union prisoners, but the fortunes of all prisoners of war turned on their fate until the final two months of the war. Not until then did Gaskins's captivity end.

In late February 1865, Gaskins was exchanged with other severely wounded prisoners held at Danville. He spent the next eight months in military hospitals until his discharge that November. In later years Gaskins had ample cause to marvel that he had survived the war. Even more extraordinary, he had survived captivity. Of the thirty-one men of the Twenty-Ninth Illinois who were taken prisoner along with Gaskins at the Battle of the Crater, only Gaskins and thirteen others lived to savor freedom.

CHAPTER TEN

# ALLEVIATION?

## (1864–1865)

In September 1864, a month after Andrew Riddle photographed the thronged city of Andersonville, Dr. Joseph Jones arrived at the prison. While navigating the labyrinthine paths between lean-tos and earthen hovels in the stockade, he encountered "an exact daguerreotype" of a man stretched out upon the urine-saturated soil. A perfect silhouette of the figure's nose, mouth, and beard could be discerned. Puzzled by the grotesque tableau, Jones queried nearby prisoners and learned that the body of a dead prisoner had lain on the spot overnight. A hard downpour had cleansed the body of accumulated filth and soot from the pinewood that prisoners used for cooking, leaving behind the uncanny likeness. The bizarre postmortem apparition was a vivid marker of the alien world of Andersonville.

Jones was not a greenhorn when it came to the carnage of warfare. Thirty years old and a three-year veteran when he set up his primitive laboratory at Andersonville, he had witnessed countless bodies ravaged by disease and combat. The camp had beckoned to him as an ideal site in which to study the diseases that were rapidly thinning the prison ranks. His research, he hoped, would inform improved medical care for Confederate soldiers.

The affliction he observed in the prison pen outstripped his powers of description, an unusual plight for a man sometimes mocked for his verbosity. The heat of the unrelenting sun, which one prisoner complained "melts men down like transplanted plants," fatigued Jones. The camp's inescapable

Dr. Joseph Jones's research tent at Andersonville. (Tulane University Archives)

stench and filth nauseated him. The swarming insects harassed him. The variety and scale of human agony overwhelmed him.

Jones pondered what could be done to ameliorate these conditions. He and other military doctors confronted the challenge of reconciling their ethical obligations with the exigencies of modern war. The therapeutic mission—to heal all and harm none—was the emerging creed of doctors in an era when they struggled to overcome long-held popular skepticism of their craft. Warfare on the scale of the Civil War, however, presented them with situations that confounded ordinary morality and ethics.

Common sense and expediency, as much as any moral obligation, prompted Union and Confederate staffs to supply medical care to captives. The expectation was that all wounded men on the battlefield would receive medical attention. So too, should prisoners while in captivity. Failure to attend to ill prisoners was a provocation for retaliation against any prisoners the enemy held. Both sides had an additional incentive to minister to ill prisoners while general prisoner exchanges were ongoing. The sooner prisoners were healthy enough to travel, the sooner they could be exchanged and their captors relieved of their burdensome care.

The unprecedented size of Civil War military and prison camps, many located near civilian communities, gave added urgency to the prevention of contagious diseases in the camps. Experience had taught military staff that soldiers' camps were breeding grounds for diseases and posed as great a threat to soldiers' well-being as the enemy's weapons. Veterans of the war with Mexico recalled that ten American soldiers had died of disease for each soldier killed in battle. More recently, disease had accounted for a similar toll during the Crimean War in Europe.

The medical care of soldiers and prisoners alike was haphazard during the first year of the war. The scale of the struggle quickly demonstrated the inadequacies of existing facilities. In 1861 no military medical infrastructure existed in the United States. The largest prewar military medical facility, located in Kansas, had forty beds. The only hospital in the nation's capital was a small six-room building used to isolate smallpox patients.

Just as the Civil War inspired Americans to experiment with imprisonment on an unprecedented scale, so too it obliged them to administer medical care on a new scale. Among the most significant and far-reaching innovations was the general hospital, which had few prewar antecedents in the United States. In the American imagination, hospitals had provided the ailing poor and hopeless with places to die. Thomas Jefferson expressed the conventional wisdom when he observed that "it is poverty alone which peoples hospitals." Everyone else who was sick was advised to recuperate at home while attended by private physicians. However, the number of ill soldiers and their dispersal over half a continent rendered traditional methods of care impractical.

Both sides fashioned medical facilities on the fly. The earliest Union hospitals were hastily built to serve Union volunteers while they trained. Few of the facilities were adequately winterized and most were cramped, understaffed, and shabby. The ill-suited warehouses, mills, and commercial buildings that Confederates recycled to serve as hospitals were no better.

Union and Confederate officials recognized an urgent need for new medical facilities on a grand scale. The Confederacy acted with uncharacteristic alacrity and in Richmond built Chimborazo Hospital, the largest hospital complex of the age. With a capacity of thirty-six hundred, the facility incorporated lessons drawn from the Crimean War, which had sparked a new recognition of the importance of ample space, light, and ventilation in hospital design. Union Surgeon General William H. Hammond, who assumed his office in April 1862, championed similarly giant hospitals. Hammond Hospital at Point Lookout, with fourteen hundred beds distributed among sixteen spacious and well-ventilated wards, was a prototype of the state-of-the-art military hospital.

Facilities at prison camps remained makeshift. Few Union prisoners in Richmond were admitted to Chimborazo Hospital. Instead, most were assigned to crude infirmaries in former tobacco warehouses, places that were indistinguishable from the prisons themselves. The medical facilities at Union camps, including Camps Douglas, Morton, and Chase, were similarly overcrowded, dank, and inadequate. Only the advent of prisoner exchanges during the summer of 1862 prevented the failings of these facilities from devolving into full-blown humanitarian crises.

When general prisoner exchanges halted and both sides began creating massive prison camps, prison authorities finally began to expand prison medical facilities. Union officials made long-requested improvements at several sites. For more than a year, the hospital at Camp Chase had been condemned as decrepit and too small. With the completion of a new facility in early 1864, the hospital was declared to be "quite satisfactory." Even

Union soldiers recuperating in the McClellan Hospital in Philadelphia in 1865. (Library of Congress)

Confederate prisoners acknowledged the improvement. At Fort Delaware the medical facilities for prisoners in 1863 included four dilapidated infirmaries and two old and battered hospital tents. By the end of the year, a new six-hundred-bed hospital won the praise of both Union inspectors and Confederate prisoners. Inslee Deaderick, a Tennessee cavalryman who spent a year in the prison, vouched to his family that the hospital was indeed "a very good one." He concluded, "The best I ever saw."

Yet there were limits to the Union's commitment to improving medical facilities for prisoners. Concerns about expense and mounting outrage over Confederate mistreatment of Union prisoners provided Secretary of War Edwin Stanton with a pretext to reject requests for improvements at Point Lookout in 1864. Facilities there were stretched to their limits as the prison population swelled to twenty thousand. Out of necessity, prison medical staff adopted a crude system of triage. Prisoners infected with smallpox were isolated in a small impromptu hospital outside the northern boundary of the stockade. Captives with other life-threatening conditions, at the rate of twenty to thirty per day, were sent to the nearby model Hammond Hospital, where they apparently received the same care as Union patients. The largest number of sick prisoners were ensconced in eighteen hospital tents arranged in two rows at the southern end of the stockade. The tents had earthen floors, were unheated, and often bulged with patients. A medical inspector conceded that severe "complaint and suffering" prevailed in them. The dispensary for the tent hospital was "a poor apology for one, having little or nothing but a few empty bottles." Patients, the inspector reported, huddled together in "a motley crew, which to be appreciated must be seen."

As bad as the tent hospital at Point Lookout was, almost all Confederate facilities were worse. Had the hospital at the prison in Cahaba, Alabama, been typical, the claims of Confederate authorities that the facilities for Union prisoners were comparable to those provided for Confederate soldiers might have been plausible. With no room for a medical facility within the cramped prison stockade at Cahaba, Confederate authorities requisitioned a nearby former hotel. Reflecting its previous purpose, the building was comparatively spacious and comfortable. Quirks of Confederate procurement ensured that the facility received supplies of both food and medicines. Prisoners confined there experienced amenities that were unimaginable in the prison stockade itself or anywhere else in the Confederate prison system. The recovery rate of prisoners admitted to the hospital at Cahaba compared favorably with that of any hospital of the day.

Elsewhere, Confederate inspection reports revealed stark disparities in the medical treatment of Confederates and prisoners. The Confederate policy of crowding prisoners together in the smallest possible space extended to hospitals. By March 1864 the three prison hospitals in Richmond held more than twice as many patients as they were intended to house. Federal patients at the Belle Isle prison hospital had only half as much room as Confederate patients at nearby Chimborazo Hospital.

Representative was the hospital at Salisbury prison, which a Union prisoner described as "heart-rending beyond expression." Rows of sick prisoners lay on loose straw the full length of the first floor of the crude facility. So great was the clutter of prisoners and straw that the hospital's dirt floors could not be cleaned. Vermin crawled around "like ants on an ant-hill," tormenting the weakest patients. Disease and illness ripped through the prison in late 1864, claiming the lives of four thousand prisoners—37 percent of those held there—within four months.

Even more egregious failings were on display at Andersonville, where the medical facilities were inhumane in every regard. During the first two months of the camp's operation, the sick were clustered within hospital tents in the stockade. As long as the hospital remained there, patients were assailed by the stench and filth of the stockade as well as by fellow prison-

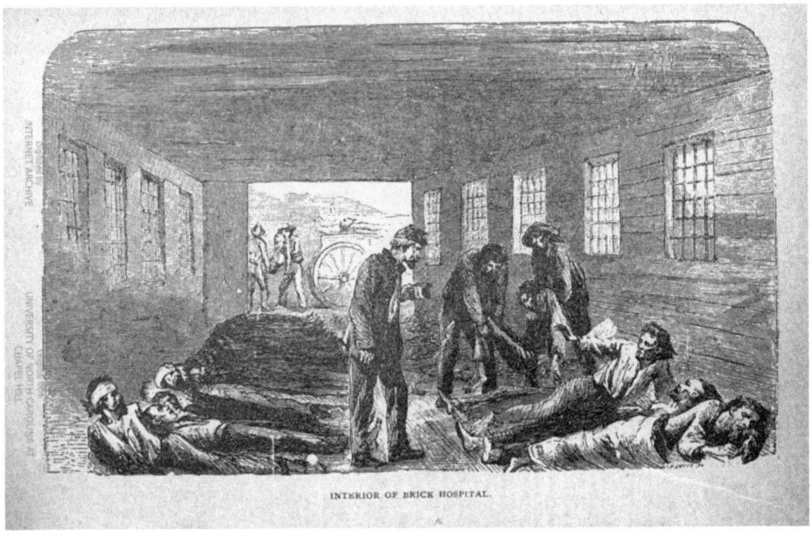


The hospital at the Salisbury prison camp also served as a death house, with the corpses on the left and the sick on the right. (From B. F. Booth, *Dark Days of the Rebellion, or, Life in Southern Military Prisons*, 1897)

ers who mercilessly stole their rations, clothing, and private possessions. After withering criticism of the stockade hospital by medical inspectors, Andersonville authorities had twenty-nine dilapidated tents erected a short distance outside the southern wall of the stockade. Doctors admitted sick inmates from the stockade to these tents when "spaces" within them were vacated by the death or, unlikely as it was, the recovery of a patient.

The hardships associated with the triage of prospective patients were harrowing, as even prison authorities conceded. Sick prisoners spent days crowded near the South Gate of the stockade, clamoring for the attention of the doctors who conducted the morning sick call. The weaker the inmate, the worse his odds of being able to claw his way through the scrum of other prisoners to reach a doctor. The exhausting ordeal of trekking back and forth to the sick area each day added to the agony of ailing prisoners.

The futility of awaiting medical care in the camp was forcefully demonstrated to George Hitchcock by the deaths of twelve of his messmates between June and September 1864. A war-weary veteran of the Twenty-First Massachusetts Volunteers, he watched as his friends succumbed without ever having been admitted to the camp hospital. A thirteenth member of his circle finally was admitted, only to die five days later of scurvy. The morbid spectacle that Hitchcock had witnessed was in no way atypical. Sometimes the deaths in the prison outnumbered those in the hospital. During one week that September, 336 prisoners succumbed within the stockade and 334 in the hospital.

Doctors admitted prisoners who were on the threshold of death to the hospital. Such was the fate of Jones Sherwood, who suffered from chronic diarrhea. His comrade Charles Holbrook, who struggled with the same disease, devotedly cared for him. After lugging Sherwood to the hospital several times, Holbrook recorded in his diary, with evident relief, that he "finally succeeded in getting him in." Days later Sherwood died, to be followed in a few weeks by Holbrook himself.

The inevitable consequence of the crude triage enforced at the Andersonville hospital was, as prisoner David Kennedy reported, "Many goes but few return." The odds of surviving a stay in that hospital were dismal and substantially worse than the odds of surviving combat. Nearly 18,000 prisoners were admitted to the hospital between February 24, 1864, and April 17, 1865. Out of this number, 12,541, or 70 percent, died there. Everyone at Andersonville understood that the hospital was effectively a death house.

Only extreme desperation can explain the resolve of sick prisoners at Andersonville to get into the camp hospital. Most days, a staff of four or fewer doctors tended the thousand or more patients who crowded into the hospital tents. Routine sanitary precautions were wholly absent. Most of the prisoners were so weakened that they had to excrete in crude bins that hospital stewards then dumped along the perimeter of the hospital area. Wounds were dressed with rags that were not washed between uses. The sick, Joseph Jones observed, were "encrusted with dirt." "Of vermin or lice," another prison doctor recalled, "there was a very prolific crop there." Like an Old Testament plague, dense swarms of insects tormented patients and staff in the hospital, leaving patients so stung by mosquitos that they appeared to be suffering from measles. In a graphic passage in his report, Jones described flies depositing maggots in the wounds of the living and in the mouths of the dead.

David Kennedy was among the small number of prisoners who survived their convalescence in the Andersonville hospital. The unabated agony of fellow patients and the days punctuated by the deaths of comrades crushed his spirits. "Theire is more miserey heire," he observed of the hospital, "than could be emagin." He returned to the stockade with relief.

Prison camps, like all military camps, were fertile incubators of disease. A single statistic illustrates how lethal the camps were: about two and one half times as many soldiers endured the hazards of the prison camps as were exposed to the dangers of battle at Gettysburg, yet the camps killed nearly ten times as many as were killed at Gettysburg. Whenever soldiers were densely assembled in environments to which they were not acclimated, they shared infections for which many had no immunity. Prisoners, who were often weakened by bad diets and dire living conditions, were especially prone to illness and vulnerable to contagious diseases.

Union and Confederate prison doctors battled the same diseases within their respective camps. The proportions claimed by the various maladies differed, however, underscoring at once the common and distinctive threats that prisoners on each side faced.

Among Confederate prisoners the leading causes of death were dysentery and chronic diarrhea. The Surgeon General's Office recorded the deaths of 30,716 Confederate prisoners of war. Of these, 7281 were from diarrhea and dysentery. At some camps, including Johnson's Island and Fort Warren, the toll of dysentery and diarrhea was negligible. At Camp Douglas, in contrast, 698 deaths due to dysentery were reported. Elmira prison reported 1394 deaths. Pneumonia (which was often labeled inflammation of the lungs or pleurisy) claimed the lives of more than 5000 Confederates. Smallpox, measles, scarlet fever, and erysipelas killed another 3400. A variety of other diseases claimed the remainder of the prisoners.

Dysentery and chronic diarrhea likewise were the leading causes of death among Union prisoners. Hospital records from Andersonville, Salisbury, Danville, and Cahaba prisons establish the devastation wrought by dysentery and diarrhea. Of the 12,541 deaths recorded at Andersonville, 5605 were traced to diarrhea and dysentery. At Danville, diarrhea and dysentery were responsible for 592 of the 1084 deaths in the hospital. Scurvy was the second most common cause of death in the Confederate prisons. At Andersonville, dysentery and scurvy combined for nearly three-quarters of the prison deaths.

That diarrhea and dysentery killed thousands of prisoners and debilitated many more was predictable, even inevitable. Conditions in almost every camp promoted the spread of diarrheal illness. Most sufferers probably contracted amoebic dysentery, which is caused by a one-celled animal that lodges in the intestine, then enters the circulatory system and eventually invades the liver, lungs, and brain. Dehydration and the rapid loss of vital minerals leaves sufferers weak and susceptible to pneumonia and other infectious diseases. While their bodies attempt to rid themselves of the organism through the intestinal tract, victims are highly contagious. Scrupulous personal hygiene is essential to prevent spreading the organism to others. Otherwise, even fleeting personal contact—especially with common food, cookware, or eating utensils—is likely to transmit the illness. Stringent hygiene was difficult at most prison camps, and impossible at some, especially Andersonville, where dysentery and chronic diarrhea stalked virtually every prisoner.

Doctors had no effective cures for diarrheal illness. The commonly administered "cures"—lead acetate, sulfuric acid, calomel, and silver nitrate—were usually ineffective and occasionally lethal. Prospects for survival were better if patients avoided doctors and their remedies. Union prisoners complained bitterly of the paucity of remedies for diarrheal illnesses in Confederate camps, but they probably fared no worse when Confederate doctors administered improvised concoctions made from "indigenous roots and bark." Desperate prisoners themselves experimented with folk recipes. When diarrhea became chronic at Salisbury prison during the fall of 1864, prisoners made tea from the bark of oak trees. Soon the oak trees within the stockade were stripped of bark as high as men could reach. When the bark supplies faltered, prisoners foraged for blackberry roots, which purportedly mitigated some of the symptoms of diarrhea. But the supply of roots was far too limited to meet the prisoners' needs. These rustic remedies, at most, provided only a temporary respite from the debilitating effects of digestive diseases.

Doctors were equally ineffective at combating other maladies in the prison camps. Hospital gangrene, which infected patients in all Civil War hospitals, confounded prison doctors and resisted cures. An explanation for its transmission eluded doctors. That it spread with devastating speed from patient to patient was apparent. Beginning with a small black spot on the skin surrounding a wound, the disease quickly turned the smallest abrasion into a frightful and putrid mess. Doctors experimented with all manner of topical agents, some of which temporarily arrested the advance of the disease but also destroyed healthy tissue. Doctors relied on successive amputations of diseased areas to slow the disease's spread.

The incidence of gangrene was of particular interest to Joseph Jones during his trip to Andersonville. His research there convinced him that doctors often misdiagnosed it. Confronted with a disease outside of their experiences, doctors apparently lacked the etiological awareness to accurately diagnose the badly diseased bodies of their patients. At Andersonville, Jones identified 266 cases of fatal hospital gangrene, a number that he considered "far below the truth."

Recognizing the ineffectiveness of the doctors' remedies, prisoners experimented with their own cures. Prisoner John England had more success than most. A battlefield wound that had not healed properly flared up while he was imprisoned in Andersonville. "At last, by much ado, I succeeded in getting into the hospital for the purpose of having it amputated." Fearful that he would not survive the amputation, he instead burned the wounded area with nitric acid and nitrate of silver before applying turpentine and linseed meal. After enduring six weeks of "infinite pain," he apparently rid himself of gangrene.

Other diseases should have posed much less of a threat to the prisoners. Smallpox claimed the lives of thousands of prisoners, even though by the mid-nineteenth century physicians understood how contagious the disease was and had effective measures to prevent its spread. Nevertheless, prison staff throughout the war repeatedly dithered when faced with outbreaks of the disease.

When Confederate prisoners captured at Chattanooga in December 1863 were shuttled north, inattentive Union doctors along the route of their forced migration failed to cull those who showed signs of smallpox. Instead, they were funneled to Rock Island, where cases of smallpox erupted three days after the first prisoners arrived. The prison was wholly unprepared. Although its walls now held more than 6000 prisoners, only 600 smallpox vaccines were on hand. None of the camp's administrators, including the camp's aged and overwhelmed surgeon, had taken the precaution of establishing an adequate "pest house" where contagious prisoners could be isolated. Instead, the surgeon and his two assistants distributed infected prisoners among five barracks within the prison. This shuffling hastened the spread and increased the lethality of the epidemic.

By the end of January 1864, seven weeks after the opening of the prison, 635 of the 6000 prisoners were sick, and 325 had died. More than 1000 prisoners perished during the prison's first four months of operation. By February, nearly a quarter of the prison's population were receiving medical treatment from the prison's overwhelmed medical staff. Two months after the beginning of the outbreak, a medical inspector was appalled to find infected prisoners still mingling with other prisoners. Not until March did a newly appointed prison surgeon and his staff make the improvements in facilities and care necessary to quell the epidemic. Exacerbated by poor planning, ineptitude, and an apparent lack of urgency among the camp's officials, the epidemic killed more than 500 prisoners.

Doctors at Elmira proved no more competent when an outbreak of smallpox struck their camp. In this instance, the most charitable explanation for the deadly flare-up is that prison staff failed to diagnose the first instance of the disease and so neglected to swiftly segregate infected prisoners. Or perhaps, as some Confederate prisoners alleged, doctors deliberately allowed the carrier of the deadly infection to remain in the overcrowded prison barracks. When some of the victims of the epidemic were buried in the camp enclosure, risking further contamination of the camp's inhabitants, the prisoners' worst suspicions seemingly were confirmed. Before the epidemic ran its course, smallpox was the third leading cause of death at Elmira.

Even the prophylactic measures that prison staffs took to prevent smallpox posed a threat to prisoners. Both Confederate and Union authorities decided to vaccinate prisoners against smallpox. But stocks of vaccine were insufficient to meet the pressing demands during the war so both Union and Confederate authorities instituted programs to obtain the scabs from healthy children who were inoculated with smallpox. The scabs removed from their infections were used to produce what doctors called pure vaccines, which were presumably uninfected by blood-borne ailments that circulated among adults, especially soldiers. But when these vaccine drives proved inadequate to meet demand, military doctors resorted to using the scabs from recently vaccinated men to vaccinate other soldiers.

The risks of using vaccines derived from adults were compounded when the vaccinations took place in prison settings, where patients were already weak and vulnerable to illness. Even worse, so-called spurious vaccinations contaminated with blood-borne diseases, including syphilis, spread fatal diseases among prisoners. Joseph Jones tried to calculate the toll of spurious vaccines at Andersonville, where substantial numbers of prisoners developed adverse reactions to vaccines. He speculated that contaminated vaccines were especially toxic among prisoners who suffered from scurvy and were exposed to hospital gangrene. Among these patients, the site of the vaccine on the prisoners' bodies flared into open ulcers dripping with "decomposing pus and blood." In short order, severe tissue destruction in the surrounding areas necessitated amputations. Jones estimated that at Andersonville one hundred prisoners suffered amputations and another two hundred died because of faulty vaccines.

The threat of smallpox forced prisoners to make a terrifying choice. They could place their trust in the competence of prison doctors and risk vaccination, or refuse vaccination and remain unprotected against one of the most feared diseases of the age. Each instance of a prisoner who suffered the horrible effects of a spurious vaccine or succumbed to an adverse reaction to inoculation reminded prisoners of the tenuousness of their control over their bodies.

The death toll of scurvy among prisoners, even more than that of smallpox, was an indictment of the prison camps. Prisoners and doctors knew how to prevent scurvy and prisoners went to great ends to do so. Although Civil War–era physicians did not know about vitamins C, $B_6$, or niacin, they recognized the need for antiscorbutic food to treat and prevent scurvy. The symptoms had been understood for more than a century before the war. A deficiency of vitamin C resulted in muscle pain, fatigue, an increased susceptibility to infection, anorexia, weakening of bones and cartilage, swollen and bleeding gums, and loss of teeth. Niacin deficiency led to skin lesions, delirium, depression, anxiety, and fatigue, while a deficit of vitamin $B_6$ produced muscle weakness, numbness and pain, usually in the hands and feet, impaired immunity, and anemia.

Prisoners were almost always vitamin deficient, even when they were not starving. These deficiencies became acute in Confederate prisons in

1864, and even appeared in some Union camps. Nowhere was scurvy more prevalent than Andersonville. By May 1864, two months after the camp's opening, scurvy cases had advanced to the point that ailing prisoners were losing their teeth and suffering swollen limbs. More and more afflicted prisoners were unable to eat their rations, especially any meat they received. Within another month, growing numbers began to die from the disease.

Prisoners devoted pages of their diaries to cataloging the accumulating symptoms of scurvy. In September 1864, prisoner George Hitchcock noticed that his gums were swollen and had turned dark purple. He anticipated his prognosis: "Where others have it and do not recover, this swelling spreads in a few days until the face and neck turn black as if blood settled all over it; then the teeth drop out—the jaws become set and a general rotting process is the last stage." For some, the symptoms appeared in the limbs first, "rendering them stiff and helpless." Hitchcock confessed to having already succumbed to "complete lassitude and low spirits."

Hitchcock's torment was both preventable and treatable. Joseph Jones acknowledged as much in his report, conceding that "nine tenths" of the deaths in Andersonville could be traced directly or indirectly to "scurvy arising from sameness of food and imperfect nutrition." Confederate prison inspector Daniel Chandler reached the same conclusion, assailing camp officials for making little if any effort to arrest the scourge by procuring proper food. As one of the camp physicians reported to his superiors that September, as long as the nutritional shortcomings prevailed, "all the skill that can be brought to bear" by him and the other medical staff "will avail nothing."

Scurvy cut a much smaller swath through the ranks of Confederate prisoners in Union camps. Although ample antiscorbutic provisions were readily available at every Union camp, preventable cases of malnutrition proliferated during 1864. Prison doctors who raised concerns about reductions of rations were ignored. At Elmira, where dysentery already ravaged the ranks of prisoners, the incidence of scurvy mounted that summer. Eugene F. Sanger, the camp surgeon, who displayed uncharacteristic concern for the camp's residents, urged "an increase of quantity and variety of antiscorbutics" and asked for permission to provide an extra weekly ration of "potatoes, cabbage, or onions" for all prisoners and a daily ration for patients suffering from scurvy. To Sanger and other surgeons fell the task of dealing with the consequences of retaliation without the discretion or power to redress the root causes of scurvy.

Medical staff were similarly impotent with regard to overcrowding in camps. In Union prison camps, the calculus of retaliation and Colonel Hoffman's habitual stinginess constrained any remedies proposed by camp doctors. Acute overcrowding in Confederate camps, of course, was condoned at the highest levels of the Confederate government. William Carrington, the prominent physician who rose to be medical director of all of Virginia's hospitals, informed a colleague, "The refusal of proper accommodations to sick Federal prisoners was one of state policy." By the late summer of 1864, he recalled, he had "adopted the conviction that the existing state of things was known and approved" by Confederate Secretary of War James Seddon. Samuel Preston Moore, the Confederate surgeon general, reached the same conclusion, observing that General Winder dismissed concerns about the alarming mortality rate and overcrowding at Confederate prison hospitals with a quip that "mortality is incident to prison life."

A dearth of competent doctors compounded the deficits and shortcomings that beset prison-camp health care. At the war's start, the United States army had just over one hundred surgeons and assistant surgeons, a quarter of whom resigned and joined the Confederate services. Five score doctors was patently inadequate to attend more than a million men who served in the Union ranks. To augment this tiny number of regular army doctors, the Union relied on doctors assigned to volunteer units and contracted civilian doctors. Eventually about twelve thousand doctors served in the Union army. Facing similar staffing problems, the Confederacy mustered just over three thousand doctors into its ranks.

Neither side apportioned their best doctors to oversee prisoners' health. Happenstance rather than design determined the composition of medical staffs at most prisons. The training, skills, and competence of military doctors in general were alarmingly varied. Neither side enforced consistent standards when appointing medical staff. A few New England states carefully vetted volunteers with medical credentials, while Wisconsin deemed a medical examining board to be a needless encumbrance: virtually anyone nominated to serve as a doctor for the state's troops was appointed. The justification for this open-door policy was that formal training should not be "the measure of practical ability." Confederate examining boards were little better and had unenviable reputations for favoritism, medical obscurantism, and general unpleasantness. Many doctors had no formal medical education. Others, including practitioners of homeopathy and folk healing methods, lacked expertise relevant to the illnesses they encountered in uniform. Few had surgical experience and almost none had familiarity with combat injuries.

Whatever the credentials claimed by prison doctors, prisoners had ample reason to worry about their competence. Confederate Private Walter D. Addison, who was captured during the Wilderness campaign in 1864 and sent to Elmira prison, observed with mounting alarm the care provided by the medical staff while working in the prison hospital. Years later he railed against the "deplorable ignorance of the medical men in charge." He bolstered his claim by recounting an error by an assistant surgeon named Ira Van Ness, who mistakenly gave a dose of forty-five drops of arsenic, instead of four *or* five, to three patients and promptly killed them.

The attitudes of many practitioners complicated the challenge of coaxing them to serve in the prison camps. Doctors were no more keen to tend prisoners than soldiers were to guard prison camps. The war, Joseph Jones explained, aroused "prejudices" that inhibited medical officers from voluntarily tending "captive enemies, who are the representatives of those who are seeking to conquer and desolate their native land."

Nowhere was the need for medical expertise more acute than Andersonville, yet doctors actively resisted serving there. J. M. Dossler, a doctor from Montgomery, Alabama, was a case in point. He requested another assignment because he was "opposed upon principle" to tending Union prisoners of war. When surgeon H. H. Clayton of Augusta, Georgia, was ordered to Andersonville, he whipped up a petition campaign by colleagues and others to protest his transfer there. The point of a bayonet was needed to persuade Dr. John C. Bates to join the Andersonville staff. Until 1864 he had been exempted from Confederate service because of his age, his existing medical practice in Macon, and, perhaps, his tepid loyalty to the Confederacy. Born in Ohio, he had received medical training in Cincinnati before moving to Florida and finally settling in Georgia. While working at a hospital in Macon in August 1864, he was arrested on unknown charges. Given the choice of serving in the Confederate army as an acting assistant surgeon or being drafted as a regular soldier, Bates reluctantly agreed to go to Andersonville.

High turnover among prison medical personnel compounded the problems associated with inadequate staffing. At Camp Chase in Columbus, Ohio, for instance, ten different men occupied the position of post surgeon between February 1863 and March 1864. Little continuity in oversight or procedures was possible under such conditions. Desperation to fill vacancies drove both Confederate and Union officials to hire local practitioners to bolster stretched medical staffs. Contract doctors acquired especially bad reputations. A Union inspector branded them "irresponsible," while prisoners perceived them to be incompetent mercenaries who avoided the front lines while pocketing an officer's salary. Some indeed treated their prison assignments as sinecures. A contract doctor at Camp Morton in Indianapolis devoted less than a half hour a day to scores of ill prisoners and the rest of his working hours to his private practice.

Chronic personnel shortages resulted in crushing workloads for any conscientious prison doctor. An earnest surgeon at Camp Chase complained in August 1864 that his duties were of an "almost Herculean magnitude" because of inadequate staffing. Overwhelmed with patient examinations, he grumbled that he had no time for other important tasks. At Andersonville, conditions reached absurd proportions. With only a handful of doctors often on duty, each surgeon was assigned to examine as many as five hundred prisoners daily. As one staff doctor acknowledged to his wife, these examinations were laughably perfunctory, amounting to little more than passing glances. A prisoner complained that although "some of the doctors appear to be kind hearted men" their examinations were "nothing but a farce just for show."

Adding to the frustrations of prison physicians were prisoners who failed to conduct themselves in a manner the doctors deemed proper. Incensed doctors condemned prisoners themselves for many of their hardships. Even as doctors acknowledged the toll of enervating diseases that left prisoners listless and disoriented, they still chastised prisoners for their polluted living conditions and unhealthful habits. At Johnson's Island, a Union officer expressed both surprise and disgust that Confederate inmates "should be willing to live in such filth." Another commented that only "a resort to brute force" could compel the prisoners there to adopt healthy behaviors. Union prisoners were denounced similarly. At Andersonville, Isaiah H. White, the chief surgeon, announced that the prisoners were "utterly devoid of humanity" and were responsible for many of the shortcomings of the camp's hospital. Joseph Jones concurred, complaining that prisoners were "utterly callous" to filth and that the only likelihood of maintaining "proper hygienic rules" was to post guards within the stockade to enforce them.

From the prisoners' perspective, doctors exercised fearsome power over them. They chose who was admitted to prison hospitals. Depending on the prison, a sojourn in the camp hospital might afford a prisoner access to medicines and a respite from the overcrowding, choking odors, and disagreeable rations in the stockade. Heated hospital wards had obvious appeal for prisoners otherwise confined in frigid tents and prison barracks during the coldest winter months.

Doctors also had the responsibility for culling ill prisoners for periodic special medical exchanges, which occurred even after regular exchanges were halted. During the last year of the war, these transfers of the sickest prisoners were the only reprieves from the prison pens other than death, escape, or enlisting in the enemy army. At a time when conditions in Confederate prisons deteriorated dramatically, both Confederate doctors and Union prisoners recognized that doctors wielded the power of life and death when they made their selections.

Doctors bestowed these medical transfers capriciously. In theory, medical staff identified those inmates who were too ill to return to active duty for the enemy yet were healthy enough to travel. But prisoners reported that some doctors accepted bribes from healthy prisoners who finagled to be included among the exchanged. Other medical staff were lackadaisical about selecting prisoners suitable for medical exchanges, as the experience of fourteen hundred Confederate prisoners transferred from Elmira in October 1864 demonstrated.

Stuffed into sixty unheated boxcars, the "ghastly tide" of "skeleton bodies" and human wreckage from the Elmira prison took thirty-five hours to reach Baltimore. Five prisoners died during the ordeal. An outraged doctor who observed the arriving prisoners protested that the prisoners' condition was "distressing in the extreme" and decried that they had been sent on the journey in the first place. If the prisoners had in fact been inspected by doctors before leaving Elmira, he lamented "it was most carelessly done." At least sixty of the prisoners were immediately sent to a hospital in Baltimore. Another forty were deemed too feeble and emaciated to survive the journey back to the Confederacy. But because Baltimore's hospitals were full and the sick prisoners could be accommodated on the ships bound for Virginia, they were sent south.

Prisoners subjected to the trek from Elmira concluded that the intent of medical staff was to hasten their death while in transit. At the very least, camp surgeons took the transfer as an opportunity to rid the camp of hundreds of sick and injured prisoners, regardless of whether they could survive the journey. An aghast medical officer declared that the debacle demonstrated "criminal neglect and inhumanity." After investigating the transfer, Colonel Hoffman concurred, concluding that in their handling of the prisoners the commanding officer and medical officers at Elmira "had neglected the ordinary prompting of humanity."

Many prison doctors recognized the systemic failings in the camps. Only willful denial could have prevented them from doing so. But their abilities, power, and disposition to ameliorate the plight of prisoners were limited. Even in circumstances far better than the prison camps, their remedies were often ineffectual and their efforts futile. Both day-to-day operations and commanding officers in the prisons regularly reminded doctors how little control they had over their circumstances. Some found the resolve and stamina to prevent harm to prisoners. The largest number, however, clung to their wartime loyalties and accommodated themselves to the prisons with only muted grumbling.

A sense of powerlessness contributed to the jaundiced attitude of prison medical staff. Scrupulous doctors were subject to prison protocols that emphasized efficiency and economy. Medical staff struggled against constraints beyond their control and enjoyed little power relative to the camps' military officers. Earnest doctors inveighed against prison overcrowding and persistent shortages of personnel and supplies but to little effect. Meanwhile, their commanding officers refused their requests and ignored their complaints. After encountering repeated frustrations, prison doctors on both sides could be excused for concluding that the health of prisoners was not a priority for their superiors.

Eugene Sanger in Elmira reached such a conclusion after butting his head repeatedly against what he called the "red-tapeism" of the Union military bureaucracy. Within a week of assuming his duties at Elmira, the surgeon was pestering his superiors to do something about a one-acre pond situated in the midst of the camp. Before the establishment of the camp, the pond had been used as a latrine and general garbage dump by Union soldiers in training. Sanger predicted that the contaminated lagoon would breed diarrhea, dysentery, and cholera. In nearly a dozen subsequent letters and reports, he continued to warn of these dangers but the pond remained "green with putrescence" while he awaited approval of his remedy. His warning proved prescient. Among Union camps nowhere was diarrheal illness as acute as at Elmira, where it killed twice as many Confederates as it did at other similarly sized Union prisons and had a higher fatality rate there than at any other northern facility. Not until late October 1864 did

Colonel Hoffman approve a plan to flush the pond with water from a nearby river and not until early January 1865 was the plan completed. By then the body of stagnant water was believed to have contributed to thousands of cases of chronic diarrhea and hundreds of deaths among the prisoners.

Isaiah White, the chief surgeon at Andersonville, confronted similar frustrations during the summer of 1864, when he attempted to cut through the bureaucratic obstacles that contributed to chronic shortages of medicines and other necessities. Regulations, for instance, required that hospital requisitions be sent to Atlanta before any supplies would be delivered from Macon. Lengthy delays inevitably occurred as the requests and approvals meandered through official channels. Even when requisitions were approved, the quantities of supplies sent were seldom adequate. White's pleas to the Confederate surgeon general in Richmond were dismissed or ignored, leaving White and his skeleton staff at Andersonville to their own devices.

Even as their pleas went unanswered, prison medical staff were subject to periodic scrutiny from camp inspectors. These investigators displayed varying degrees of urgency and competence in conducting their oversight.

Ambitious for glory, Eugene Sanger was the head surgeon at Elmira prison. (Maine State Archives)

Some submitted pro forma reports that did little more than fulfill a bureaucratic imperative to endorse efficiency and compliance with regulations. Other inspectors, such as the Union doctors outraged by the careless and cavalier transfer of ill Confederate prisoners from Elmira to Baltimore, displayed surprising rigor and candor. Likewise, the smallpox epidemic at the Rock Island prison during 1864 prompted a withering inspection report from a surgeon dispatched by Colonel Hoffman to assess the crisis. Charging "gross neglect of duty," the inspector fingered individual prison staff for censure.

The assessment of an inspector sent to Andersonville in September 1864 was even harsher. With orders from the inspector general's office in Richmond to report on conditions in the prison, Lieutenant Colonel Daniel Chandler toured the stockade before writing a scathing indictment of medical care at Andersonville, citing limited facilities and a shortage of commissioned surgeons. The "absence of all regularity in the prison grounds" made adequate hygiene in the camp impossible. "The sanitary condition of the prisoners is as wretched as can be." He condemned the daily conduct of the sick call in the camp as inhumane. So too, he contended, was the failure of camp authorities to supply either adequate rations or housing.

In this and many other instances, ranking authorities either ignored or watered down the charges and recommendations of prison inspectors. The medical inspector's report at Rock Island hastened some improvements at the prison. But the complaints regarding the transfer of prisoners from the Elmira camp had no lasting impact. Colonel Hoffman urged Secretary of War Stanton to dismiss both the camp surgeon and the camp commandant, but both retained their positions. Perhaps Stanton was distracted by the press of other business. Or perhaps, with an eye to "military necessity," he deemed it unwise to censure or dismiss surgeons when the demand for medical staff was acute. Or maybe he considered the prisoners' deaths as inconsequential. Whatever the case, Sanger, the camp surgeon, secured a long-sought transfer from Elmira in December 1864 and rose to the rank of lieutenant colonel before he completed his service the following year. After the war, he bore no stigma and he finally sated his thirst for recognition when he became one of the preeminent physicians in New England.

Chandler's report on Andersonville accomplished nothing beyond sparking a minor controversy within the corridors of the Confederate capital. General Winder responded furiously, defaming Chandler as unprofessional and insubordinate while dismissing his charges as unfounded. Instead of censuring Winder, authorities in Richmond expanded his portfolio and appointed him commissioner of Confederate prisons in November 1864.

Prison doctors had even less to fear from the scrutiny of independent observers, or what we now label nongovernmental organizations. On occasion, especially during the 1864 political campaign season, a few editors of northern Democratic newspapers expressed outrage about the medical care provided to Confederate prisoners in Union prisons. J. B. Danforth of the *Rock Island Argus*, for instance, accused prison authorities at Rock Island of the "deliberate torture and death" of Confederates held there. But his diatribes were so blatantly partisan that they aroused little public comment outside of Democratic circles. Newspapers friendly to the Union cause, in contrast, countered with glowing testimonials by enemy prisoners. The *Hammond Hospital Gazette*, a newspaper published at the Point Lookout hospital, remained silent about the medical care in the prison camp just beyond the hospital grounds, while attesting to the boundless charity that hospitalized Confederates received.

No independent body conscientiously surveilled doctors and their treatment of prisoners of war. In subsequent conflicts the International Red Cross undertook the task and by World War I, it was compiling and publicizing allegations of inhumane treatment of prisoners by all sides.

To a degree, however, during the first two years of the Civil War, the Sanitary Commission anticipated the role subsequently filled by the Red Cross. Founded by a cadre of prominent Union reformers and "men of influence," the commission mobilized to prevent public health and medical calamities like those that had decimated European forces during the Crimean War. Appalled by the "slovenliness" and disorganization that plagued the early mobilization in the North, the commissioners set out to impose order, efficiency, and "system" wherever and whenever possible in the Union war machine. The commission's first public announcement proclaimed baldly, "We cannot afford to waste life." It pledged to defer only to expertise while ignoring parochial allegiances or hidebound traditions. (The Confederacy had no counterpart to the commission; instead, southern communities organized disjointed campaigns to support their troops.) By bringing to bear modern scientific and management methods, the commission vowed that the Union's mobilization would be intelligent, orderly, and efficient.

Prisoners of war were never the primary focus of the Sanitary Commission. Instead, concern for prisoners of war evolved out of its practice of dispatching physician inspectors to survey the healthfulness and organization of military encampments. Of special interest to the organization was the construction of purpose-built military hospitals and adoption of up-to-date measures to prevent and treat diseases among the troops. Above all, assuring basic creature comforts to Union soldiers in the field preoccupied the commission.

Anxious about the public health hazards that many Union prison camps had become, the commission began in 1862 to direct its attention to prison pens. Touting its devotion to the principles of Christian charity, it displayed interest in the welfare of Confederate prisoners. At the same time, the commission undertook campaigns to provide clothing and other essentials to Union soldiers imprisoned in the Confederacy.

From the outset, the Sanitary Commission was viewed with suspicion by Union officials. President Lincoln groused that it was certain to be a "fifth wheel" to the coach of the Union. A brittle and sometimes adversarial relationship developed between the commission and the administration. For Colonel Hoffman and Union prison commandants, the commission's interest in prison affairs was irksome. Prison officials could not blithely ignore the commission's counsel without risking controversy with an organization that wielded considerable influence across the North and performed important services for all Union soldiers, including Union prisoners. Consequently, during 1862 and 1863, Union officials at the very least made gestures of deference to the commission and its experts. Although Hoffman must have gnashed his teeth when he received unsolicited reports on Union prisons, he nevertheless forwarded them to prison commandants and ordered them to consider whatever measures their resources and budgets would allow.

To the relief of Union authorities, the Sanitary Commission proved to be too invested in Union victory to persevere in its impartial humanitarianism. By 1864 any previous concern for the fate of Confederate prisoners gave way to full-throated denunciations of the Confederacy for profligate war crimes. Outrage over the condition of the former Union prisoners who had been granted medical exchanges during the spring and summer of 1864 hastened the commission's marked shift. When scores of filthy, louse-ridden, nearly naked, and alarmingly skeletal former prisoners began arriving at Union lines, the commission inspectors who greeted them were horrified. So widespread and acute were the scenes of suffering among former prisoners that in May 1864 the commission established a committee to assess the culpability of Confederate authorities.

The Sanitary Commission avowed its impartiality and freedom from political "prejudices" even as the controversy surrounding general prisoner

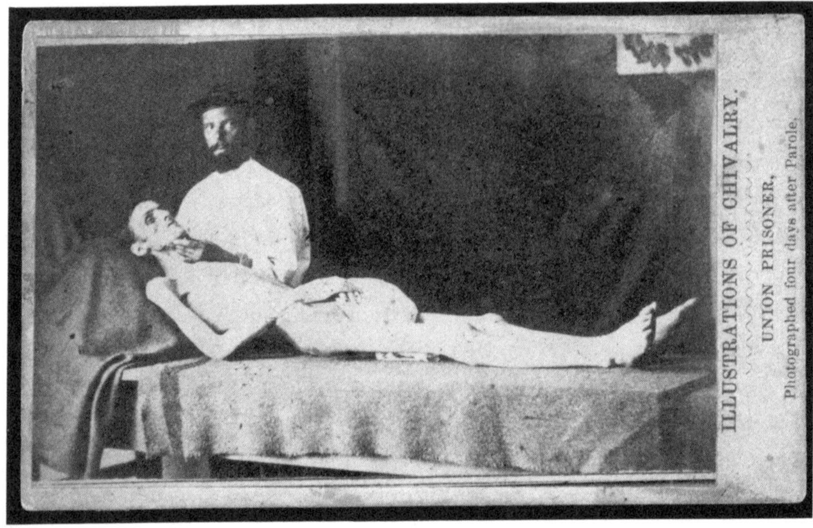


This image of an unidentified emaciated former prisoner of war from the Belle Isle camp fed mounting demands in the North for a resumption of prisoner exchanges. (Library of Congress)

exchanges intensified. In its report, which was published and widely circulated in September 1864, the commission stressed that its investigation had been conducted by "professionally competent" experts who could "read the unerring testimony of nature in the physical condition of the men."

For all the testimonials to its impartiality, the committee drew a Manichaean contrast between Union and Confederate prisoner-of-war camps. The Confederate camps were excoriated; Union prisons extolled. After cataloging the egregious failings of Confederate prisons, the commission's report vouched that Confederate prisoners received every "consideration and kindness that could be expected of a humane and Christian people." Imprisoned Confederates were "contented and cheerful." Their rations were so "generous and abundant" that, the commission avowed, they were equal to the fare served at leading hotels and resorts. So too, medical care in Union prisons was compassionate and meticulous. The only restraints that Confederate prisoners endured were those necessary to police men with "gross and filthy habits." Meanwhile, the report concluded that Confederate authorities "designedly inflicted" outrageous "privations and sufferings" upon Union prisoners. The Sanitary Commission dismissed any defenses that might absolve Confederate officials of their responsibility for the mistreatment of Union prisoners.

The report did not exaggerate the suffering of Union prisoners, which were grievous, but it grossly misrepresented the conditions experienced by Confederate prisoners. Every hardship in Confederate camps was an intentional act of malice, whereas any shortcoming in the treatment of prisoners in northern camps was inadvertent. So suffused with righteousness was the Union cause that northern patriots dismissed as trivial any infractions at Camp Chase, Point Lookout, Elmira, and elsewhere. Commission members interpreted the evidence before their eyes in accordance with their wartime loyalties.

Within the files of the commission itself were numerous reports of prison-camp inspections that itemized the failings of Union prison facilities. The commission's report was similarly silent regarding the routine dehumanization of Confederate prisoners while in transit to and from prisons in the North. The juxtaposition of the Union's alleged exemplary benevolence and the Confederacy's disgraceful inhumanity amplified the report's conclusion that the Confederates pursued a deliberate policy to exterminate Union prisoners. Contemporaries could be excused for interpreting the report as a tacit endorsement of the Lincoln administration's policies regarding prisoners of war.

In the absence of consistent and principled oversight, each prison doctor in effect had to chart his own course, tethered only by his conscience and whatever notion of professional ethics he embraced. Neither warring side had a meaningful code of conduct to guide doctors in uniform. Professional medical ethics were in their infancy and were not a focus of what little education most war-era doctors had received. Indeed, many practicing physicians had never taken a professional oath. Even the American Medical Association, then a fledgling organization that advocated a nascent professional esprit de corps among its membership, acknowledged that the only "tribunal" to determine a physician's responsibilities was his own conscience.

Military doctors, especially those working in prison camps, had to harmonize their responsibilities as soldiers and doctors. When conducting triage on the battlefield or within prison stockades, physicians had to balance the medical needs of the wounded and ill with wartime circumstances and military objectives. Predictably, military necessity often superseded concern for enemy patients' well-being and dignity.

How doctors calibrated their moral and ethical responsibilities when dealing with prisoners is only occasionally glimpsed. While captive officers and soldiers filled letters, diaries, and, later, memoirs with reflections on their prison experiences, few prison doctors did so. Most confined their comments on the camps to official channels, otherwise remaining stubbornly mute about the scenes they witnessed.

For Eugene Sanger, professional ambition trumped all else, hardening him to the casual dehumanization of prisoners. Compassion was not one of the many virtues that Sanger boasted he possessed. In July 1864, after two years of service mainly along the Gulf Coast, Sanger reported to the newly established prison camp in Elmira, where he became the chief surgeon. Sanger quickly earned the contempt of the prisoners, including Anthony Keiley, who described him "as a club footed little gentleman, with an abnormal head and a snaky look in his eyes." Vain, ambitious, and quarrelsome, Sanger had spent the previous three years of the war nursing grievances and lamenting the failure of his superiors to acknowledge his many triumphs. In October 1864, in a letter angling for a transfer and promotion, Sanger boasted that he had responsibility for the medical care of ten thousand prisoners at Elmira, "a very worthy occupation for a patriot." With a nod to the prison's rapidly rising mortality rate, he added, whether in jest or in earnest, "I think I have done my duty having relieved 386 of them [prisoners] of all earthly sorrow in one month."

Confederate surgeon John Howell lost whatever capacity he had for compassion after his arrival at Andersonville. Born and raised in a nearby county, he enlisted as a surgeon in the Confederate army in April 1862 and joined the prison's staff in July 1864. When he was assigned to the camp, he felt acutely his separation from his wife and the interruption of his career as a physician. His initial response to the conditions in the prison was horror. In a letter to his wife, he described the dilapidated facilities and the shocking appearance of "sick and emaciated, naked, ragged and dirty" prisoners. He saw "awful cases of gangrene" and other conditions but conceded that he could "give you no idea" of the "sufferings like these." He observed, "In comparison an ordinary death is pleasant to contemplate."

Within weeks Howell subdued any disquiet he felt and thereafter displayed little sympathy for the prisoners who surrounded him. His professional responsibilities did not weigh heavily on him; they were dreary but neither challenging nor taxing. Each day he selected for admission to the camp hospital the sickest prisoners from those gathered inside the prison gate. This tedious chore was lightened by his clerk, a Union prisoner, who maintained the relevant documents and recorded any prescriptions Howell ordered. "I am usually engaged from 8 to 12," he explained to his wife, but was routinely free of all duties on days when the hospital was full or when no medicines were on hand (which was commonplace).

That hundreds and hundreds of sick received medical care in name only during Howell's extended daily leisure while he conducted "his own affairs"—reading, eating, letter writing, and socializing—did not weigh on his conscience. In answer to his wife's query about the number of prisoners in the stockade, he estimated about thirty thousand. But he observed with no evident regret that "we bury about a thousand" every ten days, so "it would take but a short time (comparatively) to bury the whole of them." He sympathized with a doctor colleague who, having discovered lice crawling on his body, blamed the prisoners for his plight and vowed that he would "physic no more Yankees." Howell even found humor in a downpour of biblical intensity that lashed the camp, collapsed a portion of the stockade, and drowned a few prisoners in their earthen shebangs. His only lament was that his wife could not see the comically sodden and, for once, clean prisoners.

Joseph Jones, like other conscientious doctors, felt the tug of professional and moral responsibility for prisoners. Jones's hard-earned member-

Despite his close study of the Andersonville camp, Joseph Jones remained an unrepentant Confederate for the remainder of his life. (Tulane University Archives)

ship in the international community of scientists was keenly important to him. He was a graduate of the University of Pennsylvania medical school and a former professor of medicine. Ambitious, cocky, and eager for acclaim, he nurtured a national reputation as an expert on southern diseases and a surgeon of "fine acquirements."

His scientific rigor, of which he was inordinately proud, compelled him to acknowledge the inadequacies of Andersonville. During his brief tenure at the camp, he saw what prison doctors there observed daily—the ruinous impact of camp conditions on prisoners. His description of the prison in his report was as frank and damning as any in the diaries of prisoners themselves. Those who read it could have had no delusions about the conditions at Andersonville.

Yet, having looked into the abyss and seen the horrors at Andersonville, Jones refused to impugn the cause he served. An early champion of "southern independence" and a zealous Confederate to the war's end and beyond, he had violent contempt for the Union cause; any pity he felt for the denizens of the prison pens was tempered by that contempt. He never questioned his duties as a Confederate soldier and readily accepted the necessity of prisoner-of-war camps. He absolved the Confederacy of responsibility for Andersonville while blaming the Union for the hardships imposed on all prisoners, be they Union or Confederate.

Any personal discomfort that surfaced in his report on the medical conditions at Andersonville was contained and, ultimately, inert. He did not lobby for improvements at the camp. Nor did he draw public attention to the prison's shortcomings. Only after the existence of his report on Andersonville was publicized during the postwar trial of Captain Henry Wirz, the camp warden, did Jones publish it. When he grudgingly did so, he took pains to mitigate his own conclusions about the origins of the conditions in the camp. The priority Jones placed on restricting the dissemination of his damning report was a testament to his own conviction that his duty as a Confederate soldier came first.

---

Whether the care captives received was attentive or indifferent, competent or inept was the equivalent of a grim lottery. Even at Andersonville, luck might place a prisoner in the hands of a resolute doctor. George Hegeman had no doubt that the attentions of a Confederate surgeon at Andersonville in June 1864 prevented his death from smallpox. Weeks after he was admitted to the prison hospital, he regained enough strength to scrawl in his diary that his doctor was "one among a thousand." But fortune might place a prisoner at the mercy of a bungling or callous surgeon like the Elmira doctor whom James Huffman overheard boasting that he had "killed more Rebs than any soldier at the front."

Few if any prison doctors were prepared for the circumstances they confronted within the camps. They quickly learned that prison medicine was not the same as civilian medicine. Most lacked any relevant training and few had experience providing care in the aggregate. As prewar physicians they had been responsible to individual patients; as prison doctors they practiced their medicine on thousands of men. No training could have prepared doctors for the extent of sickness and misery that prevailed at Belle Isle, Andersonville, and Salisbury. Nor could they look to professional tradition for guidance while maintaining large numbers of prisoners of war over extended periods. Just as the camps were unprecedented, so too were the challenges that prison doctors confronted. That many doctors struggled to chart a path in these circumstances was predictable.

Not until the early twentieth century did the U.S. army begin to clarify the responsibilities of military physicians. When the army did so, military considerations took precedence over health concerns. Military doctrine affirmed that the aim of military medical care was the "preservation of the strength of the Army in the field." The care of individual soldiers was subsumed within the larger objective of maintaining "unit strength," of fielding the largest war machine. Lower yet in priority was the welfare of wounded enemy soldiers and prisoners. The principal handbook for military medical staff explained that medical officers must promote the troops' welfare "by collective general measures" and recognized that "this subordination of a patient's interests is shocking to humanitarian and professional instincts and sympathies, but it is inevitable in the stern activities of war." A half century earlier, in the absence of any formal mandate, Joseph Jones and many of his prison-camp medical peers had already countenanced the subordination of humanitarian and professional sympathies to the "stern activities of war."

CHAPTER ELEVEN

# The Winter of Desolation

## (1864–1865)

Calamity stalked Chester Berry. Even before he suffered through the death throes of the Confederacy, he endured exceptional hardships. In 1862, a few weeks after turning eighteen, he enlisted in the Twentieth Michigan Infantry. His regiment was hustled east to join the Army of the Potomac. He soon was struck down by typhoid fever but recovered in time to join the Fredericksburg campaign. His regiment was then transferred to Kentucky for a brief spell, before joining the siege of Vicksburg. Next, they were shuttled to Tennessee, where they bolstered the army marching against Knoxville. The following spring Berry and his unit were transferred back east to join the Army of the Potomac during its grim advance on Richmond. Then, in June 1864, he was taken prisoner at Cold Harbor.

Berry was dispatched south to Andersonville, where he spent three months coping with the miserable conditions in the camp. In September, he and most of the prisoners at Andersonville were, as one Confederate officer put it, "squandered in every direction" to other hastily created prison camps.

During the next three months Berry spent time in four different camps in Georgia. He was transferred to Millen, a prison near a village of the same name. From there, he was sent south to Blackshear, a poor, mean hamlet of three hundred inhabitants that unspooled along railroad tracks. He spent several weeks there, huddled in the woods under guard. Next, he and several thousand prisoners were loaded onto railcars and sent west to Thomasville. They again languished in the open for several weeks before they were

Chester Berry, a latter-day Odysseus, survived not only an extraordinarily arduous captivity at Andersonville but also the explosion of the steamboat *Sultana*. (From Chester Berry, *Loss of the Sultana*, 1892).

marched sixty miles overland to Albany. Their trek concluded after Berry and his compatriots boarded boxcars destined for Andersonville. Late on Christmas Eve 1864, they reentered the stockade they had left months earlier.

Berry's odyssey was not over. With the resumption of general prisoner exchanges in late February 1865, he and other prisoners at Andersonville deemed healthy enough to survive transit were shipped by boxcar to Montgomery, then steamboat to Selma, and finally railcars to Jackson, the closest railhead to the exchange site in Mississippi. At the end of their six-day journey, they were marched west about forty miles to their destination. During ten months as a Confederate prisoner, Berry had traveled by train, steamboat, and foot nearly two thousand miles—the distance from Boston to Salt Lake City.

After months of enforced privation, he awaited the rations and creature comforts of the exchange camp with sublime anticipation. He later recalled that he had "never experienced a happier day in my life" than when, as a free man, he tasted his first cup of coffee and gnawed on hardtack. Miffed by the stingy rations that he received, Berry thought better of them when he heard that the first prisoners to arrive at the camp had gorged themselves and, as a result, "there was a number of deaths before night."

Berry lingered in the camp for three weeks until he secured passage on a northbound steamboat departing from Vicksburg. With two thousand other former prisoners, he squeezed onto the riverboat, which had been built to accommodate fewer than four hundred passengers. Such overcrowding was a minor inconvenience to men recently liberated from the prison pens of Andersonville and Cahaba. To the steamboat operators, the masses of impatient ex-prisoners clamoring to return north represented a bonanza of easy profit. The grossly overloaded vessel, the *Sultana*, took two days to churn its way up the swollen Mississippi River to Memphis where, on the morning of April 21, its boiler exploded. The blast hurled Berry into the water and sparked a conflagration that quickly consumed the boat. Although suffering from a shattered skull that tormented him for the remainder of his life, Berry managed to drift to the shore. Already a survivor of the war's most notorious prison pen, Berry was now a survivor of the war's worst maritime disaster, which claimed the lives of as many as fifteen hundred passengers.

Berry's ordeal, at least prior to the catastrophe on the *Sultana*, was typical of prisoners in Confederate prisons during the last six months of the war. Having previously concentrated the suffering of prisoners in a few prison pens, Confederate authorities during the final months of the conflict dispersed their Union charges pell-mell to camps that were as deficient and primitive as Andersonville. Meanwhile, the conditions at the older camps, especially at Salisbury and Danville, deteriorated yet further.

The hardships in Union prisons paled by comparison. But Confederate prisoners took little solace in their fortune as the Union policy of retaliation continued to bear down on them. Their eventual release from Union prisons was unduly helter-skelter. Indeed, Union and Confederate prisons closed in much the same fashion—fitfully and with little regard for the prisoners themselves.

The impact of General William Sherman's invasion of Georgia on the Confederate prison system was lasting and irreversible. Between December 1863 and September 1864, Confederate General William Winder had orchestrated the consolidation of most Union prisoners of war in the eastern theater at Danville, Salisbury, Cahaba, and especially Andersonville. However disastrous for the prisoners, this expedient policy had been more systematic than any previous scheme to deal with Union prisoners. Sherman's advance across Georgia, as inexorable as flowing lava, upended virtually everything.

Fearful that Sherman might send forces south to liberate the thirty thousand prisoners of war at Andersonville, who might then avenge themselves on helpless civilians, Secretary of War James Seddon and General Winder concluded that removing the prisoners from Sherman's path took precedence over all other considerations. As they had repeatedly done in the past, they sped prisoners to new facilities before they had been readied. At Savannah and Charleston, the first destinations selected for many relocated prisoners, commanding officers vented exasperation and desperation when notified of the impending prisoner transfers. General Lafayette McLaws in Savannah warned that he lacked manpower to secure the prisoners and necessities to accommodate them. He protested, "I cannot keep them." His entreaties were ignored.

In Savannah, a hastily mustered force of impressed slaves erected a crude stockade on the grounds of the city jail. Work began on the afternoon of September 8 and by the following evening enough of the stockade was completed to secure the several thousand prisoners who were already on hand. Within a week the prison held about six thousand men, while another nearby stockade confined three thousand Union officers who had been transferred from Macon.

Charleston began receiving more than three thousand prisoners from Andersonville on September 12. Authorities there, who had had no time to prepare for their inundation, hustled the prisoners to the grounds of the city's race course. Foreshadowing prisons to come, the impromptu camp was an open field. Confederates plowed a furrow around the perimeter of the field to demarcate a dead line beyond which prisoners were forbidden. Nonplussed, prisoner Samuel Gibson observed, "We are not in any prison, but simply under guard."

Charleston and Savannah were never viable long-term prison sites. Neither city possessed a large facility suitable to hold prisoners, and both were under direct threat from Union forces. Heightening the anxieties of local authorities was the prospect that Union prisoners would unleash disease on their hosts. The arrival of the prisoners in Charleston coincided with outbreaks of smallpox and yellow fever. Consequently, three weeks later, the relocated prisoners were escorted to a new camp in Florence, about ninety miles north of the port city. The Savannah stockades began to be emptied of prisoners during the second week of October, and within days all but the sickest prisoners had been dispatched to the new camp at Millen, about seventy miles northwest. Meanwhile, the Union officers transferred to Savannah were reposted to Columbia, South Carolina.

The prison camp at Millen, less often referred to as Camp Lawton, had been planned as a replacement for Andersonville. In late July, when Andersonville's population neared its peak and conditions there had reached their nadir, General Winder had hastened two subalterns to identify a new prison site somewhere in eastern Georgia. By August 5 they selected a spot along the Augusta Railroad near Millen. Within days, the general was imploring speedy completion of the new camp. He ordered the impressment of slaves, wagon teams, and materials in the new prison's environs. Scores of Union prisoners were recruited in the Savannah prison camps to augment the hundreds of slaves at work on the site.

The layout of the new camp confirmed that General Winder had lost none of his enthusiasm for concentrating as many prisoners as possible into one facility. In basic design, the new prison was a facsimile of Andersonville. Winder boasted that, when completed, the camp would be "the largest prison in the world." Its dimensions were staggering. Its stockade was roughly a quarter mile square and enclosed the equivalent of thirty football fields. Here, Winder vouched, the Confederacy could house forty thousand prisoners securely, efficiently, and cheaply.

Discounting the challenges inherent in such a massive undertaking, Winder forecast that the prison would be ready to receive prisoners within a month of breaking ground. But more than four thousand trees had to be felled to form the nearly one mile of stockade walls. Then each twenty-foot log had to be stood upright, side by side, in a five-foot trench in the ground. Beyond this colossal task, Winder's plan envisioned a profusion of buildings to house the camp's administrators, doctors, and guards.

Not until October 8 was the Millen stockade completed. Cooking and hospital facilities had yet to be erected. Nevertheless, Richmond officials asked with evident impatience, "Cannot part [of the camp] at once be prepared before the completion of the whole prison grounds?" Beginning on October 11, trainload after trainload of prisoners began arriving. Within weeks the camp confined more than twelve thousand prisoners.

The opening of the camps in Columbia and Florence were even more chaotic. Flummoxed Confederate authorities in Columbia, who had no facility suitable to hold the incoming Union officers, corralled them on a four-acre field a few miles west of the city's downtown. A fragmentary border of small branches laid on the ground marked the camp's dead line. Aside from scrub pine that cluttered the site, prisoner John Hadley found it utterly desolate: "there was no stockade, no fence, no water but from a brook, no shelter not even for the sick." To the extent that Confederates subsequently improved the site, they did so with an eye to security. While nothing was done "inside" the camp itself, the brush around the perimeter was cleared and replaced by lines of guards and well-positioned artillery.

The camp at Florence was created almost overnight without any meaningful planning. A village of about a hundred inhabitants at the start of the war, Florence had only one evident advantage: it was adjacent to several important rail lines that had yet to be disrupted by Sherman's advance. Otherwise, an unfriendly visitor to the town described it as a "name rather than a place" and little more than a "railroad eating-house with sleeping-rooms attached."

On September 14, three days after a Confederate officer scouted the Florence site, the first prisoners began tumbling out of railcars there. For two weeks the prisoners hunkered in an open field surrounded by a line of guards, another line of pickets, and a few artillery pieces. Prisoners detained within the field watched while impressed slaves gradually erected the crude log wall that, by October 2, enclosed their twenty-three-acre world.

Prisoners were cautiously optimistic that their hardships would ease in the new camps. Few envisioned that conditions could be worse than they had been at Andersonville. Instead of the squalor at Andersonville, prisoners found themselves on virgin ground as yet unsoiled by a crush of prisoners. Giddy with relief, Sergeant Francis J. Hosmer judged the Savannah prison to be "fairly wholesome." Private Henry H. Adam of the Sixteenth Connecticut felt similarly about Florence, which he labeled "a very pleasant place." At Millen, John Ransom enthused that he had finally landed in "a pleasant and healthy location." A day later, he reported that "everyone is pleased with this place and are cheerful."

These favorable impressions proved fleeting. The new camps lacked the concentrated misery of Andersonville but were in other regards as bad or worse. The officers herded onto the field in Columbia soon mockingly christened it "Camp Sorghum," in honor of the unappetizing grain that made up their rations. The camp in Millen elicited déjà vu in John McElroy; "this looks like Andersonville all over again," he groused. Two days after Henry Adam described the Florence camp as "very pleasant," he scrawled with emphasis in his diary, "we do not *get enough to eat*." (Five days later he died.)

Prisoners did not have long to enjoy whatever comparative virtues the new camps possessed. Confederates emptied Camp Sorghum in December, displacing the prisoners to a new site in Columbia or to the prison at Salisbury. Millen—the apotheosis of Winder's carceral vision—operated for barely six weeks. On November 19, as Sherman's army pressed east from Atlanta, Confederate General William Hardee ordered prisoners evacuated to Savannah. On November 22, the last prisoners boarded railcars heading south. Days later, advancing Union troops reached the camp, the first major Confederate prison facility to fall to them.

The abandoned prison at Millen stirred strong emotions among those who toured it. Accompanying the Union troops who entered the site was George N. Bernard, an official army photographer. Unable to photograph the prison, he recorded his impressions in his journal. He marveled at the immense stockade, surveyed the prisoners' deserted shebangs, and glimpsed the corpses of unburied prisoners on the litter-strewn grounds. Reflecting on the experience, Bernard remarked that he had harbored grave reservations about the Union army's destruction of civilian property. But after what he observed in the Millen pen, he confessed, "I shall not be much troubled by it." For Sergeant Rice C. Bull and his comrades in the 123rd New York, witnessing the camp provoked them to meditate on their preferred fate should they ever face capture. Many vowed never to surrender, as they would rather "be shot than put in such a place." As if to expunge the possibility itself, Union soldiers razed the site before continuing their push toward Savannah.

Having abandoned the prison at Millen, Confederates again faced the dilemma of relocating prisoners. With Savannah and Charleston having already proven unsuitable, authorities hastened roughly seven thousand prisoners north to Florence and the remaining five thousand south to Blackshear, Georgia. So nondescript was Blackshear that prisoner John Ransom concluded that "a barn and a hen-coop comprise the place." It was wholly unsuited to accommodating thousands of prisoners and so isolated that Ransom surrendered hope that "the Yankee army would ever find us here." The camp, which was a mere clearing in a pine forest, was a prison in name only.

Colonel Henry Forno, the officer responsible for the prisoners in Blackshear, must have been at his wit's end. How were he and a small guard force to secure the prisoners while careening around south Georgia? The eventual disposition of his prisoners, moreover, had yet to be settled. Only two days after moving prisoners to Blackshear, Forno had to send about one thousand north to the prison in Florence. In urgent need of a secure site, he sent another sixteen hundred prisoners by rail to Thomasville in the southwestern corner of the state, where he made plans to build a new prison camp. By December 12 he had transferred all his prisoners to Thomasville. A week later, he marched his travel-weary prisoners to Albany, where they boarded trains to Andersonville.

Farther west in the Confederacy, conditions in Texas prison camps were equally chaotic and dire. Prior to 1864, Confederates accumulated only a few hundred Union captives in Texas. By June 1863, the collapse of general exchanges left Confederates scrambling to find a secure prison site. Several hundred prisoners were corralled at Camp Groce, a former training camp near Hempstead, Texas. The next month, Confederates began fashioning another prison, Camp Ford, near Tyler in east Texas. The new camp was as primitive as the camps that the Confederates would erect at Millen, Florence, and elsewhere to the east. Camp Ford initially was not enclosed by any stockade and prisoners had no tents or barracks. Prisoners quickly built shelters out of the one resource that was abundant: pine trees. An influx of about three thousand new prisoners in April 1864 swamped the camp's already inadequate facilities, reducing many new arrivals to burrow into the ground in search of shelter from the Texas heat. Confederate predictions that the surrounding countryside could provide ample provisions for the camp proved to be unfounded and prisoners complained of scant rations not fit to feed "a cur."

By the end of December 1864, previous plans to consolidate prisoners at an *uber*-prison were in tatters. Winder, nonetheless, remained resolute. He now proposed to build another camp eighteen miles north of Columbia, on the rail line to Charlotte. All the prisoners from Georgia and the Carolinas finally would be enclosed in a single camp. Yet again, events overtook Winder's scheme. Land for the new prison was secured, but by the time impressed slaves had erected the stockade, Sherman's troops were overrunning Columbia. Lying directly in the invaders' path, the unfinished prison was the last monument to Winder's command. And so, throughout the final months of the war in the eastern theater, Union prisoners remained scattered across the remnants of the Confederacy, from Alabama to Virginia.

These haphazard relocations created almost insurmountable challenges for Confederates. Maintaining communications proved to be a vexing chore for itinerant subordinates tasked with relocating prisoners. For six months starting in August 1864, General Winder himself wandered from camp to camp, from Andersonville to Macon to Millen and eventually to Florence. His migrations ended only in early February 1865, when he died of a massive heart attack while inspecting the prison at Florence. (The news of Winder's death provoked "great rejoicing" among prisoners in Florence and Columbia.)

Within the prisons, life was upended by the constant commotion of serial relocations. Already stretched prison staffs had to make preparations to relocate thousands of prisoners and then sufficient troops had to be scrounged to guard them while in transit. Upon arrival in the new camps, prison officers and guards had to restore some semblance of routine and order. The process then had to be repeated during the next migration.

Union prisoners in transit provided a grim and apparently unforgettable spectacle. While scuttling to keep out of the path of Sherman's army, Rebecca Latimer Felton and her patrician family passed cars laden with Andersonville prisoners. More than a half century later, she recalled scanning the faces of "those ragged, smoke begrimed, haggard and miserably filthy men." That evening, she reflected, "I became an eyewitness to their enforced degradation, filth and utter destitution."

This headlong dispersal of Union prisoners overtaxed the creaky Confederate rail system. Between scant rolling stock, decrepit equipment, and depleted fuel supplies, train schedules in the Confederacy were now willful flights of fancy rather than realistic forecasts. Prisoners spent days in slow motion, wedged in packed cars, overcome by the tang of their filthy comrades, rocked by the rhythm of the train, and numbed by the tedious clatter of steel wheels on tired rails and infirm roadbed. More hours drained away while prisoners waited for tardy locomotives or idled on side tracks. All too often, derailments compounded the ordeal of relocation. No accurate tallies of the number of prisoners who died in transit are extant, but prisoners' diaries and memoirs indicate that the toll was high.

Medical care in the new camps was as primitive as at Andersonville. At Millen, a corner of the interior of the stockade was set aside for triage of ill prisoners, but otherwise no shelter was provided. Outside the prison walls, a crude tent hospital served the deathly ill. At Florence the "hospital" was a rustic arbor infirmary made from boughs of trees. According to prisoner Charles Smedley, who "entered" it soon after reaching the camp, the hospital offered "poor protection, excepting from the sun." Eventually, crude sheds were erected. But neither beds nor cots were provided, so Smedley and the other sick prisoners were deposited on piles of pine needles.

For tens of thousands of Union prisoners, much of the fall of 1864 was consumed in fashioning shelter after shelter as they moved from camp to camp. No housing for the prisoners was erected at any of the new Confederate camps. Having learned by necessity, many prisoners were adept at improvising shelters. They transformed leftover sticks, branches, and stumps, or even what one prisoner described as the "offal of the stockade construction," into walls and roofs. At Millen, Samuel Gibson began collecting surplus wood to construct a temporary shelter soon after his arrival. Two weeks later, he set to work on more substantial quarters, "half cave & half tent." His work had only recently concluded when Confederates emptied the camp and Gibson faced the necessity of staking out another campsite and erecting yet another shelter.

Each relocation intensified the impoverishment of Union prisoners. By the end of the harried and haphazard dispersal of prisoners that last autumn of the war, few prisoners retained much of value beyond their clothes and, if they were fortunate, a blanket. Charles Smedley's estate when he reached Florence, for instance, included the clothes that he wore, a coat, a Bible, his diary, a small booklet of family photographs, a pocket knife, an improvised tool he used to carve bone trinkets, and a watch. He sold the brass buttons from his coat and then his pocket knife for a portion of sweet potatoes. When he died in November, his sole possession was his watch, a gift from his father, which he had refused to part with.

Relocation compounded the deadly uncertainty of prisoners' lives. At each new camp, prisoners had to learn a new camp etiquette. At Savannah, as at Andersonville, the dead line lay a few feet inside the stockade. Prisoners had long familiarity with dead line protocol in such circumstances. But at the Charleston race course, Blackshear, Camp Sorghum, and early on at Florence, no stockade existed. Ditches or small sticks on the ground served as a crude approximation of a dead line. Only by trial and error did prisoners learn whether Confederate guards would enforce an invisible dead line inside of the demarcated dead line. In such circumstances, potentially lethal boundaries were alarmingly indefinite, and dead line etiquette took on surreal qualities. At Blackshear, for instance, two stakes driven in the ground marked the "gate" in an imaginary stockade. Prisoners who had been granted permission to leave it to gather firewood were required to pass through the gate. On at least one occasion, a guard shot a prisoner who carelessly stepped across the imaginary dead line beside this gate.

With each relocation prisoners seized any occasion for flight that arose. Desperate prisoners concluded that the odds of surviving a prison escape were no worse than those of surviving in the camps. In the estimation of a Wisconsin prisoner named H. M. Davidson, the prospect of spending "another terrible winter" in an improvised prison camp made escape "simply a case of self-preservation." During hurried preparations to abandon camps, prisoners hid in hopes of being left behind. While in transit, they threw themselves off moving trains into rivers or down embankments. When trains stood idle on sidings, they sprinted off into woods and swamps. While marching on city streets to train stations or holding pens, they melted among the spectators and absconded.

Once installed in new camps, prisoners methodically probed the security arrangements. If they were allowed outside the stockades to collect firewood, some slunk off. Plenty became tireless tunnelers and burrowed their way to freedom. A few uncommonly brazen prisoners postured as hired hands or Confederate soldiers and bamboozled witless guards into setting them free. At those camps that lacked stockade walls, prisoners took advantage of darkness to creep across the dead line and scamper into the surrounding thickets. On other occasions prisoners shunned subtlety altogether. During the early days at Florence, more than four hundred prisoners bull-rushed the tiny guard force and scattered into the surrounding countryside.

By one estimate, nearly three thousand Union prisoners escaped during the last six months of the war. Once free, prisoners charted a course to Union lines. Those near the coast headed for waterways plied by Union naval vessels. In this fashion more than three hundred men managed to reach Union lines near Hilton Head, South Carolina. Other intrepid fugitives set out on overland routes to the Appalachian Mountains in hopes of reaching Union lines in Tennessee. They subsisted on the generosity of sympathetic enslaved Black people and white Unionists. Most escapees experienced only a few days of freedom before being seized again by Confederates. Recaptured prisoners seldom remained long in the camps before attempting another escape. Only a small fraction of the prisoners held in Confederate prisons escaped and reached Union lines, but Confederate civilians and soldiers were tormented by visions of avenging escapees marauding across the Confederacy's shrinking hinterland.

While the Confederate prison system was unraveling, the Union prison system was operating as efficiently as it ever would. Colonel Hoffman's challenges bore no resemblance to those faced by General Winder. The process of funneling captured Confederates to prisons in the North was predictable and routine. Aside from the scare prompted by General Jubal Early's northern foray in 1864, Confederate forces posed no threat to Union prisons. Hoffman discerned no pressing need to establish any major new camps after the opening of the Elmira prison in July 1864.

The operations of the Union camps had an altogether different appearance to Confederate prisoners. For them captivity was defined by privation and their captors' casual indifference to their circumstances. Such was the experience of Samuel Beckett Boyd, a thirty-six-year-old Confederate ordnance officer. On December 14, 1864, he was swept up during a Union raid in southwestern Virginia. The next day he began a circuitous 800-mile journey to Camp Chase in Ohio. He and two hundred other prisoners endured a six-day forced march to Knoxville, nearly 120 miles to the south. During the day they trudged through heavy rains while at night they huddled in the open. If his diary can be trusted, they received no rations. From Knoxville they were transferred by train to Chattanooga and, once there, to a holding pen. On January 5, he and about one hundred comrades boarded boxcars bound for Nashville. Sixty miles from their destination, the train jumped the tracks. They tarried for hours until the cars were restored to the tracks. Under way again, Boyd rode for the remainder of the trip on the roof of a car while a cold drenching rain froze his clothes to his body. In Nashville, he was forced to stand for hours in freezing rain before he and four hundred other prisoners were marched to the unsheltered grounds of the state penitentiary. Desperate for asylum from the elements, he noted sourly in his diary, "first time I ever desired to be in a penitentiary." Two days later, he and the others were rousted before dawn, only to shiver for hours in the cold before boarding northbound trains. Sixteen hours later, and after another train mishap, they reached Louisville. Boyd spent the next six days in a prison that, to his surprise and relief, offered small comforts. On January 14, he again climbed aboard a boxcar, this time en route to Columbus, Ohio. Much of his journey was spent in an open car in freezing weather during which he "suffered severely." The next day, a month after his capture, Boyd finally reached Camp Chase, where he would spend the remainder of the war.

During his monthlong transit, Boyd joined the more than thirteen thousand Confederate prisoners whom Union forces had amassed in Tennessee between September 1864 and January 1865, after a string of ruinous

Confederate prisoners in transit, Chattanooga, 1864. (Library of Congress)

Confederate defeats. In terse diary jottings, Boyd recorded the prevalence of sickness among his comrades, but, to his surprise, he avoided serious illness. He was better clad than most prisoners and his clothing, except for his boots, held up during his trek north. Many others, especially those captured on the battlefield, were not so fortunate. Few Union soldiers had encountered Confederate prisoners who were as fatigued, ragged, and, in the words of one appalled Union officer, "so filthy that we could smell them as plainly as a flock of sheep on a June day." By the same officer's estimate, more than a third were without shoes. None of the prisoners, including Boyd, were equipped for the rigors of the exceptionally harsh winter of 1865.

Union prison policies bore down especially on these recently captured prisoners, who were destitute and enfeebled before they entered the prison camps. Restrictions on the sale of foodstuffs by camp sutlers rendered new prisoners dependent on their prison rations, which had been reduced as part of the Union policy of retaliation. Prisoners at Rock Island, many of whom battled scurvy, complained that while they were allowed to purchase vegetables from the camp sutler, "so few prisoners have money that comparatively little benefit is derived from the privilege." The ban on packages from families to prisoners left them "entirely cut off from home supplies."

William Hoffman and other Union officials were apprised of the dire straits of these recent Confederate captives. On the same day that Boyd was transferred to Nashville, Colonel Hoffman was in the Tennessee capital, where he inspected the ranks of ragged Confederate prisoners. They were, he acknowledged, in a very destitute condition. Yet their circumstances prompted no change in policy to ameliorate their suffering. Simultaneously, mounting evidence of the destitution and suffering of prisoners of war in the Confederacy stiffened his and Secretary of War Edwin Stanton's resolve to maintain the retaliatory policies they had previously imposed.

Hoffman found a further pretext to ignore the desperate needs of prisoners in an elaborate scheme that the two sides initiated during the fall of 1864. Self-appointed Good Samaritans had periodically pressed Union and Confederate officials to ameliorate the plight of prisoners. Union General Daniel Sickles, for instance, entreated President Lincoln to refrain from retaliatory measures that had failed to moderate Confederate policy. Instead, the Union should propose to provide supplies for its soldiers in Confederate hands. Confederate officials had entertained a similar notion.

Such a scheme offered benefits to both warring slides. Each would unburden itself of some of the expense and responsibility of caring for prisoners of war. For the Confederacy, the proposition offered a cost-free solution to its inability to provide the essentials to Union prisoners. For the Union, the scheme would ease the suffering of Union prisoners without surrendering its demand that all prisoners, Black and white, be exchanged. Equally important, the scheme would rebut election-year accusations that the Lincoln administration was insensitive to the plight of Union prisoners. Between August and October, Robert Ould, the Confederate exchange agent, and Major John Mulford, a Union assistant agent of exchange, sketched the outlines of a quid pro quo arrangement. By the middle of November, the principals in the negotiations and their superiors, including General Ulysses S. Grant, Secretary of War Stanton, and Confederate General Robert E. Lee, had approved it.

The agreement, on its face, was straightforward. Each side would enjoy the privilege of supplying clothing and supplies to its soldiers held by the enemy. Neither side, however, would be relieved from the obligation to feed and clothe the prisoners it held. Henceforth, if prisoners suffered from want of essentials, their plight would no longer be the sole responsibility of their captors.

In practice, the agreement was devilishly complicated to implement. Back in late 1863, General Ethan Allen Hitchcock had been prescient when he dismissed a similar proposal as unworkable. A year later, he could muster no enthusiasm for the agreement but reluctantly conceded “the experiment might be tried.” Stockpiling supplies to send to Confederate prisons posed no challenges to Union officials. The distribution of the supplies entailed no major obstacles either. The Sanitary Commission already had experience distributing clothing to prisoners in Confederate prison camps. But few Union officials had confidence that when the supplies reached Confederate prisons, they would be distributed to the prisoners. General Hitchcock pointed out that previous attempts to distribute supplies to prisoners had been undercut by Confederate prison staff, who either absconded with the supplies or refused to allow their distribution. Moreover, supplies intended for prisoners inexorably ended up in the hands of their captors, because famished Union prisoners bartered anything that came into their possession for food.

Despite these concerns, the Sanitary Commission began shipping blankets and clothing southward. During November and December 1864, some prison diarists noted the diffusion of the blankets and clothing in their camps. At Florence, the supplies unquestionably mitigated the sufferings of some prisoners. At Andersonville, prisoners derived little benefit because the prison staff apparently hoarded the shipments. Even where the supplies were issued, they were seldom sufficient in quantity to aid more than a small portion of the prisoners.

Confederate prisoners derived even less benefit from the agreement. It seems inconceivable that Confederate officials failed to anticipate the obvious obstacles to the timely completion of the plan. The Confederacy lacked any philanthropy comparable to the Sanitary Commission to distribute supplies to Union prisons. To Confederate General William Beall fell the task of overseeing the execution of the arrangements. A prisoner at Johnson’s Island since his capture in 1863, he was paroled in early December 1864 to perform his stipulated duties. He opened an office in New York City, solicited bids for supplies from northern vendors, and began planning the eventual distribution of the supplies.

Until Confederate authorities raised funds to pay for the requested supplies, none of Beall’s hard work served any purpose. The Confederacy was destitute and neither its factories nor artisans had the wherewithal to produce supplies for prisoners. The quid pro quo agreement tacitly acknowledged this dilemma by allowing the proceeds from the sale of one thousand bales of Confederate cotton to be used for prisoner welfare. Beall was responsible for the sale of the cotton.

Winter weather, red tape, and sundry complications hindered Beall's endeavor at every step. The shipment of cotton from Mobile to New York was delayed. Some New Yorkers took umbrage at General Beall's operations in the city, prompting Secretary of War Stanton to revoke his parole and have him sequestered in prison again. When the cotton finally arrived, Beall regained his parole and negotiated its sale. The cotton, however, was of poor quality and sold for less than half the sum that Confederates had anticipated. Worse yet, Beall had to pay federal revenue taxes on the sale.

Not until early February 1865, three months after the agreement was finalized, did Confederate prisoners finally begin to receive supplies purchased with the cotton proceeds. Within a month, Beall had overseen twenty-six shipments to Union prisons. But through March and April Confederate officers who supervised the distribution of the supplies complained repeatedly of delayed or lost shipments. Because of the delays, the supplies began arriving in prisons simultaneously with the acceleration of general prisoner exchanges during the final two months of the war. Desperately needed blankets and clothes reached prisons after their ranks of prisoners had already been drastically reduced.

Colonel Hoffman, moreover, violated the spirit if not the terms of the agreement. He repeatedly used the agreement as an excuse to withhold supplies for Confederate prisoners. When he was alerted that thousands of prisoners bound north from Tennessee were in desperate need of blankets and clothing, he directed the commandant of Camp Chase to "not furnish them; the Confederacy will supply them." In early January, when describing the dire circumstances of prisoners in Nashville, Hoffman acknowledged they were "in much want of clothing." But he shirked the responsibility, instead advising that General Beall be notified of the prisoners' circumstances. "No clothing, including blankets shall be issued," he announced.

The quid pro quo scheme to provide clothing and supplies to prisoners was at best a stopgap measure until either prisoner exchanges resumed or the war ended. Throughout 1864 Union and Confederate negotiators continued to dicker over the same issues that had halted general exchanges since the previous year.

With a mixture of resignation and relief, Hitchcock relinquished responsibility for negotiating with Ould to General Benjamin Butler in December 1863. That Butler now assumed the duties of a "special exchange agent" was testament to how little confidence the Lincoln administration had in the prospects for successful negotiations. By appointing Butler, Secretary of War Stanton displayed his characteristic brinkmanship. He recognized that Butler was a popular Democratic politician-turned-general who avidly sought and usually attracted public interest. If he somehow successfully restored general prisoner exchanges in a manner consistent with Union policy, the administration could claim credit for his appointment and success. If he proved inept, Lincoln could hardly be faulted for his willingness to explore every option to revive exchanges. And if Confederate officials refused to negotiate with Butler, they, and not the Union, would bear the onus for the continuing impasse.

Stanton knew that no Union official or general was more offensive to Confederate sensibilities than Butler. During the first two years of the war, Butler had repeatedly outraged Confederates, especially with his heavy-handed administration of New Orleans following its capture in 1862. So reviled was Butler that the epithet "Beast" invariably accompanied his name in Confederate newspapers, and Confederate President Jefferson Davis had declared him a felon who, if captured, was to be executed.

Happenstance, rather than design, placed Butler at the nexus of the prisoner-of-war stalemate during 1864. After exhausting the patience of the Lincoln administration with his conduct in New Orleans, Butler had been exiled to the command of the Army of the James in the comparatively sedate military department of Tidewater Virginia and North Carolina. Although prisoners of war were not a major responsibility in this command, Butler did oversee both the prison at Point Lookout and the site for the exchange of prisoners in the eastern theater. Thus, even if Butler had shown no special interest in prisoners of war, he could not wholly ignore them.

Yet Butler did display interest, for reasons both sincere and opportunistic. Observers noted that his stout build, drooping eyelids, and watery eyes belied his brash and energetic nature. Notorious for his "talent for turbulence," he was, above all, self-aggrandizing. In his mind, if he restored prisoner exchanges, he would garner acclaim, burnish his tarnished reputation, and provide succor to Union prisoners. Generous observers judged his "ability to adapt himself to any circumstances" to be a virtue. A less charitable assessment described him as "a general without capacity, a man

During the last two years of the war, General Benjamin F. Butler tried unsuccessfully to restore general prisoner exchanges. (Library of Congress)

without character." Even his critics, of whom there were many, agreed that he was an adroit administrator and a cunning lawyer. And not all his principles were fungible. He was resolute that in all matters, Black soldiers and civilians should receive the same treatment and protection as whites. "No one will go farther in exerting every power of the Government in protecting the colored troops and their Officers than myself," Butler vowed.

In December 1863, Butler seized on an outbreak of smallpox among Union prisoners at Belle Isle prison in Richmond to initiate communications with Robert Ould. Butler sent sufficient "vaccine matter" to the Confederate capital to inoculate about six thousand individuals. Confederates accepted the vaccines but took umbrage at Butler's enterprise, interpreting it as a deliberate affront. Ould threatened not to cooperate with him, fuming to his longtime nemesis Hitchcock that "self-respect requires that the Confederate authorities should refuse to treat" with Butler.

In a canny gambit that defied Confederates to maintain their embargo on dealing with him, Butler informed Ould on Christmas Day 1863 that he had more than five hundred Confederate prisoners at hand awaiting exchange for an equal number of Union prisoners. As an emollient, he assured Ould of his earnest hope to avoid the contentious issues that had vexed previous negotiations regarding prisoners. Butler deliberately left the issue of Black prisoners to be determined in the future, while advocating the prompt restoration of exchanges until the Confederate prisons were emptied.

Butler's maneuvering confounded Confederate officials. As Butler anticipated, Ould could not rebuff this proposal. But the Confederate agent continued to refuse to negotiate with Butler and instead directed all correspondence to Butler's assistant. Meanwhile, the Confederate Cabinet was divided over whether to parley with "Beast" Butler. Richmond's newspapers were similarly split, with some dismissing him as a "negro and felon" while others judged him to be sincere.

Butler and Ould continued to circle each other from January to March 1864 before reaching a détente of sorts. They successfully negotiated several special exchanges of small numbers of officers, which they looked upon as auspicious gestures. By the end of March, Butler boasted to Stanton that he had secured the exchange of nearly one thousand enlisted men and more than sixty officers. He was, he forecast, on the verge of restoring routine prisoner exchanges.

Butler's optimism was unfounded. Having conciliated Ould on almost all points, Butler took up the issue of the exchange of Black prisoners. He had sought to box Confederates in by leaving them with only two options: either to surrender their refusal to exchange Black prisoners or to retain their stance and sabotage prospects for resumed exchanges. Butler had no grounds to conclude that Ould would surrender "the ditch" that he had vowed to defend at all costs—namely, his opposition to the exchange of former slaves in Union blue. Ould instead hoped that if he continued to hold the line against exchanging "recaptured slaves" and impeded Union efforts to confirm "any well-authenticated case of the retention of a negro prisoner," the Lincoln administration would cave on its demands.

Before Ould's intransigence could be exposed, General Grant brought Butler's maneuvering to a halt in April 1864. Grant, who was now the commander of all Union forces, knew from his experience after the fall of Vicksburg that Confederates would restore any exchanged prisoners to their army ranks as quickly as possible. Meanwhile, Confederates likely would return Union prisoners who were too emaciated and enfeebled to take up arms again. Grant was adamant that Confederate forces during the current campaign season not be augmented by exchanged prisoners. During a personal meeting with General Butler and in subsequent orders, Grant stressed that "at all hazards exchanges are to be halted" and that Butler was to "decline all further negotiations."

With no prospects for general exchanges, the only remaining course to end the ordeal of captivity was to conduct periodic special exchanges. On September 9 Butler made a proposition to Ould that balanced Grant's military concerns with humanitarian considerations. Butler invited the two sides to exchange "from time to time" sick and wounded prisoners who would likely remain unfit for duty for sixty days. Only those on death's door would be granted their freedom; the rest would be left to their fate in the camps. "I trust and believe," Butler wrote, "that this measure of obvious humanity will meet your agreement." Ould assented. Confederates were more than willing to send prisoners who were wracked by diarrhea, scurvy, and other illnesses that left them alive only because they were not yet dead.

In early November, Confederate and Union officials reached an agreement to exchange sick prisoners at Savannah, which would allow General Winder to empty the camps in Georgia and South Carolina of the sickest prisoners. Within days, ten Union ships were anchored near Savannah with more than three thousand sick and wounded Confederate prisoners. Simultaneously, Confederate doctors began selecting Union prisoners to be exchanged and stuffing them aboard trains to Savannah. On November 13 and 14, Union transports unloaded Confederate prisoners, and a few days later Confederates delivered prisoners from Millen to the waiting Union ships. Special exchanges also took place at Charleston. By the end of December, nearly eleven thousand sick and wounded Union prisoners had been exchanged at the two sites. A smaller number of just over eight thousand Union prisoners were exchanged on the James River in Virginia. Meanwhile, the Union turned over twenty thousand Confederate prisoners at the exchange site in Virginia.

For those men selected for these special exchanges, the combination of relief and exultation they experienced was overwhelming and beyond description. George Hitchcock, who had survived the summer at Andersonville and the fall at the Florence prison camp, had the good fortune to be exchanged in Charleston harbor on December 10. "Men shouted, cheered, laughed like idiots, cried like babies. Others danced, hugged each other and the whole was one scene of perfectly wild enthusiasm." Kendrick Howard, a soldier from Vermont, declared the occasion of his exchange "the happiest day of my life."

Released Union prisoners of war on board the USS *New York*, as depicted by William Waud, relished the opportunity to shed their prison rags. (Library of Congress)

These so-called medical exchanges relieved the suffering of some of the sickest prisoners. But prison-camp populations quickly swelled again as both sides captured new prisoners, including the more than thirteen thousand soldiers who had been in Confederate General John Bell Hood's army in Tennessee. Moreover, the dire condition of many of the exchanged Union prisoners intensified the urgency to resume general exchanges.

In January 1865, both sides softened their intransigence. On January 13, General Grant approved a proposal made by Ould four months earlier that both sides release all prisoners held in close confinement. Less than two weeks later, Ould made an offer to exchange all prisoners in Confederate hands, "man for man and officer for officer," for those held by the Union. The offer dealt with the problematic question of Black prisoners by adopting Butler's previous stratagem—ignoring it. On February 2 Grant informed Secretary of War Stanton that he was "endeavoring to make arrangements to exchange about 3000 prisoners per week." On the sixteenth Grant sent formal word that he accepted Ould's proposal.

By then Confederates were desperate to be relieved of the burden of feeding and guarding prisoners of war. Sherman's relentless advance through the Carolinas and the dire shortage of every essential supply convinced Winder that the best remaining course was the immediate parole of all Union prisoners. Any option that freed the Confederacy of its prisoners should be considered. Simultaneously, the Confederate Congress was in the final stages of adopting plans to enlist and arm Black soldiers. Having done so, the Confederacy could hardly treat Black men in Union uniforms as less than soldiers while it was preparing to field Black soldiers.

Grant meanwhile no longer had any military objections to exchanges. If carefully controlled, exchanges would not bolster the ranks of the shrinking Confederate army. He requested that William Hoffman ensure that Confederate prisoners from states firmly under Union control would be released first. Grant also ordered that Confederates unfit for duty be exchanged before healthy prisoners. Grant remained concerned about Black prisoners in Confederate hands, but he was confident that the impending collapse of the Confederacy would soon return them to freedom.

Confederates and Union authorities began exchanging prisoners as was feasible. Confederates struggled with the logistics required to exchange tens of thousands of men. Masses of frantic people were in motion across the crumbling Confederacy. Any Confederate railroad that continued to operate was packed with troops deployed to slow the Union advance as well as civilians in flight with whatever property they could carry. Streams of exiles and deserters crowded the region's byways. Now Union prisoners joined in this exodus.

Even prisoners seasoned by past journeys in the Confederacy were unprepared for the hardships of their exchange. The hegira of the prisoners from the Salisbury prison in North Carolina was a case in point. On February 16, the prison commandant was informed that his prisoners should prepare to be transported to the town of Goldsboro, almost two hundred miles to the east. From there the prisoners would be exchanged near Wilmington, where Union forces had established a beachhead. Rail lines connected Salisbury and Goldsboro, but General Robert E. Lee ordered that it and other crucial rail routes be reserved for supplies. Because the railroad on the first leg of the prisoners' journey, from Salisbury to Greensboro, was a strategic route, the commandant had to make alternative plans. On February 26, a column of more than twenty-eight hundred prisoners, stretching more than three miles, set off on foot. Over the next five days, the "army of skeletons" tramped toward Greensboro. Rain showers drenched them and slowed their progress. A train wreck prevented supplies from reaching them, leaving many to forage for food as they marched. Weakened by illness and hunger, hundreds of prisoners had to be abandoned along the march. Eventually, more than five thousand prisoners followed the route, emptying Salisbury camp of all but its sickest inhabitants.

At Greensboro the marchers were loaded onto flatcars bound for Raleigh. Traveling at a crawl, the prison train reached Raleigh twelve hours later. After a lengthy layover, the prisoners climbed aboard more flatcars for the final leg to Goldsboro. When they reached their destination, they clustered in the open while under guard, awaiting parole and transportation to the exchange site. Many prisoners had to loiter for days before the Confederates dispatched them to Union lines. Many did not gain their freedom until March 10, two weeks after their departure from Salisbury.

Prisoners at Andersonville fared little better. The largest portion followed the same route that Chester Berry had taken to the exchange site near Vicksburg. The three thousand prisoners who remained in the camp in late March, however, were directed to Jacksonville, Florida, for exchange. By then Confederates deemed this route to be "less fatiguing" for the prisoners than the alternatives. On April 4 a train carried the first detachment of prisoners to Albany, Georgia. From there they marched for three days to Thomasville, reversing the route that many had taken four months earlier. But the Union general who commanded the forces in Jacksonville had no orders to receive the prisoners, so Confederates returned them to Andersonville. On April 17, only days after their return to the camp, they yet again boarded trains, this time bound for Savannah. While under way, Confederates learned that Union forces threatened their path so the train turned around and headed back to Andersonville. (Although General Lee had surrendered at Appomattox, Virginia on April 9, the war in Georgia and Florida did not end until several weeks later.) The itinerant prisoners were again routed to Jacksonville by way of Thomasville. From there they set off cross-country to Lake City, Florida. There they huddled outdoors awaiting their paroles from their captors. Finally, their Confederate guards marched them in the direction of Jacksonville, before melting into the landscape and leaving them to make the remainder of the journey to the Union lines on their own.

Confederate prisoners endured their own ordeals because Union authorities emphasized expediency in their handling of exchanges. To achieve General Grant's pledge to return three thousand prisoners a week required the equivalent of dispatching sixty railcars, ten steamships, or a flotilla of six or more riverboats stuffed with prisoners every week. At the same time that Union officials were sending prisoners south, they were simultaneously transporting thousands of newly captured Confederates north. In February, for instance, nearly fifteen hundred prisoners were sent south from Elmira but more than seven hundred new captives entered the camp.

Decades after the war, Walter Addison recalled with anger his return trip to Richmond from Elmira. On an intensely cold, snowy February day, he and other prisoners were marched to the Elmira train depot, where they were packed into cattle cars. They spent the next forty-eight hours in the unheated cars. When they finally reached Baltimore, they were herded through the snowbound streets to the harbor, where they boarded a dilapidated government transport that carried them down the Chesapeake Bay and up the James River to the exchange site. During the voyage, the sickest prisoners shivered belowdecks in stalls that had previously held cattle. Addison and other comparatively healthy prisoners huddled on the ship's deck, where their only protection against wind, sleet, and snow was their flimsy blankets.

With so many prisoners in motion during the late winter and spring of 1865, it was inevitable that scores experienced tragedy on the threshold of, as one prisoner put it, "being among humans again." Each transportation disaster had its tragic particularities, but they all shared the common feature of homeward-bound prisoners perishing because of rattletrap machinery, reckless ship captains, and incompetent train engineers.

On March 31, 1865, the *General Lyon*, a steamship carrying hundreds of paroled Union prisoners, burned and sank off Cape Hatteras, North Carolina, during a storm. Of an estimated six hundred passengers and crew, only twenty-nine survived. Three weeks later, the *Massachusetts*, an older sidewheel steamship, left Alexandria, Virginia, carrying three hundred recently released Union prisoners. With men crammed onto the decks, the ship collided with a coal barge near Point Lookout. Among the estimated eighty-seven victims of the collision were men who had survived the prison camps of Andersonville, Millen, and Florence. Five days later, the boiler of the overloaded *Sultana* exploded, plunging Chester Berry into the Mississippi River and killing fifteen hundred former prisoners.

A month later, the second deadliest inland maritime disaster in the nation's history claimed yet more returning prisoners. Most of the passengers on the *Kentucky*, a steamboat on the Red River in Louisiana, were Confederate prisoners from Missouri, Arkansas, and Louisiana who had been paroled two days earlier and were eager to get home. The ship was uncon-

*The Sultana*, loaded with Chester Berry and nearly two thousand ex-prisoners, on the day before its sinking, April 26, 1865. (Library of Congress)

scionably overloaded, with eight hundred passengers. On the night of June 9, the *Kentucky* struck a sunken log between Shreveport and New Orleans. Within minutes it sank, taking with it perhaps several hundred passengers. Passenger James T. Wallace, a recent parolee, reflected, "It seemed especially hard that this sad thing should happen just when we were on our way home."

After April 1865 the logistics of exchange gave way to the dismantling of prisoner-of-war camps. Between April 9, when General Robert E. Lee surrendered at Appomattox, and June 2, when General Edmund Kirby-Smith surrendered the remaining Confederate forces west of the Mississippi River, the Union army was restoring peace in some parts of the Confederacy while hostilities continued in other areas. As long as these conditions persisted, the emptying of prison camps was necessarily piecemeal.

By the end of May, most Union prisoners of war had been liberated. Among the last Union prisoners to reach Union lines were prisoners from Camp Ford in Tyler, Texas. On May 27, they began hobbling into Fort Smith, Arkansas, after trudging nearly three hundred miles. The Confederate guards at the prison camp had apparently bolted for home when they learned of the Confederacy's defeat, leaving the prisoners unattended and free to wander off. Many Black prisoners who had been re-enslaved by the Confederacy military also had made their way to Union lines by May. More than twelve hundred at Camp Ford who were either sick or intimidated by the prospect of hiking to Union lines finally were placed on a steamboat for Shreveport on May 17. Meanwhile, those Black prisoners who had been re-enslaved by private citizens, especially in Texas, remained captive for months after Appomattox.

The logistics of transporting liberated Union prisoners northward were little different from those needed to disperse the immense army of a million and a half men that the Union had accumulated to suppress the rebellion. Between April and November 1865, while the war's prisons were being emptied, more than eight hundred thousand Union soldiers were transported home. In terms of numbers, the liberated Union prisoners were a minor consideration and inconvenience. In the eastern theater, Union authorities readily transported most liberated Union prisoners on government-owned or -leased vessels. On the Mississippi, where private steamboats thronged the river, the government contracted for former prisoners and returning soldiers to travel on private steamboats, like the ill-fated *Sultana*.

The return to the South of more than sixty thousand Confederate prisoners scattered among more than twenty different northern facilities dragged on for more than three months. General Grant sought the release of Confederates as quickly as possible on the grounds that, once home, "they may still raise something for their subsistence for the coming year and prevent suffering next winter." The drawn-out surrender of Confederate forces thwarted Grant's plans. Union authorities gave priority to the movement of Union forces and returning Union prisoners. They also were cautious about sending war-tested rebel veterans back into the South while law and order had yet to be restored and most necessities of life were scarce. In addition, Union officials prudently halted the release of Confederate prisoners in the immediate aftermath of Abraham Lincoln's assassination, recognizing that Confederates in transit would be a provocation to any grieving northerners intent on vengeance.

At the end of May, Colonel William Hoffman proposed releasing fifty prisoners a day, a rate that would require months to empty the nearly fifty thousand Confederates in Union hands. More than eighteen thousand still remained at Point Lookout. In late June, Andrew Johnson, Lincoln's successor, accelerated the discharge of prisoners by ordering the release of all enlisted Confederate prisoners of war who took the oath of allegiance.

Hoffman reported in early July that most Union prisons had been emptied, and by early the following month, fewer than two hundred Confederate prisoners remained incarcerated. With the prisons now virtually vacant, Hoffman set about shuttering them. Anything of value was sold at auction and then the prison sites themselves were returned to their owners. With characteristic attention to detail, Hoffman settled up his accounts and reported in late October that only four prisoners remained in custody, all at Fort Lafayette in New York. On November 3, 1865, Hoffman was relieved of his duties as the Union's commissary general of prisoners.

For Confederate prisoners, the protracted experience of release was excruciating. Beyond the tedium of waiting, they had to take the oath of allegiance, a ritual that aroused complex emotions in many prisoners. At Point Lookout, Samuel Pickens of the Fifth Alabama Infantry submitted to what he mockingly described as the "machine where U.S. citizens are made out of rebel soldiers." On June 16, he and a throng of other prisoners recited an oath of allegiance, kissed the Bible to affirm their oath, and stood under a huge U.S. flag canopy while they completed their documents. Pickens found humor in the ceremony but other prisoners found the experience humiliating.

Once released, Confederate prisoners journeyed southward with varying degrees of Union assistance. Prisoners from Point Lookout and New York's military prisons, including Elmira and Governors Island, were furnished train and ship transportation to Richmond or other major southern points. Others, especially those held in midwestern prisons, were left to their own devices. Prisoners with private means traveled home in as much comfort as they could afford. Indigent prisoners scrounged for work, food, and charity while they made their way south.

William G. B. Morris's day of release was June 12. Morris was a carpenter and millwright from Dallas, North Carolina, who had served in the Sixty-Fourth North Carolina Infantry and been captured at Gettysburg and sent to Johnson's Island. "Oh what a happy day to be at liberty once more," he rejoiced. He spent three days traveling by train from Sandusky to Baltimore. Then he embarked on a Chesapeake Bay steamer to Fortress Monroe. From there he made his way to Richmond, where he waited two days for a train to nearby Petersburg. After three more days of rail travel, he reached Charlotte, then continued his journey on foot. Four days later and two weeks after his release, Morris returned home.

Chester Berry's war odyssey came to an end weeks after Morris's return. After recovering from the trauma of the sinking of the *Sultana,* Berry had to muster the courage to board another steamboat to travel upriver to Cairo,

Illinois. From there, he continued by rail to Mattoon, Illinois, where he waited for a train to Indianapolis. "Here I was obliged to go hungry, or beg from the citizens, although I had a meal ticket at the eating house given me by the Sanitary Commission, but the landlord refused to honor it." (Other returning prisoners received similar receptions in some communities. When members of the Ninth Minnesota who had been imprisoned returned home, they too were forced to sleep on the streets and beg for food.) Berry continued eastward to Columbus, Ohio, where he spent two weeks in a hospital recovering from his head injury. On June 7, almost three years after he had donned a uniform as an eighteen-year-old, he was finally mustered out of service in Detroit. His return home came as a shock to his mother, who had received notice months earlier that her son had been killed on the *Sultana*. The false report of Berry's death proved to be a major inconvenience in years to come. Because he was listed in the Michigan Adjutant General's Report for 1865 as having died on the *Sultana,* he had to persuade skeptical federal pension officials that he had, in fact, survived and was very much alive.

CHAPTER TWELVE

# GIVING THE HISTORY AND WHOLE TRUTH

## (1865–1867)

On the morning of November 10, 1865, Captain Henry Wirz bade farewell to his spartan quarters in the Old Capitol Prison, located a short distance from the Capitol in Washington, D.C. He left behind a few articles of clothing, some tobacco, a little whiskey, a Bible, a book of a Scottish clergyman's meditations on the pending end-times, and a cat, which had been his companion since May. He left no record that he reflected on the conditions he experienced as a prisoner or those that Union soldiers had endured while he presided as commandant at Andersonville.

The occasion for Wirz's exit—his pending execution for acts of violence and cruelty against Union prisoners—could hardly have been more solemn or grim. While awaiting the final preparations for the execution, Wirz was granted a reunion with Captain Richard Winder, the former quartermaster at Andersonville who was incarcerated while awaiting trial. The two men had a long conversation, during which they reminisced about their military service, their time together at Andersonville, and the injustice of their prosecution. Later, while shuffling to the gallows, Wirz passed James W. Duncan, a former factotum at Andersonville, and Major John Gee, the former commander of Salisbury prison. They, too, awaited prosecution for their acts while in charge of Union prisoners. Shouts of "Hang him" and "Remember Andersonville" greeted Wirz's appearance at the gallows. For Winder, Duncan, and Gee, Wirz's reception and impending fate was a bleak harbinger of their own possible destinies.

By ten a.m., when Wirz was positioned on the scaffold, several hundred spectators, who had begun gathering at dawn, most of whom were soldiers, crowded into the prison yard. So keen was public interest that officials had sought to restrict admission by printing two hundred yellow tickets like those commonly offered for stage shows. When the tickets ran out, would-be spectators climbed trees along the exterior of the prison wall and clambered onto roofs of neighboring buildings.

On the scaffold, Wirz listened as his crimes and sentence were read aloud. Observers scrutinized Wirz for signs that "the worm of conscience" was troubling his soul and some final insight into how the "weak, nerveless figure" on the gallows had exercised "power and cruelty in unparalleled excess." Two Catholic priests ministered to him until finally, at 10:32, with his hands and legs pinioned by straps and the noose adjusted around his neck, the trapdoor underneath him was sprung. Ten minutes later, a doctor pronounced Wirz dead. The soldiers crowding the streets around the prison greeted the news that "the jailer of Andersonville" was no more with a loud ringing cheer.

The execution of Wirz was understood, both then and since, to be a land-

Preparing Captain Wirz for his Execution, November 1865. (*Frank Leslie's Illustrated Weekly*)

mark event. At the time, Wirz's prosecution for war crimes was anticipated to be the first of many. In fact, it proved to be one of only a handful of trials of former Confederates. In subsequent decades it would be recalled, inaccurately, as the only execution of a Confederate for violating the laws of war.

Wirz's prosecution became, and remains, a Rorschach test of attitudes about the Confederacy and the war to preserve the Union. For the survivors of the camps as well as family and friends of the more than thirteen thousand men who died at Andersonville, Wirz's execution was emphatically merited. He warranted no pity and the cause that he served deserved no respect. For Wirz's apologists, and especially former Confederates, the cheers from the voyeurs at his execution ghoulishly showcased the scapegoating of a blameless soldier in a noble cause.

That Andersonville and other prison pens inspired formal prosecutions of violators of the laws of war was fitting. In the spring of 1865, Union officials confronted the question of whether to charge former Confederates for violations of the laws of war that had been codified in General Orders No. 100 in 1863. Especially egregious in the eyes of Union military prosecutors had been the mistreatment of Union prisoners of war. Since 1862, allegations of deliberate cruelty against Union prisoners had accumulated and influenced Union policies. Now, victory presented the opportunity to affirm the principle that transgressions by enemy combatants would be punished. Union officials recognized that their decisions to prosecute Wirz and other former Confederates would establish a precedent in not just American but also international law. In one of the most pronounced ironies of the war, the much maligned trial of Wirz has since been cited and even celebrated by jurists as the origin of the modern prosecution of war crimes.

In the weeks immediately following Appomattox, Union prosecutors anticipated trials of dozens of former Confederates, almost all of whom had been responsible for prisoners of war. Judge Advocate Joseph Holt, who served as the Lincoln administration's chief arbiter of military law, stressed the urgency of prosecuting Confederate officials. Among those arrested were Wirz, Winder, Gee, and other Confederate officers who had served at prison camps.

The trajectory of Holt's life, at first glance, would seem to have predisposed him to reflexive sympathy for the concerns of white southerners. He was the scion of a slaveholding family in Kentucky and had amassed a fortune practicing law in Mississippi during the 1830s. He subsequently returned to Kentucky, where he rose in prominence as a conventional "states rights" Democrat. As the onetime owner of more than a dozen slaves, Holt viewed the rise of abolitionism and the Republican Party with alarm. During the mid-1850s he excoriated "Black Republicans" for jeopardizing the union through their hostility to slavery.

Yet Holt was a complex man who never wavered in his loyalty to the Union as the sectional crisis intensified. He eventually concluded that slavery itself was the most immediate threat to the republic. While in James Buchanan's Cabinet, he persuaded the President to condemn secession as an illegal act. Holt, however, was unable to induce Buchanan to take any decisive steps to avert the nation's rupture. When Lincoln took office, Holt returned to Kentucky and worked to keep the state out of the Confederacy. By the time Lincoln appointed him judge advocate in 1862, he had wholly revised his views on slavery. He now urged the destruction of the institution as a war aim and championed the equal treatment of all Americans, including the formerly enslaved, under the law. As early as 1862, Holt began acting on the principle that Black Americans were citizens and referred to them as such. Having arrived at these positions, he held them resolutely.

Skeptics and critics of the prosecution of former Confederates, both then and since, have charged that Holt was animated by paranoia and a thirst for vengeance upon the former Confederacy. Holt's disposition was steadfastly grim, his countenance melancholy, and his demeanor brusque. Gideon Welles, a colleague in the Lincoln administration and fellow Democrat, described him as a "stern, stubborn, relentless man." Lincoln's successor, Andrew Johnson, was less charitable, declaring Holt to be as "cruel" and "remorseless" as the notorious ancient Greek lawmaker Draco or the infamous Roman emperor Nero.

Holt's resolve to punish Confederates for war crimes was more than a wild-eyed crusade for retribution. The traumatic assassination of President Lincoln by John Wilkes Booth unquestionably hardened Holt's resolve. Booth, a Confederate sympathizer, had previously conspired to kidnap the President to ransom him for the release of Confederate prisoners. That Booth had also met with Confederate agents in Canada confirmed Holt's suspicion that Confederates had planned and waged far-flung campaigns of murder, arson, and mayhem. A failure to prosecute the worst Confederate violators, Holt avowed, would encourage violations of the laws of war in the future, perhaps by the same former Confederates who had fomented rebellion.

Judge Advocate Joseph Holt anticipated the trial of Henry Wirz as the first of many prosecutions of Confederates for violating the laws of war. (Library of Congress)

Holt believed that prosecutions of Confederate officials were essential to deprive the rebellion and its architects of any residue of legitimacy. As official postmortems of the rebellion and its leaders, the trials would be decisive in shaping the historical memory of the prison camps. As one prosecutor explained, trials were "the means of bringing to light and giving the history and whole truth" regarding Confederate prisoner-of-war policies. Holt himself vouched that trials were crucial to prevent "one of the most important chapters in the annals of the rebellion" from being "lost to history."

Having made the decision to prosecute former Confederates, Holt and his subalterns had to decide on the best means to do so. He did not seek summary executions or stage show trials of accused Confederates. If crass revenge was his principal motivation, Holt adopted a cumbersome, unreliable, and controversial judicial process—the military commission—to achieve it. The military tribunals that he extolled proved as likely to result in acquittal as in conviction.

The resort to military tribunals to adjudicate alleged war crimes was both practical and political. Military commissions had been first used during the war with Mexico when occasion arose to discipline U.S. soldiers for offenses contrary to the laws of war while in Mexico. The intent of the military courts was to formalize procedures and ensure legal protections for Americans charged with violations when state courts did not exist or were not operating. Tribunals in essence provided constitutional protections in circumstances otherwise unaddressed in the federal Constitution. With the precedent established more than a decade before the first salvo of the Civil War, military tribunals became commonplace during the conflict. Between 1862 and 1865, probably more than four thousand tribunals were convened, including scores that addressed alleged violations of the laws of war.

The logic of using military tribunals to punish former Confederate prison keepers was straightforward. Once a conflict concluded, there was no recognized power to determine and enforce criminal responsibility for war crimes by the defeated enemy. Nor was there any legal infrastructure in civilian courts to handle such cases. Holt declared military tribunals indispensable "in cases of which the local criminal courts could not legally take cognizance, or which by reason of intrinsic defects of machinery, they are incompetent to do so." Attorney General James Speed concurred and issued an opinion that illegal acts of war could be tried only in military courts.

The resort to military tribunals was also a consequence of General Orders No. 100. That 1863 directive, it may be recalled, had established expectations for the waging of war. Subsequently, the War Department's Bureau of Military Justice assumed the administration of the newly codified laws of war. Although Confederate government officials had dismissed the order as a travesty, it forewarned them of the conduct the Union expected them to uphold. Now at the war's end, after having established the administrative capacity to adjudicate the laws of war, Holt and his staff applied themselves to prosecuting the most egregious violators of those laws. Trials by military commission, Holt vouched, were the "most powerful and efficacious instrumentalities" for imposing justice on Confederate "malefactors" who would otherwise escape punishment.

Holt understood that the postwar tribunals would have to clarify the practical application of General Orders No. 100. Although the order established broad principles, it left crucial details undefined. What specific violations of the laws and customs of war by Confederates merited prosecution? Was the prosecution of accused Confederate violators a choice or the duty of the victors? What punishments were appropriate for their violations? Was a claim to have followed a superior's orders a legitimate defense for an accused violator of the laws of war?

Holt's confidence in the legitimacy of military tribunals was not universally shared. In the eyes of many, military tribunals were unwarranted and arbitrary. When the war ended, ongoing disputes over the constitutionality of military courts became entwined with new controversies over the reconstruction of the former Confederacy and the reestablishment of civilian courts there. Just as many Democrats had denounced military tribunals during the war as unconstitutional precursors to tyranny, so too did opponents of ambitious reconstruction policies in the former Confederacy oppose the use of military tribunals to protect the formerly enslaved and to prosecute former Confederates. To the extent that the jurisdiction of military courts shrank with the reopening of state courts across the South, prospects for punishing former Confederates also diminished. After all, no one was likely to seek justice in a southern court against any Confederate accused of war crimes. There was even less likelihood that a southern white jury would convict an alleged Confederate war criminal.

Because of the contested legitimacy of military tribunals, Holt and Secretary of War Edwin Stanton recognized that any prosecutions of former Confederates had to be both justifiable and compelling. On these grounds Henry Wirz, the commandant of Andersonville prison, was the first alleged war criminal to be tried. Since 1862 Union prisoners had leveled accusations of cruelty against Wirz and since 1864 he had presided over the most reviled prison in the nation's history. Had General John Winder survived the Civil War he almost certainly would have been the first Confederate brought before a military tribunal. In lieu of Winder, a credible case against Wirz would advance Holt's larger aim of stripping the Confederacy of any esteem or honor that it still retained.

Union cavalry arrested Wirz on May 7, 1865, at Andersonville. In less than two days, a fraction of the time that it had taken Union prisoners to reach Andersonville, he was transferred to Washington, D.C. There he was held in the Old Capitol Prison awaiting trial for conspiring "to impair the lives of Union prisoners." A special military commission, composed of nine Union officers, with Major General Lew Wallace presiding, was convened. Colonel Norton P. Chipman, a trusted assistant to Holt, served as judge advocate during the trial.

The trial began on August 23 and continued for two months. As Holt had hoped, it received front-page coverage in the nation's newspapers and attracted extensive international interest. More than 150 witnesses, including prisoners, ex-Confederates, and residents of communities near Andersonville, described in unprecedented detail the conditions in the prison, the methods Wirz used to discipline prisoners, and the chain of command that prevailed at the camp. The trial testimony provided the first comprehensive portrait of Andersonville and of Confederate policies toward prisoners of war. Not until three decades later, when the federal government began publishing the wartime records relating to prisoners of war, would the American public gain a fuller documentary portrait of Andersonville.

At the outset, Chipman worked to establish a conspiracy among Confederate leaders, extending from Confederate President Jefferson Davis down the chain of command to Wirz, to incapacitate, starve, and kill Union prisoners. Doing so would have bolstered plans to try Davis and others. Chipman made this point explicitly, observing that those "sufficiently high in authority to have prevented these atrocities, and to whom the knowledge of them was brought" were as culpable as were Wirz and others who followed illegal orders. Applying the same logic of military command, former prisoner Robert Kellogg testified regarding the perspective of prisoners: "We saw that we were badly treated and miserably provided for; and we naturally supposed that he, the commandant of the prison, was in a great degree at least, responsible for it; we supposed, of course that somebody was responsible for it."

Wirz adamantly denied that he had any intent to mistreat prisoners. He had been scrupulous in following the orders of his superiors and had done so without animus toward the imprisoned. He and defense witnesses convincingly argued that he was not responsible for the inhumane medical facilities at Andersonville; he had not commanded the hospital, where camp surgeons had outranked him. Nor was he responsible for the deplorable rations in the camp, which were the obligation of the commissary general's office.

Wirz could not so easily deflect other changes of culpability in the mistreatment of prisoners. No one denied his authority over prison discipline at Andersonville. Of the accusations of Wirz's cruelty by former prisoners, Chipman dwelled on instances of shootings of prisoners who strayed near the dead line in the prison stockade. The line itself, the prosecution conceded, was not a "crime in itself." Union prisons had also imposed dead lines. The enforcement at Andersonville, however, had been reckless and arbitrary. Witnesses described numerous examples of prisoners with no nefarious intent who had been shot down while meandering near or reaching across the dead line. Wirz had manifested no concern about these shootings and apparently never disciplined any guards for them. Courtroom testimony regarding the shootings left a deep impression on the trial audience, not least the tribunal's titular head, General Wallace. He was moved to render the testimony he heard into an uncommonly stark sketch and painting that remains one of the grimmest contemporary renderings of the war.

The prosecution bolstered its case by calling a string of witnesses who told of severe punishments ordered by Wirz. They recalled instances when the entire camp had been deprived of rations as a collective punishment. They recounted being confined in stocks for hours without water or shade, being whipped for refusing to perform prison labor, and being mauled by vicious guard dogs.

The prominence given to Wirz's mistreatment of Black prisoners was conspicuous. The court heard of Wirz's abuse of Black prisoners and of the work they were forced to do. Chipman also drew attention to Wirz's use of dogs that had been trained to track fugitive slaves. This scrutiny to the mistreatment of Black prisoners almost certainly reflected Chipman's deep-seated abolitionist convictions. But he and Holt also were intent on establishing the precedent of Black witnesses testifying against whites in a court of law. Had Wirz been tried in any civilian court in the South in the summer of 1865, the testimony of Black prisoners would have been inadmissible. Equally important, by invoking the violence of slavery, Chipman impugned the ethical legitimacy of the cause that Wirz had served. Images conjured by testimony of prisoners fleeing dogs and of whips lashing the backs of prisoners corroborated claims that the South's "system of human slavery" had "trained its devotees to acts of cruelty." As the *Chicago Tribune* observed during the proceedings, not just Wirz but also "southern barbarism" was on trial.

The defense counsel had no rebuttal for many of these accusations of cruelty. Wirz's case was not helped by citing a ruling by a justice of the Georgia Supreme Court that condoned the use of dogs to track escaped slaves and convicts. Chipman mocked the precedent, pointing out that state law was irrelevant to Wirz's case and that the Georgia judge's ruling was, at most, "evidence to the extent to which a naturally strong mind may be warped and turned from a strict view of justice when compelled to square it with a system of slavery." Wirz's prewar stint as a homeopathic physician and overseer for about one hundred slaves on a plantation at Milliken's Bend, Louisiana, gave credence to the accusation that he had transferred skills acquired as a taskmaster for the enslaved to his duties as a jailor of Union prisoners of war.

The most tenuous charges leveled against Wirz were of murder. A few trial participants repeated hearsay about Wirz murdering prisoners, but only one witness claimed to have personally seen the Confederate commandant do so. Wirz refuted the accusations while complaining they were

The trial of Captain Wirz, "the Andersonville Jailer," filled the columns of the nation's newspapers for weeks during the late summer and fall of 1865. (From *Harper's Weekly*, October 21, 1865)

so "vague and indefinite" that no effective defense was possible. Testimony from defense witnesses and Wirz's protestations of innocence persuaded the military commission to acquit him of the charges of deliberate murder.

The trial ended in early November 1865, by which time Wirz was ill and bedridden. Protesting that he had simply followed orders, Wirz insisted that his motive—to be a good soldier—had been mundane. If he revealed no traces of psychopathy, no sadistic pleasure from inflicting pain, he also displayed no capacity to acknowledge personal responsibility for Andersonville. He presented himself as one small, seemingly impotent figure in a large and arcane war bureaucracy.

The commission found Wirz guilty of ten charges and sentenced him to death. He appealed to Andrew Johnson for clemency, but the President demurred and the sentence stood. By the morning of his execution Wirz had accepted his fate. While on the gallows, the *New York Herald* reported, there was "something in his face and step which, in a better man, might have passed for heroism."

Wirz's conviction strengthened Judge Advocate Holt's resolve to prosecute "sundry rebel officials" for their cruel treatment of Union prisoners. The next target was Confederate General Hugh W. Mercer. In January 1866 he was brought before a military commission for the murder of seven Union prisoners of war near Savannah in December 1864.

The case against Mercer was weak. Unlike Wirz, Mercer had a reputation as a conscientious and honorable soldier. His father was a Revolutionary War hero and Mercer was a West Point graduate who had served on General Winfield Scott's staff. His alleged crime crumbled under scrutiny. Prosecutors conceded that the executed Union prisoners of war had been in the Confederate ranks when they were executed. But, the prosecution argued, they had only joined the rebel cause to "avoid starvation" in the Millen and Florence camps. Their offense, the prosecution asserted, had been to plan an escape to Union lines when General William Sherman's forces advanced on Savannah. Traditional laws of war provided no justification for executing the men for attempting to escape.

Almost as soon as the trial began, the evidence exonerated Mercer and embarrassed the prosecution. No firm evidence demonstrated that Mercer had ordered the executions or had even been present when the prisoners had been court-martialed and executed. Even more damaging to the case was testimony provided by both prosecution and defense witnesses that the executed men had indeed volunteered for Confederate service; the defense contended that the men had switched sides not out of hunger but out of frustration and anger over the Union's failure to secure their exchange. Witnesses confirmed that the men had been executed not for desertion (or escape) but for having planned to capture their commanding officer during their escape. The executed men were, in Confederate eyes and in conventional military law, guilty of mutiny.

The trial generated national coverage, almost all of it favorable to Mercer and some of it highly critical of the prosecution. When the military court acquitted Mercer on all counts, newspapers across the South, as well as Democratic journals in the North, applauded the court for its wisdom and fairness. The judge advocate's office, in contrast, was the target of blistering criticism for bringing the case in the first place.

Prosecutors had a much stronger case against Confederate General George Pickett, who had ordered the hanging of twenty-one prisoners of war in North Carolina in February and March 1864. Pickett's planned prosecution shared the didactic intent of the other prosecutions advocated by Holt. Pickett had been a prominent Confederate officer even before he commanded the ill-fated charge against Union lines on the final day of the Battle of Gettysburg. After the 1864 executions, his intemperate language in letters to his Union counterpart in North Carolina strongly suggested that malice had motivated his execution order. Compounding his offense, the men executed on Pickett's orders had been North Carolina Unionists. Pickett's viciousness toward them was another chapter in the brutal oppression of Unionists by Confederate authorities, which Republicans and many northern newspapers had condemned throughout the war. Pickett's intent, his accusers asserted, had been "to terrify the loyal people of North Carolina; to make them subservient to the scheme of rebellion, and to bring contempt upon the Government its victims represented." Reflecting his aim to terrorize the families and neighbors of the executed men, Pickett had allowed the corpses of the executed men to be dishonored. Some had been stripped of clothes and left unprotected until they were collected by their families, some thrown in a mass grave at the base of the gallows, and some given to doctors for dissection.

Shifting political winds and influence saved Pickett from prosecution. Had he been in federal custody in late 1865, he almost certainly would have been arraigned. But by then he and his family had absconded to Canada. In his absence, prosecutors gathered testimony that left ambiguous the status of the executed men. These ambiguities initially discouraged Holt from pursuing the case against Pickett. Subsequently, after receiving additional evidence, Holt changed his stance and endorsed prosecution. But by the spring of 1866, Secretary of War Stanton had diminishing confidence in military commissions to punish war crimes or former Confederates. Meanwhile, Andrew Johnson, who perceived Holt and the Bureau of Military Justice as allied with his own political enemies, was actively opposed to further prosecutions of Confederates. Decisive in tamping down enthusiasm to try Pickett was the intercession of General Ulysses S. Grant on behalf of his longtime friend. Grant acknowledged that there was no justification for the executions that Pickett had ordered but vouched that Pickett was "an honorable man." Eager to put the strife of the war behind the nation, Grant asked what public good would be advanced by Pickett's trial.

While Pickett's case hung in the air, a military commission in Raleigh, North Carolina, considered charges against Major John Gee, the Salisbury prison commandant. Gee had been arrested the previous fall and imprisoned in Washington, D.C. His prosecution finally began in February 1866 and continued until June. The tribunal eventually collected hundreds of pages of testimony from Gee, Confederate soldiers, and former prisoners.

As commandant of one of the deadliest Confederate prisons, Gee must have seemed a deserving target of prosecution. Despite the horrific conditions that prevailed at Salisbury during Gee's tenure, the defense demonstrated that Gee had strenuously complained of prison conditions to his superiors. He had not resorted to any of the punishments that Wirz had applied at Andersonville and had tried to curb trigger-happy guards. In one instance, when a Union officer was shot near the dead line at the prison, Gee had considered punishing the guard responsible but concluded that the ambiguous location of the dead line provided no basis to do so. When the prisoners staged their breakout attempt in November 1864 and guards answered with indiscriminate firing, Gee ordered an immediate ceasefire as soon as he arrived on the scene. He also prevented local citizenry, who had joined with the guards, from acting on their "very decided disposition" to gun down the prisoners.

The trial, in a manner wholly unanticipated by Holt, vindicated Gee. During Gee's long captivity, sympathizers and Confederate loyalists in Florida proclaimed him a martyr and held fund-raising pageants to subsidize his legal expenses. While his trial ground on, southern newspapers printed transcripts of the proceedings, which bolstered white southern prejudice against his and other prosecutions. When the prosecuting counsel called for an end to the proceedings and the commission announced that Gee was not guilty on all counts, white southern newspapers feted the acquittal as a referendum on "southern civilization." A Raleigh newspaper crowed that "no man in the South represents a higher or more enviable character for all the virtues which ennoble human nature than Major Gee."

Even as the prosecution of Gee ended in acquittal, military prosecutors secured the conviction of James Duncan, a lowly private and jack-of-all-trades at Andersonville. Exiled from occupied New Orleans, he had served as a clerk in the quartermaster's office at the prison, overseen the prison cookhouse, where the daily rations were cooked, and supervised prison burials. These duties made him a reviled presence in the daily lives of prisoners. He also had been a habitual and shameless war profiteer, withholding supplies and rations, especially salt, and then selling them to prisoners. His penchant for larceny escalated when Wirz appointed him temporary sutler in 1864. By then, Duncan was looting food and supplies destined for the prison hospital. When prisoner exchanges were reestablished in early 1865, Duncan expanded his operations and began bartering with prisoners to move their names up the list of prisoners to be exchanged. The evidence of Duncan's thievery and violent abuse of prisoners, though not exhaustive, was presented over five days of testimony to a military commission in March 1866. Having witnessed Wirz's execution, Duncan must have been relieved when, in July, the tribunal sentenced him to fifteen years of hard labor. White southern newspapers were silent about any larger significance that Duncan's conviction held.

The aborted prosecution of Pickett and the handful of other trials for Confederate war crimes accomplished only some of Holt's ambitions. The testimony gathered during Wirz's and Duncan's trials reinforced the notoriety of Wirz and the Andersonville camp. The prosecutions also established important and enduring precedents. First, an officer of a belligerent taken into custody after the close of military operations could be tried by a military commission for violations of the rules of war committed within enemy lines. Second, a war criminal so tried could be sentenced to execution.

The trials, however, were a disappointment to Holt and many others. The prosecutions of Mercer and Gee illustrated that there was no simple way of assuring that the facts revealed in court and the verdicts delivered would discredit the former Confederacy. To the contrary, the trials provided a venue for Wirz and other former Confederates to blame the Union for the horrors endured by Union prisoners of war. Such posturing could not save Wirz. But when promoted in defense of Mercer and Gee, who came across as honorable men groundlessly persecuted, these claims acquired greater plausibility.

That Confederate Secretary of War James Seddon and President Jefferson Davis escaped trial was an especially significant failure of the prosecution. The trials confirmed the old adage that only little thieves are hanged, while great ones remain free. Despite the best efforts of the prosecution to diagram a conspiracy, the trials of Wirz and Duncan failed to demonstrate clear evidence of collective culpability of senior Confederates. Along with General Winder, Seddon and Davis were the officials most responsible for Confederate prisons. Seddon had been repeatedly apprised of the disarray and severe suffering in the prison camps, especially at Andersonville, Florence, and Salisbury. Yet he never took any steps to address those conditions. Davis displayed no evident concern about the operation of his nation's prison camps. No evidence demonstrated that Seddon and Davis conducted their nation's prisons with an explicit intention to kill or starve Union prisoners of war. But their intentions should not outweigh the effect of their inaction. At the very least, a strong case could have been made that they were culpable of the sin of omission rather than commission.

Seddon and Davis, moreover, were directly responsible for the Confederacy's explicit policy of enslaving Black prisoners of war. Both men tenaciously affirmed the policy, even after it proved fatal to the fragile prisoner exchange regime and the Union declared it to be a violation of the laws of war. Neither man expressed compassion for the several thousand Black citizen soldiers whom the policy condemned to enslavement.

Judge Advocate Chipman contended that the strongest basis upon which to prosecute Davis was his complicity in the horrors of Andersonville. But Duncan's trial put an end to the prospect of further prosecutions of Confederates. President Johnson exhibited little inclination to try Davis even before the struggle over postwar policy between the White House and Congress intensified. With the aim of ending military jurisdiction in the South, the President formally declared the war over in April 1866. His proclamation, in which Johnson admonished that military tribunals during peacetime were "dangerous to public liberty," stripped the legitimacy of any further prosecutions by the Bureau of Military Justice.

In the same month, the Supreme Court ruled in *Ex parte Mulligan* that military tribunals were unconstitutional where civil courts were functioning. The decision had no direct bearing on the South, but it further undercut the legitimacy of military courts and left open the possibility that the court might rule against future military commissions in the former Confederacy. Soon thereafter, Johnson appointed Henry Stanbery, who endorsed restoring power to state courts across the former Confederacy, as Attorney General. Chipman retained hope that Johnson's successor, Ulysses S. Grant, might revive the prosecution of Davis. But having already shown questionable leniency in his plea for mercy toward George Pickett, Grant ignored Chipman's wishes. Davis and Seddon, consequently, never had to defend themselves or Confederate treatment of prisoners of war before a court.

Many Union veterans were galled by the feeble prosecution of Confederates. The broad amnesties offered to surrendering Confederates, they fumed, had provided unwarranted immunity for alleged war crimes. Even worse, the leniency shown by Johnson, Grant, and others toward the leaders of the rebellion disgraced the nation's sacrifice. General Rush C. Hawkins, who took umbrage at the failure to prosecute General Pickett, fretted that the Union's leaders had lost their moral bearings and succumbed to a misguided "indiscriminate magnanimity." For Hawkins and many Union veterans, justice was sacrificed in pursuit of craven reconciliation.

Because the trials did not accomplish their intended aims to the satisfaction of many northerners, congressional Republicans in 1867 established a special committee to "thoroughly investigate" Confederate treatment of prisoners of war. The committee was staffed by four northern Republicans and one northern Democrat. All were Union veterans who had been elected to Congress after the war. They solicited and received thousands of letters from former prisoners and families of prisoners, with accounts of imprisonment from the earliest months to the last days of the war. Committee members also collected depositions from nearly one hundred former prisoners. Two years after its creation, the committee completed a twelve-hundred-page report that was a pastiche of official records, excerpts from published prison memoirs, letters, and depositions.

At the outset of the document, the committee members addressed skeptics who asked, "What is to be gained by spreading before this country and the world a picture so terrible, and an experience so sickening and loathsome in its details?" The committee answered that the topic was of such import for "the civilization of the age" that it demanded "an enduring record, truthful and authentic, and stamped with the national authority." Unconstrained by the legal formalities that had prevailed in the military tribunals, the committee members demonstrated to their satisfaction that the mistreatment of Union prisoners was the direct and inevitable result of "slavery, treason, and rebellion." The need to affirm and publicize this conclusion was urgent, the committee regretted, because "the rebels and their sympathizers" had "infused in the public mind" that "destitution and want of supplies" drove Confederates "to the fearful expedient of starving Union prisoners of war," whereas the Lincoln administration, by halting exchanges, engaged in "willful neglect of the prisoners in their hands" and "a wanton disregard of the strongest dictates of duty and humanity" toward Union prisoners. The committee claimed that its report provided "a full, complete, and convincing refutation of these." It also demonstrated, the committee affirmed, that "the highest as well as the subordinate officers of the confederacy" were "guilty of atrocities for which Wirz suffered on the gibbet."

When the committee's report was issued in 1869, it aroused little interest or commentary in the nation's newspapers. The testimonials augmented the grim and familiar portrait of Confederate prison pens, but they offered only further accusations rather than proof of Confederate design. To the extent that Union prison camps were mentioned in the report, they were described as models of humane charity. Congress revealed no zeal to scrutinize the Union's prisoner-of-war policies and their implementation. Instead, they displayed an unwarranted assurance that Union policy had been the most humane in history.

Inspired by recent events, representatives of fifteen countries met in 1874 in Brussels to draft an international agreement on the laws of war. The conference chairman acknowledged that they drew inspiration from "what happened in the United States during the Civil War." Of particular influence was General Orders No. 100, which its author, Francis Lieber, had shared with his large circle of academic and legal peers throughout Europe. Several prominent participants in the meeting had already touted its significance. Johann Bluntschli, a scholar of international law at the University of Heidelberg, had translated the order into German. Russian jurist Fyodor de Martens, who compiled a draft agreement that circulated before the Brussels conference, drew heavily from Lieber's work.

With the Civil War and the recent Franco-Prussian War in mind, the participants were convinced of the ineffectiveness of retaliation as a deterrent to violations of the laws of war. Having already glimpsed modern warfare during the Crimean War (1854–1856) and the Austro-Sardinian War (1859), Europeans were dismayed by the scale and perceived cruelty of the American bloodletting. They noted the pernicious escalation of retaliation during the American conflict, culminating in measures that established worrisome precedents. Charles Cornwallis Chesney, an influential British military scholar and man of letters, lamented that "the horrors of the Thirty Years' War have been revived to the disgrace of the boasted civilization of the age." Reflecting the views of many European elites, the *Saturday Review* deplored the "retrograde" precedents established during the war and concluded that "if America is really to be the model of the world, it will be a very cruel and pitiless world."

Beginning at the Brussels conference and culminating at the 1899 Hague Convention, delegates from the major European powers and a smattering of other nations gradually demoted retaliation as the principal means of enforcing the laws of war. They also agreed on the first international convention on the treatment of prisoners of war. The sixteen articles addressing prisoners of war closely aligned with Union policy during the Civil War. They included perfunctory acknowledgment of the tradition of paroles and exchanges while explicitly condoning mass internment of prisoners. None of the articles discouraged prisoner-of-war camps.

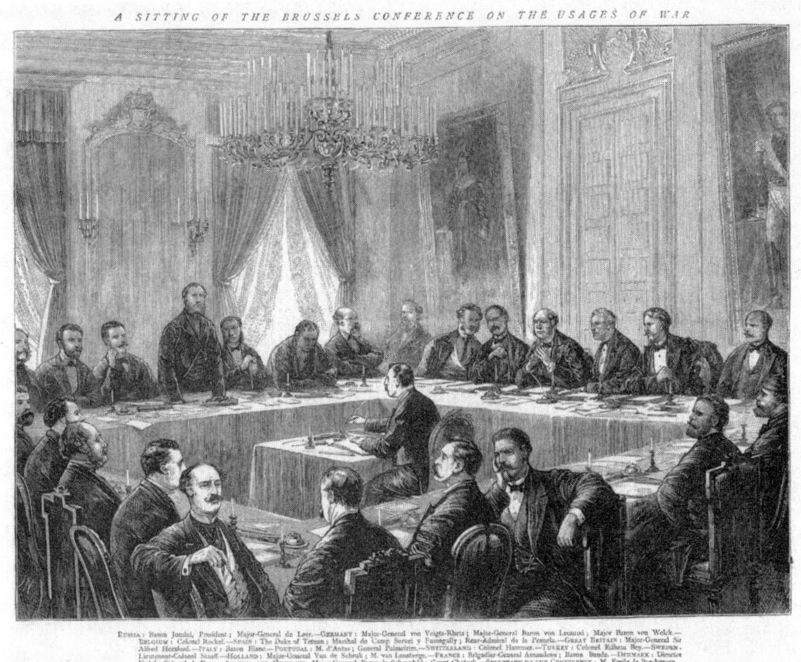


European observers drew inspiration from the American Civil War when they began to codify modern laws of warfare at the Brussels conference in 1874. (Bridgeman Images)

To compensate for the diminished importance assigned to retaliation as a means to discourage violations of the laws of war, humanitarians advocated new prominence for neutral relief organizations. The conduct of various Union and Confederate commanders during the Civil War, as well as that of German officers during the Franco-Prussian War, demonstrated that military leaders could not be trusted to conform to the laws of war. Gustave Moynier, a Swiss jurist and cofounder and president of what later grew to be the International Committee of the Red Cross, looked to public sentiment, mobilized by his and similar organizations, to induce military leaders to conduct lawful warfare. While negotiators at The Hague were wary of conceding too much influence to Moynier and his ilk, they acknowledged the value of formalizing the work of relief agencies, especially in monitoring the treatment of prisoners of war.

Negotiators recognized that sterner incentives than aroused public opinion were required to compel compliance with the laws of war. In the intervening years between the American Civil War and the Hague Convention, a growing number of prominent legal scholars endorsed the principle that, as the American law reformer David Dudley Field argued in 1872, a nation was obligated "through its military or other tribunals" to prosecute individual soldiers accused of war crimes. This new emphasis on the individual accountability of combatants elevated the precedents established by General Orders No. 100 and the postwar American military commissions. Although the trials of former Confederates during 1865 and 1866 were unknown to most foreign observers, they recognized that the trial and conviction of Captain Wirz affirmed that belligerents could assign criminal liability for war outrages. Especially during and after World War I, when debate over the prosecution of alleged war criminals took on a new urgency, the Wirz trial acquired landmark status in the evolution of modern laws of war.

The scope of individual criminal responsibility for violations of the laws of war remained unclear. Wirz had defended himself by claiming to have merely followed orders while serving as prison commandant at Andersonville. His trial failed to resolve whether an inferior officer was criminally responsible for obeying orders that violated the laws of war. Many jurists during the early twentieth century absolved subordinates who carried out illegal acts, while holding their commanding officers accountable. But prosecuting senior officers for war crimes, as the stillborn prosecutions of Jefferson Davis and James Seddon demonstrated, was exceedingly difficult. The appropriate allocation of culpability for superiors and subordinates would remain unresolved until the war crimes trials following World War II.

Advocates of the 1899 Hague Convention and later agreements celebrated them as the triumph of benevolence and reason. But they proved to be inadequate to contain, let alone prevent, the carnage of World War I. Despite the articles in the 1899 Convention regulating the treatment of prisoners of war, captive soldiers in subsequent wars experienced many of the same hardships as their predecessors during the Civil War. Tangles of barbed wire replaced the dead lines of the Civil War era. Military necessity, bureaucratic ineptitude, and the casual dehumanization that accompanies mass confinement fostered prisons camps that differed in degree, not kind, from Civil War camps.

Neither Americans nor Europeans voiced reservations about the innovation of large custodial prison camps. Working on the assumption that they now were a feature of modern warfare, statesmen integrated them into the formal laws of war. Militaries anticipated their need in future conflicts and planned accordingly. A few legacies of the older system of prisoner parole and exchange persisted, but henceforth few captured soldiers had any cause to anticipate escaping long-term confinement.

The institutionalization of prisoner-of-war camps across the Western world coincided with the proliferation of other custodial camps. Just as asylums, penitentiaries, and workhouses had been the harbingers of modern methods of social control during the first half of the nineteenth century, prison camps and various types of internment camps later in the century presaged the unprecedented coercive power that states would exercise during the twentieth century. The far-flung internment camps established at the dawn of the new century, from the Philippines to India and South Africa, were not facsimiles of the prison camps of the American Civil War. Nor were they the direct or inevitable issue of those prison pens. Instead, they were products of the needs and logic of late-nineteenth-century imperialism. Yet, in important regards, the rationales for all massive custodial camps, whether of imprisoned soldiers or interned civilians, reflected the expanding ambitions and capacities of modern Western states.

For Western governments contending with irregular combatants and what we now call asymmetrical warfare, prisoner-of-war camps, internment camps, and the codification of the laws of war became tightly intertwined. The problem of armed resistance by irregular forces plagued most of the major Western military powers of the day. Confederate partisans had harassed Union soldiers throughout the Civil War, and resolute bands of American Indians continued to torment the United States army until the last decade of the nineteenth century. In the new century, American soldiers contended with guerrillas and "bandits" while occupying the Philippines and Haiti. Europe's imperial powers simultaneously conducted exhausting counterinsurgency campaigns along the frontiers of their expanding empires.

The absence of any alternative to large custodial prisoner-of-war camps during the half century after the Civil War is telling. Earlier in the nineteenth century, the detention of a few hundred inmates in an asylum or penitentiary was sufficient to tax the capabilities of many state bureaucracies. But both the Union and Confederacy demonstrated that modern transportation networks and administrative capacities made it possible, indeed advantageous, to detain hundreds of thousands of humans for years at a time. Internment on a massive scale was now not only imaginable but also feasible. To the extent that any debate arose over custodial camps, it was not whether to operate them but how.

CHAPTER THIRTEEN

# Can These Be Men?

## (1865–1910)

More than a century before neuropsychiatrist Bessel van der Kolk observed that "the body keeps the score" of the trauma it has endured, John W. January anticipated the axiom. He came as close to becoming a celebrity as did any survivor of Andersonville. He was not shy about displaying the scars of his captivity. Until his death in 1906, he was a familiar presence at local and national veterans' meetings, where he described his prison experiences and peddled photographs of himself and his war wounds.

The testimony of January's body bespoke his suffering and resilience. He was born in Clinton County, Ohio, in 1845. Seven years later he and his parents moved west to Illinois. In January 1864, at the age of nineteen, he enlisted as a private in the Fourteenth Illinois Volunteer Cavalry. He was then a robust farm reared youth, five feet eight inches tall and weighing about 165 pounds. Weeks later, his unit was attached to General George Stoneman's forces during General Sherman's campaign to capture Atlanta. On July 31, Stoneman and five hundred Union cavalrymen, including January, were captured during battle north of Macon. Had they prevailed, they might have reached their planned objectives of Macon and Andersonville. Instead, January and his comrades were themselves soon confined along-side the prisoners they had intended to liberate.

January spent three months in Andersonville before he was transferred, by way of Charleston, to the Florence prison. Four comrades from his company died during his time in Andersonville; more than fifty members of his regiment died in Confederate prisons before the end of his captivity. January himself was given up for dead in February 1865, when he was stricken with scurvy and "swamp fever" (probably the blood infection leptospirosis). Compounding his agony, his feet and ankles became infected with gangrene, leading his legs to molt necrotic flesh. Anxious to prevent its spread and certain his death was imminent, he pleaded with prison medical staff to operate on him. They dismissed his entreaties on the grounds that no intervention was likely to extend his life. Desperation drove January, as he later told the story, to do the unthinkable. While inside the Florence stockade and unaided by equipment or any pain relief, he used a pocket knife to hack off his own gangrenous feet.

January miraculously survived these impromptu amputations and at the war's close was exchanged in Wilmington, North Carolina. He remained there until he was transferred to a military hospital in New York. By then he purportedly weighed forty-five pounds, having shed more than one hundred pounds since his capture. Despite predictions of his certain death, he slowly recovered and seven months later was released from the hospital.

Within a few years of his release from Confederate prisons, John January began tirelessly spreading the story of the amputation of his feet at the Florence prison camp. (Library of Congress)

He bore more than physical scars of his service. As he explained in a deposition two years after the war, he had entered the Union ranks "full of hope" and "flushed with health and strength." He came home "worn down with sickness and suffering, and a cripple for life, with nothing to comfort me" other than the belief that "my sufferings were for a good cause."

Within a month of his liberation from Confederate custody, January began garnering national notoriety. During a speech in New York City in May, a Union veteran offered January's horrific experience as a vivid illustration of Confederate barbarism. In June, *Harper's Weekly*, the nation's most widely read magazine, published an etching of a skeletal January recumbent on a hospital bed. Although images of amputees had become commonplace by the war's end, the rendering of January was singular. *Harper's* engravers omitted all superfluous background details, isolating January in a sketch-like manner. He appears as a barely human object, his body a decrepit and shriveled vessel seemingly too depleted to sustain life. With returning prisoners like January as inspiration, poet Walt Whitman asked, "Can these be men—these little, livid brown, ash-streaked monkey-looking dwarfs? Are they not really mummied, dwindling corpses?"

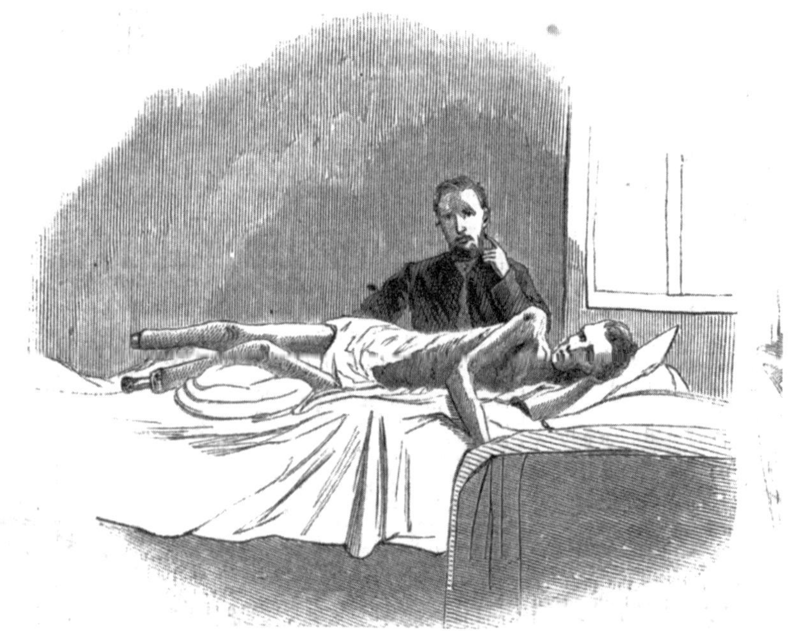

John January first attracted national attention when his skeletal image was depicted in a story about Confederate atrocities in *Harper's Weekly*. (From *Harper's Weekly*, June 17, 1865)

January's depiction in *Harper's* extorted sympathy for January and for countless prisoners mutilated by their captivity. Whether January was a willing subject for the rendering is unknown. Some maimed veterans tired of public scrutiny. The amputee, wrote a mordant veteran who had lost a leg, "is looked upon as public property" by curious strangers. In January's case, he likely was among scores of Union prisoners that Union surgeons photographed to document their appalling physical condition upon their release from Confederate camps. The author of the accompanying *Harper's* article affirmed that January's hospital portrait and the other engravings were "exact facsimiles of photographs."

January began embellishing his ordeal during the decade after the war. He was hardly exceptional in embroidering his war record, but when he did so, he amplified not just his own mettle, but also the wretchedness of the prison camps. Unlike some of his prison comrades, January did not write a prison memoir. Instead, his public lectures and numerous newspaper accounts kept his story before the public. The nation's preeminent prosthetics manufacturer, A. A. Marks of New York City, claimed January as a satisfied client and periodically planted stories in newspapers recounting his wartime ordeal, miraculous return to the world of the living, and postwar accomplishments. In the version of his prison stint that he widely repeated and that graced the photographs of his disfigured body that he hawked, January claimed to have joined the Union cause in 1861 as a sixteen-year-old, rather than when he was nineteen. In his retelling, he was a war-weary veteran rather than a greenhorn when he was captured. And he invariably recounted amputating his own feet, whereas, for several years after the war, he quietly acknowledged that another prisoner had wielded the pocketknife that lopped off his feet.

January's career as a veteran raconteur was of a piece with his generation's labors to make sense of the war, the most traumatic event in the young nation's history. The war precipitated a reappraisal of what it meant to be a citizen soldier when modern warfare consumed between one-third and one-half of the able-bodied male population of the United States. The predicament of former prisoners of war was an especially acute variation of the problem that all veterans faced: how to secure individual recognition and honor after the nation's first experience of mass warfare and slaughter on a previously unimaginable scale. But January and other prison survivors recounted not just another war story; they bore witness to the unique inhumanity of the camps—of life suspended, of living to eat, of dwelling in one's filth, of the casual cruelty, and of being powerless to prevent a friend's suffering. Former prisoners insisted that their prison experiences were so far outside the ken of their contemporaries, even other veterans, as to be almost incomprehensible.

Americans eventually resolved the dilemma of how to commemorate the anonymous valor of the war's citizen soldiers. Sculptures of battle-ready, well-clad, and resolute anonymous soldiers came to crowd the public spaces of the North and South alike as a celebration of the valor of common soldiers. These ubiquitous monuments, however, rendered the dirty, emaciated, disease-ravaged, and listless prisoner of war invisible. Hundreds of thousands of men during the war had experienced capture and imprisonment, but they fretted that a creeping national amnesia threatened to erase their ordeal and sacrifice from the national memory.

The first order of business for returning prisoners of war was to readjust to daily life outside of the prison yards. After enduring months or years of captivity, simple acts of personal agency were novel, often intoxicating, and sometimes overwhelming. The freedom to meander, to repose in private, to savor the fellowship of church services, and to undertake otherwise mundane activities at will could be heady experiences for men who had endured life within the dead line.

Former prisoners discovered that captivity had indelibly marked them. Habits that William H. Lightcap had acquired in Andersonville periodically resurfaced later in his life. He had joined the Fifth Iowa Cavalry when he was nineteen and had served only a few months before he was captured, in July 1864. From then until the end of the war he was imprisoned in Andersonville. He returned home to the Midwest, where a few years later he boarded with a family in Galesville, Illinois. One evening after dinner he found the lady of the house examining crumbs that he had carefully segregated to the side of his dinner plate. His time in Andersonville had instilled in him a phobia about the vermin that infested rice and bean rations there. Lightcap thereafter unthinkingly culled his food of anything that resembled bugs. Mortified by his eccentric custom, he explained to his hostess when and where he had acquired it. Later in life, decades after his military service, he still caught himself combing his food.

Even mundane accoutrements of everyday life proved disorienting to some former prisoners. The sensation of fabric against skin might stir prison memories of armies of crawling lice. Creature comforts that war veterans might have expected to relish after the privations of captivity could instead prove irksome. They did so for Henry Clay Mettam, a Marylander who served in the First Maryland (Confederate) Cavalry. Within the span of a few weeks, he went from imprisonment at Camp Chase to camping alone in the woods during his journey home to Maryland and then to the comforts of home. So accustomed had he become to rough living during his time at Camp Chase that he had difficulty readjusting to those domestic comforts. From being yet another prisoner among thousands, he abruptly became, as he recalled fondly a half century later, "the real thing," when he was "feasted and petted and almost spoiled." But he could not shed some of his prison ways. "It was quite a while before I could sleep on a feather pillow," he later recalled. Instead, he preferred pillows stuffed with straw like those he had improvised during his captivity.

Many former prisoners returned to civilian life with a yearning for the comforting security of family. The solitude and loneliness that Henry "Harry" Lloyd White experienced while imprisoned in Richmond and at Salisbury provoked him to reflect on his prewar conduct with contrition. When he was captured near Winchester, Virginia, in June 1863, he could claim many accomplishments. Born into a prominent family in western Pennsylvania, he graduated from Princeton, was admitted to the bar, and was elected to the state legislature before he was twenty-five. In 1862, when he marched off to war, he left behind his wife and a daughter. After a bout of intense self-reflection while in the Salisbury prison he had an epiphany: "Ambition has been my god." He regretted that he had given himself over to "my love of the world and its excitements" but now the privation of home life animated a wrenching transformation of his "emotional nature." He testified, "Turning myself into myself, I have felt to the fullest that I am a husband and a father." In early 1865 he returned home to his wife and daughter with a fresh devotion to his domestic obligations.

Although lacking White's apparent advantages and saddled with conspicuous infirmities, John January was similarly keen to marry and establish a family. After he recovered sufficiently to leave the military hospital in New York, he returned to his parents' home in Illinois. Two years later, he married Elizabeth Spence, and over the next decade their household grew to include six children and his elderly parents. Despite his severe physical handicap, he rose within the ranks of farm laborers until he gradually amassed a modest landholding. In 1882 he was the beneficiary of a sinecure appointment as the postmaster of the Illinois House of Representatives.

A decade later he moved his family to Dell Rapids, South Dakota, a small but flourishing farming community. By then, he was a proficient raconteur who subsidized his family's income by recounting his prison story to paying audiences, selling photographs of himself, and peddling patent medicines. As one contemporary account of his life reported, he could boast of more than two decades of "activity and breadwinning."

The urgency with which January, White, and many other ex-prisoners threw themselves into their roles as patriarchs and breadwinners was not exceptional. Many harbored an anxiety that their service and captivity had come at the cost in years lost that could never be regained. This sense of acute loss was evident within the committee of prison survivors charged by the Connecticut General Assembly in 1905 with designing a monument to honor men from the state who were buried at Andersonville. The committee wanted the monument's sculptor to portray the stolen youth of the men held within the camp. When the monument was unveiled it depicted a "typical New England lad" waiting his fate with calmness and resignation.

The postwar lives of White and January illustrate the resilience displayed by many former prisoners. Their record of sacrifice and ability to

Sculptor Bela Pratt's Connecticut Memorial at Andersonville, dedicated to "Lost Youth," is a poignant reminder that most prisoners were teenagers or men in their early twenties. (From *International Studio*, 1897)

withstand hardship fed their self-confidence and sharpened their resolve. John England, a member of the Second New York Cavalry and an Andersonville survivor, traced his newfound purposefulness to his ordeal as a prisoner, when he had been "chastened, humbled, and purified by the absolute experience of misery." Now, he explained, "the humblest of God's blessings" inspired his rapture. His outward appearance had been altered only slightly, but he was now "wiser and better"—although "somewhat sadder." With a logic common among nineteenth-century Americans, England attested that his "suffering" had hastened his rehabilitation and forged his newfound moral maturity.

While most former prisoners coped with their return to civilian life, a substantial minority did not. Ill health was the most conspicuous cause for the postwar struggles of ex-prisoners. Having survived the battlefield and prison yard, many arrived home sick and physically wrecked. Veterans collectively were more likely to suffer than the general population from tuberculosis, heart disease, rheumatism, chronic diarrhea, and dysentery after the Civil War. These maladies were especially acute among former prisoners of war, who ran a higher risk of death during the 1870s than did their peers, a risk that grew with each passing year. By the tens of thousands, they suffered from weakened teeth, ravaged gums, and other lingering results of malnutrition.

The effects of repeated and prolonged psychological trauma upon some prisoners hindered their adjustment to freedom. Among veterans, soldiers who served in units with high casualty rates were substantially more likely to develop chronic medical problems. Because so many Civil War soldiers enlisted with family, friends, and neighbors in local volunteer units, every death around them was likely to be of a close acquaintance or even kin. Soldiers captured during the last year and a half of the war, especially Union soldiers, had to come to terms not only with the casualties they had witnessed on the battlefield, but also with the deaths they saw daily within prison camps.

The distinction between "lived time" and "objective time," proposed by the French philosopher Henri Bergson, helps clarify the psychological trauma experienced by prisoners of war. Objective time, Bergson explains, is chronological and can be precisely tracked with watches and calendars. Lived time is a subjective experience of time as it is felt by individuals. It is shaped by specific memories of the past and anticipation of the future. Almost to a man, former prisoners recalled the glacial pace of the passage of time and their inchoate but consuming anxiety about the future while they were in the camps. After the war, this lived time in captivity manifested itself unbidden in the day-to-day activities of former prisoners.

When William Lightcap picked over his food a quarter century after his captivity, he experienced the lived time of his captivity simultaneously with the present moment. When Henry Lubker, a survivor of Andersonville, wandered the streets of Quincy, Illinois, eyeing suitable locations for prison escape tunnels, he remained trapped within the prison dead line from which he had been liberated years prior. Waitstill "Wait" Hastings apparently could never place enough distance between himself and the Salisbury stockade, where he had been held prisoner for a year. Captured at Chickamauga, he had tunneled his way to freedom and escaped to Union lines. Thereafter he was ever alert for fear of being recaptured. He hid from strangers and fretted that bloodhounds were on his trail until, at the age of forty-seven, he shot himself in the head.

Lightcap found the experience of his temporal duality embarrassing but not debilitating. For Lubker and Hastings the tenacious memory of their lived time in captivity was crippling and reduced them to tragic figures in their communities. In these and other instances, memory of the prison camps left survivors hollowed out, their ability to work curtailed, their capacity for joy imperiled, their ability to love compromised, and their most fundamental natural instinct—the will to live—undermined.

David Penman, by all accounts, was among those prisoners who saw and endured too much too quickly while in the camps. When only eighteen he enlisted in the Seventh New York Heavy Artillery. In the month prior to his capture in 1864, he and his unit saw almost continuous combat during the relentless campaign for Richmond. At its start they numbered slightly more than 1800 men. During the ensuing three months the Seventh suffered some of the highest casualties of any Union unit during the war. During the first month of the campaign alone, more than 250 of Penman's comrades were killed or missing in action, more than 550 wounded, and nearly 300 captured. On June 16, during the opening assault on Petersburg and almost one month to the day after Penmen first experienced enemy fire, he was captured. A week later he entered Andersonville, where he remained until he made the grueling trek to Jacksonville in April 1865.

Penman's first exposure to combat apparently troubled him less than the maelstrom of Andersonville. Examining doctors had no explanation for his mental distress but noted that "his friends claim it as due to long confinement in the prison." His ten months there "affected his youthful mind so much that he never forgot them." The suffering that most distressed him was that of his comrades. He was joined in the camp by nearly 400 members of the Seventh, 163 of whom died during Penman's captivity. He later complained often of "the terrible shock" he suffered when witnessing fellow prisoners kill "their own buddies" for stealing rations from one another. He never regained his mental equilibrium after the war and eventually had to be institutionalized.

Prisoners like Penman who manifested severe trauma from combat and captivity returned home ill prepared to face life events likely to amplify their despair and anxiety. Financial uncertainty exacerbated the stress and depression experienced by many former prisoners, especially Confederates. Within the span of months, James C. McCue was captured in the closing days of the war, sent to Point Lookout, suffered a protracted illness, and returned home to Virginia, in July 1865, only to learn that he was no longer the prosperous farmer he had been when he volunteered in 1861. Exhausted, sick, and defeated, he now faced impending destitution. When his efforts to restore his family's solvency failed, "his mind began to give way."

These and similar bouts of mental distress among ex-prisoners cannot be traced solely to repercussions of captivity. The effects of imprisonment can seldom be isolated from the cumulative traumas that soldiers experienced. Determining the precipitating event that drove John E. Jackson to shoot himself in July 1873 is perhaps impossible. Death hounded his family throughout his life. His mother had died when he was six, and one of his own children died in infancy before the war. A brother died in battle in 1862, and another was captured, imprisoned, and exchanged before dying in battle days before Lee's surrender. After the war two more of Jackson's children died as infants, and then his father, who was living with him, died eight months before Jackson took his own life.

Jackson had witnessed firsthand the war's toll while serving in the Twelfth Virginia Infantry. Early in the war, his unit had numbered nearly one thousand, but battle casualties, sickness, and desertion shrank it to fewer than two hundred by the end of his service. He also underwent the ordeal of captivity twice. During his first stint, from October 1864 to March 1865, he was confined at Point Lookout. On April 5, 1865, less than two weeks after his exchange and return to the Confederate ranks in Virginia, he was recaptured and sent to Hart's Island prison in New York City. Three months later, he was released and returned to Virginia.

Contemporary accounts of Jackson's suicide made no mention of either his Civil War service or his imprisonment. Neither was per se exceptional. Most southern white men of his age had served in the Confederate army, and many had experienced captivity. To posit battlefield trauma and captivity as possible triggers for suicidal impulses among former soldiers would have contradicted prevailing confidence in masculine grit. So too, an acknowledgment that Jackson's service might have contributed to his self-destruction would have raised troubling questions about the likelihood of future suicides among Jackson's comrades. Instead, his community elected to dwell on his personal culpability for his mental illness. He displayed defects of character when he surrendered to his recently acquired "vicious appetite" for alcohol. His recurring intoxication sent him into "gloomy and depressing melancholy" and cost him his job shortly before he took his life. No one publicly voiced a more humane explanation for Jackson's demise—that he had endured too much death and disappointment in his brief life.

Not all former prisoners could be expected to possess the seemingly unbounded optimism and exceptional tolerance for pain and distress that enabled John January to overcome his scarring during his imprisonment. He mustered uncommon physical stamina and mental resolve to nurture a large family, repeatedly revisit his prison ordeal, and display a much admired bonhomie. Yet even he, when not rehashing his prison ordeal for fellow veterans or paid audiences, could not escape unwelcome reminders of his captivity. Every few hours, for the remainder of his life, he had to remove his prosthetics to allow the swelling in his leg stumps to subside.

Amid the human devastation left by the war, former prisoners of war struggled for recognition. By one estimate, one million men on both sides were "torn and shattered" by their war experiences. On the Union side alone, 60,000 had been killed by dysentery and diarrhea. Nearly 30,000 had, like John January, surrendered a body part to amputation. More than 250,000 had received gunshot wounds, and another 225,000 had been discharged for serious ailments.

Former prisoners of war were not altogether absent in postwar medical discourse. The case files of John Shaw Billings, who would subsequently become one of the most influential surgeons in the nation, are illustrative. Billings was a recent graduate of the Medical College of Ohio in April 1862, when he was commissioned first lieutenant in the Union army. During the Peninsula campaign that year, he was responsible for the treatment of more than 150 gunshot wounds. As a newly minted surgeon, his interest was aroused by "special cases" that tested his skills and could be later written up and published. The circumstances of his patients, who were captured Confederates, warranted only passing mention. That they were exhausted, in severe pain, and "despondent at being prisoners" was acknowledged only because those factors influenced the patients' prospects for postoperative survival. The measured tone and clinical language evident in Billings's case histories suffused other medical discussions of prisoners of war, with nary a hint of the vitriol so common in other postwar mentions of the prison camps.

Horace Porter was one of the few voices within the medical community that urged recognition of the unique distress that former prisoners had experienced. A graduate of Yale, he served as a surgeon in the Seventh and Tenth Connecticut Infantry and oversaw a Union hospital at Beaufort, South Carolina. By 1889 he believed ample evidence demonstrated that disease, combat, and "the torments of Confederate prisons" had left many veterans with symptoms of an "incurably diseased nervous system." The "neural atrophy" of former prisoners had been "born in prison pens, while Infinite Mercy slept." The "after effects" might not become apparent until long after the precipitating trauma. But, he warned, they were certain eventually to emerge. Few of Porter's colleagues heeded his advice.

Had it not been for the federal pension program for Union veterans, former prisoners of war might well have become almost invisible to doctors. In 1862, Congress pledged to provide pensions to soldiers who had been injured or wounded and had incurred a disability while in service. The prerequisite for a pension was proof of a disability that had originated during the war and had been reported or observed by witnesses at that time. To secure a pension, a claimant had to substantiate his service, describe his disability and, if necessary, supply witnesses who could attest to his service and disability. The applicant then submitted to a physical examination by an approved physician, and a pension board finally considered his application. These protocols elevated examining physicians to de facto stewards of federal pensions charged with ensuring that only deserving veterans benefited from the nation's generosity.

Nothing in the 1862 pension law singled out ex-prisoners of war for special consideration. Soldiers who had suffered debilitating battlefield wounds were the intended beneficiaries of the program, but those who were disabled by chronic illnesses contracted while in captivity were also eligible for pensions. John January, for instance, had no difficulty securing a pension. No examining doctor could question the severity of his disability or its origins; he had walked into the Florence prison pen on his own two feet, but when he reached Union lines months later he had severed limbs and ailments that left him at death's door. His subsequent treatment had been charted in his extensive military medical files.

Other former prisoners confronted myriad problems satisfying examining doctors and pension officials. Whereas wounds on the battlefield or serious illnesses in military camps were typically recorded in soldiers' military records, the medical histories of Union prisoners while in Confederate hands were fragmentary, if they were even extant. Many chronically ill prisoners, moreover, had not received any medical care, especially during the last year of the war. When they later applied for a federal pension, their inability to confirm the origin of their disability or "to show treatment where none was to be had" provided grounds for pension officials to dismiss their applications. In these instances, the only recourse available to claimants was to resubmit their applications bolstered with testimonials attesting to their captivity and its contribution to their disability.

Ex-prisoners complained bitterly about the "red-tapeism" and fastidiousness displayed by examining physicians and pension officers who interpreted pension guidelines narrowly while ignoring the distinctive circumstances of former prisoners. The *National Tribune*, a newspaper devoted to the interests of Union veterans, protested in 1884 that the skepticism displayed by the pension bureaucracy toward the claims of former prisoners was unwarranted and heartless. The treatment that prisoners suffered at the hands of Confederates, the newspaper editorialized, "was in itself calculated to wreck the strongest constitution, [and] should be held as proof presumptive" that former prisoners' disabilities were the result of their imprisonment. While testifying before the congressional committees responsible for oversight of the pension program, William H. Mattingly of Indiana insisted that only the willfully obtuse or callous would deny that the ex-prisoner who retained his health during captivity was "a miracle of bodily and mental endurance." Former prisoners contended that even a cursory analysis of data regarding the diseases that had afflicted them in the camps and of their postwar morbidity would confirm their claims that Confederate prisons had been incubators of postwar disabilities. Instead, each application was considered in isolation, leaving each applicant to convince the examining doctors that his disability originated and manifested itself in the camps.

These requirements displayed a cavalier disregard for the realities of the prison experience. In some instances, skeptical pension officers required former prisoners to provide evidence of their physical "soundness" not just prior to captivity but also prior to enlistment. For many applicants, the only proof they could offer were testimonials of witnesses. But how, a former prisoner named John Richland wondered, was he expected to locate witnesses when so many of them had died in the camps or had scattered widely at the war's end? His own unit illustrated the challenges for applicants. Richland and forty-seven other soldiers in Company B of the 111th Ohio Infantry had been captured at Lenoir City, Tennessee, in September 1863. Thirty-five had eventually been transferred from prisons in Richmond to Andersonville. There, twenty-one of them had died. Only Richland and ten others had answered the last roll call in the camp. It was no small matter for pension applicants to track down possible witnesses among camp survivors, comrades from whom they had been separated during the chaotic dispersal of prisoners to new prisons and the haphazard exchanges at the end of the war.

The pension system was even less sympathetic to applicants who claimed to suffer from mental illnesses that they traced to imprisonment. During the postwar era, there was no common vocabulary to describe war-induced psychosis. Nor was any systematic investigation of the mental health of veterans or former prisoners undertaken. To the degree that there was discussion of the subject, it was by administrators of the nation's insane asylums. In the war's immediate aftermath, they were sanguine that, as the superintendent of the Government Hospital for the Insane in Washington, D.C., explained, the conflict "has not been marked, as such struggles have usually been, by any increase or peculiarity of mental derangement." Reflecting this wisdom, doctors and pension officials were inclined to dismiss veterans' claims of mental trauma.

To former prisoners fell the task of persuading pension officials to consider "diseases of the nervous system" in awarding pensions. This lobbying spurred a gradual and informal liberalization of the pension system. By the end of the 1880s, nearly a quarter of pension recipients had no record of either illness or injury. Applicants, especially former prisoners of war, interpreted this loosening of pension requirements as further evidence of the arbitrariness of pension protocols. Throughout the 1880s, ex-prisoners of war campaigned for specific provisions in the pension laws to address their circumstances and speed the awarding of pensions to them. But the proposed revisions never enjoyed sufficient political support to overcome opposition from other veterans who took offense that ex-prisoners without evident disabilities might receive pensions. Many Democrats, some of whom had served in the Confederate army, were also opposed to the expansion of pensions for Union veterans and especially former prisoners whose claims for public support impugned Confederate prisons.

When significant pension expansion finally occurred in 1890, former prisoners received no special consideration. The Dependent and Disability Act did, however, allow veterans to claim pensions for any debilities that "incapacitated" them "for the performance of manual labor," regardless of when or how they were incurred. Pension examiners evidently adopted their own subjective interpretations of the pension protocols and in more and more instances displayed a new sympathy for the former prisoners they examined. The panel that assessed the pension claim of Michael Nellis, who had served in the First New York Mounted Rifles, noted that he had endured "a history of great suffering" while imprisoned at Andersonville. They concluded that the nervous disease that incapacitated him probably had its origins "from this experience." Similarly, the doctors who examined William George Farrar divined that "his nervous system [was] completely broken down by prison life" in Andersonville.

Despite the expansion of eligibility, former prisoners had to display dogged determination when they attempted to navigate the pension application process. The burden of proof was especially daunting for Black applicants. Nothing in the law mandated that pension candidates be white, and eventually thousands of Black veterans secured pensions. Indeed, Black former prisoners were largely successful in securing pensions, with perhaps three-quarters of applicants doing so. But they had to run a gauntlet that may have discouraged many other Black veterans from seeking pensions.

Black ex-prisoners faced unique difficulties in producing the legal evidence required to substantiate their pension applications. They had been less likely to be assigned combat roles and less likely to receive medical care when they were injured. As a result, they often lacked corroborating medical records. Their experiences in captivity could not easily be confirmed because most had been re-enslaved by the Confederate government or private slave owners. These enslaved prisoners were seldom formally exchanged and therefore had difficulty substantiating the length of their captivity as well as the origins of any disabilities. In some instances, Black pension applicants had to secure the testimony of their former enslavers to confirm their captivity. Even when Black claimants provided adequate documentation, they still could not be assured that white examining physicians would endorse their applications.

James Myers, a veteran of the Forty-Third United States Colored Infantry, encountered all manner of frustrating delays and challenges when he applied for a pension in 1890. He was among the Black troops captured during the Battle of the Crater and, like most of them, was compelled to work for the Confederate army. He subsequently was confined in a Danville prison until March 1865, when he was transferred to a Confederate hospital. On his pension application he claimed that he had developed rheumatism "from abuse while in prison of confederates [sic], having received blows from officers in charge at High Bridge, Virginia." He also complained of muscle pain and joint inflammation, diminished mobility, and heart problems.

Affidavits from witnesses confirmed much of Myers's application. They testified that he had been "sound" when he joined the army, had been taken prisoner, and had returned from captivity afflicted by symptoms of rheumatism. But Myers lacked witnesses who could attest to his experiences during captivity. Worse yet, the white doctor in Savannah, Georgia, who examined Myers in May 1891 was contemptuous of him and his claims. Dismissing them as typical of Black men eager to shirk work, the examiner vouched that no disability prevented Myers from performing manual labor.

During the next eight years Myers underwent further medical examinations and gathered additional witness testimony until he finally secured an affidavit from Dr. S. Palmer Lloyd, the first Black physician in Savannah, attesting to his limited mobility and feeble breath. Myers then submitted to another examination with doctors who confirmed his disabling ailments. Nine years after filing his first application and less than a year before his death, Myers received his pension.

Fifteen years after his release from Confederate captivity, John January gave an account of his self-mutilation at the Florence prison to a gathering of the Andersonville Prison Survivors Association in Chicago. It was one of countless veterans' meetings he attended and addressed. For January and the other attendees, these meetings provided unique camaraderie because there was "no other comradeship like that of ex-prisoners of war." Among their fellow camp survivors, Union ex-prisoners found sympathetic audiences for their musings on captivity, their readjustment to civilian life, and the nation's unmet debt to them.

Confederate ex-prisoners displayed no comparable impulse to form organizations of prison comrades. Those who sought fellowship with other former prisoners did so within regimental organizations or, eventually, the United Confederate Veterans, which was founded in 1889. Unlike their Union counterparts, Confederate ex-prisoners had little practical incentive to establish associations of former prisoners. Organizing to secure federal veterans' pensions was pointless because federal revenues were never going to support aging rebels. Perhaps of greater consequence, the huge proportion of former Confederates shared the experience of captivity during the final months of the war. Although they may not have endured long stints in Union prisons, they shared the common experience of surrender and defeat. By way of contrast, Union ex-prisoners, including many who had survived harrowing experiences as captives, were outliers among their comrades. Thus, while Confederate ex-prisoners sought solace and affirmation with other veterans, some Union ex-prisoners sought out comrades who had undergone similar wartime ordeals.

Two organizations sought to rally Union ex-prisoners. The earliest, the Andersonville Prison Survivors Association, was founded in 1865 by former denizens of the Georgia prison who gathered in Washington, D.C., to testify during Captain Wirz's trial. Their stated objective was to provide aid to widows and orphans of prisoners who died in Andersonville, as well as to former prisoners themselves "when their circumstances demand it." In 1874 two hundred former prisoners gathered in Worcester, Massachusetts, and founded the National Union of Andersonville Survivors. After struggling to muster members and experimenting with several purportedly more inclusive names, that organization finally settled on Union Ex-Prisoners of War Association.

Neither of the Union ex-prisoners organizations mustered a significant portion of the population of former prisoners. For all the jockeying over its name, the Union Ex-Prisoners of War Association claimed just two thousand members at its peak during the late 1880s. The largest annual gatherings of either organization attracted between two and three hundred members; state and local meetings drew far fewer. With cause, organizers lamented any delay in recruiting new members; each year the pool of potential members shrank as prison survivors died off prematurely. Of the twenty-five ex-prisoners who founded the Andersonville Prison Survivors Association in 1865, only six were alive to hear January's address at the 1880 meeting.

We can only speculate as to why more Union ex-prisoners did not join these organizations. Perhaps many ex-prisoners preferred not to wallow in prison yard nostalgia with other former prisoners. John January readily relived his prison ordeal, but other former prisoners, like William Lightcap, only reluctantly acknowledged theirs. The likeliest explanation is that most Union ex-prisoners sought community not with other ex-prisoners but in the Grand Army of the Republic (GAR), the largest and most influential Union veterans' organization. Within it, their primary identity was as victorious saviors of the republic, not as beaten-down and aggrieved captives.

Within its broad ambit, the GAR accorded ex-prisoners conspicuous respect. Founded in 1866, the GAR by the century's close had more than four hundred thousand members, gathered in hundreds of "posts" across the country. Former prisoners of war Paul Van Der Voort, John G. B. Adams, and Ivan N. Walker were among those elected to one-year terms as president of the organization, and other ex-prisoners held state and national leadership positions. The organization's ceremonies awarded prisoners of war a central place in the war's memory. During the early years, new members were blindfolded, shrouded in a "disfigured" army blanket (to represent the suffering of the prisoner of war), and ordered to kneel before coffins that bore the name of Union prisoners of war. The initiates were informed that before them were the remains of "brother patriots" who had starved to death in the "demon den" of Andersonville and then been interred by their friends in unmarked graves. The lurid tableau made visceral the motto of the GAR: "Fraternity, Charity and Loyalty." There evidently could be no greater sacrifice than that made by the men who died at Andersonville, no greater loyalty to the republic than was displayed by them, and no more noble charity than that shown by prisoners to their prison comrades.

The symbiotic relationship between the GAR and the Republican Party also periodically elevated Union ex-prisoners. During the 1870s and 1880s, northern Republicans repeatedly invoked the memory of Andersonville to mobilize the electorate. Sometimes the acknowledgment of ex-prisoners was crassly opportunistic and revealed the party's desperation to rouse voters. In 1868, for instance, Georges Clemenceau, the future prime minister of France, observed the spectacle of a huge Republican parade in Philadelphia that included a wagon stuffed with former prisoners from Andersonville "who seemed to excite special enthusiasm along the route of the parade." On other occasions, Republicans recalled the horrors of Andersonville to remind Americans of the nation's debt, contracted during the war, to Union

Like most ex-prisoners, these survivors of Confederate prisons found fellowship with other veterans of the camps at Grand Army of the Republic encampments, in this instance in Minneapolis in 1884. (Library of Congress)

veterans. Any reluctance to fulfill this debt could be interpreted as an intentional slight that discredited the sacrifices of the war, and specifically the exceptional sacrifices of the former prisoners of war.

James G. Blaine, a congressman from Maine and perennial Republican presidential candidate, repeatedly invoked Andersonville to advance his party's fortunes. In 1877 he sabotaged plans of the new Democratic majority in the House of Representatives to restore full citizenship rights to those former Confederates who had not yet regained them. Blaine justified his opposition by observing that the bill would restore citizenship to Jefferson Davis, whom Blaine described as "the author, knowingly, deliberately, guilty, and willfully, of the gigantic murders and crimes at Andersonville." On other occasions Blaine denounced the Democratic Party's opposition to pensions for Union veterans and made a point of "reciting anew in the face of the rehabilitated South the story of Andersonville."

These gestures of recognition, however, did not still powerful currents of grievance and disquiet evident when Union ex-prisoners gathered. They perceived themselves to be unappreciated or wrongly ignored. The members of the Kansas Association of Union Ex-Prisoners wrung their hands that their sufferings, which "made up the blackest pages of the late war," were "untold—and by the world almost forgotten." John McElroy expressed the frustration of many former prisoners when he observed that more Union soldiers died in prisons than on the battlefield during the last year of the war. While the public was well versed in the "heroism and sacrifices" of those who died in battle, "it has heard little of the still greater number who died in the prison pen," he lamented. Former prisoner Charles M. Smith complained that major battles preoccupied the popular memory of the war. Overlooked was the "valiant service" and "fortitude, courage and heroism" of prisoners who had lived in "circumstances more trying and fatal" than did soldiers who never endured captivity.

Some former prisoners also acknowledged a lingering sense of failure. While dedicating a monument to Michigan soldiers who died in Andersonville, Governor Aaron Bliss hinted at the torment that he experienced while imprisoned there. "To suffer day by day, to see death strike right and left, and to realize that one is helpless to do aught but endure it all as best one can; while outside the walls marches are made, battles are fought, and deeds are done for home and flag."

An undercurrent of guilt also surfaced in the musings of former prisoners. Having survived the camps while friends, and sometimes family, did not, ex-prisoners pondered their survival at the same time that they wondered whether they had done enough to help those around them. John Ransom reflected, "When taken prisoner [I] was fleshy, weighing about one hundred and seventy-five, round faced, in fact an overgrown, ordinary, green-looking chap of twenty. [I] had never endured any hardships at all and was a spring chicken." He was grateful that he possessed "an iron constitution" and a resolute disposition. But when he reflected on the "thousands and thousands of thorough-bred soldiers [who died in the prisons], tough and hearty and capable of marching thirty, forty, and even fifty miles in twenty-four hours and think nothing of it, I wonder and [keep] wondering that it can be so—that I am alive."

CHAPTER FOURTEEN

# The Only True and Correct Picture

## (1865–1965)

While recuperating at home in Connecticut during the fall of 1865, Robert Kellogg wrote *Life and Death in Rebel Prisons.* Three years before, as an eighteen-year-old, he had joined the Sixteenth Connecticut. Weeks later and without any training to speak of, he was sent into battle at Antietam and severely wounded. In the spring of 1864, he and 400 men from his regiment were captured at Plymouth, North Carolina, and sent to Andersonville, where 150 of his comrades died.

Kellogg's account of his year in Confederate prisons was the prototype for hundreds of subsequent memoirs by ex-prisoners. Its subtitle aptly summarized its content: *Giving a Complete History of the Inhuman and Barbarous Treatment of Our Brave Soldiers by Rebel Authorities, Inflicting Terrible Suffering and Frightful Mortality, Principally at Andersonville, Ga., and Florence, S.C.* Kellogg provided an extensive litany of incidents, strung together in rough chronological order, of the typical prisoner's struggles to survive overcrowding, disease, exhaustion, food shortages, and mistreatment. Anticipating that readers might suspect that he exaggerated the horrors of the camps, Kellogg affirmed his trustworthiness. Located before the title page in the book is a testimonial from eighteen former prisoners, listed by name, rank, and unit, who vouch that Kellogg's description of prison life is in "nowise an exaggeration." On the title page itself, Kellogg quotes John 3:11, a biblical verse with layers of meaning: "We speak that we do know, and testify that we have seen." The passage affirms that Kellogg's eyes witnessed the scenes he described.

Yet, as Kellogg lamented, his words could not conjure fully the reality of life in the camps. In the decades after the war, the spectacle of the prison camps begged to be rendered for an American public that avidly consumed visual sensations. This appetite ensured that Andrew Riddle's photographs of Andersonville were widely copied to illustrate books and magazines. Exhibits of broken canteens turned into primitive plates, of wood scraps hewn into eating utensils, and of crude buckets used to hold soup rations were further evidence of this impulse (see page 147). To be in the mere presence of such mementos of misery apparently could enable observers to span the chasm of time and to be transported out of the familiar comforts of civilian life into the confines of the stockade, if only temporarily and incompletely.

Kellogg's publisher recognized the visual possibilities of the prison saga and scattered graphic images throughout it. The prison scenes complemented Kellogg's testimonials by depicting specific instances of suffering, identified by page number. Like historic relics, the illustrations were visual facts that enabled viewers to experience vicariously the ordeal of captivity.

The artistic renderings of the prison experience, displays of curated prison artifacts, and published accounts by ex-prisoners testified to the long shadow that the camps cast over the memory of the war. These disparate

THE MIDNIGHT STORM: OUR MISERABLE LODGINGS.—PAGES 196-218

"Midnight Storm" and other illustrations in Kellogg's memoir vividly evoked the hardships borne by prisoners at Andersonville. (From Robert H. Kellogg, *Life and Death in Rebel Prisons*, 1866)

renderings belied the ballyhooed postwar progress toward national reconciliation. Americans could agree that the prison camps had been a tragic innovation—nobody in 1861 had imagined that they could exist in such numbers over such a long period. But everything else about the camps and the prison-camp experience was contested. White southerners were little inclined to concede the Confederacy's responsibility for the trauma that Robert Kellogg and tens of thousands of other Union prisoners endured. Northerners, basking in victory and the moral certainty that it provided, were no less loath to absolve the Confederacy's prisoner-of-war policies.

Felix de la Baume vouched on his print *Let Us Forgive but Not Forget* that it was "the only true and correct picture of the horrible Slaughter Pen" of Andersonville. He was an implausible figure to corroborate the trustworthiness of anything related to his military service. Born in Saxony, he immigrated to the United States shortly before the outbreak of the Civil War. In 1861, while using the name Felix Oesser, he enlisted in the Seventh New York Infantry. In February 1862 he deserted. The following December he enlisted under his real name in an independent New York infantry regiment. A few months later he was discharged with a disability. In November 1863 he enlisted yet again, this time in the Thirty-Ninth New York Infantry. The explanation for his serial enlistments was simple: each time he enlisted he collected another bounty, a monetary reward that was being offered to entice men into the Union ranks as the war dragged on. (He apparently also dabbled in forgery and attempted to pad his back pay.) His chicanery came to an end during the summer of 1864, when he was captured in Virginia and sent to Andersonville. He remained there until the war's end.

Whether de la Baume's stint in Andersonville tempered his criminal inclinations is unclear, but it did give him an identity as an ex-prisoner of war that he embraced for the remainder of his life. He was among the ex-prisoners who founded the Andersonville Survivors Association in 1865. For years thereafter, his signature graced its gaudy membership certificates. He also augmented his income as a clerk in Chicago by selling his pictorial rendering of Andersonville. Based on his own sketch, the print was rendered for publication by George Frederick Keller, another German-born Union veteran. (Keller would later earn a living in San Francisco as one of the popular

Felix de la Baume carved out a role as a postwar advocate for Andersonville survivors.

and virulently anti-immigrant cartoonists of the late nineteenth century.) John January, the inveterate ex-prison raconteur, served as de la Baume's publicity agent.

The print sold well. De la Baume likely intended it to grace the walls of veterans' clubhouses as well as the parlors of patriots. (Original copies of the print are still routinely sold at auction and can be found in many present-day archives.) By comparison, only a few published prison narratives, including Kellogg's, enjoyed wide circulation and steady sales. Most memoirs by ex-prisoners had small print runs or appeared in local newspapers, obscure veterans' journals, and regimental histories.

With renderings of the prisoners' suffering and the malevolence of Confederate officials, *Let Us Forgive but Not Forget* comes as close as any single image to encapsulating the Union prison memory. Exhibiting a documentary intent, de la Baume crowded the print with images of specific individuals, including Robert Kellogg, and notorious incidents of cruelty, each identified in captions at the bottom of the print. Rather than shield the viewer's gaze from the misery in the stockade, de la Baume obstinately drew attention to it. Even the margins of the print provide space for grisly vignettes, including a detail of hounds mauling a prisoner and a reproduction of the *Harper's* image of an emaciated and near death John January. As

Inspired by de la Baume, the lithograph *Let Us Forgive but Not Forget* offered a panoramic display of Confederate atrocities at Andersonville.

further confirmation of the authenticity of the scenes depicted, de la Baume vouched that the drawing from which the print was derived had served as "important evidence" during the trial of Captain Henry Wirz.

Like de la Blume's print, with its scenes of willful wickedness, ex-prisoners devoted page upon page in their postwar writings to cataloging the iniquities of Captain Wirz, General William Winder, and other prison commandants. Union memoirists traced their treatment in the prisons to pathologies that distorted white southern civilization. De la Baume himself invoked the violence of slavery with images of prisoners being whipped and guard dogs charging across the stockade and mauling prisoners. These and other examples of moral corruption, Alonzo Cooper explained in his prison memoir, illuminated "the brutalizing effect of the system of human slavery," which had nurtured "total depravity" in the souls of slaveholders.

De la Baume's print and the memoirs of Union ex-prisoners were paeans to the resolve and stoicism of prisoners. The attention lavished on the heroic conduct of prisoners almost certainly revealed a lingering anxiety that some veterans and civilians questioned the mettle of men who had surrendered or allowed themselves to be captured. This same anxiety may explain the inordinate space devoted to attempted prison escapes in prison narratives. Drawing on the familiar conventions of slave narratives and antislavery fiction, memoirists cast the prison-camp escapee as exemplifying the dauntless resistance of prisoners to their captivity.

So resolutely does de La Baume's print focus on depicting physical suffering and brutality that it reveals no glimpse of the interior, private experience of captivity that modern observers may expect or seek. In the present day, when the individual psyche is our preoccupation, we may assume that prisoners of war ruminated about the psychic trauma of their captivity. They did so, but in a manner that displayed little of the brooding cynicism and disillusionment that suffuse many personal reflections on more recent wars. Their accounts testify to the importance they attached to masculine self-control in the face of hardship and suffering. Memoirists refused to acknowledge the possibility that the anonymous deaths, unmarked graves, and suffering in the camps had been a pointless waste. Instead, they displayed a guileless sentimentality while cluttering their memoirs with what may sound to modern ears as simplistic platitudes.

De la Baume dedicated his print to the memory of the fourteen thousand "martyrs" who died at Andersonville. Other prison narrators also invoked the language of martyrdom to describe their ordeal. Whereas many prison diarists during the war had assailed the moratorium on prisoner exchanges after 1863, postwar memoirists recast it as a regrettable but essential element of Union strategy. Their sacrifice in the camps had ensured that the ranks of the Confederate army had not been replenished with exchanged prisoners. As testament to their resolve and loyalty in the face of extremity, Union ex-prisoners repeated the motto "Death before dishonor," a slogan that was sprinkled throughout prison narratives and graced the letterhead of the Ex-Prisoners of War Association.

Etched on the stockade wall in de la Baume's print is the Latin maxim "*Fiat justitia ruat caelum*" (Let justice be done though the heavens fall). Prison memoirists demanded justice. During the war's immediate aftermath, former prisoners used their memoirs to urge the prosecution of Confederates for mistreatment of captives. By the 1880s Union ex-prisoners conceded that the time for retribution had passed, and that, as the title of de la Baume's print urged, magnanimity was now required. But de la Baume and other former prisoners held firm that no meaningful national reconciliation could occur until the "true history" of the Confederate prison camps, as they understood it, was acknowledged by the nation and acceded to by former Confederates.

In April 1891 *Century Magazine* published another Civil War reminiscence. The magazine, which was the most popular illustrated monthly journal of the era, had thrived during the 1880s by publishing a series of articles devoted to firsthand accounts of the war. Like its predecessors, the 1891 account was accompanied by lavish illustrations, including a striking prison scene entitled "Selling Bread." It depicts an auction of a piece of bread by a barefoot entrepreneur clad in tattered clothes. Only his battered hat, adorned with a dangling tassel, suggests his status as a soldier. Participating in the bidding are four men whose clothing is similarly vestigial. Three of them emerge from the darkness of crude, shelflike bunks where they repose. A shabby and ripped blanket, the only bedding in evidence, hangs down from an occupied pallet. So lethargic or weak are two of the men that they seem fatigued by the effort to raise their hands to confirm their bids. Several other men display no interest in the transaction and remain ensconced in their bunks with only their bare feet in evidence.

SELLING BREAD.

The illustration "Selling Bread" depicted a scene familiar to prisoners in both Union and Confederate prison camps. (From *Century Magazine*, April 1891)

The illustration depicts a strategy for survival devised by prisoners. By the last decade of the century, prison memoirists had made familiar the sometimes feverish prison yard bartering common in the camps. William Shelton, the illustrator for the *Century* article, knew firsthand of the commerce that he depicted in the scene. A talented painter, illustrator, and writer, he had served in the First New York Light Artillery. At the Battle of the Wilderness he was badly wounded and taken prisoner. While imprisoned in Macon, Charleston, and Columbia, he made several escape attempts, until finally succeeding on the day of Abraham Lincoln's second inauguration. An account of Shelton's own adventures appeared in *Century Magazine* just months after the publication of "Selling Bread."

In one crucial regard, the illustration was unlike any the journal had previously published. The desperation it depicted was of Confederate rather than Union prisoners of war. The author of the illustrated reminiscences was James A. Wyeth, who was then a prominent surgeon in New York; however, three decades earlier, he had served in the Confederate cavalry. In the fall of 1862, as a sixteen-year-old in Alabama, he had enlisted. In October of the following year he was captured and sent to Camp Morton in Indianapolis, where he remained until the war's end.

Wyeth's article was part of a deliberate change of course by *Century Magazine.* Until then the magazine and most other popular journals had

John A. Wyeth, here as he appeared in 1861, wrote a widely read riposte to Union denunciations of Confederate prisons. (From John A. Wyeth, *Sabre and Scalpel*, 1914)

shied away from controversial topics that might cause offense on either side of the Mason-Dixon Line, including treatment of prisoners of war. In 1890 new proprietors of *Century* were eager to duplicate the success of the journal's earlier war series. Sensing an opportunity to increase circulation by generating controversy, they began publishing articles on Civil War prisons, beginning with Wyeth's memoir.

Wyeth's article is the archetype of Confederate prison narratives, just as Kellogg's account had been for Union prison memoirs. Little in Wyeth's account was likely to have surprised ex-Confederates. It was a distillation of claims and charges they had been making since the war. But Wyeth's prominence as a renowned medical practitioner and the magazine in which his article appeared combined to give his account uncommon significance.

Wyeth's intent in writing the article was typical of Confederate memoirists. "The Southern side of prison life has not yet been fully written," he announced. For Wyeth, fealty to truth compelled him to take up the pen and provide "the truth" of his prison experience. During the previous two decades, northern accusations of Confederates' cruelty had aroused defenders of the Confederacy to take up their pens. Especially tireless was J. William Jones, a former Confederate chaplain who was the guiding force behind the founding of the Southern Historical Society. So urgent was the need for a rebuttal of northern accusations that in 1876 Jones devoted several of the earliest issues of the society's journal to refuting "the slanders against our Government and people." But Jones's rejoinder to Union ex-prisoners had reached only the small audience of former Confederates who subscribed to his journal. Wyeth, in contrast, carried the battle to the national audiences who read *Century Magazine*.

Equal parts counterthrust and apologia, Wyeth's article echoed almost point by point the accounts of Union ex-prisoners, including a reminiscence of Andersonville that *Century Magazine* had recently published, only a few issues back. Wyeth dismissed northern accounts of prison camps that had been broadcast by de la Baume, Kellogg, and others. He did not deny that Union prisoners had suffered during the war. But he was adamant that he and other Confederate prisoners had suffered as much as their Union counterparts and that the conditions he had experienced in Camp Morton differed only in degree from those in Andersonville. Without adequate blankets or clothing, he and his comrades had lived in barnlike, barely heated barracks. Chronic hunger had driven Wyeth's prison mates to devolve into near hogs who hunted vermin to eat and fought over the refuse thrown in the swill tubs in the hospital kitchen. Wyeth himself had been so emaciated that when he returned home after his imprisonment his mother and sisters had not recognized him. Like a scene inspired by de la Baume's print, Wyeth described capricious and cruel Union guards who beat prisoners without provocation.

Wyeth traced the suffering of both Union and Confederate prisoners to the Lincoln administration. Union prisoners were victims of the Union blockade of the Confederacy, which had resulted in chronic shortages across the South. However, southerners who lacked every necessity had little to spare for Union prisoners. Meanwhile, Confederate prisoners in the wartime North endured deliberate privation. Wyeth recalled watching day after day "the progress of emaciation" among his prison comrades. "It seemed strange," he observed, "that human beings were actually starving to death in a country rich in the necessaries of life." By shifting focus to Lincoln and the federal government, Wyeth redistributed the blame for prisoners' suffering, relieving Confederates of responsibility while magnifying the cruelty of Union policies.

Wyeth swaddled his outrage in the language of sectional comity. He assured readers that he had no intention of stoking sectional discord. The treatment of prisoners by both the Union and Confederacy, he vouched, had been "characterized either by indifference or neglect," which amounted "in many instances to criminality." Wyeth's claim of equality of suffering among prisoners was confirmed by the illustration "Selling Bread," which provided no visual clue as to the identity of the depicted prisoners. The scene of haggard prisoners, tattered clothing, and the simultaneously pitiful and comical auctioning of bread could have occurred at Cahaba, Libby Prison, Camp Chase, or Elmira.

When his article elicited a storm of denunciations by Union ex-prisoners, Wyeth was quick to accuse his northern detractors of allowing sectional prejudice to blind them to objective truth. Reconciliation, Wyeth implied, was not possible unless the charges of both sides received equal credence. The *Atlanta Constitution*, like many white southern newspapers, applauded the import of Wyeth's article, predicting that "in the course of a few years northern histories of the war will be thrust aside." To occupy Wyeth's common ground, northerners would have to surrender the memory that de la Baume and his comrades had spent years tending.

Some defenders of the Confederacy were no more willing than Wyeth's northern critics to embrace his claim of common suffering. They dismissed Union ex-prisoners' accounts as exaggerated sectional propaganda and expressed no contrition for the Confederate prison camps. Instead, they dug in their heels and elevated Captain Wirz as a convenient symbol to vindicate the Confederacy and its conduct of the war.

Amid the frenzy of Confederate commemoration at the turn of the twentieth century, white southern clubwomen launched a campaign to commemorate Wirz, whom they anointed an innocent victim of vengeful hysteria. In 1905, the Georgia Division of the United Daughters of the Confederacy (UDC) proposed a monument to Wirz to "rescue his memory," restore him to his "rightful place" among military heroes of the war, and counter "the slanders and falsehoods" regarding Andersonville. After fundraising and debating appropriate locations for the monument, the UDC in 1909 unveiled a commemorative obelisk in the center of the town of Andersonville. The monument provided a convenient location to vent Confederate grievances and rebut northern calumny. Etched on its pedestal is the charge that responsibility for the tens of thousands of graves at Andersonville and the other wartime prisons lay with neither the Confederacy nor Wirz, but with "the policy of the [Union] foe."

Winslow Homer was an unlikely documentarian of Andersonville. Raised in an antislavery milieu in Boston, he displayed no strong political inclinations before he became an artist-correspondent for *Harper's Weekly* in October 1861. While in the employ of the magazine, he traveled with the Army of the Potomac to gather material in person. His illustrations from the front lines quickly distinguished him as the war's foremost artist. Later in life, his métier became depictions of the nation's elite at play. Even so, he displayed an enduring interest in Americans on the margins of society.

His sympathetic imagination made possible his rendering of *Near Andersonville*, a scene he had not witnessed. In the painting Homer directs the viewer's eyes to a grave, statuesque young Black woman. Adorned in an elaborate, dark-colored day gown with ornamental piping, she stands in the door of a rustic wooden cabin. On the painting's left in the distance a band of armed Confederate soldiers, with the rebel battle flag waving above them, escorts Union captives to prison.

The female subject and her placement in the painting are striking. She is the only Black woman in any of Homer's Civil War–era paintings. Employing the Western aesthetic convention of locating evil on the left side of a scene and virtue on the right, Homer places the Confederates on the left and

Winslow Homer's painting *Near Andersonville* (1865–1866) was unusual in linking the fates of Union prisoners and Black southerners.

the Black spectator on the right. Left ambiguous is the status of the Union captives. Are they escapees whose flight has ended in their recapture? Or are they new arrivals about to be thrust into the maelstrom of the prison stockade? Also ambiguous is the status of the Black woman. Is she enslaved? Her rendering betrays none of the conventional caricature of Black humanity that distorted most depictions of Black people by white artists. Her clothing, seeming African headdress, black skin, and the crude cabin setting in the Confederate hinterland all suggest that she is enslaved.

Her presumed enslavement is, indeed, crucial to the painting's central conceit. The Black witness to the prisoners' trek emerges from the cabin's gloom and stands on the threshold of the more brightly lit exterior. By juxtaposing light and dark, inside and outside, Homer conveys the pending liberation of his Black subject. Yet while she will soon experience freedom, the Union captives she observes are marching toward their thralldom at the newly established prison at Andersonville.

The painting is one of the most haunting postwar meditations on the moral relationship between the sacrifice of Union prisoners of war and the extension of freedom's reach to Black Americans. Homer implies an ethical and existential equality between the ordeals of slavery and Andersonville. He seems to posit that the suffering of prisoners of war was the cost to expiate the national sin of slavery. The prisoners' loss of freedom made possible the Black woman's freedom. Or perhaps Homer was suggesting that while the prisoners' captivity was a tragedy of war, it should not obscure the larger imperative of destroying slavery.

When *Near Andersonville* first attracted public attention in 1866, it was acknowledged to be "full of significance." But thereafter the painting quickly disappeared into private hands, where it would remain for a century. Had it remained accessible to the public, it likely would have garnered ongoing interest, as did Homer's other war paintings.

The disappearance of the painting from public consciousness for generations is a metaphor for the waning acknowledgment of the link between the fate of prisoners of war and the freedom of enslaved Black people. By the turn of the century, fewer and fewer Americans recognized these coupled fates that had been evident to Homer in 1864. This fading recognition reflected a broad retreat from the egalitarian ambitions of the Reconstruction era. Even during the war, many Union soldiers had denied the destruction of slavery as an appropriate war aim and had bitterly opposed the Lincoln administration's insistence that the Confederacy exchange Black prisoners. During the two decades after Appomattox, the Republican Party's priorities shifted from remaking the former Confederacy to consolidating the party's own future. Champions of racial equality still found a home within its ranks, but the party increasingly attracted defenders of wealth and white privilege. The pursuit of national reconciliation discouraged discussion of any topic likely to revive sectional rancor, ranging from the morality of slavery to the treatment of prisoners of war. The resulting sectional détente required that northerners and southerners display public deference to their respective shibboleths. The price of this comity was a gradual expunging of Black people as active participants in the war.

Veterans and ex-prisoners contributed to this advancing amnesia. After the war, Union ex-prisoners increasingly played up the Union's responsibility for the moratorium of prisoner exchanges. Indeed, some dismissed purported Union outrage over Confederate treatment of Black prisoners as a convenient pretext to halt exchanges. Confederate apologists, meanwhile, seldom mentioned slavery or Black prisoners of war. In the tit-for-tat struggle over the memory of the prison camps, neither white Union nor Confederate veterans found it advantageous to linger on the issue of Black prisoners.

Conspicuously absent from the postwar contest over the memory of the camps were the voices of Black ex-prisoners. Only rarely did white newspapers and magazines devote space to Black ex-prisoners, as in the case of Isaac Gaskins, the Black veteran who was captured during the Battle of the Crater. Of the hundreds of memoirs published by ex-prisoners, none are by a Black veteran. This apparent silence may be partially explained by the illiteracy and obscurity of many previously enslaved Black soldiers. Thousands of Black soldiers had been re-enslaved or forced to work for the Confederacy, but only a few hundred Black veterans had experienced the prison camps that were the focus of national discussion.

Black historians had little to say on the topic either. In fairness, they could not have easily reconstructed a full history of Black prisoners with the records at their disposal. They also preferred to devote their attention to the battlefield exploits of Black men. Several veterans—most notably, Christian A. Fleetwood, George Washington Williams, and Joseph T. Wilson—published important accounts of Black wartime service. But none of these authors had been a prisoner of war. Nor had they been a member of a regiment that suffered large numbers of captives. Only Williams, in his *History of the Negro Troops in the War of the Rebellion*, devoted a chapter to Black soldiers in the hands of the Confederacy. His account, however, sheds no light on their actual experiences, but instead revisits the horrors of Andersonville, which only a very small number of Black prisoners experienced. The remainder of his account summarizes the warring sides' policies on prisoner exchanges and the Confederate troops' penchant for committing atrocities against Black troops. The cumulative effect of these silences was that Black prisoners of war, like Homer's striking painting, virtually disappeared from the broader national consciousness.

Until 1930 the discordant memories of the Civil War withstood the drift of national reconciliation. In that year, William B. Hesseltine published *Civil War Prisons: A Study in War Psychology*, which proved to be the single most important work on Civil War prisons during the twentieth century. Few books on any facet of the war have exerted comparable influence over so many decades. For more than a half century, it was often singled out by scholars as a crucial starting point for any understanding of Civil War prisons.

The enduring stature of Hesseltine's book reveals much about the evolution of American understandings of the Civil War. It also reveals the preoccupations of its author and his generation. Unacknowledged at the time of its publication and seldom noted since then, Hesseltine's book is as much a product of post–World War I disillusionment as it is a careful investigation of Civil War prisons.

The topic of Civil War prisons must have appealed to Hesseltine's professional ambitions and iconoclastic predisposition. Until then, no historian of note had addressed the treatment of Civil War prisoners of war. Surely there was no topic regarding the Civil War more in need of rigorous consideration than prison camps. The lodestar for Hesseltine and his academic peers was the reconstruction of the past through rigorous objectivity. When Hesseltine entered the professoriate, academic historical scholarship, with the pretenses of a scientific enterprise, was less than a half century old. Hesseltine's borderlands background—he was born and raised in the northernmost county in Virginia and trained in Ohio—made him an ideal candidate to address the divisive topic. By the standards of the day, his regional prejudices were mild. He did complain about "the damned Yankees all around on all sides" while a graduate student at Ohio State University and he condescended to his Black academic peers. He was not, however, a Confederate apologist. At the outset of his career, he had savaged the circle of Nashville-based intellectuals known as the Agrarians and displayed no tolerance for their Confederate hagiography. He mocked sectional chauvinism, romantic renderings of the Civil War, and anything that smacked of fervid idealism or patriotism.

Over a three-decade-long career, which ended prematurely when he died suddenly in December 1963, Hesseltine was a prolific author who wrote with the verve, certainty, and clarity of a gifted polemicist. He published several well-regarded works, but it was his grip on the interpretation of Civil War prisons that defined his enduring reputation. From his first book in 1930 until the introduction to a collection published after his death, Hesseltine held fast to the interpretation that he had arrived at during the 1920s.

In a 1935 article, published in the first issue of the newly established *Journal of Southern History*, Hesseltine distilled his argument into a single paragraph. Civil War prisoners of war, he contended, "remembered their hardships and invented atrocities to fit their hypothesis of 'Yankee' or 'Rebel' cruelty." Their lurid accounts of suffering, more than any other influence, kept alive "the bitter psychosis of the Civil War." During and after the war, reports of prison cruelty had "fed the fires of hate and inspired war-crazed peoples with savage impulses" just as stories of German atrocities in Belgium had done during World War I.

The wartime psychosis that Hesseltine so lamented was fundamental to his interpretation and it figured prominently in everything he wrote about Civil War prisons. Eschewing a rigorous definition of the psychosis, Hesseltine instead presumed that it was self-evident that wartime deceit and propaganda had fomented a disordered, irrational, and violent state of mind in the populace. This line of analysis exposed the deep, lingering cynicism among many Americans, especially intellectuals, about the legitimacy of American participation in World War I. Hesseltine was among a cohort who, as the essayist Bernard De Voto later observed, had been "young and impressionable at a time when an intellectual fashion was developing the (erroneous) thesis that the United States could and should have stayed out of the First World War and the (false) theorem that we were betrayed into it by propaganda." To these influences could be traced Hesseltine's understanding of Civil War prisons no less than to his impassioned pacifism and, before World War II, his ardent isolationism.

Having identified the wartime psychosis that was the engine of the calamity of Civil War prisons, Hesseltine next identified its wellspring. Strikingly, it was exclusively a northern pathology. Elsewhere in his writings he took southern secessionists to task, but the tragedy of the prison camps was manufactured in the North. Reflecting his hostility to moralism in public life, Hesseltine traced northern "prison atrocity stories" to "abolitionist propaganda," which posited that slavery promoted tyranny and contempt for human life. Deceit amplified this exaggerated portrait of southerners. The Svengali of the psychosis was Secretary of War Edwin Stanton. In the summer of 1863, Hesseltine explained, Stanton had encouraged "a quarrel over technical matters" between the Union and Confederate exchange agents as a pretext to sabotage prisoner exchanges. Stanton's motivations were "venom and coldbloodedness," as well as a cynical scheme to discourage Union soldiers from deliberately surrendering to the enemy. Stanton and his allies flooded the North with "propaganda" that pictured conditions in Confederate prisons in the "blackest colors" and Confederates as committed to destroying the lives of their prisoners. The reporting of "atrocity stories" became "an act of high patriotism" which forestalled northern criticism of Lincoln administration policies that were "devoid of humanitarianism."

Hesseltine's diagnosis of the Union wartime psychosis was a curious conclusion for a historian who professed to scoff at so-called psychohistory. He placed responsibility for suffering of prisoners squarely on the Union even while he mitigated that responsibility by tracing it to a pathology. In this fashion he trivialized the Union cause by associating it with irrational impulses and cynical propaganda. His distrust of Union motivations is nowhere more manifest than in his curious charge that Secretary of War Stanton used "a quarrel over technical matters" to sabotage prisoner exchanges. Apparently, the Confederacy's stated policy of enslaving or executing Black prisoners of war was a technical matter rather than a humanitarian violation.

Hesseltine's silence about the predicament of Black prisoners of war was coupled with surprising credence for claims of Confederate altruism. Hesseltine did not ignore the suffering in Confederate prisons, so much as he excused it. To the degree that Union prisoners did suffer, it was, he explained, because of the failure of the Confederacy's transportation system, the "inefficiency" of its prison system, and its wartime poverty, all of which were exacerbated by the Union blockade of southern ports. Faced with these circumstances, the Confederacy, as any polity would have, directed its scarce resources to its armies rather than to its captive enemies. Hesseltine assured his readers that Confederate officials had "struggled valiantly" to get supplies, but they had been unobtainable.

In Hesseltine's hands, Captain Wirz —sickly, harassed, and assigned a task beyond anyone's capacity—was a figure cast in a Greek tragedy. His postwar execution was the tragic culmination of wartime psychosis. His persecutor, Norton P. Chipman, was consumed by the psychosis and conducted the prosecution without regard for rules of evidence or perjured testimony. Because the psychosis, and Secretary of War Stanton, required a scapegoat, Wirz was "found guilty of conspiring with Jefferson Davis and Robert E. Lee to destroy the prisoners." (In fact, Wirz was not found guilty of conspiring with Davis and Lee but rather of specific acts of violence and mistreatment.)

Once stirred into existence, the wartime psychosis was apparently eternal. To Hesseltine's evident disgust, it suffused the groaning shelves of prison memoirs and soldiers' diaries published since the Civil War. Because the passion of prisoners of war could not be reconciled with "objective" history, Hesseltine summarily dismissed accounts by ex-prisoners as largely worthless partisan special pleading. Even worse, the motivations that prompted ex-prisoners to set down "their real or imagined experience" had been crass. Beyond cashing in on the wartime psychosis, Union veterans hoped that their prison reminiscences would sustain and enrich "their series of pension raids on the national treasury." By dismissing prison diaries and memoirs as so much hackneyed and duplicitous "charlatanry," Hesseltime avoided the need to analyze them.

Hesseltine's interpretation of Civil War prisons proved so enduring because it was consonant with the ascendent explanation of the Civil War during the mid-twentieth century. Hesseltine fulfilled the crucial requirement of "objective" scholarship by defending neither side in the conflict. His ambivalence about the war did not evince sympathy for the Confederate cause. But nor did he celebrate the Union triumph. His silence on the dispute over Black prisoners of war and ambivalence on the Union cause resulted in a work that southern historians could use to vindicate the Confederacy. Not surprisingly, they readily embraced it. Hesseltine's interpretation also meshed seamlessly with the argument that the Civil War had been a "needless war" that resulted from inept statecraft and irresponsible sectional extremism. Many of the leading historians of the era contended that a "blundering generation" had allowed a regrettable combination of "fanaticism" and "bogus leadership" to push the nation over the precipice of civil war.

Hesseltine's account of the prison camps allowed little foothold for alternative interpretations. Reflecting his prejudices, Hesseltine had relied exclusively on official records from the war. Any scholar who contested Hesseltine's approach by drawing on prison memoirs risked perpetuating the "wartime psychosis" and violating the dictums of "objective" history. So too, any scholar who introduced "moralism" into the discussions of wartime prisons by questioning Confederate motivations and conduct was certain to offend prevailing professional standards of impartiality.

With his dismissal of the "myth of Andersonville," Hesseltine completed the marginalization of prisoners of war that ex-prisoners had anxiously anticipated since the war. What had happened in the camps and the experiences of the captives themselves were never of abiding interest to Hesseltine. Instead it was the "war system itself," as he called it, and the psychosis it had manufactured that riveted his attention. Yes, Andersonville had been an atrocity, but, Hesseltine announced, "it was a minor part of the total atrocity which the war committed against the reason of men."

Had James A. Wyeth lived long enough to witness the centennial of the Civil War, he likely would have been gratified that the "myth of Andersonville" had been vanquished. By then the prevailing wisdom regarding the camps was consonant with Wyeth's claims that had provoked such controversy in 1891. During the intervening decades, Hesseltine gave scholarly credibility to the dismissal of Andersonville as a singularly gross violation of humane warfare. In 1959, on the eve of the centennial, Bruce Catton endorsed and parroted Hesseltine's conclusions. Catton, who was the most widely acclaimed and read Civil War historian of the day, published his account in *American Heritage*, a hugely popular history magazine that graced coffee tables across the nation. Catton's essay opened with a telling caption: "Andersonville was merely the worst of a bad lot." Robert Kellogg, Felix de la Baume, and other Andersonville survivors would have recoiled at any use of "merely" in conjunction with Andersonville. Catton passed over the innovation that the camps had represented and the combination of resources and planning that had made them possible. Instead, he pointed to "hasty action" prompted by wartime pressures, "human blundering," and "administrative red tape" as the impetus behind the prison camps and the misery in them. But the real culprit, he concluded, was "war itself."

A decade later, a widely used text on the Civil War reached a similar conclusion, assigning the camps to the list of tragic blunders that had sparked the war and sustained its carnage. The text's authors cautioned the "fair minded observer" from offering "sweeping reproach" to either warring side. "Whatever be the message of the dead at Andersonville and Rock Island," they warned, "that message is not to be read as the mandate for the perpetuation of sectional blame and censure."

By then so complete was the exculpation of responsibility for the camps that many scholars dismissed prisoners' accounts of their captivity as hysterical, partisan, and dishonest. This scholarly contempt for prisoners' testimony was conspicuously displayed during the centennial, when a team of noted historians surveyed the vast body of writings on the Civil War. Included in the multivolume work was an extensive inventory of firsthand accounts of the prison camps compiled by Frank L. Byrne, whose graduate advisor at the University of Wisconsin had been William Hesseltine. Channeling his mentor's perspective, Byrne provided pithy reviews of hundreds of firsthand prison memoirs. He praised a select few as "fairly objective," "temperate," and "unembittered." But he dismissed many others on the grounds of the authors' perceived partisanship, earning his reproach as, for instance, "bitter," "very partisan," "lurid," "rabidly hostile to Confederates," "exaggerated," "biased," or "hate-filled."

Historians, in the name of "objective history," comforted Americans with claims that the camps had been an unintended consequence of an unprecedented war. As long as ex-prisoners had survived, their memory of the camps could not be expunged. But as time took its toll on the ranks of former prisoners, the memory of the camps was sequestered and pushed to the margins of the nation's history. In its place a consensus about the camps emerged: in our contemporary parlance, historians acknowledged that "mistakes were made." When historians did so, they helped clear the way for the triumph of a heroic and romantic memory of the war that would have been unrecognizable to Robert Kellogg and his prison comrades.

CHAPTER FIFTEEN

# Places of Shadows

A tombstone bearing the name of Leander Farnham, whose burial Andrew Riddle photographed, remains to the present day. After Farnham succumbed to malnutrition, his corpse was assigned the number 5851. He was preceded in a mass grave at Andersonville by E. A. Johnson (dysentery) and was followed by D. Palmer (malnutrition). (When his brother and fellow prisoner Lorenzo Farnham died of prolonged sun exposure four days later, his burial number was 6264.) The placement of Farnham's tombstone (and most of the other thirteen thousand tombstones) almost certainly has little relationship to the precise location where his spent body was laid in the ground. But, at a minimum, his sacrifice and presence there are acknowledged.

The cemeteries that hold the bodies of Farnham and tens of thousands of other prisoners who died in the camps are among the only remaining vestiges of the Civil War prisons. Since the late nineteenth century, Americans have preserved nearly 60,000 acres, or roughly ninety square miles, of Civil War battlefields. Less than 750 acres associated with Civil War prisons, in contrast, are maintained as historic sites. Andersonville National Historic site accounts for most of that total, while the rest mainly consists of cemeteries scattered on both sides of the Mason-Dixon Line. These cemeteries, which endure in obscurity, betray the curious mixture of indifference and solicitude that Americans have displayed toward the prison camps.

The cemeteries that hold the Confederate prisoners who died at Camp

Leander Farnham's gravestone. (Kevin Frye Andersonville Historian)

Douglas, Camp Chase, and Point Lookout are illustrative. During the war more than 3800 deceased Camp Douglas prisoners were interred in the potters' field in the Chicago city cemetery (now Lincoln Park). In 1866 they were dug up and moved to the Oak Woods Cemetery, located south of the former prison site. At the time, no individual headstones marked the location of graves, so the human remains became hopelessly jumbled. During the succeeding decades Confederate associations began fund-raising campaigns to erect a memorial to the dead in the cemetery. On May 30, 1895, in an event symbolic of the spirit of sectional reconciliation that was then waxing, President Grover Cleveland and his Cabinet attended the dedication of a cemetery monument commemorating the Confederate prisoners. An act of Congress in 1903 provided federal funds for the improvement of the so-called Confederate Mound, including erecting plaques listing the names of 4243 known Confederate soldiers interred in what is perhaps the largest mass grave in the nation. Another 2000 may rest there, but spotty records foil an exact count.

At Camp Chase, a two-acre prison cemetery holds an estimated 2168 remains. In the decades following the war, it too fell derelict—until William H. Knauss, a wounded Union veteran, recruited Union and Confederate veterans' organizations to renovate it. In 1904, Congress allocated funds for the maintenance of the cemetery. Ensconced in a residential neighborhood, it presently is bordered by a baseball field, a hair salon, and an ice cream stand.

At Point Lookout the remains of more than 3000 deceased prisoners were scattered in three cemeteries. Their graves initially were marked with wooden headboards, but all semblance of order was lost when bodies were haphazardly exhumed by families of the deceased. Confusing matters further, in 1870, the state of Maryland purchased the former prison site and removed 3404 Confederate dead to a mass grave in a nearby cemetery. A modest marble obelisk marked the new grave site. Thirty years later, a federally funded effort to document individual graves proved futile. Instead, an eighty-five-foot granite obelisk was erected on a burial mound. The exact number of individuals buried in the mass grave is unlikely ever to be determined.

At Elmira and Rock Island, conscientious grave tending ensured that the Confederate dead did not disappear into unmarked mass graves. So precise were the records kept by John W. Jones, the ex-slave who served as the cemetery sexton in Elmira, that when federal funding subsidized the rehabilitation of the prisoners' graves in 1907, only 7 of the 2973 Confederate graves could not be identified. Those who died at Rock Island were also buried in coffins with headboards marking each grave. In 1871, Lieutenant Martin Luther Poland, who was assigned to the federal arsenal on Rock Island, mapped all the graves. Nearly four decades later, when the cemetery was resurveyed, Lieutenant Poland's handiwork ensured the accurate placement of marble headstones inscribed with the name and regiment of each deceased Confederate.

The graves of Union prisoners of war typically fared worse. An exception was those prisoners who died while in transit through Lynchburg, Virginia. They were so conscientiously buried that federal officials readily identified their remains when they were disinterred after the war. Confederates elsewhere displayed marked indifference to the burial of Union prisoners. At the Salisbury prison, Confederates piled deceased prisoners in eighteen 240-foot-long trenches in a former cornfield. In the absence of any accurate records, the number of prisoners buried willy-nilly is unknown. After the war, aggrieved northerners estimated that as many as 11,700 lay in the ground and inscribed that total on the granite obelisk commissioned by the U.S. Congress in 1873 to honor the unknown soldiers buried there. (Present-day estimates of the number of interments in the mass graves run about 3800.) At Florence, 2802 Union soldiers were buried in unmarked trenches on land later purchased by the federal government. In Richmond, Union prisoners who perished in the city's hospitals and prisons were buried helter-skelter, including in a cemetery otherwise reserved for Black residents of the city. After the war their remains were consolidated in a newly created national cemetery.

Without a prodigious reclamation effort, the graves of Farnham and the other thirteen thousand dead at Andersonville would have become unidentifiable. Because Farnham and the other occupants of the mass graves there were identified only by weather-worn numbered wooden stakes, any effort to catalog the graves required an accurate list of the names of the dead and their identifying numbers. Fortunately, Dorence Atwater of the Second New York Cavalry surreptitiously maintained a register of prison deaths while he was a prisoner. Captured in the aftermath of the Battle of Gettysburg, eighteen-year-old Atwater was sent to Belle Isle and then transferred to Andersonville in late February 1864. After a bout of chronic diarrhea

Memorial to the Unknown Dead, Salisbury National Cemetery. (Library of Congress)

secured his admission to the prison hospital, he was tasked with maintaining the camp's death register. Convinced that Confederate officials would never willingly reveal the death register, he secretly copied it. When he was exchanged in February 1865, he smuggled his copy of the register out of the camp. After his return north he notified Union officials of his record of Andersonville burials, prompting federal plans to mark the graves at the Georgia prison.

While the grave-site expedition was still being planned, Atwater contacted Clara Barton, who had gained international renown first as a tireless nurse during the war and then for her efforts to locate missing soldiers. Keen to assist the work at Andersonville, Barton asked Secretary of War Edwin Stanton if she too could join the expedition. In July and August 1865, while laborers erected wooden headboards and tidied the prison burial grounds, Atwater and Barton undertook the painstaking task of notifying families of men who had died in the prison. The work of compiling an accurate cemetery record continued for the remainder of the century (and, indeed, to the present), ensuring that fewer than five hundred of the more than thirteen thousand prisoners buried at Andersonville remain unidentified.

Few Americans exhibited a comparable compulsion to preserve the prisons themselves. Happenstance and expediency explain most of what remains of the prisons. That northerners showed no interest in preserving the prisons that had held Confederates was unsurprising. Northerners displayed neither embarrassment about the prisons nor any explicit intent to erase them from the landscape. In an era when deliberate historical preservation was rare, northerners attached no enduring historical significance to the campsites.

After the war the U.S. army had use for only a few of its erstwhile prison camps. Rock Island, Fort Warren, and Fort Delaware remained active installations, but their prison facilities were either dismantled or repurposed. At Rock Island, the army razed the last prison buildings in 1907. Elsewhere, no steps were taken to preserve the Union prison camps that had no military utility. The dismantling of Camp Chase, for example, began three months after the defeat of the Confederacy. On July 14, 1865, as per Colonel William Hoffman's orders, the prison commandant sold everything of value at public auction, netting $3200 for federal coffers. By the middle of the following year, the camp had been emptied of government property, leaving behind rows of derelict prison barracks that a visiting journalist described as a desolate "skeleton." A group of investors subsequently bought the site, stripped the barracks of any remaining lumber, and then razed them along with the prison walls. In 1905 a real estate company purchased most of the former prison grounds and divided it into residential lots. Since then, the development has evolved into the Westgate neighborhood.

Condominiums, apartments, and a shopping center cover the site where Camp Douglas once stood in Chicago. Between July and November 1865, the army sold everything of value, and scavengers made off with the rest. By 1878 a local history enthusiast found it impossible to determine the precise site of the former prison. For most of the twentieth century, the one-time existence of the prison in the so-called Douglas neighborhood went unacknowledged. In 1990, Ernest Griffin, the patriarch of a family-owned funeral home, erected a memorial to Civil War soldiers, including the Confederate prisoners held in Camp Douglas. He had become fascinated by the Civil War and the prison after he learned that his grandfather, Charles H. Griffin, a free Black man, had enlisted in the Twenty-Ninth Colored Regiment in 1864 at Camp Douglas. Along with Issac Gaskins and the other soldiers in the unit, Charles Griffin had stormed into the Crater in 1864. But, unlike Gaskins, Griffin had escaped capture. He had remained with his unit when it was transferred to Galveston, Texas, where he had been present on June 19, 1865, when General Gordon Granger announced the freeing of all slaves in Texas.

When Ernest Griffin dedicated his memorial wall more than a century later, he was questioned as to why the grandson of a Black Union veteran was honoring Confederates. He responded, "They were the sons of God before they were the sons of man." He subsequently added a Confederate battle flag, at half-staff, to the memorial. After the flag was repeatedly torn down, Griffin defended its display as "a symbol of respect for a dead human being." The memorial remained standing until 2007, when the family sold their property to developers and the memorial was dismantled. Seven years later the Illinois Historical Society erected a small plaque at Thirty-Second Street and Martin Luther King Drive, marking the first permanent acknowledgment of the former prison camp where it had once stood.

At Johnson's Island the surplus equipment and materials, the buildings, and the stockade walls were auctioned off in 1866. Most of the lumber was salvaged, and some of the smaller buildings were dragged to the mainland, across Sandusky Bay when it froze during the winter. For three decades after the war, much of the island, including the site of the prison, was devoted to an orchard and farmland. By the end of the century all visible reminders of the prison depot had disappeared.

Nature, as much as human action and neglect, was responsible for obliterating the remnants of Point Lookout. The most primitive of all Union prison camps, Point Lookout had few structures that were likely to survive without human intervention. Even then, the relentless waters of the Chesapeake Bay during the past century and a half would have taken their toll. At least half of the original site of the prisoner-of-war stockade has now been consumed by shoreline erosion.

On April 4, 1865, two days after Confederate forces evacuated Richmond, Abraham Lincoln and a small entourage toured the smoldering ruins of the former Confederate capital. When they passed Libby Prison, which only Andersonville exceeded in notoriety, the President paused to gaze at the site. A crowd of whites and Blacks greeted him with shouts of "We will pull it down!" Apparently overwhelmed by sorrow, Lincoln responded, "No, leave it as a monument."

Lincoln's request, alas, was not fulfilled. Northerners might have been expected to preserve the Confederacy's most notorious prison camps as vivid symbols, along with whips, manacles, and slave auction blocks, of the cruelty of the southern civilization that had sundered the republic. As Lincoln suggested, the former camps might also have served as memorials to the men who had endured the singular hardships of captivity. Northerners, however, showed only fitful interest in their preservation.

For a time, Libby Prison appeared destined to become a memorial. From April 1865 until August 1868, federal authorities jailed Confederates in the former warehouse-cum-prison. Even so, its notoriety attracted a steady stream of curious travelers keen to glimpse its infamous chambers and to pocket mementos. By 1888, they had "picked it to pieces." This persistent interest in the site inspired a group of Chicago investors, including Charles F. Gunther, a candy tycoon, to purchase the warehouse, dismantle it, then ship its six hundred thousand bricks to Chicago on 132 railroad cars. There in 1889 it was rebuilt to serve as the home for Gunther's massive collection of Civil War artifacts, historical curios, and such oddities of dubious provenance as the preserved skin of the serpent from the Garden of Eden. For almost a decade crowds ogled the shrine's hodgepodge.

But when public interest in the old prison waned, it was torn down again. Many of the prison's bricks became souvenirs, while others were used to construct a wall of the Chicago Historical Society. The beams, timbers, and most of the wood were sold to a farmer who used them to build a massive barn, which remains standing near Hamlet, Indiana. Thus, while building materials from Libby Prison endure to the present day, no one since the end of the nineteenth century has been able to amble through its rooms, touch its walls, peer out its windows, or experience the frisson of occupying space that once held thousands of desperate prisoners.

Almost all the other Civil War prisons vanished from the landscape long before Libby Prison was transported, brick by brick, to Chicago. Salisbury and Millen prisons were ransacked even before the end of hostilities. Sherman's troops razed the remnants of the Millen camp during their March to the Sea in 1864. When Union General George Stoneman and his troops reached Salisbury in April 1865, the prison had been emptied and was being used as a supply depot. Stoneman ordered the prison structures burned and a wood fence built around the mass graves. Of the buildings that once constituted the prison, only one house, believed to be a guardhouse, survived. The remains of the Camp Ford prison compound in Texas were destroyed in July 1865 by a detail of the Tenth Illinois Cavalry. In Danville, Virginia, the repurposed warehouses that had made up the prison facilities there were returned to their previous commercial purposes. Only one of the prison warehouses, much altered during the intervening years, remains standing. It is not open to the public and, aside from a small plaque on one of the exterior walls, is unlikely to attract the attention of any passerby. At Florence, the few permanent structures that Confederates had erected quickly vanished, leaving a landscape that betrays no evidence of the onetime prison camp.

Andersonville alone aroused a preservationist impulse among northerners. In the war's immediate aftermath, the prison cemetery was a focus of northern interest. Meanwhile, the prison grounds became an impromptu haven for several hundred formerly enslaved Black families. Through a combination of intimidation, violence, and litigation, the prewar white owner eventually regained control of the prison grounds. He took no measures to preserve the site. A visitor in 1873 noted that "a rich growth of bushes, trees, and plants" covered prison grounds that once had been utterly barren of any vegetation. Many of the crude wells dug by parched prisoners also remained, posing hazards to any visitors intrepid enough to trek to the forlorn site. The

Stockade at Andersonville Prison, 1868. (Library of Congress)

dead line that had once been the terror of prisoners was repurposed to discourage foraging cattle from wandering into the creek where prisoners had once bathed and relieved themselves. The stockade remained standing, but anyone could "pass through it at almost any point." Within three years, the visitor predicted the entire stockade would collapse upon the ground.

While the prison site was reclaimed by nature, the cemetery became a destination where formerly enslaved people of southern Georgia and southeastern Alabama gathered every national (as opposed to Confederate) Memorial Day to commemorate the war and the sacrifice of the Union soldiers who had fought in it. These raucous celebrations of Union valor and victory galled white Georgians, who pointedly ignored Memorial Day.

During the 1880s white Union veterans evinced a newfound interest in Andersonville. In 1890, the Grand Army of the Republic (GAR), Department of Georgia, bought the former prison grounds with the intention of maintaining the site as a shrine. But the organization quickly concluded that it lacked adequate resources to do so and in 1896 deeded the site to the Woman's Relief Corps (WRC), the women's auxiliary of the GAR. Under the auspices of the WRC, the prison grounds were cleared and a spate of monument building followed. Between 1899 and 1916 nine cemetery monuments, funded by various states, were erected commemorating soldiers who had been imprisoned or perished at Andersonville. An additional twelve monuments were dedicated within the prison grounds between 1901 and 1934.

Even as white veterans and their female allies assumed control over the prison grounds at the turn of the century, the participation of Black people in Memorial Day celebrations continued to rile local whites. Beginning in 1902, the sheriff, bolstered by "a posse of hand picked men" and state militia, supervised the thousands of Black excursionists who gathered at the cemetery. Local authorities pressured railroad companies to end reduced excursion fares for Black revelers. The cumulative effect of white harassment was unmistakable; white news accounts applauded when the military kept away "the disorderly colored element" and at the same time drew "the increased attendance of the white people." Within a few years, Black celebrants had been largely exiled from the Memorial Day traditions that they had initiated at Andersonville.

In 1910, on the verge of the orgy of national reconciliation that accompanied the fiftieth anniversary of the war, the WRC donated the prison grounds to the federal government. Far off the beaten path in southern Georgia and viewed with marked hostility by many white southerners, the Andersonville prison site was an unwelcome and awkward charge for federal officials. Any development of the site that foregrounded the suffering of Union prisoners was certain to spark immediate denunciations by Confederate heritage groups and white southern politicos. (The year prior, the Georgia United Daughters of the Confederacy had erected their memorial to Henry Wirz in the village of Andersonville.) With neither funding nor any clear mandate, federal officials made only token enhancements, leaving the site effectively unimproved for much of the twentieth century.

Not until 1970 were significant federal resources devoted to the interpretation of Andersonville. Motivated by the allure of tourist dollars, influential local whites pushed for the site to be declared a National Historic Site. But, reflecting deference to long-standing white southern sensibilities, the mission of the site was *not* the exclusive interpretation of the Andersonville prisoner-of-war experience but rather "the role of prisoner-of-war camps in history," and "the sacrifice of Americans who lost their lives in such Camps."

Despite its new elevated status, the site remained severely underfunded and without significant exhibit space or even a visitor center. If not for the national preoccupation with Vietnam War prisoners of war, it is possible that Andersonville would have remained undeveloped. In 1984, the National Park Service reached an agreement with a group called the American Ex-Prisoners of War to jointly raise funds for a new National Prisoner of War Museum to be built on the prison grounds. Fourteen years later, the museum, which now serves as the site's visitor center, opened.

During the museum's first two decades, its exhibits focused on the long history of American prisoners of war rather than the ordeal of prisoners who once lived literally outside the doors of the museum. The museum exhibits dwelled little on why Andersonville and the other massive Civil War prison camps came into existence in the first place, why conditions were so appalling at Andersonville, why the Confederacy refused to exchange Black prisoners of war, or why Henry Wirz had been executed. More recently, National Park Service staff at Andersonville have made laudable progress in tackling these crucial, if awkward topics. Visitors to the Andersonville website can now read concise and trenchant commentary on the history that hitherto had been carefully avoided.

The museum's founding mandate, however, continues to constrain its capacity to present fully the history of the Andersonville prison camp. As the only federally funded historical site that specifically interprets the Civil War prison-camp experience, Andersonville remains conspicuously underdeveloped. Rather than an immersive experience, a visit to the site places a premium on the visitor's imagination and familiarity with the prison's history. Andersonville prison was a landscape built by Confederates, enslaved people, and prisoners of war, but contemporary visitors encounter a natural landscape with only barely visible vestiges of the prison. The present-day verdant landscape bears no resemblance to the desertlike world that prisoners inhabited and that Andrew Riddle photographed in August 1864. Even with the aid of Riddle's photographs, it is difficult to envision the prison stockade on the landscape. Neither the scant portion of the stockade that has been reconstructed nor the inconspicuous stakes that mark the boundaries of the original stockade can begin to conjure the looming presence of the walls and dead line that confined the lives of prisoners. Nor can the handful of re-created shebangs evoke the oppressive congestion and disorder that overwhelmed prisoners. The physical site of the prison has been preserved, but otherwise it remains mute.

The awkward combination of indifference and solicitude extended to recognition of the last Andersonville survivors. Strikingly, the death of the last survivor passed without acknowledgment. Some have suggested Dennis McDonald was the last Andersonville survivor upon his death in 1945. Born a century earlier, he had served in the Fifty-Third Illinois. Some of his claims about his service—that he stood guard near the podium when President Lincoln delivered his Gettysburg Address in 1863, that he escaped from Andersonville, and that he helped bury fifteen hundred skeletons accumulated during the Battle of the Wilderness—are so suspect that they call into question his claims to have been imprisoned at Andersonville.

Others have suggested that John Wool Bartleson, born in August 1846 in the southern tip of Illinois, was the last survivor. In October 1863, at age seventeen, Bartleson enlisted in the Eighty-First Illinois Volunteer Infantry. He and 125 other members of his regiment were taken prisoners in Mississippi on June 10, 1864. During the next five months he was confined at Andersonville, Millen, and Savannah until November 26, when he had the good fortune to be included in a special exchange. He returned to Illinois, remaining there until 1872, when he moved to Kansas and took up residence in a dugout, which must have elicited memories of his prison accommodations at Andersonville and Millen. He prospered, married twice, and fathered twelve children, five of whom survived childhood. On the morning of April 18, 1944, eight decades after his imprisonment at Andersonville, Bartleson expired.

Quite possibly, William Evan Whittinghill of Kentucky was the last survivor. In March 1864, as a fifteen-year-old, he enlisted in the Fourth Regiment, Kentucky Mounted Infantry. A month later he was captured south of Atlanta and sent to Andersonville. He quickly was prostrated by starvation and sickness. During the frenzied dispersal of Andersonville prisoners in anticipation of Sherman's March to the Sea, Confederates apparently sent him to the Union lines near Atlanta. He was the last prisoner to be crammed onto a boxcar that had been used to haul salt pork. Despite his severe ill health, which was further aggravated by salt residue in the car that irritated his severe sunburn blistering from exposure in the camp, he recovered after convalescing in Union hospitals during the final months of the war. He briefly resided in Missouri before settling near Indianapolis, where he remained for the last sixty years of his life. He married in 1875 and with his wife raised six children, five of whom survived childhood. Although he served as the chaplain for the Indiana GAR, he otherwise seldom talked of the war or his imprisonment. Instead, he preferred to dwell on the "meaning of life and the value of faith." Despite suffering chronic diarrhea, dyspepsia, disease of the colon, and severe malnutrition while a prisoner, he outlived his siblings, his wife, and three of his children. He died at his home on January 2, 1949. His passing warranted a few columns in Indiana newspapers, but otherwise the death of a 101-year-old Andersonville survivor—perhaps the last—garnered no national notice.

Because most Civil War prison sites have been erased from the landscape, generations of Americans have encountered no vestiges that might inspire reflection on what Whittinghill and the hundreds of thousands of other prisoners of war endured during the most destructive war in the nation's history. The Civil War seemingly has left Americans untroubled by "the hauntingly possessive ghosts" of trauma that torment many other nations. Unless we happen upon, say, an inconspicuous historical marker in Danville, Virginia, or the memorial to the Confederate dead on Point Lookout in Maryland, when do we have a cause to ask how we know what we know about the largest prisons in this nation's history, to ponder whose voices from the camps we hear, and to acknowledge the silences about the Civil War that endure? We seldom confront the challenge William Evan Whittinghill and other prisoners faced: What of their traumatic experiences should be remembered?

Captivity profoundly marked Whittinghill, Isaac Gaskins, Frederic James, William Haigh, and the other Civil War prisoners of war who populate this book. Their public remarks, letters, diaries, and memoirs offer glimpses of the despair, suffering, camaraderie, and compassion that they experienced within the stockade. But what do we hear in their testimonies? Little imagination is required to discern evidence of the ubiquitous horrors of war or of humanity's capacity for callousness and cruelty. Violent conflict magnifies rather than mitigates the obligations of responsibility. Perhaps the laws of humanity are violated in all wars, but the pressure of circumstances during war are not license for cavalier indifference to human suffering. Or we may conclude, as many have, that the history of Civil War prison camps demonstrates how the exigencies of war inevitably create unintended circumstances, many of them tragic. But the history recounted here includes both acts of direct responsibility and acts of complicity.

Assigning responsibility for the acts that defined the captivity experienced by Whittinghill, Gaskins, James, and the others entails assessing everything from words to deeds, from abstract policies to the capricious distribution of rations. There is no evidence that either Confederate or Union soldiers conducted their prison camps as death camps or with a deliberate intention to kill prisoners of war. Prison officials, in many instances, were guilty of the sin of omission rather than commission. But their intentions should not outweigh the effect of their actions and inaction on the lives of prisoners.

It confers no moral distinction on the Union cause to remember the brutality of Andersonville while ignoring the horrors of Point Lookout. No false equivalency need be drawn between the suffering in Andersonville and the calibrated policy of retaliation adopted by the Union in 1864. Nor should either be overlooked, dismissed, or rationalized as a deplorable but unintended consequence of war. To ignore that the prison camps of the Civil War were the product of human volition is to ignore the historical record itself.

Few of the men trapped in the camps anticipated that their personal ordeals presaged the experience of captivity that millions would undergo in the century to come. By the time that William Evan Whittinghill died, Cuba, American-occupied Philippines, South Africa, and the belligerents in World War I and World War II had all hosted large custodial prison camps. What Civil War prisoners understood as an experience unique to them subsequently proved to be a feature of modern warfare and statecraft. Had the denizens of the Civil War prison camps anticipated the future, they might have cautioned future generations that a nation, whether in peace or at war, has no life outside the people who incarnate it. Undoubtedly voicing the sentiments of tens of thousands of prisoners, Robert Kellogg testified during the trial of Captain Henry Wirz that "we saw that we were badly treated" and "we supposed, of course that somebody was responsible for it."

# ACKNOWLEDGMENTS

Only recently have I come to understand the questions that have linked my interest in the past. I thought of myself as having a morbid interest in some of the darker aspects of the nineteenth- and twentieth-century United States. Not until I began researching this nation's history of torture did I recognize my abiding interest in people who have confronted acute ethical dilemmas while under extreme duress.

Delving into the experiences of Civil War prisoners of war, especially the men who experienced captivity at Andersonville, Salisbury, and Florence prisons, is to observe people under unimaginable duress. For many, the experience was profoundly dehumanizing. Many nevertheless retained their dignity and fundamental humanity. To read the prison diaries of Charles Smedley, Frederic James, and Charles Mattocks is to be humbled by the moral fortitude and compassion that their authors displayed during the ordeal of captivity.

This history acquired even greater meaning for me when I learned how many Americans had experienced captivity during the Civil War. Captivity was more commonplace during the conflict than in any subsequent war waged by this nation. Any reader whose ancestors lived in the United States during the Civil War is likely to be within three or four degrees of separation from a Civil War prisoner. I, for instance, had a great-great-uncle who was imprisoned at Fort Douglas in Illinois, an experience that apparently left lingering scars. Another great-great-uncle survived Andersonville.

Yet, this widely shared history of captivity and its myriad influences on our nation's public life (as well as on the prisoners' descendants) occupy little in any space in our national memory.

I began writing this book one month before the Covid pandemic transformed my life. If writing can be an isolating activity during "normal times," it was even more so during the pandemic. Yet, although the pandemic effectively closed many of the nation's archives and libraries during 2020 and 2021, and continued to hamper some into 2022, many librarians and archivists enabled me to continue my work through their generosity. Perhaps not until the history of the pandemic is written will the contribution of librarians and archivists to the life of the mind across the globe be fully appreciated. I am forever grateful to librarians and archivists at the Florida Atlantic University, Atlanta History Center, Vermont Historical Society, Wisconsin Historical Society, University of Missouri, University of Tennessee—Knoxville, Ohio Historical Society, University of Virginia, Emory University, University of North Carolina at Chapel Hill, U.S. Army Military History Institute, and Minnesota Historical Society, as well as anonymous librarians all over the world who made their collections available to virtual users. Numerous librarians generously provided scans of important materials that otherwise would have been inaccessible. A special word of thanks is appropriate for Angela Melton, the collections curator at the Danville Museum of Art and History in Virginia, who helped me to track down the remarkable image by Henry Van der Weyde.

I, too, am grateful to the sage advice of superb historians of the Civil War era, including Caroline Janney, Aaron Smith-Shaheen, Joe Glatthaar, David Blight, Yael Sternhell, and Randy Sparks, all of whom read some or all of this manuscript. Christopher Phillips gave the manuscript an especially thorough scrubbing. Guenter Bischof, a distinguished historian of twentieth-century Europe and the son of a prisoner of war during World War II, also offered his perspective on the manuscript. This book, in both conspicuous and inconspicuous ways, is better thanks to their wisdom. While researching this book, I was the beneficiary of excellent research assistance by Caroline Newhall, Francesca Langer, A. J. Blalock, and Rob Shappard.

I also am indebted to many wonderful historians who have written about our nation's Civil War prisons, some of whom I know but many of whom I do not. Had I written this book thirty years ago, I would have been without the benefit of the wonderful works of Lonnie Spears, Roger Pickenpaugh, Michael P. Gray, Angela Zombek, Evan Kutzler, Benton McAdams, Lorien Foote, William Marvel, Benjamin Cloyd, and others.

Special thanks are due to Sarah Gardner, who is indirectly responsible for this book. When she, and her colleagues Doug Thompson, Matt Z. Harper, and David Davis, invited me to deliver the Lamar Lectures at Mercer University, I was inspired to develop ideas that had simmered since completing an earlier book on the history of torture in the United States. Those lectures, during the pandemic, were my first opportunity to present my ideas to an audience. I remain grateful for the warm hospitality they provided.

While this book is not one that Susan would have written, she made it immeasurably better by turning her keen eye to it. She also shared the joy of life with me that made the travails of the men I was writing about especially poignant. Armistead always listened with patience to my coalescing ideas about Civil War prisons. Daphne, whose life of this planet coincides with the writing of this book, only provided distractions, however welcome they may have been. To each of them, I offer my unbounded love and gratitude.

I am grateful to John Glusman for taking on this manuscript and shepherding it through the editorial process at Norton. And I am likewise grateful to Don Fehr, my agent, for bringing my project to the attention of John. Thanks to Wickliffe Hallos at Norton. Special praise is due Trent Duffy, an exceptional copy editor.

Of my debts, few are longer in gestation and greater in scale than my debt to Stephen Schmidt. Steve did not read my manuscript, nor did we discuss it. But the lessons that I first began learning from him in his ninth-grade math class in San Jose, Costa Rica—and have continued to through the subsequent decades—have informed everything I have written. Dedicating a book to him seems like small recompense for his generosity and friendship over the years. I first encountered the writings and poetry of Pablo Neruda almost simultaneously with meeting Steve. In the years since, I have often turned to Neruda to say the things for which I do not have adequate words. Having known Steve, I understand Neruda when he writes of friendship that "widens out the boundaries of our being."

# NOTES

In these notes, the commonly used abbreviation *"OR"* refers to the 119-volume compilation, in two series, of Union and Confederate official records and documents gathered by the U.S. War Department as *The War of the Rebellion: A Compilation of the Official Records of the Union and Confederate Armies* (Washington, D.C.: Government Printing Office, 1880–1901).

## CHAPTER ONE: A PHOTOGRAPHER VISITS ANDERSONVILLE

2 **transcend his humble origins:** The little that is known about Riddle is summarized in Robert Scott Davis, "A Day Captured at Andersonville Prison Camp: The Photographs of Andrew J. Riddle," *Prologue: The Quarterly of the National Archives* 34 (Fall 2002): 212–17; William Marvel, "The Andersonville Artist: The A. J. Riddle Photographs of August 1864," *Blue & Gray Magazine* 10 (August 1993): 18–23.

3 **"Such a picture":** *Richmond Whig*, August 29, 1864, 1.

4 **"perspiration started":** Roger Fenton, "Narrative of a Photographic Trip to the Seat of War in the Crimea," *Humphrey's Journal* 1 (March 1856): 334.

7 **"certifying experience":** Susan Sontag, "On Photography," *Essays of the 1960s and 70s* (New York: Library of America, 2013), 534.

7 **"Verbal representations":** Alexander Gardner, *Gardner's Photographic Sketch Book of the War* (Washington, D.C.: Philp & Solomons, 1865-1866), vol. 1, title page.

7 **"We speak that":** Robert H. Kellogg, *Life and Death in Rebel Prisons: Giving a Complete History of the Inhuman and Barbarous Treatment of Our Brave Soldiers by Rebel Authorities, Inflicting Terrible Suffering and Frightful Mortality* (Hartford: L. Stebbins, 1867), title page.

8 **"were alive with vermin":** Quoted in Eliza Frances Andrews, *Extracts from the Wartime Journal of a Georgia Girl* (New York: D. Appleton, 1908), 78.

8 **"a putrefying mass":** Joseph Jones, "Observations upon the Diseases of the Federal Prisoners Confined at Camp Sumter, Andersonville," *OR*, ser. II, 8:593.

10 **"We found it crowded":** United States Sanitary Commission, *Narrative of Privations and Sufferings of United States Officers and Soldiers While Prisoners of War in the Hands of the*

*Rebel Authorities: Being the Report of a Commission of Inquiry, Appointed by the United States Sanitary Commission; With an Appendix, Containing the Testimony* (Boston: Office of Littell's Living Age, 1864), 260.

11 **"hardly room to lie down":** Henry Devillez, "Reminiscences of the Civil War: Andersonville," *Indiana Magazine of History* 11 (June 1915): 144.

11 **photographs imprison reality:** Sontag, "On Photography," 643.

12 **"formidable batteries":** *Richmond Whig*, August 26, 1864, 1.

13 **"this gigantic mass of human misery":** Jones, "Observations upon the Diseases," ser. II, 8:623.

14 **"hopeless misery . . . ghastly corpses":** Jones, "Observations upon the Diseases," ser. II, 8:603, 604.

15 **"The blame of this appalling misery":** *Richmond Whig*, August 29, 1864, 1.

15 **"all the agonies":** *Richmond Whig*, August 29, 1864, 1.

17 **Other innovations:** David Montgomery, *Beyond Equality: Labor and the Radical Republicans, 1862–1872* (New York: Vintage, 1972), 47; James M. McPherson, *Battle Cry of Freedom: The Civil War Era* (New York: Oxford University Press, 1988), 859.

18 **"the civil war in America":** J. F. C. Fuller, *The Generalship of Ulysses S. Grant* (London: John Murray, 1929), viii.

19 **"the quarry from which":** Stephen C. Neff, *Justice in Blue and Gray: A Legal History of the Civil War* (Cambridge: Harvard University Press, 2010), 58.

21 **"here is where I can see":** Entry for May 7, 1864, George R. Crosby Diaries, January–June 1864, folder 13, MSA 84, Leahy Library, Vermont Historical Society, Barre.

## CHAPTER TWO: IN ACCORDANCE WITH THE CUSTOMS OF WAR

24 **to repel Union troops:** The military maneuvers leading up to and following from Pegram's defeat are described in W. Hunter Lesser, *Rebels at the Gate: Lee and McClellan on the Front Line of a Nation Divided* (Naperville, Ill.: Sourcebooks, 2004), 85–120.

24 **"jaded and reduced condition":** *OR*, ser. I, 2:210.

25 **"In the meantime":** *OR*, ser I, 2:250–51.

25 **"to do all in my power":** *OR*, ser. I, 2:250–51.

25 **"should be conducted upon":** George B. McClellan to Abraham Lincoln, July 7, 1862, in Edward McPherson, *The Political History of the United States of America, During the Great Rebellion, from November 6, 1860, to July 4, 1864* (Washington, D.C.: Philp & Solomons, 1864), 385–86.

26 **"The prisoners are beyond measure":** George B. McClellan, *McClellan's Own Story* (New York: Charles L. Webster, 1887), 62.

27 **"himself generally useful":** Lawrence Sangston, *The Bastilles of the North* (Baltimore: Kelly, Hedian, and Piet, 1863), 83.

27 **"Our mess continues":** Sangston, *Bastilles of the North*, 96.

27 **"roast turkies":** Sangston, *Bastilles of the North*, 76.

27 **eight more of the two thousand prisoners:** See Minor H. McLain, "The Military Prison at Fort Warren," *Civil War History* 8 (June 1962): 136–51; Minor H. McLain, "Prison Conditions in Fort Warren, Boston During the Civil War" (PhD diss., Boston University, 1955).

27 **"Dressed as a tourist":** Theo F. Rodenbough, ed., *From Everglade to Cañon with the Second Dragoons* (New York: D. Van Nostrand, 1875), 253.

29 **Romans seized the town of Uspe:** See Brian Campbell, *War and Society in Imperial Rome, 31 BC–AD 284* (London: Routledge, 2002), 75.

29 **"wonderful sight":** August. C. Krey, *The First Crusade: The Accounts of Eyewitnesses and Participants* (Princeton, N.J.: Princeton University Press, 1921), 261.

29 **"Once captured don't kill him":** Horace, *The Satires, Epistles, and Ars Poetica*, translated by A. S. Kline, bk. 1, epistle 16 ("The meaning of true goodness"), https://romanhistorybooks.typepad.com/files/horace-satires-epistles-ap.pdf, accessed February 10, 2024.

29 **"Prisoners taken in War":** Charles Molloy, *De Jure Maritimo et Navali: Or, a Treatise of Affairs Maritime, and of Commerce in Three Books* (London, 1676), 386.

30 **maintained a lavish lifestyle:** Barbara Tuchman, *A Distant Mirror: The Calamitous 14th Century* (New York: Knopf, 1978), 168–69.

30 **Droyle's subsequent ransom netted Sadeler:** E 358/6, fol. 5v, https://www.medievalsoldier.org/dbsearch/, accessed July 2, 2024.

30 **"to put an end to quarrels":** Jean-Claude Faucon, ed., *La Chanson de Bertrand Du Guesclin de Cuvelier* (Toulouse: Editions Universitaires du Sud, 1990), 1:470.

30 **had no evident ransom value:** Edmond de Dynter, *Chronique des Ducs de Brabant*, ed. P. F. X. De Ram (Brussels: M. Hayez, 1854–1860), 3:303–4. See also Anne Curry, *The Battle of Agincourt: Sources and Interpretations* (Woodbridge, Eng.: Boydell and Brewer, 2000), 243–45, 432–33; Rémy Ambüh, "A Fair Share of the Profits? The Ransoms of Agincourt," *Nottingham Medieval Studies* 50 (2006): 142–48.

31 **"As soon as your enemy":** Emmerich von Vattel, *The Law or Nations; or Principles of Natural Law* (London: G.G. and J. Robinson, 1797), bk. 3, chap. 8, sect. 140.

31 **Preventing the slaughter:** Stephen C. Neff, *War and the Law of Nations: A General History* (Cambridge, Eng.: Cambridge University Press, 2005), 295.

31 **among the least horrific in the continent's history:** David A. Bell, *The First Total War: Napoleon's Europe and the Birth of Warfare as We Know It* (Boston: Houghton Mifflin Harcourt, 2007), 5–7.

33 **he was exchanged for 1047 privates:** Kevin J. Weddle, *The Compleat Victory: Saratoga and the American Revolution* (New York: Oxford University Press, 2021), 342–43.

34 **Not until 1758 were the last:** Fred Anderson, *Crucible of War: The Seven Years' War and the Fate of Empire in British North America, 1754–1766* (New York: Knopf, 2007), 150–58; Timothy J. Shannon, "French and Indian Cruelty? The Fate of the Oswego Prisoners of War, 1756–1758," *New York History* 95 (Summer 2014): 381–407.

34 **"we treat them as Friends":** W. W. Abbot, ed., *The Papers of George Washington*, Colonial Ser. (Charlottesville: University Press of Virginia, 1983), 1:165.

37 **Washington scrupulously hewed to European methods:** Bruce Buchan, "Pandours, Partisans, and Petite Guerre: The Two Dimensions of Enlightenment Discourse on War," *Intellectual History Review* 23 (2013): 329–47.

38 **"severe and exemplary punishment":** Jared Sparks, ed., *The Writings of George Washington: Being His Correspondence, Addresses, Messages, and Other Papers, Official and Private, Selected and Published from the Original Manuscripts; With a Life of the Author, Notes and Illustrations* (Boston: American Stationers'/John B. Russell, 1837), 3:90.

38 **treated "with humanity":** Worthington Chauncey Ford et. al., eds., *Journals of the Continental Congress, 1774–1789* (Washington, D.C.: Government Printing Office, 1937), 3:400.

38 **Washington warned his British counterpart:** George Washington to William Howe, December 18, 1775, George Washington Papers, ser. 3, Varick Transcripts, 1775–1785, subser. 3E, Enemy Officers and British Subjects, 1775–1783, letterbook 1: August 11, 1775–December 1, 1783, Library of Congress, Washington, D.C.

38 **"base usage of our people":** Michael J. Crawford, William J. Morgan, and William B. Clark, eds., *Naval Documents of the American Revolution* (Washington, D.C.: Naval History Division, Department of the Navy, 1964), 2:877.

38 **"old, unsightly, rotten hulk":** Thomas Andros, *The Old Jersey Captive: Or a Narrative of the Captivity of Thomas Andros on Board the Old Jersey Prison Ship at New York, 1781* (Boston: William Peirce, 1833), 8. See also Thomas Dring, *Recollections of Life on the Prison Ship Jersey*, ed. David Swain (Yardley, Pa.: Westholme, 2010), 8; Andrew Sherburne, *Memoirs of Andrew Sherburne: A Pensioner of the Navy of the Revolution* (Providence: H. H. Brown, 1828), 115.

39 **"In a transport of joy":** Ethan Allen, *A Narrative of Colonel Ethan Allen's Captivity* (Philadelphia: Robert Bell, 1779), 45.

39 **experienced "much courtesy":** Winfield Scott, *Memoirs of Lieut.-General Scott, LL. D* (New York: Sheldon, 1864), 71.

40 **"would not fail to look":** Scott, *Memoirs*, 72.

40 **Threats of retaliation mounted:** United States House, *Report on the Spirit and Manner in Which the War Has Been Waged by the Enemy, 1813* (New York: Garland, 1978).

41 **"are under the safeguard":** War Department of the United States, *General Regulations for the Army, or, Military Institutes* (Philadelphia: M. Carey and Sons, 1821), 139.

41 **no pity toward Mexican guerrillas:** Peter Guardino, "The Constant Recurrence of Such Atrocities: Guerrilla Warfare and Counterinsurgency During the Mexican-American War," *Journal of the Civil War Era* 12 (March 2022): 3–27.

41 **"I have not the means":** Steven R. Butler, ed., *A Documentary History of the Mexican War* (Richardson, Tex.: Descendants of Mexican War Veterans, 1995), 207.

42 **General Andrew Jackson and his troops:** Thomas Kanon, "'A Slow and Laborious Slaughter': The Battle of Horseshoe Bend," *Tennessee Historical Quarterly* 58 (Spring 1999): 14–15.

42 **his successors promptly adopted extreme measures:** John K. Mahon, *History of the Second Seminole War, 1835–1842* (Gainesville: University Press of Florida, 2017), 274–93.

42 **the summary execution of Palouse captives:** Carl Paul Schlicke, *General George Wright, Guardian of the Pacific Coast* (Norman: University of Oklahoma Press, 1988), 177–96.

42 **expulsion of roughly eighty thousand native peoples:** The expulsion is eloquently described in Claudio Saunt, *Unworthy Republic: The Dispossession of Native Americans and the Road to Indian Territory* (New York: W. W. Norton, 2021), esp. chap. 5.

43 **"justify us at the tribunal":** Henry Wager Halleck, *International Law, or, Rules Regulating the Intercourse of States in Peace and War* (San Francisco: H. H. Bancroft, 1861), 425.

43 **Dorset had fulfilled his pledge:** Charles H. Ross, "Old Memories," in *War Papers Read Before the Commandery of the State of Wisconsin* (Milwaukee: Burdick, Armitage & Allen, 1891), 1:152.

## CHAPTER THREE: WHAT IS TO BE DONE WITH THE PRISONERS?

44 **"carelessness or want of system":** Entry for August 1, 1861, Charles Carroll Gray Diary, 2569-z, Southern Historical Collection, Wilson Special Collections Library, University of North Carolina at Chapel Hill.

44 **"we would be torn to pieces":** Michael Corcoran, *The Captivity of General Corcoran* (Philadelphia: Barclay, 1864), 26. See also William C. Harris, *Prison-Life in the Tobacco Warehouse at Richmond* (Philadelphia: George W. Childs, 1862), 19–20; William H. Merrell, *Five Months in Rebeldom, Or, Notes from the Diary of a Bull Run Prisoner, at Richmond* (Rochester, N.Y.: Adams and Dabney, 1862), 15; Robert Garth Scott, *Forgotten Valor: The Memoirs, Journals, and Civil War Letters of Orlando B. Willcox* (Kent, Ohio: Kent State University Press, 1999), 302.

44 **"really of heroic stamp":** Maria Lydig Daly, *Diary of a Union Lady, 1861–1865*, ed. Harold E. Hammond (Lincoln: University of Nebraska Press, 2000), 167, 180, 219.

45 **"a low-bred, uneducated, selfish":** Scott, *Forgotten Valor*, 357.

45 **Corcoran garnered international notoriety:** See "Arrival of the *Persia*," *London Daily News*, October 22, 1860, 5; "United States and Canada," *London Daily News*, November 29, 1860, 7; "Arrival of the *Persia*," *London Morning Post*, October 22, 1860, 6; "Loss of the *Connaught*," *London Standard*, October 22, 1860, 6; "The Prince of Wales in New York," *Liverpool Daily Post*, October 29, 1860, 7.

46 **"What should be done":** *Richmond Whig*, August 5, 1861, 1.

47 **The edict triggered a frenzy:** For the early history of Confederate privateers, see William Morrison Robinson Jr., *The Confederate Privateers* (1928; repr., Columbia: University of South Carolina Press, 1994), 25–88.

47 **"No treating with [Confederates]":** Sinclair Tousey, "About Prisoners of War, Privateers, &c.," *New York Times*, August 7, 1861, 2.

47 **clamored for executions of secessionists:** See "Reminiscences of Stephen A. Douglas," *Atlantic Monthly*, August 1861, 212, "What Is to Be Done with the Pirates?," *Philadelphia Inquirer*, August 16, 1861, 1.

48 **"his last Rich Mountain success":** "The President's Message," *Richmond Dispatch*, July 22, 1861, 2; "Proclamation by the President," *Richmond Dispatch*, August 16, 1861, 2.

48 **"They might as well work":** *OR*, ser. II, 3:715.

48 **a macabre solution:** *OR*, ser. II, 3:716. See also Charles Lanman, ed., *Journal of Alfred Ely, a Prisoner of War in Richmond* (New York: D. Appleton, 1862), 49–50.

48 **The inglorious voyage of the *Savannah*:** Robinson, *Confederate Privateers*, 49–58.

49 **another privateer, the *Jefferson Davis*:** Robinson, *Confederate Privateers*, 59–78.

49 **Davis sent a public letter:** *OR*, ser. II, 3:5–6.

50 **"Practically, there is none":** Charles P. Daly, *Are the Southern Privateersmen Pirates? Letter to the Hon. Ira Harris, United States Senator* (New York: James B. Kirker, 1862), 4–5.

50 **"he will recognize us":** "A Dilemma," *Raleigh Register*, July 24, 1861, 3.

50 **"the family of nations":** D. F. Murphy, *The Jeff Davis Piracy Cases: Full Report of the Trial of William Smith for Piracy, as One of the Crew of the Confederate Privateer, the Jeff Davis: Before Judges Grier and Cadwalader, in the Circuit Court of the United States, for the Eastern District of Pennsylvania, Held at Philadelphia, in October 1861* (Philadelphia: King & Baird, 1861), 92.

50 **"convicted felons":** J. P. Benjamin to John H. Winder, November 9, 1861, in *OR*, ser. II, 3:738–39.

51 **"There is I think no doubt":** Scott, *Forgotten Valor*, 315–16. On Corcoran's early captivity, see Daly, *Diary of a Union Lady*, 102; Paul Joseph Revere to "Dear John," November 11, 1861, Revere Family Papers, reel 3 (microfilm), Massachusetts Historical Society, Boston; Corcoran, *Captivity*, 86–87.

51 **"inaugurate systematic measures":** "Another Letter from Colonel Corcoran," *New York Times*, August 12, 1861, 8; "The War Movements," *Baltimore Sun*, August 16, 1861, 1; Lanman, *Journal of Alfred Ely*, 25, 135.

51 **"It is a great compliment":** Daly, *Diary of a Union Lady*, 77.

51 **"strenuous efforts being made":** Corcoran, *Captivity*, 89.

51 **The campaign reached its climax:** "The Release of Colonel Corcoran," *Richmond Dispatch*, December 20, 1861, 2; George Opdyke to Abraham Lincoln, "Wednesday, Sends Resolutions Concerning Release of Colonel Michael Corcoran," February 5, 1862, Abraham Lincoln Papers: ser. 1, General Correspondence, 1833 to 1916, Library of Congress, Washington, D.C.

52 **Captain Timothy O'Meara:** Scott, *Forgotten Valor*, 339. For subsequent reports of hostages, see these accounts in *Richmond Dispatch*: "Exchange of Prisoners," April 25, 1862, 1; "Held as a Hostage," February 13, 1863, 1; "Held as a Hostage," May 21, 1863, 1; "The Traitor Rucker," May 25, 1863, 1; "Held as a Hostage," May 26, 1863, 1; "From Tennessee," July 22, 1863, 1; "Latest from the North," November 16, 1863, 1; "The Recent Expedition of the Enemy to Elizabeth City, N.C.," January 2, 1864, 1; "Northern Item," February 23, 1864, 1; "Yankee Outrages—Retaliation," August 18, 1864, 2.

52 **beneficiaries of individual exchanges:** "From Norfolk," *Richmond Dispatch*, September 21, 1861, 3; "Discharge of Union Prisoners, &c.," *Richmond Dispatch*, October 7, 1861, 2; William J. Crossley, *Extracts from My Diary, While Boarding with Jefferson Davis in Three of His Notorious Hotels* (Providence: Rhode Island Soldiers and Sailors Historical Society, 1903), 20.

53 **"I am hourly assailed":** *OR*, ser. 2, 3:539, 568–69, 604, 779.

53 **Wilcox heard rumors:** Scott, *Forgotten Valor*, 317, 320–21.

53 **"I hope you are all striking":** George W. Kenney to father, December 27, 1861, George W. Kenney Papers, 1860–1865, Rubenstein Library, Duke University, Durham, N.C.

54 **"the Irish Lion":** Scott, *Forgotten Valor*, 337.

54 **Winder was an improbable figure:** On Winder's life, the essential source is Arch Fredric Blakey, *General John H. Winder, C.S.A.* (Gainesville: University Press of Florida, 1990).

56 **"his face was a picture":** Edward A. Pollard, *Life of Jefferson Davis, with a Secret History of the Southern Confederacy* (Philadelphia: National Publishing, 1869), 218. For other impressions of Winder, see Lanman, *Journal of Alfred Ely*, 24, 96, 104, 125; Scott, *Forgotten Valor*, 311–12.

56 **"a man of no experience":** Charles Marshall, *An Aide-de-Camp of Lee* (Boston: Little, Brown, 1927), 46–47; C. Vann Woodward, ed., *Mary Chesnut's Civil War* (New Haven: Yale University Press, 1981), 124.

57 **Northrop's previous experience:** The essential resource to understand Northrop is Jerrold Northrop Moore, *Confederate Commissary General: Lucius Bellinger Northrop and the Subsistence Bureau of the Southern Army* (Shippensburg, Pa.: White Mane, 1996).

57 **"famished and pinched with hunger":** W. A. Abbott, "Experience of W. A. Abbott, Late Acting Ensign United States Navy, as a Prisoner of War," in William H. Jeffrey, *Richmond Prisons 1861–1862: Compiled from the Original Records Kept by the Confederate Government, Journals Kept by Union Prisoners of War, Together with the Name, Rank, Company, Regiment and State of the Four Thousand Who Were Confined There* (St. Johnsbury, Vt.: Republican Press, 1893), 98.

57 **"do not remain long enough":** *OR*, ser. 2, 3:694.

58 **"incipient moustache":** William Dandridge Turner, "The Libby Lion," *The Black Swan* 4 (August 1929): 29; "Well Arranged," *Richmond Dispatch*, March 31, 1862, 2.

58 **"awkward and inefficient":** J. T. W. Hairston, in Jeffrey, *Richmond Prisons 1861–1862*, 88.

58 **"lamentably deficient":** "Prison Guards," *Richmond Dispatch*, July 25, 1862, 1.

58 **"not very formidable fellows":** Jeffrey, *Richmond Prisons 1861–1862*, 155.

58 **"the essence of authority":** Harris, *Prison-Life in the Tobacco Warehouse*, 135.

58 **"a very strict disciplinarian":** Hairston, in Jeffrey, *Richmond Prisons 1861–1862*, 86. See also "The Infamous Capt. Todd," *New York Times*, February 27, 1862, 8; Lanman, *Journal of Alfred Ely*, 44–45; Jeffrey, *Richmond Prisons 1861–1862*, 83, 111–12; J. B. Jones, A Rebel War Clerk's Diary: At the Confederate States Capital, ed. James I. Robertson Jr., vol. 1, April 1861–July 1863 (Lawrence: University Press of Kansas, 2015), 30; Robert E. Krick, *Staff Officers in Gray: A Biographical Register of the Staff Officers in the Army of Northern Virginia* (Chapel Hill: University of North Carolina Press, 2003), 325–26.

58 **"the tented field and blood 'galore'":** Todd's record as a prison commandant is detailed in Stephen Berry, *House of Abraham: Lincoln and the Todds, a Family Divided by War* (Boston: Houghton Mifflin, 2007), 83–98.

59 **"not only one of the most gallant":** *Richmond Enquirer*, June 17, 1862, 1. See also Frances H. Casstevens, *George W. Alexander and Castle Thunder: A Confederate Prison and Its Commandant* (Jefferson, N.C.: McFarland, 2004), 45.

59 **"an intense and bitter hatred":** Harris, *Prison-Life in the Tobacco Warehouse*, 128.

59 **stuffed into "sweatboxes":** The scandal, investigation, and verdict are surveyed in Casstevens, *George W. Alexander*, 97–124.

59 **"foul and scurrilous abuse":** Jeffrey, *Richmond Prisons 1861–1862*, 13–15, 131; "Capt. Todd and the New York Press," *Richmond Dispatch*, October 16, 1861, 1.

60 **their jailer and other Freemasons:** Corcoran, *Captivity*, 41–42, 91–94.

60 **The duties of a "prison keeper":** Hairston, in Jeffrey, *Richmond Prisons 1861–1862*, 85–87.

61 **"being forced by my foes":** Corcoran, *Captivity*, 40.

61 **"We are apparently destined to rival":** Entry for May 14, 1862, Gray Diary.

61 **In other regards, the city was ill suited:** Stephen V. Ash, *Rebel Richmond: Life and Death in the Confederate Capital* (Chapel Hill: University of North Carolina Press, 2019), esp. 37–80.

62 **Eventually, almost a quarter:** Lonnie R. Speer, *Portals to Hell: Military Prisons of the Civil War* (Lincoln: University of Nebraska Press, 1997), 21.

63 **"close confinement":** "White Girls in Tobacco Factories," *Hunt's Merchants Magazine*, April 1859, 522–23.

63 **"the unwholesome and destructive atmosphere":** A Farmer, *The South*, January 7, 1858, 3.

63 **"a mere hog pen":** Entry for September 2, 1861, Willard W. Wheeler Diary, William L. Clements Library, University of Michigan, Ann Arbor.

63 **"Feeding a drove of swine":** Lanman, *Journal of Alfred Ely*, 24.

63 **"the mortality among the Abolition prisoners":** *Richmond Dispatch*, August 9, 1861, 2.

64 **Henceforth, the plan was:** "Prisoners of War to Be Sent South," *Richmond Enquirer*, November 19, 1861, 2.

64 **"murderers, thieves, mail robbers":** Quoted in Speer, *Portals to Hell*, 28.

64 **Confederate authorities looked to civilian jails:** "The Prisoner Account," *Richmond Dispatch*, November 4, 1861, 2; Lanham, *Journal of Alfred Ely*, 108–11; Scott, *Forgotten Valor*, 309.

65 **"a grim little place":** Entry for September 18, 1861, Gray Diary

65 **The second stint at the fort:** "Letter from a Yankee Prisoner at Charleston," *Charleston Daily Courier*, Dec. 13, 1861, 4.

66 **Stung by the public outcry:** For background on this portion of Corcoran's saga, see John Benjamin Christiansen, "'Valley Forge Was Paradise Compared to It': A Community Study of Columbia, South Carolina's Civil War Prisoner of War Camps" (master's thesis, University of South Carolina, 2004).

67 **"more dismal ware-house":** Entry for March 26, 1862, Gray Diary. See also entries for March 26, 29, April 11, 1862, Gray Diary.

67 **"streams of filthy matter":** Scott, *Forgotten Valor*, 322. See also "C.S. Military Prison," *Richmond Dispatch*, March 27, 1862, 4; Joseph Ferguson, *Life Struggles in Rebel Prisons: A Record of the Sufferings, Escapes, Adventures and Starvation of the Union Prisoners* (Philadelphia: James M. Ferguson, 1865), 33–34.

68 **"very undesirable":** Entry for May 17, 1862, Gray Diary.

68 **fourteen hundred captives:** The prison population is derived from rosters in Jeffrey, *Richmond Prisons 1861–1862*, 161–269.

69 **the Confederacy lost irreplaceable:** Harold D. Woodman, *King Cotton and His Retainers: Financing and Marketing the Cotton Crop of the South, 1800–1925* (Lexington: University of Kentucky Press, 1968), 210.

70 **The extended ordeal of Willard W. Felton:** This account of Felton's travels is derived from the Willard W. Felton Diary, 1862, Wisconsin Historical Society, Madison.

71 **"an abscess on the side":** Inscription in the Felton Diary, 1862.

72 **Corcoran's subsequent military career:** See *OR*, ser. II, 4:394, 395, 400, 437.

## CHAPTER FOUR: WHERE IS GENERAL BUCKNER?

74 **"Where is General Buckner?":** *OR*, ser. II, 3:298.

74 **a flurry of increasingly anxious telegrams:** See *OR*, ser I, 7:33, 36–37, 155; ser. II, 3: 267–71; ser. I, 7:161, 336–37; ser II., 3:267–71, 275–88, 298–99, 312, 320, 325.

75 **At Camp Randall:** Colonel William Hoffman to Charles Whipple, May 7, 1862, Records of the Office of the Commissary General of Prisoners 1861–67, RG 249, Letters Sent (hereafter CGPLS), National Archives, Washington, D.C.; Hoffman to Martin Smith, May 7, June 25, August 15, 1862, CGPLS; Hoffman to James Mulligan, May 7, 16, 1862, CGPLS; Hoffman to Edwin Stanton, May 26, 1862, CGPLS.

75 **"the amount of standing water":** *OR*, ser. II, 4:106. See also *OR*, ser. II, 1:110–11, 129; *OR*, ser. II, 3:403; *OR*, ser. II, 4:107–8, 172–73, 238, 253, 279–81; *OR*, ser II, 8:986–1001; Hoffman to General Montgomery Meigs, July 1, 10, August 1, 1862, CGPLS; Hoffman to Lorenzo Thomas, July 1, 1862, CGPLS; Hoffman to Joseph Tucker, July 9, 12, August 1, 1862, CGPLS.

75 **"the mean whiskey":** *OR*, ser. II, 3:410–11, 417, 498–500; *OR*, ser. II, 4:18.

78 **"It is to be expected":** *OR*, ser. II, 2: 8.

78 **"Mr. Stanton was fond of power":** Howard K. Beale, ed., *Diary of Gideon Welles: Secretary of the Navy Under Lincoln and Johnson* (New York: W. W. Norton, 1960), 1:67.

78 **"careless and indifferent":** Quoted in Walter Stahr, *Stanton: Lincoln's War Secretary* (New York: Simon and Schuster, 2017): 58.

79 **"black terrier":** Montgomery Blair, quoted in Edgar T. Welles, ed., *Diary of Gideon Welles* (New York: Houghton Mifflin, 1911), 1:127.

80 **Union armies were better provisioned:** Mark R. Wilson, *The Business of Civil War: Military Mobilization and the State, 1861–1865* (Baltimore: Johns Hopkins University Press, 2006), 5–33.

80 **"the office and duties of commissary-general":** *OR*, ser. II, 3:156.

80 **"Up to this time generals":** *OR*, ser. II, 3:390.

80 **"is placed, entirely under Colonel William Hoffman":** *OR*, ser. II, 4:30.

81 **General Grant, for example:** Hoffman to Ulysses S. Grant, April 21, 1863, CGPLS; Hoffman to Orlando Wilcox, June 11, 1863, CGPLS.

81 **"simply to give orders":** *OR*, ser. II, 4:152–53. See also Hoffman to David Tod, July 7, 1862, CGPLS; Hoffman to [Joseph Darr], July 7, 1862, CGPLS; Hoffman to Meigs, July 8, 1862, CGPLS; Hoffman to Thomas, July 8, 1862, CGPLS; Hoffman to James A. Ekin, August 4, 1862, CGPLS; H. M. Lazelle to John J. Freedley, July 20, 22, 1862, CGPLS.

82 **"There is scarcely a record left":** Tucker to Hoffman, July 1862, CGPLS. The shuffling of camp commanders at several other camps, especially Camp Chase in Columbus, was only slightly less frenetic: see *OR*, ser. II, 5:535; *OR*, ser. II, 7:680–81; Hoffman to Thomas, July 1, 1862, CGPLS.

83 **"very kind man":** Hoffman to Samuel R. Curtis, November 14, 28, December 11, 1862, CGPLS; Hoffman to Stanton, November 27, 1862, CGPLS.

84 **"The idea of keeping five thousand prisoners":** "An Absurd Rumor," *Chicago Tribune*, February 14, 1862, 4.

84 **"want of discipline":** See Hoffman to Whipple, May 7, 1862, CGPLS; Hoffman to Smith, May 7, June 25, August 15, 1862, CGPLS; Hoffman to Mulligan, May 7, 16, 1862, CGPLS; Hoffman to Stanton, May 26, 1862, CGPLS; *OR*, ser. II, 3:647–48; *OR*, ser. II, 4:112–14, 130–31, 216–17, 504.

84 **"experienced man of business":** Hoffman to Ekin, June 24, August 14, 1862, CGPLS.
84 **"all the liquors":** *OR*, ser. II, 3:54. See also *OR*, ser. II, 4:195–208, 763–65; Hoffman to Thomas, July 12, 1862, CGPLS; Hoffman to Lazelle, August 10, 1862, CGPLS; *OR*, ser. II, 4:291; *OR*, ser. II, 5:367, 388–89, 435, 720; Hoffman to John Christopher, June 5, 1862, CGPLS; Hoffman to Ekin, March 23, 1862, CGPLS; Hoffman to Edwin W. H. Read, June 9, 1862, CGPLS; Hoffman to Tucker, June 29, 1862, CGPLS; Hoffman to D. Garland Rose, July 19, August 1, 1862, CGPLS.
85 **"entirely without experience":** H. M. Lazelle to William Hoffman, July 13, 1863, in *OR*, ser. II, 4:197.
85 **"a strong antislavery Republican":** *OR*, ser. II, 3:412.
85 **"utterly ignorant":** *OR*, ser. II, 4:195–208. See also *OR*, ser. 2, 4:313, 319–20, 341–42, 367–71.
86 **The prison Hoffman designed:** Leo E. Oliva, "Fort Atkinson on the Santa Fe Trail, 1850–1854," *Kansas History* 40 (Summer 1974): 212–33.
88 **In St. Louis, Union officials:** *OR*, ser. II, 3:574–75.
88 **conversion of the abandoned Alton Prison:** *OR*, ser. II, 3:169, 216, 237, 247, 257.
89 **an ideal place for a military camp:** On Camp Butler, see Helen Edith Sheppley, "Camp Butler in Civil War Days," *Journal of the Illinois State Historical Society* 25 (January 1933): 285–317; Camilla A. Corlas Quinn, "Forgotten Soldiers: The Confederate Prisoners at Camp Butler, 1861–1863," *Illinois Historical Journal* 81 (Spring 1988): 35–44; William S. Peterson, "A History of Camp Butler, 1861–1866," *Illinois Historical Journal* 82 (Summer 1989): 74–92; Mark Flotow, "Early Civil War Camp Butler and William Tecumseh Sherman: Persistence of a False Narrative," *Journal of the Illinois State Historical Society* 116 (April 2023): 42–55.
89 **Camp Chase had ample space:** *OR*, ser. II, 3:33–36, 348–49, 375.
90 **"deplorable condition":** *OR*, ser. II, 3:363, 367.
91 **"carelessness and willful neglect":** *OR*, ser. II, 4:197.
91 **"Ten thousand men should certainly":** *OR*, ser. II, 4:107–8, 172–73, 238, 253, 279–81, 341–42; *OR*, ser. II, 8: 986–1002; Hoffman to Meigs, July 1, 10, August 1, 1862, CGPLS; Hoffman to Tucker, July 9, 12, August 1, 1862, CGPLS.
91 **Segregating officers and the ranks:** *OR*, ser. II, 3:539–41.
92 **"without any stove":** Randal W. McGavock, *Pen and Sword: The Life and Journals of Randal W. McGavock*, ed Herschel Gower and Jack Allen (Nashville: Tennessee Historical Commission 1959), 598.
93 **"The more I see of this dirty":** McGavock, *Pen and Sword*, 599.
95 **"great desire has been":** *OR*, ser. II, 4:324.
95 **"a temporary and cheap character":** *OR*, ser. II, 7:468.
95 **"At best it must fall far short of perfection":** *OR*, ser. II, 6:773.
95 **"such clothing as may be":** *OR*, ser. II, 4:152–53. See also *OR*, ser. II, 6:773; *OR*, ser. II, 3:32, 50, 316–17; *OR*, ser. II, 4:152, 406, 457–58; Hoffman to Joseph A. Potter, July 12, 1862, CGPLS; Hoffman to William W. Treadway, July 4, 1862, CGPLS; Hoffman to Meigs, August 1, 1862, CGPLS; Hoffman to Tucker, August 6, 1862, CGPLS.
95 **"judiciously withholding":** *OR*, ser. II, 3:361, 432. See also Hoffman to Ekin, March 18, 23, 29, 1862, CGPLS; Hoffman to Tucker, June 29, 1862, CGPLS; Hoffman to William S. Pierson, June 23, July 13, 1862, CGPLS; Hoffman to Foster, May 11, 1862, CGPLS; Hoffman to Mulligan, May 17, 1862, CGPLS; Hoffman to John Christopher, June 5, 1862, CGPLS.
96 **"to make the prisoners as comfortable":** *OR*, ser. II, 4:367.
96 **But elsewhere they bought items:** See *OR*, ser. II, 4:291; *OR*, ser. II, 5:367, 388–89, 435, 720; Hoffman to Christopher, June 5, 1862, CGPLS; Hoffman to Ekin, March 23, 1862, CGPLS; Hoffman to Read, June 9, 1862, CGPLS; Hoffman to Tucker, June 29, 1862, CGPLS; Hoffman to Rose, July 19, August 1, 1862, CGPLS.
96 **nearly two million dollars:** Leslie Hunter, "Warden for the Union: General William Hoffman (1807–1884)" (PhD diss., University of Arizona, 1971), 158–60.
96 **"bureaucracy develops the more perfectly":** Max Weber and Stephen Kalberg, *Max Weber: Readings and Commentary on Modernity* (Malden, Mass.: Blackwell, 2005), 200.

## CHAPTER FIVE: UPON TERMS OF PERFECT EQUALITY

97 **"from the walls of their prison":** *OR*, ser. II, 6:171–72.

98 **plea reached Welles in July 1863:** United States, Naval War Records Department, *Official Records of the Union and Confederate Navies in the War of the Rebellion* (Washington, D.C.: Government Printing Office, 1894–1922), ser. I, 8:543; ser. I, 13:563; ser. II, 6:121, 188; ser. II, 5: 721, 845.

100 **"a binding love for the South":** William M. Dickson, quoted in William B. Styple, *McClellan's Other Story: The Political Intrigue of Colonel Thomas M. Key, Confidential Aide to General George B. McClellan* (Kearny, N.J.: Bellegrove, 2012), 22.

101 **"firm, but temperate":** "Thurlow Weed's Reminiscences," *New York Tribune*, April 23, 1879, 8.

101 **"a very, very wise man":** William O. Stoddard, *White House Sketches*, No. 5, quoted in Michael Burlingame, ed., *Inside the White House in War Times: Memoirs and Reports of Lincoln's Secretary* (Lincoln: University of Nebraska Press, 2000), 162.

102 **"For that portion of our Northern":** A. C. Avery, "On the Life and Character of Lieut.-General D.H. Hill," Memorial Address to the Ladies' Memorial Association, May 10, 1893, in *Southern Historical Society Papers* 21 (1893): 116.

102 **After six months of intermittent dickering:** C. P. Wolcott (Assistant Secretary of War) to John A. Dix, July 12, 1862, and General George McClellan to Dix, July 13, 1862, John A. Dix Correspondence and Autograph, Manuscript Division, Library of Congress, Washington, D.C.; Dix to Edwin Stanton, July 16, 19, 23, 1862, Edwin McMasters Stanton Papers, 1818–1921, Manuscript Division, Library of Congress.

103 **Within weeks the exchanges accelerated:** Dix to Stanton, July 25, 26, 1862, Stanton Papers.

104 **"our blood has almost ceased to circulate":** Andrew Jackson Campbell, *The Civil War Diary of Andrew Jackson Campbell*, ed. Jill K. Garrett (Columbia, Tenn., 1965), 57, 64, 76.

104 **"The boys were nearly worn out":** Entry for September 20, 1862, John K. Farris Diaries, MS 343, Stuart A. Rose Manuscript, Archives, and Rare Book Library, Emory University, Atlanta.

105 **These sudden impositions of parolees:** See *OR*, ser. II, 5:191, 198, 216, 231, 237–38, 301–2, 330–40.

105 **"pay no respect":** *OR*, ser II, 4:865–66.

107 **"more annoyance and trouble":** *OR*, ser. II, 4:940–41; see also 773, 852–54, 935, 949–50.

107 **"Butler shall have met":** "Proclamation," *Richmond Dispatch*, December 24, 1862, 1; *OR*, ser. II, 4:770–71; ser II, 5:19, 20, 795–97.

108 **"clerical air":** Ben Perley Poore, *Reminiscences of Sixty Years in the National Metropolis* (Philadelphia: Hubbard Brothers, 1886), 2:27.

108 **His house boasted some:** One of Ould's daughters would be a celebrated postwar "belle." See Virginia Tatnall Peacock, *Famous American Belles of the Nineteenth Century* (Philadelphia: J.P. Lippincott, 1901), 230–38; Mary Boykin Chesnut, *A Diary from Dixie, as written by Mary Boykin Chesnut, Wife of James Chesnut Sr., United States Senator from South Carolina, 1859–1861, and Afterward an Aide to Jefferson Davis and a Brigadier-General in the Confederate Army*, ed. Isabella D. Martin and Myrta Lockett Avary (New York: D. Appleton, 1906), 302.

109 **"Let God judge between us":** Robert Ould to William H. Ludlow, April 11, 1863, *Southern Historical Society Papers* 1 (1876): 306.

109 **"taxing their ingenuity":** Lynda Laswell Crist, ed., *The Papers of Jefferson Davis*, vol. 9, *January–September 1863* (Baton Rouge: Louisiana State University Press, 1997), 106–7.

109 **"an ass":** Crist, *The Papers of Jefferson Davis*, 9:109.

109 **"Were I in your place":** *OR*, ser. II, 5:703.

110 **"perverting the truth":** "The Exchange of Prisoners: Gen. Meredith's Reply to Commissioner Ould," *New York Times*, November 23, 1863, 9.

110 **"I am not in my proper vocation":** Ethan Allen Hitchcock, *Fifty Years in Camp and Field: Diary of Major-General Ethan Allen Hitchcock, U.S.A.*, ed. W. A. Croffut (New York: G.P. Putnam's Sons, 1909), 47, 162.

111 **"so utterly reckless of integrity":** *OR*, ser. II, 6:403.

112 **one hundred Black "servants":** Colonel William Hoffman to Governor David Tod, April 21, 1862, CGPLS; *OR*, ser. II, 5:35–36; *OR*, ser. II, 6:397–98.

112 **State legislators demanded:** U.S. Senate, "Resolutions of the Legislature of Ohio Relative to Rebel Officers in Columbus and Camp Chase Prisons," Document No. 94, *Miscellaneous*

*Documents of the Senate of the United States for the Second Session of the Thirty-Seventh Congress, 1861–'62* (Washington, D.C.: Government Printing Office, 1862).

113 **"remorseless revolutionary struggle":** *OR*, ser. III, 1:718.

113 **"to get along without touching":** Abraham Lincoln to John A. McClernand, January 8, 1863, Abraham Lincoln Papers: ser. 1, General Correspondence, 1833 to 1916, Library of Congress.

113 **"they may be found competent":** "Militia Act of 1862," *U.S., Statutes at Large, Treaties, and Proclamations of the United States of America* (Boston, 1863), 12:597–600.

113 **military necessity compelled him to strike:** Abraham Lincoln to Major General John A. McClernand, January 8, 1863, in Roy P. Basler, ed., *The Collected Works of Abraham Lincoln* (New Brunswick, N.J.: Rutgers University Press, 1953), 6:48–49.

114 **"This army will sustain":** *OR*, ser. I, 24:157.

114 **"the heaviest blow yet":** Ulysses S. Grant, *The Papers of Ulysses S. Grant*, ed. John Y. Simon (Carbondale: Southern Illinois University Press, 1982), 9:196.

114 **"as many persons of African descent":** Abraham Lincoln, "To the Senate and House of Representatives," July 17, 1862, in Basler, *Collected Works of Abraham Lincoln*, 6:330.

114 **"we will soon have a waiter":** Stephen E. Ambrose, ed., *A Wisconsin Boy in Dixie: The Selected Letters of John K. Newton* (Madison: Wisconsin State Historical Society, 1961), 28.

114 **"an eagle on his button":** "Speech of Frederick Douglass," *Liberator*, July 6, 1863, 118.

114 **"would drive many of our friends":** Daniel Ullman, *Address by Daniel Ullman, L.L.D., Major General, U.S.V., Before the Soldiers and Sailors' Union of the State of New York, on the Organization of Colored Troops and the Regeneration of the South, Delivered at Albany, February 5, 1868* (Washington, D.C.: Great Republican Office, 1868).

115 **"would be treated worse":** *Boston Journal* quoted in *National Intelligencer and Washington Advertiser*, May 30, 1862.

115 **"the most execrable measure recorded":** *OR*, ser. II, 5:808.

116 **"abandonment of all rules":** *OR*, ser. II, 11:45.

116 **"an invitation to murder":** "Lincoln's Proclamation," *Charleston Daily Courier*, October 3, 1862, 1.

116 **"no alternative but success":** Robert E. Lee to James A. Seddon, January 10, 1863, in Clifford Dowdey, ed., *The Wartime Papers of R. E. Lee* (Boston: Little, Brown, 1961), 390.

116 **"severe retaliatory measures":** James V. Orville, *The History, Civil, Political and Military, of the Southern Rebellion: From Its Incipient Stages to Its Close; Comprehending, Also, All Important State Papers, Ordinances of Secession, Proclamations, Proceedings of Congress, Official Reports of Commanders, Etc., Etc.* (New York: J. D. Torrey, 1861), 3:359.

116 **"Let the execution be made":** Quoted in Horace Greeley, *The American Conflict: A History of the Great Rebellion in the United States of America, 1860–'64* (New York: O. D. Case, 1866), 2:523.

117 **whites in northwestern Mississippi executed:** Louis Hughes, *Thirty Years a Slave: From Bondage to Freedom; The Institution of Slavery as Seen on the Plantation and in the Home of the Planter* (Milwaukee: South Side, 1896), 154.

117 **"taken in arms":** *Journal of the Congress of the Confederate States of America, 1861–1865* (Washington, D.C.: Government Printing Office, 1904), 3:387.

117 **"swift and terrible punishment":** *OR*, ser. II, 4: 945–46, 954.

118 **"white men and jentalmen":** Thomas Livingston to James M. Williams, June 13, 1863, Record Book, Seventy-Ninth U.S. Colored Troops, vol. 2, Records of the Adjutant General's Office, RG 94, National Archives, Washington, D.C.

118 **"If we were insane enough":** "Exchange or No Exchange," *Richmond Enquirer*, August 25, 1863, 4.

118 **"the colored prisoners":** *OR*, ser. I, 22:219. See also Kansas Adjutant General's Office, *Official Military History of Kansas Regiments During the War for the Suppression of the Great Rebellion* (Leavenworth, Kans.: W. S. Burke, 1870), 410.

118 **Black men and women who were abducted:** "Running Negroes South," *Harper's Weekly*, November 8, 1862, 718.

118 **"We are trying to find out":** Gustavus V. Fox to Admiral S. F. DuPont, February 26, 1863, in Robert Means Thompson and Richard Wainwright, eds., *Confidential Correspondence of*

*Gustavus Vasa Fox, Assistant Secretary of the Navy, 1861–1865* (New York: Naval History Society, 1920), 1:185.

119 **"I would regard it nothing":** *OR*, ser. I, 14:468–69.

119 **Eight members of the Eleventh Louisiana:** Proceedings of a Board of Officers, March 14, 1866, and Department of Mississippi, SO 62, March 17, 1866, both in Forty-Ninth U.S. Colored Infantry (USCI), U.S. Colored Troops Regimental Papers, entry 57C, RG 94, National Archives.

119 **They were transported to Texas:** Deposition, Samuel Anderson, June 23, 1896, in Pension File SC959813, Samuel Anderson, Forty-Sixth U.S. Colored Infantry, Civil War Pension Application Files, RG 15, National Archives; Descriptive Books, Companies E and G, Forty-Sixth U.S. Colored Infantry, and HQ Forty-Sixth U.S. Colored Infantry, SO 65, December 2, 1865, both in Forty-Sixth U.S. Colored Infantry, Regimental Books, RG 94, National Archives.

119 **"very large number of negroes":** *OR*, ser. II, 6: 21–22. See also *OR*, ser. I, 24:425, 443–44, 459.

119 **"I consider it an unfortunate circumstance":** *OR*, ser. I, 24:450, 466.

120 **Union officers of Black soldiers:** *OR*, ser. II, 6:213, 264; Albert Allen to George B. Drake, August 6, 1864, War Department, Adjutant General's Office, Military Service Record of Albert Allen, U.S. Colored Troops: Seventy-Eighth U.S. Colored Infantry, RG 94, National Archives; Charles E. Page to George B. Drake, July 26, 1864, Consolidated File for Second Lieutenant Charles E. Page, Eighty-First U.S. Colored Troops Infantry Regiment, RG 94, National Archives.

121 **"do not cease on this account":** Francis Lieber, *Instructions for the Government of Armies of the United States in the Field, Prepared by Francis Lieber, LL.D.* (originally issued as General Orders No. 100), Adjutant General's Office, 1863 (Washington, D.C.: Government Printing Office, 1898), article 15.

121 **"a case for the severest retaliation":** Lieber, *Instructions for the Government of Armies*, articles 27, 58.

122 **"a relapse into barbarism":** "Order of Retaliation," in Basler, *Collected Works of Abraham Lincoln*, 6:357.

122 **"if they [Blacks] are in the army":** William Whiting, quoted in Michael Vorenberg, "Abraham Lincoln's 'Fellow Citizens'—Before and After Emancipation," in William A. Blair, and Karen Fisher Younger, eds., *Lincoln's Proclamation: Emancipation Reconsidered* (Chapel Hill: University of North Carolina Press, 2009). 161.

122 **"Now while colored men are admitted":** "Colored Troops: Opinion of Wm. Whiting, Esq., Solicitor to the War Department," *New York Times*, July 31, 1863, 8.

123 **"You have not a foot":** William Ludlow to Robert Ould, June 14, 1863, in *OR*, ser. II, 6:18.

123 **"die in the last ditch":** H. Ex. Doc. 32, 37th Cong., 1st sess., 32.

124 **"all exchanges have now ceased":** *OR*, ser. II, 6:452–55, 582–83.

124 **Confederates' refusal to exchange Black prisoners:** *OR*, ser. II, 6:594–600.

125 **three Confederate prisoners be held:** *OR*, ser. I, 14:199–202; *OR*, ser. II, 5:708, 823–27; *OR*, ser. II, 6:171–72, 188; Elon A. Woodward, comp., *The Negro in the Military Service of the United States—A Compilation*, M-858, roll 5, 4224, National Archives.

125 **"The rebellion exists":** *OR*, ser. II, 7:119.

125 **the three sailors languished:** *OR*, ser. II, 7:956, 1007; *OR*, ser. II, 8:146, 257.

## CHAPTER SIX: THE ACCUMULATION

126 **"The few that did get away":** Quoted in Mark H. Dunkelman, *Brothers One and All: Esprit de Corps in a Civil War Regiment* (Baton Rouge: Louisiana State University Press, 2004), 132.

127 **"a few of us have reached":** Newell Burch, "The Civil War Diary and Related Sources of Corporal Newell Burch, 145th New York Volunteers, Covering the Period August 25, 1862, to April 21, 1865," ed. John Q. Imholte, 88, Friedsam Memorial Library, St. Bonaventure University, St. Bonaventure, N.Y. On the retreat, see Kent Masterson Brown, *Retreat from Gettysburg: Lee, Logistics, and the Pennsylvania Campaign* (Chapel Hill: University of North Carolina Press, 2005), 177–78, 273–74, 295–97, 369–70.

129 **"Everywhere there is a wrangling":** "City Intelligence. The Libby Prison and Its Contents," *Richmond Enquirer*, February 2, 1864, 3.

129 **"very pleasant spot":** "Prisoners of War," *Richmond Enquirer*, July 11, 1862, 2. See also "War Gossip in Richmond," *Charleston Mercury*, August 2, 1862, 1.

130 **"better satisfied than they would be":** *Richmond Sentinel*, May 13, 1863, 1.

130 **"a dirty lousy hole":** William Dolphin, *William Dolphin's Civil War Diary, August 15, 1863, Through April 4, 1864* (Ossining, N.Y.: Ossining Historical Society, 1991), 20.

130 **"Not a spear of grass growing":** John A. Stoneham and Mary Jane H. Wilson, eds., *Diaries and Letters of Horace Aurelius Smith: October 15, 1862, to December 31, 1867* (privately pub., 2001) (entry for July 14, 1863).

130 **"winds and wrapped in fogs":** "Union Prisoners at Richmond," *Harper's Weekly*, December 5, 1863, 779.

130 **"irregular mass of old dilapidated":** Gregory A. Coco, ed., *From Ball's Bluff to Gettysburg . . . and Beyond: The Civil War Letters of Private Roland E. Bowen, 15th Massachusetts Infantry 1861–1864* (Gettysburg, Pa.: Thomas, 1994), 176.

130 **"we found about 3000 ahead of us":** Burch, "Civil War Diary," 89–90.

131 **"the rebs have taken everything":** Dolphin, *William Dolphin's Civil War*, 20.

131 **"slept cold last night":** Dolphin, *William Dolphin's Civil War*, 29.

131 **"like pigs just as close":** Coco, *From Ball's Bluff to Gettysburg*, 176.

131 **"The silent hours of night":** Coco, *From Ball's Bluff to Gettysburg*, 176–77.

131 **"sleep more [at] nights":** Burch, "Civil War Diary," 108.

131 **"one fourth of the filth":** Coco, *From Ball's Bluff to Gettysburg*, 184.

131 **"too much crowded":** *OR*, ser. II, 6:587–88.

131 **Four months later, the prison's:** *OR*, ser. II, 6:1087–88.

133 **"that (in such a crowded place as this is) if a person":** Quoted in Dale Fetzer and Bruce Mowday, *Unlikely Allies: Fort Delaware's Prison Community in the Civil War* (Mechanicsburg, Pa.: Stackpole, 2000), 112 (Jenkins's diary entry for July 11, 1863).

133 **"It is a first rate place to see":** Quoted in Fetzer and Mowday, *Unlikely Allies*, 117.

134 **"washings of the hands":** *OR*, ser. II, 6:1124.

135 **"it costs the Confederacy":** "Treatment of Prisoners," *Richmond Dispatch*, April 9, 1863, 1.

135 **General Winder exacerbated:** "Impressment of Flour," *Richmond Dispatch*, March 12, 1863, 1.

135 **"Looks about as usual":** Bergun H. Brown Diary, Bergun H. Brown Papers (C3798), 59, State Historical Society of Missouri Research Center, Columbia.

136 **"so freely as to make it seem":** George R. Sherman, *Assault on Fort Gilmer and Reminiscences of Prison Life* (Providence: Rhode Island Soldiers and Sailors Historical Society, 1897), 41.

136 **"could always take in a few more":** James S. Anderson, *Nineteen Months a Prisoner of War in the Hands of the Rebels: Experience at Bell Isle, Richmond, Danville, and Andersonville* (Milwaukee: Starr and Son, 1865), 42.

136 **"could scarcely find room":** Entry for March 28, 1864, William Tritt Diary, Wisconsin Historical Society, Madison.

137 **"There were enough vacancies":** George H. Putnam, *A Prisoner of War in Virginia, 1864–5* (New York: G.P. Putnam's Sons, 1914), 35.

137 **the water turned muddy**: Homer B. Sprague, *Lights and Shadows in Confederate Prisons: A Personal Experience, 1864–5* (New York: G.P. Putnam's Sons, 1915), 116; entries for May 13, 14, 1864, George R. Crosby Diaries, January–June 1864, folder 13, MSA 84, Leahy Library, Vermont Historical Society, Barre.

137 **"were obliged to make their evacuations":** Henry M. Davidson, *Fourteen Months in Southern Prisons: Being a Narrative of the Treatment of Federal Prisoners of War in the Rebel Military Prisons of Richmond, Danville, Andersonville, Savannah and Millen* (Milwaukee: Daily Wisconsin, 1865), 95; Solon Hyde, *A Captive of War* (New York: McClure, Phillips, 1900), 125.

137 **"most wretched conditions":** *OR*, ser. II, 6:888–90.

137 **"should be put up in the roughest":** Quoted in Benton McAdams, *Rebels at Rock Island: The Story of a Civil War Prison* (DeKalb: Northern Illinois University Press, 2000), 23.

138 **"no water yet in prison yard"**: McAdams, *Rebels at Rock Island*, 35.

138 **"dirty, ragged, careworn looking":** *Davenport (Iowa) Union*, December 11, 1863, 2.
138 **Stunned prisoners who hailed:** McAdams, *Rebels at Rock Island*, 46.
140 **"digestive and intestinal derangements":** *OR*, ser. II, 5:742.
140 **"that clung to me like a leech":** George M. Neese, *Three Years in the Confederate Horse Artillery* (New York: Neale, 1911), 340.
141 **"miserable affairs":** James T. Wells, "Prison Experience," *Southern Historical Society Papers* 7 (1878): 327.
141 **"seen so much service":** Charles T. Loehr, "Point Lookout," *Southern Historical Society Papers* 18 (1890): 116.
142 **confirmed by one of Hoffman's inspectors:** *OR*, ser. II, 6:743.
142 **"it soon got to be the same":** Burch, "Civil War Diary," 120, 127.
142 **Andersonville was the solution:** The essential work on Andersonville and its founding is William Marvel, *Andersonville: The Last Depot* (Chapel Hill: University of North Carolina Press, 1994).
143 **"salubrity" and abundance of water:** Jefferson Davis, *The Rise and Fall of the Confederate Government* (New York: D. Appleton, 1881), 2:596.
143 **"no difficulty will be encountered":** "Change of Base," *Richmond Sentinel*, December 30, 1863, 1.
143 **"an old prison officer":** "Trial of Capt. Wirz," *New York Times*, August 31, 1865, 1.
143 **In 1862 he joined:** "Execution of Wirz," Washington *Evening Star*, November 10, 1865, 1.
145 **Private William Hawkins:** Dunkleman, *Brothers One and All*, 121.
146 **"which nearly smothered us":** Charles Smedley, *Life in Southern Prisons: From the Diary of Corporal Charles Smedley of Company G, 90th Regiment, Penn'a Volunteers* (Fulton, Pa.: Ladies' and Gentlemen's Fulton Aid Society, 1865), 16–21.
146 **Newell Burch and his friend:** Burch, "Civil War Diary," 121.
146 **Charles Smedley spent:** Smedley, *Life in Southern Prisons*, 22.
147 **"an elephant of immense magnitude":** "886 Northern Prisoners in Macon," *Macon Telegraph*, May 2, 1862, 1.
147 **"At a time when it is difficult":** "Prisoners of War," *Macon Telegraph*, May 3, 1862, 2 (italics in original).
148 **local wrote to President Jefferson Davis:** Richard W. Iobst, *Civil War Macon: The History of a Confederate City* (Macon, Ga.: Mercer University Press, 1999), 278.
148 **The best solution, he contended:** *OR*, ser. II, 7:167–69.
148 **Chandler urged that no more prisoners:** *OR*, ser. II, 7:546–50.
149 **he continued to fire off:** *OR*, ser. I, 38:877; *OR*, ser. II, 7:469, 471, 473.
150 **"rebel prisoners are treated as well":** *Baltimore American* quoted in *Hammond (Ind.) Gazette*, November 3, 1863, 1.
150 **"have more to eat here":** *Hammond Gazette*, January 27, 1864, 1.
150 **Such was the case at Rock Island:** "The Treatment of Prisoners During the War Between the States," *Southern Historical Society Papers* 1 (1876): 290–91.
150 **"strict retaliation would be practiced":** Colonel A. J. Johnson, "Letter from the Commandant of Rock Island Barracks," *Rock Island (Ill.) Argus*, November 25, 1864, 2; *OR*, ser. II, 8:17.
150 **"scrupulously clean and neat":** "Treatment of Prisoners," *Richmond Dispatch*, April 9, 1863, 1.
151 **"You yourself see":** *OR*, ser. II, 6:80, 104, 113.
151 **"monstrous pretension":** Dunbar Rowland, ed., *Jefferson Davis, Constitutionalist: His Letters, Papers, and Speeches* (Jackson, Miss.: Little & Ives, 1923), 5:405.
151 **"sufficiently reduced by death":** *OR*, ser. II, 7:524–25, 551–53.
152 **"the very great sympathy":** *OR*, ser. II, 7:755–62.
152 **"drawn out of shape":** Burch, "Civil War Diary," 127.

## CHAPTER SEVEN: A MIXTURE OF INDIFFERENCE AND HALF-WITTED CRUELTY

153 **"chastening providence":** Jefferson J. Hammer, ed., *Frederic Augustus James's Civil War Diary: Sumter to Andersonville* (Rutherford, N.J.: Fairleigh Dickinson University Press, 1973), 49–50.

154 **"territories of the self":** Erving Goffman, *Asylums: Essays on the Social Situation of Mental Patients and Other Inmates* (Chicago: Aldine, 1962), 23.

156 **"scum" of the North's mongrel:** Henry C. Dickinson, *Diary of Capt. Henry C. Dickinson, C.S.A.* (Denver: Williamson-Haffner, 1914), 47.

157 **"a sickening blotch upon humanity":** Jesse Hawes, *Cahaba: A Story of Captive Boys in Blue* (New York: Burr, 1888), 259–60.

157 **"without discipline":** *OR*, ser. II, 7:549.

157 **"thoroughly demoralized":** *OR*, ser. II, 7:548.

157 **"good, steady, obedient & willing men":** Quoted in Roger Pickenpaugh, *Captives in Gray: The Civil War Prisons of the Union* (Tuscaloosa: University of Alabama Press, 2009), 130.

157 **"the most unpromising subjects":** *OR*, ser. II, 7:65.

158 **Regulations in Union and Confederate:** See, for example, the Camp Chase "Instructions to Prison Guards," in *OR*, ser. II, 7:1.

158 **the force that patrolled the stockade:** U.S. Congress, H. Ex. Doc. 23, *Trial of Henry Wirz: Letter from the Secretary of War ad Interim, in Answer to a Resolution of the House of April 16, 1866, Transmitting a Summary of the Trial of Henry Wirz* (Washington, D.C.: Government Printing Office, 1868), 236.

158 **"slip-shod indifference":** Anthony M. Keiley, *In Vinculis; or, The Prisoner of War: Being the Experience of a Rebel in Two Federal Pens, Interspersed with Reminiscences of the Late War, Anecdotes of Southern Generals, Etc.* (New York: Blelock, 1866), 132.

158 **"a rather curious mixture":** George H. Putnam, *A Prisoner of War in Virginia, 1864–5* (New York, G.P. Putnam's Sons, 1914), 66.

158 **"I culd stay here contented":** Louis A. Brown, ed., "The Correspondence of David Olando McRaven and Amanda Nantz McRaven, 1864–1865," *North Carolina Historical Review* 26 (January 1949): 51.

158 **"feeal a touch of sorrow":** Brown, "Correspondence of David Olando McRaven," 81.

159 **"commenced my free-masonry":** Homer B. Sprague, *Lights and Shadows in Confederate Prisons: A Personal Experience, 1864–5* (New York: G. P. Putnam's Sons, 1915), 38–39.

159 **"the only interest manifested by any Rebel":** John McElroy, *Andersonville: A Story of Rebel Military Prisons, Fifteen Months a Guest of the So-Called Southern Confederacy* (Toledo: D. R. Locke, 1879), 377. See also Samuel S. Boggs, *Eighteen Months a Prisoner Under the Rebel Flag: A Condensed Pen-Picture of Belle Isle, Danville, Andersonville, Charleston, Florence and Libby Prisons, from Actual Experience* (Lovington, Ill.: privately pub., 1887), 38, 46; Jacob Jewell, *Heroic Deeds of Noble Master Masons During the Civil War from 1861 to 1865 in the U.S.A.* (Pueblo, Col.: privately pub., 1916), 28–29.

161 **Andersonville prisoner John Ransom:** John L. Ransom, *Andersonville Diary, Escape, and List of the Dead, with Name, Co., Regiment, Date of Death, and No. of Grave in Cemetery* (Auburn, N.Y.: privately pub., 1881), 42.

162 **Half of the escapees:** Frank E. Moran, "Colonel Rose's Tunnel at Libby Prison," *Century Magazine*, March 1888, 770–90.

162 **The logistics required to carry out:** *OR*, ser. II, 7:901–6. See also Charles E. Frohman, *Rebels on Lake Erie* (Columbus: Ohio Historical Society, 1965), 72–80.

162 **"they are becoming more strict":** Quoted in Dale Fetzer and Bruce Mowday, *Unlikely Allies: Fort Delaware's Prison Community in the Civil War* (Mechanicsburg, Pa.: Stackpole, 2000), 110 (Jenkins's diary entry for August 3, 1863).

162 **"This will undoubtedly increase the sickness":** *OR*, ser. II, 6:638.

162 **no longer had "any confidence":** Brown, "Correspondence of David Olando McRaven," 66.

163 **But they quickly retreated:** Hawes, *Cahaba*, 409–23.

163 **Early and his army withdrew:** Benjamin Franklin Cooling. *Jubal Early's Raid on Washington, 1864* (Tuscaloosa: University of Alabama Press, 2007), esp. 157–76.

163 **Meade called "desperate":** George Meade, *The Life and Letters of George Gordon Meade, Major-General United States Army*, ed. George Gordon Meade (New York: Charles Scribner's Sons, 1913), 2:167–68. See also *OR*, ser. I, 33: 183–89.

164 **"they would all be blown to Hell":** Arch Fredric Blakey, *General John H. Winder*, C.S.A. (Gainesville: University Press of Florida, 1990), 173.

164 **When a group of local white women:** Congress, *Trial of Henry Wirz*, 364.

165 **"Quite a number of visitors here to-day":** Michael Dougherty, *Prison Diary, of Michael*

*Dougherty, Late Co. B, 13th., Pa., Cavalry: While Confined in Pemberton, Barrett's, Libby, Andersonville and Other Southern Prisons* (Briston, Pa.: Chas. A. Dougherty, 1908), 44.

165 **"comical and ludicrous":** Ransom, *Andersonville Diary*, 33.

165 **"she Yankee brutes":** Entry for July 9, 1863, Robert Bingham Diary, vol. 1, June–October 1863, Robert Bingham Papers, 3731-z, Southern Historical Collection, Wilson Special Collections Library, University of North Carolina at Chapel Hill.

165 **"the refined and valorous people":** Keiley, *In Vinculis*, 94–95. See also Michael P. Gray, *The Business of Captivity: Elmira and Its Civil War Prison* (Kent, Ohio: Kent State University Press, 2001), 23–26.

166 **their notions of personal dignity:** See Julius Murray to brother, September 24, 1861, Julius A. Murray Family Papers, 1810–1855, 1861–1862, 1865, n.d., Wisconsin Historical Society, Madison.

166 **At Elmira, during the night:** Reminiscences of Berry Benson, Berry Benson Papers, 2636, Southern Historical Collection, Wilson Special Collections Library, University of North Carolina at Chapel Hill.

166 **"Every hour of the day":** Henri Pierre Clavreul, *Diary of Rev. H. Clavreul: With the Names of Dying Federal Soldiers to Whom He Ministered at Andersonville, Ga., July and August, 1864*, ed. George Robbins (Waterbury: Connecticut Association of Ex-Prisoners of War, 1910), 5.

167 **"how much we suffered":** John R. King, *My Experience in the Confederate Army and in Northern Prisons* (Clarksburg, W.V.: United Daughters of the Confederacy, 1917), 38.

167 **"on the good nature of the examining officer":** Charles Mattocks, *"Unspoiled Heart": The Journal of Charles Mattocks of the 17th Maine*, ed. Philip N. Racine (Knoxville: University of Tennessee Press, 1994), 154, 180.

167 **"cultivated a microscopic penmanship":** Keiley, *In Vinculis*, 90.

167 **thousands of letters for the prisoners:** Congress, *Trial of Henry Wirz*, 409, 410, 613.

168 **"you could have heard a pin drop":** Dougherty, *Prison Diary*, 18.

168 **"prisoners are bountifully supplied":** *OR*, ser. II, 6:489.

168 **"nothing shall be allowed":** Quoted in Leslie Hunter, "Warden for the Union: General William Hoffman (1807–1884)" (PhD diss., University of Arizona, 1971), 184.

168 **Union guards:** Dickinson, *Diary of Capt. Henry C. Dickinson*, 45.

169 **"I said nothing":** Dougherty, *Prison Diary*, 18.

169 **"throwing a feather into the wind":** Mattocks, *"Unspoiled Heart,"* 380.

169 **The tallies of tablespoons:** See John Allen Diary, 1864–1865, Virginia Historical Society, Richmond; *Henry H. Stone Diary*, Andersonville National Historic Site, Andersonville, Ga.

170 **"A careful analysis of the rations":** Fetzer and Mowday, *Unlikely Allies*, 59–60, 113, 120–21, 144.

170 **ration should be "considerably reduced":** William Hoffman to E. M. Stanton, May 19, 1864, in *OR*, ser. II, 7:150–51.

170 **"half the amount of meat":** W. F. Swalm to J. H. Douglas, November 13, 1863, in *OR*, ser. II, 6:578.

170 **"salty enough to make a hound yell":** George M. Neese, *Three Years in the Confederate Horse Artillery* (New York: Neale, 1911), 339.

170 **"much too diminutive in quantity":** Neese, *Three Years*, 339.

170 **While supplies remained scarce:** J. B. Jones, *A Rebel War Clerk's Diary at the Confederate States Capital* (Philadelphia: J. B. Lippincott, 1866), 2:11 (entry for August 12, 1863).

171 **"hungry as Satan":** William Dolphin, *William Dolphin's Civil War Diary, August 15, 1863, Through April 4, 1864*, ed. C. M. Crisfield (Ossining, N.Y.: Ossining Historical Society, 1991), 20.

171 **"could not wait to cook it":** James J. Heslin, ed., "The Diary of a Union Soldier *in Confederate Prisons*," *New York Historical Society Quarterly* 41 (July 1957): 241. See also Mattocks, *"Unspoiled Heart,"* 144.

171 **"I did not presume":** Congress, *Trial of Henry Wirz*, 40–41.

171 **Ashley V. Barrows:** Congress, *Trial of Henry Wirz*, 50.

171 **John H. Goldsmith:** Congress, *Trial of Henry Wirz*, 298, 333.

171 **"fared very well":** Congress, *Trial of Henry Wirz*, 466.

171 **"a small bit" of ham:** James, *Civil War Diary*, 78–84, 93.

172 **Prisoners traded with guards:** Congress, *Trial of Henry Wirz*, 118, 461.

173 **a postage-stamp-sized piece of bacon:** Charles Smedley, *Life in Southern Prisons: From the Diary of Corporal Charles Smedley of Company G, 90th Regiment, Penn'a Volunteers* (Fulton, Pa.: Ladies' and Gentlemen's Fulton Aid Society, 1865), 34.
173 **"no man can eat them":** Congress, *Trial of Henry Wirz*, 125.
173 **"potato peelings, cabbage stalks":** Charles T. Loehr, "Point Lookout," *Southern Historical Society Papers* 18 (1890): 116.
173 **Bales of clothing and blankets:** Congress, *Trial of Henry Wirz*, 141, 416–19.
174 **"As long as a prisoner":** *OR*, ser. II, 6:462.
174 **"There are very many sick":** *OR*, ser II, 3:636.
174 **"if we find them on you":** Amos Edward Stearns, *Narrative of Amos E. Stearns: Member Co. A., 25th Regt., Mass. Vols., a Prisoner at Andersonville*, ed. Samuel H. Putnam (Worcester, Mass.: F. P. Rice, 1887), 15–16.
174 **Private William Hawkins resorted:** Mark H. Dunkelman, *War's Relentless Hand: Twelve Tales of Civil War Soldiers* (Baton Rouge: Louisiana State University Press, 2006), 118–19.
175 **"the rebs have taken everything":** Dolphin, *Civil War Diary*, 20. See also Mattocks, *"Unspoiled Heart,"* 139, 140.
175 **"Valuables were never returned":** James T. Wells, "Prison Experience," *Southern Historical Society Papers* 7 (1879): 326.
175 **"new lot of prisoners":** John W. Robinson, "Experiences in Camp Chase Prison," *Confederate Veteran* 14 (November 1906): 514.
175 **A different danger haunted prisoners:** *Narrative of Privations and Sufferings of United States Officers and Soldiers While Prisoners of War in the Hands of the Rebel Authorities; Being the Report of a Commission of Inquiry, Appointed by the United States Sanitary Commission* (Philadelphia: U.S. Sanitary Commission, 1864), 34.
175 **"It galls them terribly":** John Whipple letter, July 1864, in Lydia M. Post, ed., *Soldiers' Letters from Camp, Battle-field, and Prison* (New York: Bunce and Huntington, 1865), 376.
175 **"we felt the insult keenly":** Benjamin Taylor Holliday, "Account of My Capture," 18, B. T. Holliday Papers, Albert and Shirley Small Special Collections Library, University of Virginia, Charlottesville.
175 **"imperious":** William Haigh to "My Dear Kate," May 27, 29, 1865, William H. Haigh Papers, 1841–1846, 1865, 02649-z, Southern Historical Collection, Wilson Special Collections Library, University of North Carolina at Chapel Hill.
175 **"insolence and brutality":** Keiley, *In Vinculis*, 70.
176 **Black guards shot more than thirty prisoners:** Richard H. Triebe, *Point Lookout Prison Camp and Hospital: The North's Largest Civil War Prison* (n.p.: Coastal Books, 2014), 24–27.
177 **"a perhaps innocent man":** *OR*, ser. II, 6:854.
177 **At Andersonville, absconding prisoners:** Congress, *Trial of Henry Wirz*, 130.
177 **Failure to report an escape:** Congress, *Trial of Henry Wirz*, 162.
177 **officers' prison in Columbia, South Carolina:** Stephen M. Weld, *War Diary and Letters of Stephen Minot Weld, 1861–1865* (Cambridge: Riverside, 1912), 383.
178 **"I must try and do something":** Alfred S. Roe, ed., *The Melvin Memorial, Sleepy Hollow Cemetery, Concord, Massachusetts, a Brother's Tribute* (Cambridge: Riverside, 1910), 123.
178 **"I procured all that I needed":** Congress, *Trial of Henry Wirz*, 110.
178 **"it is considered a great crime":** Ransom, *Andersonville Diary*, 42.
178 **"Hope they will have a good time":** Entry for May 24, 1864, James Burton Diary, MS 120, Stuart A. Rose Manuscript, Archives, and Rare Book Library, Emory University, Atlanta. See also William J. McKell, "The Journal of Sergt. Wm. J. McKell," *Civil War History* 3 (September 1957): 333.
179 **At Salisbury in November 1864:** Benjamin F. Booth and Steve Meyer, *Dark Days of the Rebellion: Life in Southern Military Prisons* (Garrison, Iowa: Meyer, 1996), 162. See also Donald F. Danker, "Imprisoned at Andersonville: The Diary of Albert Harry Shatzel, May 5, 1864–September 12, 1864," *Nebraska History* 38 (June 1957): 101, 103; Ronald G. Watson, ed., *From Ashby to Andersonville: The Civil War Diary and Reminiscences of Private George A. Hitchcock, 21st Massachusetts Infantry* (Campbell, Calif.: Savas, 1997), 191–92.
179 **"roughly handled":** James, *Civil War Diary*, 88.
179 **Utica, New York:** "Churches in the City of Utica," *Utica City Directory for 1858–9* (Utica, N.Y.: Joseph Arnott, 1858), 16; Nashville City and Business Directory (Nashville: L. P. Wil-

liams, 1860), 80; *E. Coy's City Directory, New Albany, Indiana* (New Albany, Ind..: E. Coy, 1860), 10–11.

179 **"observed as a play day":** James, *Civil War Diary*, 49; see also 41, 44.

179 **"there is no difference here":** Roe, *The Melvin Memorial*, 115.

179 **"to live once more in a land":** James, *Civil War Diary*, 44.

179 **the commandant at Camp Douglas:** David L. Keller, *The Story of Camp Douglas: Chicago's Forgotten Civil War Prison* (Charleston: Acadia, 2015), 117.

180 **"I want no advice on religious matters":** Entries for March 5, 6, June 26, 1864, William Peel *Diary*, Z/1797.000, Manuscript Collections, Mississippi Department of Archives and History, Jackson; entry for March 4, 1864, William A. Mayo Diary, 1861–1866, MS-1300, Betsey B. Creekmore Special Collections and University Archives, University of Tennessee, Knoxville; John G. Barrett, ed., *Yankee Rebel: The Civil War Journal of Edmund DeWitt Patterson* (Chapel Hill: University of North Carolina Press, 1966), 158–59.

180 **"Rebel ministers":** Albert Heffley, *Civil War Diaries of Capt. Albert Heffley and Lt. Cyrus P. Heffley, Company F-142nd Regt. Penna. Vol., Army of the Potomac* (Apollo, Pa.: Closson, 2000), 68.

180 **"a freedom shrieker":** Keiley, *In Vinculis*, 156.

180 **"had no time to waste":** Quoted in Gray, *The Business of Captivity*, 112.

181 **Reverend Isaac Handy:** Dickinson, *Diary of Capt. Henry C. Dickinson*, 33.

181 **furtive prayer groups and "religious associations":** George C. Osborn, ed., "A Confederate Prisoner at Camp Chase: Letters and a Diary of Private James W. Anderson," *Ohio State Archaeological and Historical Quarterly* 59 (January 1950): 45.

181 **ignore regulations against mingling:** William H. Peel, *Far from Home: The Diary of Lt. William H. Peel, 1863–1865*, ed. Ellen Sheffield Wilds (Bloomington, Ind.: Author House, 2009), 123–24.

181 **"prayed treason":** Dickinson, *Diary of Capt. Henry C. Dickinson*, 33.

181 **"to give victory to the loyal armies":** Henry S. White and Edward Drewry Jervey, *Prison Life Among the Rebels: Recollections of a Union Chaplain* (Kent, Ohio: Kent State University Press, 1990), 62–65.

182 **"full of sorrow for what":** Congress, *Trial of Henry Wirz*, 287–94, 426–31.

183 **"a new genre of ministry":** Report of the Diocese of Savannah, *Annales de la Propagation de la Foi*, vol. 37 (1893), 397–405. See also Thomas O'Dea, *History of O'Dea's Famous Picture of Andersonville Prison as It Appeared August 1st, 1864, When It Contained 35,000 Prisoners of War: Graphic Description of That Famous Locality, with Explanation of Key to Prison and Marginal Scenes* (Cohoes, N.Y.: Clark and Foster, 1887), 19; Robert H. Kellogg, *Life and Death in Rebel Prisons* (Hartford: L. Stebbins, 1865), 163–64; Charles Fosdick, *Five Hundred Days in Rebel Prisons* (Bethany, Mo.: Clipper Book and Job Office, 1887), 48; John B. Vaughter, *Prison Life in Dixie: Giving a Short History of the Inhuman and Barbarous Treatment of Our Soldiers by Rebel Authorities* (Chicago: Central Book Concern, 1881), 62; Augustus C. Hamlin, *Martyria, or Andersonville Prison* (Boston: Lee and Shepard, 1866), 34.

## CHAPTER EIGHT: TO BE CONTENT IN NARROW LIMITS

184 **"'grand entrée' upon the theatre":** William Haigh to "My Dear Kate," May 24, 1865, William H. Haigh Papers, 1841–1846, 1865, 02649-z, Southern Historical Collection, Wilson Special Collections Library, University of North Carolina at Chapel Hill.

184 **"that first *conscious* knowledge":** Haigh to "Kate," May 24, 1865.

184 **"sickens me":** Haigh to "Kate," May 24, 1865.

185 **"to bask in the sunshine":** Haigh to "Kate," May 24, 1865.

185 **Corporal Henry Devillez:** Henry Devillez, "Reminiscences of the Civil War: Andersonville," *Indiana Magazine of History* 11 (June 1915): 144.

185 **precious space in his pocket diary:** Entries for May 23, June 11, 1864, George R. Crosby Diaries, January–June 1864, folder 13, MSA 84, Leahy Library, Vermont Historical Society, Barre. See also Ronald G. Watson, ed., *From Ashby to Andersonville: The Civil War Diary and Reminiscences of Private George A. Hitchcock, 21st Massachusetts Infantry* (Campbell, Calif.: Savas, 1997), 183; Donald F. Danker, "Imprisoned at Andersonville: The Diary of Albert Harry Shatzel, May 5, 1864–September 12, 1864," *Nebraska History* 38 (June 1957):

42, 92; John L. Ransom, *Andersonville Diary, Escape, and List of the Dead, with Name, Co., Regiment, Date of Death, and No. of Grave in Cemetery* (Auburn, N.Y.: privately pub., 1881), 59, 110.

186 **Most colleges of the era:** Center for Education Statistics, *120 Years of American Education: A Statistical Portrait*, ed. Thomas D. Snyder (Washington, D.C.: Department of Education, 1993), 64.

186 **the foundry in Pittsburgh:** "A Great Cannon Foundry," *Scientific American*, September 10, 1864, 165.

186 **Only the largest northern textile mills:** John Leander Bishop, *A History of American Manufactures from 1608–1860, Exhibiting the Origin and Growth of the Principal Mechanic Arts and Manufactures, from the Earliest Colonial Period to the Adoption of the Constitution* (Philadelphia: Edward Young, 1861), 115, 316.

187 **"was thrown in company with prisoners":** C. W. Jones, *In Prison at Camp Lookout* (Martinsville, Va.: Bulletin, ca. 1890).

187 **prisoners hailing from six states:** Ransom, *Andersonville Diary*, 20. See also Danker, "Imprisoned at Andersonville," 110.

187 **Samuel Melvin, as he lay**: Alfred S. Roe, ed., *The Melvin Memorial, Sleepy Hollow Cemetery, Concord, Massachusetts, a Brother's Tribute* (Cambridge: Riverside, 1910), 133.

187 **"Sad indeed was the parting":** Lyle G. Adair, *They Have Left Us Here to Die: The Civil War Prison Diary of Sgt. Lyle G. Adair, 111th U.S. Colored Infantry*, ed. Glenn Robins (Kent, Ohio: Kent State University Press, 2011), 24.

187 **George A. Hitchcock:** Watson, *From Ashby to Andersonville*, 199, 216.

187 **"What agony":** Michael Dougherty, *Prison Diary, of Michael Dougherty, Late Co. B, 13th., Pa., Cavalry: While Confined in Pemberton, Barrett's, Libby, Andersonville and Other Southern Prisons* (Briston, Pa.: Chas. A. Dougherty, 1908), 20. See also David S. Whitenack, "Reminiscences of the Civil War: Andersonville," *Indiana Magazine of History* 11 (June 1915): 132.

188 **"They ordered us away":** U.S. Congress, H. Ex. Doc. 23, *Trial of Henry Wirz: Letter from the Secretary of War ad Interim, in Answer to a Resolution of the House of April 16, 1866, Transmitting a Summary of the Trial of Henry Wirz* (Washington, D.C.: Government Printing Office, 1868), 295.

188 **"strangers to each other":** John McElroy, *Andersonville: A Story of Rebel Military Prisons, Fifteen Months a Guest of the So-Called Southern Confederacy* (Toledo: D. R. Locke, 1879), 234.

188 **"amid such privation and suffering":** Amos Edward Stearns, *Narrative of Amos E. Stearns: Member Co. A., 25th Regt., Mass. Vols., a Prisoner at Andersonville*, ed. Samuel H. Putnam (Worcester, Mass.: F. P. Rice, 1887), 31. See also Robert Knox Sneden, *Eye of the Storm: A Civil War Odyssey*, ed. Charles F. Bryan Jr. and Nelson D. Lankford (New York: Simon and Schuster, 2000), 229.

189 **"neat in their habits":** Jefferson J. Hammer, ed, *Frederic Augustus James's Civil War Diary: Sumter to Andersonville* (Rutherford, N.J.: Fairleigh Dickinson University Press, 1973), 41.

189 **"the society" included "the very best":** Thomas Gibbes Morgan Jr. to "My dear Mother," December 9, 1863, Papers of Thomas Gibbes Morgan, Sr., and Thomas Gibbes Morgan, Jr., 1776–1946, David M. Rubenstein Rare Book and Manuscript Library, Duke University, Durham, N.C.

189 **"the veriest rabble I ever saw":** Entry for July 30, 1863, Robert Bingham Diary, vol. 1, June–October 1863, Robert Bingham Papers, 3731-z, Southern Historical Collection, Wilson Special Collections Library, University of North Carolina at Chapel Hill.

189 **groused about the "unwashed":** Haigh to "Kate," May 24, 1865. See also William Cary Dodson, unpublished memoir, subser. 1.2, box 8, folder 19, Civil War collection, No. 20, Stuart A. Rose Manuscript, Archives, and Rare Book Library, Emory University, Atlanta; W. C. Dodson, "Stories of Prison Life," *Confederate Veteran* 3 (March 1900): 121; James W. Anderson to Thomas, January 1865, in George C. Osborn, ed., "Writings of a Confederate Prisoner of War," *Tennessee Historical Quarterly* 10 (March 1951): 86.

189 **"men are thicker hear":** Henry Lloyd White, "War Prison Diary of Major Harry White, 1863–1864," 10, 107, White Family Papers, "Indiana, Pennsylvania in the Civil War Era" collection, Indiana University of Pennsylvania Special Collections, Indiana, Pa.

189 **"from morning until night":** John G. Barrett, ed., *Yankee Rebel: The Civil War Journal of*

*Edmund DeWitt Patterson* (Chapel Hill: University of North Carolina Press, 1966), 171–72 (entry for June 12, 1864). See also entries for July 5, 10, August 2, 9, 15, 1863, Bingham Diary.

190 **"Here is where I can see":** Entry for May 7, 1864, Crosby Diaries.

190 **"One thing that makes us all feel":** Entry for May 21, 1862, Journal of Josephus C. Moore, May 20, 1861, to September 2, 1862, 1861/1862, University of North Texas Libraries, UNT Digital Library, Denton; https://digital.library.unt.edu/ark:/67531/metapth207713/, accessed May 14, 2025.

190 **"sick enough of Rebel prisons":** Joseph Edward Hodgkins, *The Civil War Diary of Lieut. J. E. Hodgkins: 19th Massachusetts Volunteers, from August 11, 1862, to June 3, 1865*, ed. Kenneth Turino (Rockport, Me.: Picton, 1994), 109–11.

190 **"playing off, sick and going":** William J. McKell, "The Journal of Sergt. Wm. J. McKell," *Civil War History* 3 (September 1957): 331.

190 **Some healthy prisoners increased:** Mark H. Dunkelman, *Brothers One and All: Esprit de Corps in a Civil War Regiment* (Baton Rouge: Louisiana State University Press, 2004), 121.

190 **"the weak were robbed and kicked":** John England in Lydia M. Post, ed., *Soldiers' Letters from Camp, Battle-field, and Prison* (New York: Bunce and Huntington, 1865), 455.

191 **"usual number of fights":** Watson, *From Ashby to Andersonville*, 186. See also Ransom, *Andersonville Diary*, 20, 41, 63.

191 **"A fight every day sure":** Entry for July 2, 1864, William Tritt Diary, Wisconsin Historical Society, Madison. See also William A. Mayo Diary, 1861–1866, MS-1300, Betsey B. Creekmore Special Collections and University Archives, University of Tennessee, Knoxville; Danker, "Imprisoned at Andersonville," 96–97; entry for October 17, 1864, Thomas Alphonso Sharpe Diary, box 6, folder 19, Civil War Collection, MSS 20, Stuart A. Rose Manuscript, Archives, and Rare Book Library, Emory University; Charles Mattocks, *"Unspoiled Heart": The Journal of Charles Mattocks of the 17th Maine*, ed. Philip N. Racine (Knoxville: University of Tennessee Press, 1994), 167.

191 **"some men in camp who had been going":** Entry for April 5, 1864, B. Yancey Malone, *The Diary of Bartlett Yancey Malone*, ed. Sam J. Ervin and William Whatley Pierson (Chapel Hill: University of North Carolina Press, 1919), 47.

191 **So bold was one thief at Andersonville:** Ransom, *Andersonville Diary*, 69.

191 **"prowl about at night like hyenas":** Sneden, *Eye of the Storm*, 214 (entry for March 7, 1864). See also Danker, "Imprisoned at Andersonville," 98; Ransom, *Andersonville Diary*, 23, 25, 33, 43, 48.

191 **"the most horible Barberism":** Entry for June 29, 1864, Ransom Chadwick's Andersonville Prison Diary, vol. 1, Gale Family Library, Minnesota Historical Society, St. Paul.

192 **"very bold":** Entry for June 26, 1864, Crosby Diaries.

192 **they openly assaulted and robbed:** Ransom, *Andersonville Diary*, 8, 55; Watson, *From Ashby to Andersonville*, 187–88.

192 **"rather be hanged than live":** Ransom, *Andersonville Diary*, 115.

193 **"Here all is bestial":** Roe, *The Melvin Memorial*, 117 (entry for July 6, 1864).

193 **embracing "good will":** Haigh to "My Dear Kate," June 8, 1865, Haigh Papers.

194 **"semi-living state":** Entry for July 28, 1863, Bingham Diary.

194 **"one not acquainted with prison life":** Entry for May 21, 1862, Journal of Josephus C. Moore. See also Danker, "Imprisoned at Andersonville," 97.

194 **"those who keep busy stand it best":** Entry for August 14, 1864, "Civil War Diary of Sergeant Henry W. Tisdale: Company I, Thirty-Fifth Regiment, Massachusetts Volunteer Infantry, 1862–1865," http://www.civilwardiary.net/, accessed May 14, 2025.

194 **took up the study of German:** Mattocks, *"Unspoiled Heart,"* 152–53.

195 **"Our supply of books":** Quoted in Roger Pickenpaugh, *Captives in Gray: The Civil War Prisons of the Union* (Tuscaloosa: University of Alabama Press, 2009), 104.

195 **"The kind dispensation of your books":** C. W. Hayes to Amanda Gardner, March 5, 1865, quoted in Melvin Grigsby, *The Smoked Yank* (privately pub., 1888), 87–88.

196 **Prisoners elsewhere held informal lyceums:** See entries for September 15 and October 20, 1864, Sharpe Diary, box 6, folder 18.

196 **"some nights they will":** Thomas Beadles, quoted in Pickenpaugh, *Captives in Gray*, 107.

196 **Although miffed by the performance:** Ransom, *Andersonville Diary*, 42, 47; Watson, *From Ashby to Andersonville*, 188; Mattocks, *"Unspoiled Heart,"* 163.

196 **"evening entertainment by Bogus":** Earl E. Boyer, ed., *Civil War Diaries of Capt. Albert Heffley and Lt. Cyrus P. Heffley* (Apollo, Pa.: Closson, 2000): 67 (entry for November 11, 1863).

197 **"quite creditable":** Entry for September 4, 1863, Joseph Kern Diary, Joseph Mason Kern Papers, 2526-z, Southern Historical Collection, Wilson Special Collections Library, University of North Carolina at Chapel Hill.

197 **"a combination of negro minstrels":** William Peel, quoted in Pickenpaugh, *Captives in Gray*, 107.

197 **Union officers imprisoned:** Mattocks, "*Unspoiled Heart*," 151, 167.

198 **"looked on with eager interest":** Daniel R. Hundley, *Prison Echoes of the Great Rebellion* (New York: S. W. Green, 1874), 112 (entry for August 27, 1864).

198 **"amuse themselves mostly by gambling":** Entry for July 24, 1863, Bingham Diary.

198 **"Some think it is a sin":** Paul C. Helmreich, ed., "The Diary of Charles D. Lee in Andersonville and Florence Prison Camps, 1864," *Connecticut Historical Society Bulletin* 41 (January 1976): 19–20 (entries for June 6, 24, 1864).

198 **"I will be no worse off":** Entry for September 3, 1864, George E. Albee Diary, 1864, MS 41695, Library of Virginia, Richmond.

200 **"what the 'dead line' was":** Stearns, *Narrative of Amos E. Stearns*, 14, 25.

200 **"not knowing the rules":** Watson, *From Ashby to Andersonville*, 193.

200 **"free as circumstances will permit":** Ransom, *Andersonville Diary*, 22.

200 **"We slept together, ate together":** Whitenack, "Reminiscences of the Civil War," 132.

200 **"Of course I have to pony up":** Dougherty, *Prison Diary*, 19.

201 **"We are divided into detachments":** Entry for May 22, 1864, Crosby Diaries.

201 **"a rail about the camp":** Dougherty, *Prison Diary*, 32.

202 **"draw hidden money from the 'Yanks'":** Dougherty, *Prison Diary*, 30.

202 **"a most infamous lying":** Entry for February 14, 1864, Bingham Diary.

202 **"a teaspoonful of salt, 25 cents":** Dougherty, *Prison Diary*, 31.

203 **Selman chastised a Confederate soldier:** William Marvel, *Andersonville: The Last Depot* (Chapel Hill: University of North Carolina Press, 1994), 48–49.

203 **offered Union prisoners favorable exchange rates:** Mattocks, "*Unspoiled Heart*," 162.

203 **paid $4.50 for "a little lot":** Roe, *The Melvin Memorial*, 104.

203 **Bradford Sparrow:** Entry for July 16, 1864, Bradford Sparrow Diary, Bradford Sparrow Correspondence, University of Vermont Libraries, Burlington.

204 **New Yorker John Hoster:** Entry for July 12, 1864, John L. Hoster Diary, 1862–1865, Stuart A. Rose Manuscript, Archives, and Rare Book Library, Emory University. See also Watson, *From Ashby to Andersonville*, 189, 216; Stearns, *Narrative of Amos E. Stearns*, 30.

204 **"Passing up the street":** Entry for July 7, 1863, Scrapbook, folder 2, Joseph Mason Kern Papers, 1860–1865, 02526-z, Southern Historical Collection, Wilson Special Collections Library, University of North Carolina at Chapel Hill.

204 **"We have stores oppen":** Quoted in Pickenpaugh, *Captives in Blue*, 143.

204 **"a city—a marketplace"**: Congress, *Trial of Wirz*, 574.

204 **selling their skills and labor:** See Ransom, *Andersonville Diary*, 75, 77, 84; Dunkelman, *Brothers One and All*, 123.

205 **"would be a greater inducement":** *OR*, ser. II, 6:701–2.

206 **"the Ancient Mariner's experience":** Watson, *From Ashby to Andersonville*, 194, 211.

206 **"famished skeletons":** Dougherty, *Prison Diary*, 31.

206 **"I shall feel lonesome now":** Entry for January 11, 1865, George A. Clarkson Diary, Andersonville National Historic Site, Andersonville, Ga.

206 **A careful analysis of the survival rates:** Dora L. Costa and Matthew E. Kahn, "Surviving Andersonville: The Benefits of Social Networks in POW Camps," *American Economic Review* 97 (September 2007): 1467–87.

207 **"all attempts would be fruitless":** McKell, "The Journal of Sergt. Wm. J. McKell," 337–38.

208 **"transition from that place":** McKell, "The Journal of Sergt. Wm. J. McKell," 339.

209 **"committed our friend's remains to the deep":** Henry C. Dickinson, *Diary of Capt. Henry C. Dickinson, C. S. A.* (Denver: Williamson-Haffner, 1914), 164.

209 **"We see it every day":** Louis A. Brown, ed., "The Correspondence of David Olando McRaven and Amanda Nantz McRaven, 1864–1865," *North Carolina Historical Review* 26 (January 1949): 81.

209 **"The continuous sight of death":** "Etats-Unis," *Annales de la Propagation de la Foi* 37 (1865): 400.
210 **James was present to pray:** Hammer, *James's Civil War Diary*, 48–53.
211 **"sickening and heart-rending spectacle":** A. W. Mangum, *Confederate States Military Prison at Salisbury, NC* (Wake Forest, N.C.: Scuppernong, 2019).
211 **"a very solemn and impressive occasion":** Hammer, *James's Civil War Diary*, 56.
211 **"no friend to stand by":** Haigh to "Kate," May 24, 1865.

## CHAPTER NINE: ON ACCOUNT OF MY COLOR

212 **"We are learning to make fortifications":** William McCoslin, "Letter from the Front," *The Christian Recorder*, August 27, 1864, 3.
213 **"When I lead these men into battle":** *Memorial of Colonel John A. Bross, Twenty Ninth U.S. Colored Troops, Who Fell Leading the Assault on Petersburgh, July 30, 1864: Together with a Sermon by His Pastor, Rev. Arthur Swazey* (Chicago: Tribune Book and Job Office, 1865), 101.
214 **"couldn't tell what I was":** Isaac Gaskins, letter to editor, *Illinois State Journal*, October 21, 1889, 2.
215 **"we were not allowing them to surrender":** Entry for July 30, 1864, Hall T. McGee Diary, 1864–1866 (43/2223), South Carolina Historical Society, Charleston.
215 **"Most of the negroes were killed":** Jerome B. Yates to wife, August 3, 1864, in Robert G. Evans, ed., *The 16th Mississippi Infantry: Civil War Letters and Reminiscences* (Jackson: University Press of Mississippi, 2002), 281.
215 **By one estimate:** Caroline Wood Newhall, "Under the Rebel Lash: Black Prisoners of War in the Confederate South" (PhD diss., University of North Carolina at Chapel Hill, 2020).
215 **"was perfectly right":** James I. Robertson Jr., ed., "'The Boy Artillerist': Letters of Colonel William Pegram, C.S.A.," *Virginia Magazine of History and Biography* 98 (April 1990): 242–45.
215 **"soil their hands with the capture":** Quoted in Ervin L. Jordan Jr., *Black Confederates and Afro-Yankees in Civil War Virginia* (Charlottesville: University Press of Virginia, 1995), 277.
215 **"returned to their owners":** *OR*, ser. I, 22:965.
215 **"held in strict confinement":** *OR*, ser. II, 7:703–4.
216 **"shrieking, praying, and cursing":** John Herbert Claiborne, *Seventy-Five Years in Old Virginia* (New York: Neale, 1904), 208.
216 **"See the white and nigger equality soldiers!":** H. Seymour Hall, "Mine Run to Petersburg," in *War Talks in Kansas* (Kansas City, Mo.: Franklin Hudson, 1906), 231.
216 **"you will never live":** Sumner U. Shearman, *Personal Narratives of Events in the War of the Rebellion, Being Papers Read Before the Rhode Island Soldiers and Sailors Historical Society*, ser. 5, no. 8 (Providence: Rhode Island Soldiers and Sailors, 1898), 16–18.
216 **With their retransformation into property:** See, for instance, Deposition, Samuel Anderson, June 23, 1896, in Pension File SC959813, Samuel Anderson, Forty-Sixth U.S. Colored Infantry, Civil War Pension Application Files, RG 15, National Archives, Washington, D.C.; Descriptive Books, Companies E and G, Forty-Sixth U.S. Colored Infantry, and HQ Forty-Sixth U.S. Colored Infantry, SO 65, December 2, 1865, both in Forty-Sixth U.S. Colored Infantry, Regimental Books, RG 94, National Archives.
217 **"unusually well educated":** "Saved from Prisons—The Seventh Annual Reunion of the Ex-Prisoners of War of Illinois," *Bloomington (Ill.) Pantagraph*, October 22, 1885, 3.
217 **Authorities on occasion dispersed:** *OR*, ser. I, 23:294, 850; *OR*, ser. II, 7:583.
218 **nearly six hundred Black prisoners:** *OR*, ser I, 39:427–28, 548, 698, 705, 706–8, 715–16.
218 **"dark and horrible beyond description":** Isaac N. Johnston, *Four Months in Libby, and the Campaign Against Atlanta* (Cincinnati: R. P. Thompson, 1864), 57.
218 **"do the drudgery of the prison":** Johnston, *Four Months in Libby*, 58.
218 **"were marched out every morning":** Gaskins, letter to editor, 2.
219 **They worked at the train depot:** U.S. Congress, H. Ex. Doc. 23, *Trial of Henry Wirz: Letter from the Secretary of War ad Interim, in Answer to a Resolution of the House of April 16, 1866, Transmitting a Summary of the Trial of Henry Wirz* (Washington, D.C.: Government Printing Office, 1868), 179–80, 406.
219 **"anything respectable to eat":** Gaskins, letter to editor, 2.

219 **"like a hog in a farmer's yard":** Charles Mattocks, *"Unspoiled Heart": The Journal of Charles Mattocks of the 17th Maine*, ed. Philip N. Racine (Knoxville: University of Tennessee Press, 1994), 205.

219 **"give me a blow":** Gaskins, letter to editor, 2.

219 **"had to go without rations":** Luis F. Emilio, *History of the Fifty-Fourth Regiment of Massachusetts Volunteer Infantry, 1863–1865* (Boston: Boston Book, 1894), 429.

219 **"were treated worse than dumb brutes":** John McElroy, *Andersonville: A Story of Rebel Military Prisons, Fifteen Months a Guest of the So-called Southern Confederacy; A Private Soldier's Experience in Richmond, Andersonville, Savannah, Millen, Blackshear and Florence* (Toledo: D. R. Locke, 1879), 163.

219 **the whipping of a Black prisoner:** Roger Pickenpaugh, *Captives in Blue: The Civil War Prisons of the Confederacy* (Tuscaloosa: University of Alabama Press, 2013), 191.

220 **"If we lagged or faltered":** *OR*, ser. II, 8:153.

220 **Jennings was placed in the camp stocks:** Congress, *Trial of Henry Wirz*, 187.

220 **He also was restrained and gagged:** Congress, *Trial of Henry Wirz*, 279.

220 **Isaac Haskins:** Congress, *Trial of Henry Wirz*, 174, 177, 408, 518–19; William B. Styple, ed., *Death Before Dishonor: The Andersonville Diary of Eugene Forbes, 4th New Jersey Infantry* (Kearny, N.J.: Bellegrove, 1995), 90.

220 **Bardo was placed in the stocks:** Congress, *Trial of Henry Wirz*, 128, 512.

220 **"he had tried to make a nigger":** "The Union Prisoners at Andersonville, Georgia," *Cleveland Daily Leader*, October 17, 1864, 3.

221 **Out of one hundred eighty:** Gaskins, letter to editor, 2.

221 **"the negroes suffered most":** Homer B. Sprague, *Lights and Shadows in Confederate Prisons: A Personal Experience, 1864–5* (New York: G.P. Putnam's Sons, 1915), 78.

222 **"as good soldiers as any":** "Annual Message to Congress," December 8, 1863, in Abraham Lincoln, *Lincoln: Speeches and Writings*, vol. 2, *1859–1865* (New York: Library of America, 1989), 538–54.

222 **"There have been men who have proposed":** Abraham Lincoln, April 19, 1864, in Roy P. Basler, ed., *The Collected Works of Abraham Lincoln* (New Brunswick, N.J.: Rutgers University Press, 1953), 7:506–7.

223 **"It is hard on our men":** *OR*, ser. I, 120:607.

223 "**to absolutely stop exchanges":** Howard K. Beale, ed., *Diary of Gideon Welles: Secretary of the Navy Under Lincoln and Johnson* (New York: W. W. Norton, 1960), 2:171.

224 **"every soldier . . . that is killed":** *Cincinnati Daily Enquirer*, July 25, 1864.

224 **"our niggers in uniform":** "The Exchange Question," *Chicago Times*, quoted in the *Richmond Dispatch*, December 24, 1863, 1.

225 **"with the express or implied understanding":** Abraham Lincoln to Isaac M. Schermerhorn, n. d., 1864, in Basler, *Collected Works of Abraham Lincoln*, 8:2.

225 **"I did not come out to fight":** Henry P. Hubbell to Walter S. Hubbell, January 26, 1863, in Simon P. Newman, "A Democrat in Lincoln's Army: The Civil War Letters of Henry P. Hubbell," *Princeton University Library Chronicle* 50 (Winter 1989): 163.

225 **"I don't want to fire another shot":** Valentin Bechler to wife, November 11, 1862, in Robert C. Goodell and P. A. M. Taylor, eds., "A German Immigrant in the Union Army: Selected Letters of Valentin Bechler," *Journal of American Studies* 4 (February 1971): 161.

225 **"I consider my life":** Olney Andrus to Mary Andrus, in Fred A. Shannon, ed., *The Civil War Letters of Sergeant Olney Andrus* (Urbana: University of Illinois Press, 1947), 29.

226 **"we must stay here":** Entry for September 2, 1864, Kendrick R. Howard Diary, Misc 698, Vermont Historical Society, Barre.

226 **"rough that it should be necessary":** John L. Ransom, *Andersonville Diary, Escape, and List of the Dead, with Name, Co., Regiment, Date of Death, and No. of Grave in Cemetery* (Auburn, N.Y.: privately pub., 1881), 89.

226 **"I hardly know which to blame most":** Entry for July 2, 1864, Samuel J. Gibson Diary and Correspondence, MSS 5241, Library of Congress, Washington, D.C.

226 **"cannot do harm, & if it will do good":** Alfred S. Roe, ed., *The Melvin Memorial, Sleepy Hollow Cemetery, Concord, Massachusetts, a Brother's Tribute* (Cambridge, Mass.: Riverside, 1910), 120.

227 **"The everlasting niggers must be protected":** Entry for July 16, 1864, Gibson Diary.
227 **"The government should punish any man":** Styple, *Death Before Dishonor*, 89.
227 **"What the hell did they enlist":** Donald F. Danker, "Imprisoned at Andersonville: The Diary of Albert Harry Shatzel, May 5, 1864–September 12, 1864," *Nebraska History* 38 (June 1957): 121.
227 **"considerable favor":** Styple, *Death Before Dishonor*, 91.
227 **"the actual state of that hell on earth":** Hermes, "Letter from Richmond," *Charleston Mercury*, August 31, 1864, 1.
229 **the heartless Lincoln administration:** Edward Wellington Boate, "The True Story of Andersonville Told by a Federal Prisoner," *Southern Historical Society Papers* 10 (January 1882): 25–32 (originally appeared in *New York News*, July 1865).
229 **"this last dreadful sacrifice":** "Thirty-Five Thousand White Men vs. a Few Negroes," *Coshocton (Ohio) Democrat*, September 28, 1864, 4.
229 **"rot in unheard of misery":** Davenport *Quad City Times*, September 30, 1864, 2.
229 **"Oh, the humanity that weeps":** "Union Prisoners in Georgia," Wheeling *Daily Register*, September 26, 1864, 2. See also "Our Suffering Prisoners," *Detroit Free Press*, September 30, 1864, 2.
230 **Union prisoners in Savannah:** "Mass Meeting of Federal Prisoners," *Columbus (Ga.) Times*, October 7, 1864, 1.
230 **"The U.S. only asks":** Mattocks, *"Unspoiled Heart,"* 160–61, 163, 195, 211, 218.
231 **"deeply excited, and most righteously so":** Walt Whitman, "What Stops the General Exchange of Prisoners of War? Three-Fourths of Our Men Already Exchanged by Death, or Mental and Bodily Ruin, and the Rest Will Soon Follow" (letter to the editor), *Brooklyn Eagle*, December 27, 1864, 2.
231 **"so many baboons":** Walt Whitman, *Notebooks and Unpublished Prose Manuscripts*, ed. Edward F. Grier (New York: NYU Press, 1984), 6:2160.
232 **"exchanging the negro for a white prisoner":** Entries for August 30, September 6, 10, 11, 17, 1864, Thomas Alphonso Sharpe Diary, box 6, folder 19, Civil War Collection, MSS 20, Stuart A. Rose Manuscript, Archives, and Rare Book Library, Emory University, Atlanta.
233 **Andersonville as "bondage":** Entry for September 5, 1864, William Farrand Keys, Civil War Journal, 1863–1864, Special Collections and University Archives, Rutgers University, New Brunswick, N.J.
233 **"the african Slave trade":** Whitfield J. Bell, ed., "Diary of George Bell: A Record of Captivity in a Federal Military Prison, 1862," *Georgia Historical Quarterly* 22 (June 1938): 182 (entry for July 10, 1862).
233 **"like slaves in the middle passage":** "The Southern Military Prisons: Inquiry by the United States Sanitary Commission—Confirmatory Account of the Martyrdom of Our Soldiers in the South," *New York Times*, September 25, 1864, 1.
233 **"We look like a lot of colored persons":** Michael Dougherty, *Prison Diary, of Michael Dougherty, Late Co. B, 13th., Pa., Cavalry: While Confined in Pemberton, Barrett's, Libby, Andersonville and Other Southern Prisons* (Briston, Pa.: Chas. A. Dougherty, 1908), 23.
233 **"so black that we can hardly tell":** Edward Beach, *Misery on All Sides: A Union Soldier's Letters, POW Experiences, Andersonville Diary, Love Letters, and Papers*, ed. Janet Elaine Selby Marx (privately pub., 2011), 72. See also Styple, *Death Before Dishonor*, 54, 61.
233 **"could hardly be told from Mulattos":** John E. Warren, "Release from the Bull Pen—Andersonville, 1864," *Atlantic Monthly* 202 (November 1958): 136.
234 **"Free the nigger and enslave the whites":** Dougherty, *Prison Diary*, 33.
234 **"barbarous appetites on helpless captives":** Samuel S. Boggs, *Eighteen Months a Prisoner Under the Rebel Flag: A Condensed Pen-Picture of Belle Isle, Danville, Andersonville, Charleston, Florence and Libby Prisons, from Actual Experience* (Lovington, Ill.: privately pub., 1887), 3.
234 **Union prisoners understandably saw themselves:** Bell, "Diary of George Bell," 182 (entry for July 10, 1862).
234 **"This was done for mere spite":** Entry for March 17, 1864, William A. Noel Diary, Rare Book Department, Boston Public Library.
234 **"This is a taste of negro equality":** *Richmond Whig*, March 8, 1864, quoted in "The Rich-

mond Press on the Raid: The Captured Bandits; How the Prisoners Are Treated," *New York Times*, March 10, 1864, 1.

235 **"subordination is his":** Henry Cleveland, ed., *Alexander H. Stephens in Public and Private: With Letters and Speeches Before, During, and Since the War* (Philadelphia, 1866), 127.

236 **"Was there ever such a thing":** Entries for February 24, 25, 1864, "The Diary of Charles Warren Hutt of Westmoreland County, Virginia," quoted in Edwin W. Beitzell, *Point Lookout Prison Camp for Confederates* (Leonardtown, Md.: St. Mary's County Historical Society, 1972). See also John H. Hauberg and Lafayette Rogan Jones, "A Confederate Prisoner at Rock Island: The Diary of Lafayette Rogan," *Journal of the Illinois State Historical Society* 34 (March 1941): 46.

237 **"the same victims of Rebel hate":** Quoted in Lorien Foote, Rites of Retaliation: Civilization, Soldiers, and Campaigns in the American Civil War (Chapel Hill: University of North Carolina Press, 2021), 27.

237 **"was always that look":** Ezra Hoyt Ripple, *Dancing Along the Deadline: The Andersonville Memoir of a Prisoner of the Confederacy*, ed. Mark A. Snell (Novato, Calif.: Presidio, 1996), 14.

237 **"the workings of the 'peculiar institution'":** McElroy, *Andersonville*, 134.

238 **In a postwar memoir, Hadley:** John V. Hadley, *Seven Months a Prisoner* (New York: Charles Scribner's Sons, 1898), 113–27.

## CHAPTER TEN: ALLEVIATION?

240 **"an exact daguerreotype":** Joseph Jones, "Report on Conditions at Andersonville," in U.S. Sanitary Commission, *Sanitary Memoirs of the War of the Rebellion*, ed. Austin Flint (New York: Hurd and Houghton, 1867), 1:522–23.

240 **"melts men down":** Entry for June 23, 1864, David Kennedy Diary, 1864 January–September, P519, Gale Family Library, Minnesota Historical Society, St. Paul.

242 **The scale of the struggle:** Three essential works on the medical challenges that arose during the Civil War are Frank R. Freemon, *Gangrene and Glory: Medical Care During the American Civil War* (Madison, N.J..: Fairleigh Dickinson University Press, 1998); Margaret Humphreys, *Marrow of Tragedy: The Health Crisis of the American Civil War* (Baltimore: Johns Hopkins University Press, 2015); Glenna R. Schroeder-Lein, *Confederate Hospitals on the Move: Samuel H. Stout and the Army of Tennessee* (Columbia: University of South Carolina Press, 1994).

242 **"it is poverty alone":** Thomas Jefferson to Joseph Carrington Cabell, May 16, 1824, in R. J. Honeywell, *The Educational Work of Thomas Jefferson* (Cambridge: Harvard University Press, 1931), 266.

242 **With a capacity of thirty-six hundred:** Carol C. Green, *Chimborazo: The Confederacy's Largest Hospital* (Knoxville: University of Tennessee Press, 2004), 1–19.

243 **Hammond Hospital at Point Lookout:** Charles J. Stillé, *History of the United States Sanitary Commission: Being the General Report of Its Work During the War of the Rebellion* (Philadelphia: Lippincott, 1866), 123.

244 **"The best I ever saw":** Quoted in Joel D. Citron, *Confederate Prisoners at Fort Delaware: The Legend of Mistreatment Reexamined* (Jefferson, N.C.: McFarland, 2018), 105.

244 **"a poor apology for one":** *OR*, ser. II, 6:575–81.

244 **The recovery rate of prisoners:** William O. Bryant, *Cahaba Prison and the Sultana Disaster* (Tuscaloosa: University of Alabama Press, 1990), 64–78.

245 **the Belle Isle prison hospital:** *OR*, ser. II, 7:39.

245 **"heart-rending beyond expression":** Benjamin F. Booth and Steve Meyer, *Dark Days of the Rebellion: Life in Southern Military Prisons* (Garrison, Iowa: Meyer, 1996), 128–30.

245 **Disease and illness ripped through the prison:** Louis A. Brown, *The Salisbury Prison: A Case Study of Confederate Military Prisons, 1861–1865* (Wilmington, N.C.: Broadfoot, 1992), 163–65.

245 **patients were assailed by the stench:** Jones, "Report on Conditions," 1:506.

246 **The exhausting ordeal:** *OR*, ser. II, 7:546–48, 551–52, 755–56, 758–59.

246 **A thirteenth member of his circle:** Ronald G. Watson, ed., *From Ashby to Andersonville: The Civil War Diary and Reminiscences of Private George A. Hitchcock, 21st Massachusetts Infantry* (Campbell, Calif.: Savas, 1997), 233–53.

246 **During one week that September:** U.S. Surgeon General's Office, *The Medical and Surgical History of the War of the Rebellion (1861–65)*, ed. Joseph Janvier Woodward (Washington, D.C.: Government Printing Office, 1879), pt. 3, 1:34.

246 **"finally succeeded in getting him in":** Quoted in Jennifer Hopkins, "The Deadliest Ground of the Civil War—Medicine at Andersonville Prison," https://www.civilwarmed.org/andersonville-medicine/, accessed May 15, 2025.

246 **"Many goes but few return":** Entry for June 10, 1864, Kennedy Diary.

246 **Out of this number, 12,541:** Surgeon General's Office, *Medical and Surgical History*, pt. 2, 1:32–33.

246 **Most days, a staff of four:** U.S. Congress, H. Ex. Doc. 23, *Trial of Henry Wirz: Letter from the Secretary of War ad Interim, in Answer to a Resolution of the House of April 16, 1866, Transmitting a Summary of the Trial of Henry Wirz* (Washington, D.C.: Government Printing Office, 1868), 38.

247 **"encrusted with dirt":** Jones, "Report on Conditions," 1:520.

247 **"Of vermin or lice":** Congress, *Trial of Henry Wirz*, 28.

247 **flies depositing maggots:** Jones, "Report on Conditions," 1:520.

247 **"Theire is more miserey heire":** Entry for August 11, 1864, Kennedy Diary.

247 **Union and Confederate prison doctors:** Surgeon General's Office, *Medical and Surgical History*, pt. 3, 1:46.

247 **7281 were from diarrhea:** Surgeon General's Office, *Medical and Surgical History*, pt. 2, 1:36.

247 **698 deaths due to dysentery:** Surgeon General's Office, *Medical and Surgical History*, pt. 2, 1:36.

247 **Elmira prison reported 1394 deaths:** Surgeon General's Office, *Medical and Surgical History*, pt. 2, 1:37.

248 **5605 were traced to diarrhea:** Surgeon General's Office, *Medical and Surgical History*, pt. 2, 1:32–33.

248 **592 of the 1084 deaths:** Surgeon General's Office, *Medical and Surgical History*, pt. 2, 1:35.

248 **At Andersonville, dysentery and scurvy:** Surgeon General's Office, *Medical and Surgical History*, pt. 2, 1:36.

249 **But the supply of roots:** Booth and Meyer, *Dark Days*, 112, 187–88.

249 **Beginning with a small black spot:** Jones, "Report on Conditions," 1:515.

249 **"far below the truth":** Jones, "Report on Conditions," 1:530.

249 **"At last, by much ado, I succeeded":** Lydia M. Post, ed., *Soldiers' Letters from Camp, Battlefield, and Prison* (New York: Bunce and Huntington, 1865), 457.

250 **establishing an adequate "pest house":** *OR*, ser. II, 6:938–39.

250 **epidemic killed more than 500 prisoners:** Benton McAdams, *Rebels at Rock Island: The Story of a Civil War Prison* (DeKalb: Northern Illinois University Press, 2000), 48–52.

251 **Joseph Jones tried to calculate the toll:** Jones, "Report on Conditions," 1:613–18.

252 **"Where others have it and do not":** Watson, *From Ashby to Andersonville*, 219.

252 **"scurvy arising from sameness":** *OR*, ser. II, 7:546–48, 551–52, 755–56, 758–59.

252 **"all the skill that can be brought":** Congress, *Trial of Henry Wirz*, 38.

252 **"potatoes, cabbage, or onions":** *OR*, ser. II, 7:682.

253 **"The refusal of proper accommodations":** *OR*, ser. II, 7:1084.

253 **"mortality is incident to prison life":** *OR*, ser. II, 6:1051.

253 **"the measure of practical ability":** Quoted in George Worthington Adams, *Doctors in Blue: The Medical History of the Union Army in the Civil War* (Baton Rouge: Louisiana State University Press, 1996), 10.

254 **"deplorable ignorance of the medical men":** Walter D. Addison, "Recollections of a Confederate Soldier of the Prison-Pens of Point Lookout, Md., and Elmira, New York," September 30, 1889, Southern Historical Collection, Wilson Special Collections Library, University of North Carolina at Chapel Hill.

254 **"captive enemies, who are the representatives":** Jones, "Report on Conditions," 1:513.

254 **doctors actively resisted serving there:** Jones, "Report on Conditions," 1:512.

254 **H. H. Clayton of Augusta:** Schroeder-Lein, *Confederate Hospitals on the Move*, 118.

254 **Desperation to fill vacancies:** H. H. Cunningham, *Doctors in Gray: The Confederate Medical Service* (Baton Rouge: Louisiana State University Press, 1993), 37.

255 **incompetent mercenaries:** *OR*, ser. II, 6:819.
255 **A contract doctor at Camp Morton:** *OR*, ser. II, 6:424–26.
255 **"almost Herculean magnitude":** Quoted in Roger Pickenpaugh, *Camp Chase and the Evolution of Union Prison Policy* (Tuscaloosa: University of Alabama Press, 2007), 125.
255 **"some of the doctors appear":** Entry for June 21, 1864, Nehemiah Solon Diary, MS 78606a, Connecticut Museum of Culture and History, Hartford.
255 **"should be willing to live":** *OR*, ser. II, 7:484–85.
255 **"a resort to brute force":** *OR*, ser. II, 7:695.
255 **"utterly devoid of humanity":** *OR*, ser. II, 7:171.
255 **prisoners were "utterly callous":** Jones, "Report on Conditions," 1:511, 507, 522.
256 **"it was most carelessly done":** *OR*, ser. II, 7:892–93, 894.
256 **"criminal neglect and inhumanity":** *OR*, ser. II, 7:894.
257 **"had neglected the ordinary prompting":** *OR*, ser. II, 7:892.
257 **the "red-tapeism" of the Union military bureaucracy:** Eugene F. Sanger, "Elmira Prison vs. Andersonville: Statement of the Surgeon Who Had Charge of the Hospital Department at Elmira," *Portland (Me.) Daily Press*, January 24, 1876, 1.
258 **White's pleas to the Confederate surgeon general:** *OR*, ser. II, 7:426–27, 430, 524–25.
259 **"gross neglect of duty":** *OR*, ser. II, 6:938–39.
259 **"absence of all regularity":** *OR*, ser. II, 7:755.
259 **After the war, he bore no stigma:** Jesse Waggoner, "The Role of the Physician: Eugene Sanger and a Standard of Care at the Elmira Prison Camp," *Journal of the History of Medicine and Allied Sciences* 63 (January 2008): 1–22.
260 **"deliberate torture and death":** "Prisoners Released," *Rock Island (Ill.) Argus*, November 21, 1864, 3.
260 **"We cannot afford to waste life":** Katharine Prescott Wormeley, *The United States Sanitary Commission: A Sketch of Its Purposes and Work* (Boston: Little, Brown, 1863), 266. See also Allan Nevins and Milton H. Thomas, eds, *The Diary of George Templeton Strong: The Civil War, 1861–1865* (New York: Macmillan, 1952), 3:162.
261 **in May 1864 the commission established:** *OR*, ser. II, 7: 188–89, 387–88, 398, 444–45.
262 **"read the unerring testimony of nature":** Report by Commission of Inquiry, U.S. Sanitary Commission, *Narrative of Privations and Sufferings of United States Officers and Soldiers While Prisoners of War in the Hands of the Rebel Authorities* (Boston: Littell's Living Age, 1864), 4.
262 **"consideration and kindness":** Commission of Inquiry, *Narrative of Privations*, 18, 20.
262 **"gross and filthy habits":** Commission of Inquiry, *Narrative of Privations*, 20, 96.
262 **outrageous "privations and sufferings":** Commission of Inquiry, *Narrative of Privations*, 22–23, 76, 95.
263 **the only "tribunal" to determine:** Robert B. Baker, "The Medical Ethics Revolution," in Robert B. Baker et al., *The American Medical Ethics Revolution: How the AMA's Code of Ethics Has Transformed Physicians' Relationships to Patients, Professionals, and Society* (Baltimore: Johns Hopkins University Press, 1999), 17–51.
264 **"as a club footed little gentleman":** Anthony M. Keiley, *In Vinculis; or, The Prisoner of War: Being the Experience of a Rebel in Two Federal Pens; Interspersed with Reminiscences of the Late War; Anecdotes of Southern Generals, Etc.* (New York: Blelock, 1866), 138.
264 **"a very worthy occupation":** Eugene F. Sanger Papers, Records of the Office of the Adjutant General, Regimental Correspondence, 1861–1865, Maine State Archives, Augusta.
264 **"sick and emaciated, naked":** Dr. J. M. Howell to wife, July 29, 1864, John McKinney Howell Letters to His Wife, MS 3259, Hargrett Rare Book and Manuscript Library, University of Georgia Libraries, Athens.
265 **"I am usually engaged from 8 to 12":** Howell to wife, August 29, 1864, Howell Letters.
265 **"physic no more Yankees":** Howell to wife, August 29, 1864.
265 **His only lament:** Howell to wife, August 10, 1864, Howell Letters.
266 **a surgeon of "fine acquirements":** Sanford B. Hunt, "Army Alimentation in Relation to the Causation and Prevention of Disease," in Sanitary Commission, *Sanitary Memoirs*, 1:80.
266 **He absolved the Confederacy:** Jones, "Report on Conditions," 1:533.
267 **"one among a thousand":** James J. Heslin, ed., "*The Diary of a Union Soldier in Confederate Prisons*," *New York Historical Society Quarterly* 41 (July 1957): 265.

267 **"killed more Rebs than any soldier":** James Huffman, *Ups and Downs of a Confederate Soldier* (New York: William E. Rudge's Sons, 1940), 97.
267 **"this subordination of a patient's interests":** Quoted in Joseph H. Ford, *Details of Military Medical Administration* (Philadelphia: P. Blakiston's Son, 1918), 6.

## CHAPTER ELEVEN: THE WINTER OF DESOLATION

268 **"squandered in every direction":** *OR*, ser. II, 8:734.
269 **During ten months as a Confederate prisoner:** Chester D. Berry, *Loss of the Sultana and Reminiscences of Survivors* (Knoxville: University of Tennessee Press, 2005), 45.
269 **"never experienced a happier day":** Berry, *Loss of the Sultana*, 46.
270 **the war's worst maritime disaster:** For Berry's account of the sinking, see Berry, *Loss of the Sultana*, 47–55; for modern accounts of the disaster, see Gene Eric Salecker, *Disaster on the Mississippi: The Sultana Explosion, April 27, 1865* (Washington, D.C.: Naval Institute Press, 1996); Alan Huffman, *Sultana: Surviving the Civil War, Prison, and the Worst Maritime Disaster in American History* (New York, Collins, 2009).
271 **"I cannot keep them":** Lafayette McLaws to Howell Cobb, September 9, 1864, cited in Roger Pickenpaugh, *Captives in Blue: The Civil War Prisons of the Confederacy* (Tuscaloosa: University of Alabama Press, 2013), 198.
271 **"We are not in any prison":** Entry for September 12, 1864, Samuel J. Gibson Diary and Correspondence, MSS 5241, Library of Congress, Washington, D.C.
272 **the Union officers transferred:** *OR*, ser. II, 7:773, 788–89, 795.
272 **Scores of Union prisoners were recruited:** Julia Garlick, "Reminiscences of Federal Prison in Lawtonville," *Waynesboro (Ga.) True Citizen*, June 7, 1924, 10.
272 **"the largest prison in the world":** *OR*, ser. II, 7:869–70.
272 **"Cannot part [of the camp]":** *OR*, ser. II, 8:773.
273 **"there was no stockade":** John V. Hadley, *Seven Months a Prisoner, or, Thirty-Six Days in the Woods* (Indianapolis: J. M. and F. J. Meikely, 1868), 88.
273 **"name rather than a place":** Sidney Andrews, *The South Since the War* (Boston: Ticknor and Fields, 1866), 191–92.
273 **"fairly wholesome":** Francis J. Hosmer, *A Glimpse of Andersonville and Other Writings* (Springfield, Mass.: Loring and Axtell, 1896), 42.
273 **"a very pleasant place":** Entry for October 10, 1864, Diary of Henry H. Adam, Connecticut Museum of Culture and History, Hartford.
273 **"everyone is pleased":** John L. Ransom, *John Ransom's Civil War Diary: Notes from Inside Andersonville, the Civil War's Most Notorious Prison* (Mineola, N.Y.: Dover Publications, 2017), 109, 110. See also Lucius W. Barber, *Army Memoirs of Lucius W. Barber* (Chicago: J. M. W. Stationary, 1894), 178; Henry Hitchcock, *Marching with Sherman: Passages from the Letters and Campaign Diaries of Henry Hitchcock, Major and Assistant Adjutant General of Volunteers, November 1864–May 1865*, ed. M. A. DeWolfe Howe (New Haven: Yale University Press, 1927), 210.
273 **"this looks like Andersonville":** John McElroy, *Andersonville: A Story of Rebel Military Prisons* (Toledo: D. R. Locke, 1879), 453.
273 **"we do not *get enough to eat*":** Entries for October 11, 14, 16, 18, 1864, Adam Diary.
274 **"I shall not be much troubled":** Hitchcock, *Marching with Sherman*, 160.
274 **"be shot than put in such a place":** Rice C. Bull, *Soldiering: The Civil War Diary of Rice C. Bull, 123rd New York Volunteer Infantry*, ed. K. Jack Bauer (San Rafael, Calif.: Presidio, 1977), 193. See also Joseph T. Glatthaar, *The March to the Sea and Beyond: Sherman's Troops in the Savannah and Carolinas Campaigns* (New York: New York University Press, 1985), 77.
274 **"a barn and a hen-coop":** Ransom, *Civil War Diary*, 131; See also McElroy, *Andersonville*, 496.
274 **Forno had to send:** Amos W. Ames, "A Diary of Prison Life in Southern Prisons," *Annals of Iowa* 40 (Summer 1969): 2; *OR*, ser. II, 7:1204; entries for November 21–December 25, 1864, George M. Shearer Diary, 1864, Special Collections, University of Iowa, Iowa City; John W. Urban, *Battlefield and Prison Pen: Or Through the War, and Thrice a Prisoner in Rebel Dungeons* (New York: Union, 1882).

275 **not fit to feed "a cur":** W. F. Oscar Federhen, *Thirteen Months in Dixie, or, the Adventures of a Federal Prisoner in Texas: Including the Red River Campaign, Imprisonment at Camp Ford, and Escape Overland to Liberated Shreveport, 1864–1865*, ed. Jeaninne Surette Honstein and Steven A. Knowlton (El Dorado Hills, Calif.: Savis Beatie, 2022), 11. See also J. B. Leake Diary, in Roger Davis, ed., "The Camp Ford Diary of J. B. Leake," *Chronicles of Smith County, Texas* 42 (2003): 44–61; entries for April 24, May 7, 16, June 6, 1864, William Fortunatus McKinney Diary, in Howard O. Pollan and Randal B. Gilbert, eds., "The Camp Ford Diary of Captain William Fortunatus McKinney," *Chronicles of Smith County, Texas* 25 (Summer 1996): 15–25; Leon Mitchell Jr., "Camp Ford Confederate Military Prison," *Southwestern Historical Quarterly* 66 (July 1962): 1–16; James M. Smallwood, "Prison City, Camp Ford: Largest Confederate Prisoner-of-War Camp in the Trans-Mississippi," in Kenneth W. Howell, ed., *The Seventh Star of the Confederacy: Texas During the Civil War* (Denton: University of North Texas Press, 2009), 208–27.

276 **Winder's death provoked "great rejoicing":** Robert D. Allen and Cheryl J. Allen, eds., *A "Guest" of the Confederacy: The Civil War Letters and Diaries of Alonzo M. Keeler, Captain, Company B, Twenty-Second Michigan Infantry* (Nashville: Cold Tree, 2008), 169.

276 **"I became an eyewitness":** Rebecca Latimer Felton, *Country Life in Georgia in the Days of My Youth* (Atlanta: Index, 1919), 86.

276 **creaky Confederate rail system**: William B. Styple, ed., *Death Before Dishonor: The Andersonville Diary of Eugene Forbes, 4th New Jersey Infantry* (Kearny, N.J.: Bellegrove, 1995), 121; Hitchcock, *Marching with Sherman*, 209, 212; Allen and Allen, *A "Guest" of the Confederacy*, 173; Ransom, *Civil War Diary*, 147, 163; Ezra Hoyt Ripple, *Dancing Along the Deadline: The Andersonville Memoir of a Prisoner of the Confederacy*, ed. Mark A. Snell (Novato, Calif.: Presidio, 1996), 60; Robert Knox Sneden, *Eye of the Storm: A Civil War Odyssey*, ed. Charles F. Bryan Jr. and Nelson D. Lankford (New York: Free Press, 2000), 287–88.

276 **prisoners who died in transit:** Ransom, *Civil War Diary*, 132.

276 **"poor protection, excepting from the sun":** Charles Smedley, *Life in Southern Prisons: From the Diary of Corporal Charles Smedley of Company G, 90th Regiment, Penn'a Volunteers* (Fulton, Pa.: Ladies' and Gentlemen's Fulton Aid Society, 1865), 43. See also *OR*, ser. II, 7:973.

277 **"half cave & half tent":** Entries for October 3, 19, 23, 1864, Gibson Diary.

277 **his sole possession was his watch:** Smedley, *Life in Southern Prisons*, 51.

277 **stepped across the imaginary dead line:** Styple, *Death Before Dishonor*, 126, 134, 151.

278 **"simply a case of self-preservation":** H. M. Davidson, *Fourteen Months in Southern Prisons: Being a Narrative of the Treatment of Federal Prisoners of War in the Rebel Military Prisons of Richmond, Danville, Andersonville, Savannah and Millen* (Milwaukee: Daily Wisconsin, 1865), 244–45.

278 **they melted among the spectators:** Styple, *Death Before Dishonor*, 124, 128, 129; Allen and Allen, *A "Guest" of the Confederacy*, 145, 151, 171; Lessel Long, *Twelve Months in Andersonville* (Huntingdon, Ind.: Thad and Mark Butler, 1886), 88–90; Ransom, *Civil War Diary*, 147; William B. Smith, *On Wheels and How I Came There: A Real Story for Real Boys and Girls, Giving the Personal Experiences and Observations of a Fifteen-Year-Old Yankee Boy as Soldier and Prisoner in the American Civil War* (New York: Hunt and Eaton, 1892), 144; Sneden, *Eye of the Storm*, 261–63.

278 **visions of avenging escapees marauding:** These fears are skillfully explored in Lorien Foote, *The Yankee Plague: Escaped Union Prisoners and the Collapse of the Confederacy* (Chapel Hill: University of North Carolina Press, 2016).

279 **Boyd finally reached Camp Chase:** Entries for January 1–16, 1865, Samuel Beckett Boyd Diary, MS-0248, Betsey B. Creekmore Special Collections and University Archives, University of Tennessee, Knoxville.

280 **"so filthy that we could smell":** Quoted in Wiley Sword, *Embrace an Angry Wind: The Confederacy's Last Hurrah: Spring Hill, Franklin, and Nashville* (New York: HarperCollins, 1992), 385. See also John M. Copley, *A Sketch of the Battle of Franklin, Tenn., with Reminiscences of Camp Douglas* (Austin: Eugene von Boeckmann, 1893), 64, 67.

280 **"so few prisoners have money":** Douglas Southall Freeman, *A Calendar of Confederate Papers with a Bibliography of Some Confederate Publications* (Richmond: Confederate Museum, 1908), 119; see also 91, 106.

281 **"entirely cut off from home supplies":** Freeman, *Calendar of Confederate Papers*, 118.
281 **a very destitute condition:** *OR*, ser. II, 8:25.
281 **Instead, the Union should propose:** *OR*, ser. II, 6:457–58, 468, 629–30.
282 **"the experiment might be tried":** *OR*, ser II, 7:575.
282 **"He opened an office":** *OR*, ser. II, 7:926, 1008–9, 1011, 1063, 1117–18, 1121–22, 1206–7; *OR*, ser. II, 8:21–22, 40, 173–74.
283 **Beall was responsible for the sale:** *OR*, ser. II, 8:1131, 1191–92.
283 **Beall had to pay federal:** *OR*, ser. II, 7:1122, 1132, 1140–41, 1201–2, 1247, 1248–49, 1271, 1281–82, 1295, 1297, 1299; *OR*, ser. II, 8:13–15, 23, 27, 77.
283 **Desperately needed blankets and clothes:** Freeman, *Calendar of Confederate Papers*, 84; *OR*, ser. II, 8:748–749, 1000. This sad affair is concisely charted in Morgan Allen Powell, "Cotton for the Relief of Confederate Prisoners," *Civil War History* 9 (March 1963): 24–35.
283 **"not furnish them; the Confederacy will":** *OR*, ser. II, 8:1285, 1288.
283 **"No clothing, including blankets":** *OR*, ser. II, 7:1266. See also *OR*, ser. II, 8:25, 36, 106.
284 **"ability to adapt himself":** John G. Nicolay and John Hay, *Abraham Lincoln: A History* (New York: Century, 1890), 4:133.
284 **"a general without capacity":** Quoted in Elizabeth D. Leonard, *Benjamin Franklin Butler: A Noisy, Fearless Life* (Chapel Hill: University of North Carolina Press, 2022), xii.
285 **"No one will go farther":** Benjamin F. Butler, *Butler's Book: Autobiography and Personal Reminiscences of Major-General Benjamin F. Butler: A Review of His Legal, Political, and Military Career* (Boston: A. M. Thayer, 1892), appendix p. 3.
285 **"sufficient 'vaccine matter'":** Benjamin F. Butler, *Private and Official Correspondence of General Benjamin F. Butler: During the Period of the Civil War* (Springfield, Mass.: Plimpton, 1917), 3:214–15, 298–300, 311–12, 315–16, 341–42.
285 **"self-respect requires":** *OR*, ser. II, 6:768.
285 **five hundred Confederate prisoners:** *OR*, ser. II, 6:836, 867.
285 **he assured Ould of his earnest hope:** *OR*, ser. II, 6:755, 836, 867; Butler, *Butler's Book*, 586.
286 **"any well-authenticated case":** *OR*, ser. II, 7:105.
287 **"at all hazards exchanges":** Butler, *Butler's Book*, 594. See also *OR*, ser. II, 7:46–50, 53–56, 62–63.
287 **"that this measure of obvious humanity":** *OR*, ser. II, 7:794.
287 **Meanwhile, the Union turned over:** *OR*, ser. II, 8:424.
287 **"Men shouted, cheered":** Ronald G. Watson, ed., *From Ashby to Andersonville: The Civil War Diary and Reminiscences of George A. Hitchcock, Private, Company A, 21st Massachusetts Regiment: August 1862–January 1865* (Campbell, Calif.: Savas, 1997), 220.
287 **"the happiest day of my life":** Entry for November 25, 1864, Kendrick R. Howard Diary. Misc 698, Vermont Historical Society, Barre.
288 **"endeavoring to make arrangements":** *OR*, ser. II, 8:170.
289 **the Confederate Congress was in the final stages:** Bruce Levine, *Confederate Emancipation: Southern Plans to Free and Arm Slaves During the Civil War* (New York: Oxford University Press, 2007).
290 **emptying Salisbury camp:** David McRaven to wife, February 26, 1865, in Louis A. Brown, ed., "The Correspondence of David Orlando McRaven and Amanda Nantz McRaven," *North Carolina Historical Review* 26 (January 1949): 93; *OR*, ser. II, 8:296–99, 304–5, 358; Benjamin F. Booth and Steve Meyer, *Dark Days of the Rebellion: Life in Southern Military Prisons* (Garrison, Iowa: Meyer, 1996), 294–318.
290 **The three thousand prisoners who remained:** *OR*, ser. II, 8:427; entries for April 4–8, 13, 17–19, 1865, John Whitten Diary, Library of Congress; Amos W. Ames, "A Diary of Prison Life in Southern Prisons," *Annals of Iowa* 40 (Summer 1969): 18–19.
291 **fifteen hundred prisoners were sent south:** *OR*, ser. II, 8:1000.
291 **huddled on the ship's deck:** Walter D. Addison, "Recollections of a Confederate Soldier of the Prison-Pens of Point Lookout, Md., and Elmira, New York," Southern Historical Collection, Wilson Special Collections Library, University of North Carolina at Chapel Hill.
291 **"being among humans again":** Entries for April 1, 9, 1865, John Ely Diary, Ely Papers, Ohio History Connection, Columbus.
291 **estimated eighty-seven victims:** Peter Holman, *Going Home: The Short Life and Sudden*

*Death of the U.S. Army Transport Steamer "General Lyon"* (Kent, Ohio: Tower of Song and Stone, 2023), 152–65.

291 **passengers on the *Kentucky*:** New Orleans *Picayune*, June 15, 1885, 3.

292 **Within minutes it sank:** Shreveport *Journal*, July 10, 1974, D-1.

292 **"It seemed especially hard":** Entry for June 11, 1865, James T. Wallace Diary, 3059-z, Southern Historical Collection, Wilson Special Collections Library, University of North Carolina at Chapel Hill.

293 **Between April and November 1865:** Secretary of War, *Annual Report of the Secretary of War, 1865* (Washington, D.C.: Government Printing Office, 1866), 1:26–32.

293 **"they may still raise something":** *OR*, ser. II, 8:556.

294 **only four prisoners remained:** *OR*, ser. II, 8:1004.

294 **"machine where U.S. citizens":** G. Ward Hubbs, ed., *Voices from Company D: Diaries by the Greensboro Guards, Fifth Alabama Infantry Regiment, Army of Northern Virginia* (Athens: University of Georgia Press, 2003), 386.

294 **"Oh what a happy day":** Morris's journey is recounted in the entries for June 12–29, 1865, William G. B. Morris Diary, U.S. Army Military History Institute, Carlise Barracks, Pa. See also Bradley R. Clampitt, *Lost Causes: Confederate Demobilization and the Making of Veteran Identity* (Baton Rouge: Louisiana State University Press, 2022), esp. 53–82.

295 **"Here I was obliged":** Berry, *Loss of the Sultana*, 68.

295 **members of the Ninth Minnesota:** Walter N. Trenerry, "When the Boys Came Home," *Minnesota History* 38 (June 1963): 289.

295 **he had, in fact, survived:** Berry, *Loss of the Sultana*, 56.

## CHAPTER TWELVE: GIVING THE HISTORY AND WHOLE TRUTH

296 **He left no record:** *Washington Star*, November 11, 1865, 1.

297 **"the worm of conscience":** "Wirz: Details of His Execution," *New York Herald*, November 11, 1865, 1.

299 **Yet Holt was a complex man:** Joshua E. Kastenberg, *Law in War, War as Law: Brigadier General Joseph Holt and the Judge Advocate General's Department in the Civil War and Early Reconstruction, 1861–1865* (Durham, N.C.: Carolina Academic Press, 2011), 276; for an excellent portrait of Holt, see Elizabeth D. Leonard, *Lincoln's Forgotten Ally: Judge Advocate General Joseph Holt of Kentucky* (Chapel Hill: University of North Carolina Press, 2011).

299 **"stern, stubborn, relentless man":** Howard K. Beale, ed., *Diary of Gideon Welles: Secretary of the Navy Under Lincoln and Johnson* (New York: W. W. Norton, 1960), 2:370.

299 **"'cruel' and 'remorseless'":** Beale, *Diary of Gideon Welles*, 2:423; Leonard, *Lincoln's Forgotten Ally*, 41.

300 **"the means of bringing to light":** Norton Parker Chipman, *The Tragedy of Andersonville: Trial of Captain Henry Wirz, the Prison Keeper* (privately pub., 1911), 27–30.

300 **"one of the most important chapters":** *OR*, ser. III, 5:490–94.

300 **Military commissions had been first used:** Winfield Scott and H. L. Scott, General Orders No. 190, June 26, 1847 (republished General Orders No. 20 with additions), Lincoln Financial Foundation Collection, https://archive.org/details/headquartersofar00scot/page/n3/mode/2up, accessed June 5, 2024; Winfield Scott, *Memoirs of Lieut.-General Scott, LL.D* (New York: Sheldon, 1864), 2:393–97; Erika Myers, "Conquering Peace: Military Commissions as a Lawfare Strategy in the Mexican War," *American Journal of Criminal Law* 35 (Spring 2008): 201–40.

301 **more than four thousand tribunals:** Mark E. Neely, *The Fate of Liberty: Abraham Lincoln and Civil Liberties* (New York: Oxford University Press, 1991), 160–79. See also David W. Glazier, "Precedents Lost: The Neglected History of the Military Commission," *Virginia Journal of International Law* 46 (Fall 2005): 7–8, 40; John Fabian Witt, *Lincoln's Code: The Laws of War in American History* (New York: Free Press, 2012), 267.

301 **"intrinsic defects of machinery":** *OR*, ser. III, 5:490–94.

301 **Attorney General James Speed concurred:** James Speed, "Military Commissions," in J. Hubley Ashton, ed., *Official Opinions of the Attorneys General of the United States* (Washington, D.C.: W. H. & O. H. Morrison, 1869), 11:297–317.

301 **"most powerful and efficacious instrumentalities":** *OR*, ser. III, 5:493.

303 **"sufficiently high in authority":** U.S. Congress, H. Ex. Doc. 23, *Trial of Henry Wirz: Letter from the Secretary of War ad Interim, in Answer to a Resolution of the House of April 16, 1866, Transmitting a Summary of the Trial of Henry Wirz* (Washington, D.C.: Government Printing Office, 1868), 751, 773.

303 **"We saw that we were badly treated":** Congress, *Trial of Henry Wirz*, 652.

304 **"system of human slavery":** U.S. Congress, House, Special Committee on the Treatment of Prisoners of War and Union Citizens, Report No. 45, *Report on the Treatment of Prisoners of War, by the Rebel Authorities, During the War of Rebellion* (Washington, D.C.: Government Printiing Office, 1869), 5–8.

304 **"southern barbarism":** Quoted in "The Andersonville Prison-Keeper," Boston *Liberator*, September 8, 1865, 1.

304 **"evidence to the extent":** Congress, *Trial of Henry Wirz*, 771–72.

305 **"something in his face and step":** "Wirz: Details of His Execution," 1.

307 **"to terrify the loyal people":** Rush C. Hawkins, *An Account of the Assassination of Loyal Citizens of North Carolina* (New York: J. H. Folan, 1897), 16.

307 **Some had been stripped of clothes:** Hawkins, *Account of the Assassination of Loyal Citizens*; W. H. Doherty to E. D. Townsend, July 16, 1866, in "Rebel General Pickett," H. Ex. Doc. 11 (39th Cong., 2nd sess.), 5.

307 **In his absence prosecutors gathered:** "Murder of Union Soldiers in North Carolina," H. Ex. Doc. 98 (39th Cong., 1st sess.), 48–49.

307 **"an honorable man":** Ulysses S. Grant to Andrew Johnson, March 16, 1866, in "Rebel General Pickett," 9.

307 **a military commission in Raleigh:** Annette Gee Ford, *The Captive: Major John H. Gee, Commandant of the Confederate Prison at Salisbury, North Carolina, 1864–1865* (privately pub., 2000), 11–12.

308 **Gee had considered punishing:** Ford, *The Captive*, 156ff, 239ff.

308 **"very decided disposition":** Ford, *The Captive*, 239, 290ff, 443ff.

308 **Confederate loyalists in Florida proclaimed:** Tallahassee *Semi-Weekly Floridian*, May 25, 1866, 2; Tallahassee *Tri-Weekly Florida Sentinel*, June 18, 1866, 2; *Jacksonville Florida Union*, May 26, 1966, 2.

308 **"no man in the South":** "Maj. Gee's Trial," *Raleigh Sentinel*, June 2, 1866, 2.

309 **White southern newspapers were silent:** *OR*, ser. II, 8:926–28.

310 **"dangerous to public liberty":** Andrew Johnson, "Proclamation Declaring the Insurrection at an End," in Charles W. Eliot, ed., *American Historical Documents, 1000–1904* (New York: P. F. Collier and Son, 1910), 457.

310 **Davis and Seddon, consequently:** Kastenberg, *Law in War*, 260–61.

310 **"indiscriminate magnanimity":** Hawkins, *Account of the Assassination of Loyal Citizens*, 46.

311 **"What is to be gained":** House Report No. 45, *Report on the Treatment of Prisoners*, 7.

311 **"the rebels and their sympathizers":** House Report No. 45, *Report on the Treatment of Prisoners*, 8.

311 **"a full, complete, and convincing refutation":** House Report No. 45, *Report on the Treatment of Prisoners*, 7.

312 **"what happened in the United States":** Brussels Conference, *Collection of Documents from 1874 Conference* (The Hague: Les Frères van Cleef, 1890), 23.

312 **"the horrors of the Thirty Years' War":** Charles Cornwallis Chesney, *A Military View of Recent Campaigns in Virginia and Maryland* (London: Smith, Elder, 1863), 1:36.

312 **"if America is really to be":** "The Usages of War," *Saturday Review of Politics, Literature, Science, and Art*, September 12, 1863, 355.

314 **"through its military or other tribunals":** David Dudley Field, *Draft Outlines of an International Code* (New York: Baker, Voorhis, 1872), 476.

314 **the Wirz trial acquired landmark status:** George A. French, "Superior Orders and War Crimes," *American Journal of International Law* 15 (July 1921): 444–45; Stephen Strong Gregory, "Criminal Responsibility of Sovereigns for Willful Violations of the Laws of War," *Virginia Law Review* 6 (March 1920): 400–421; James F. Willis, *Prologue to Nuremberg: The*

*Politics and Diplomacy of Punishing War Criminals of the First World War* (Westport, Conn.: Greenwood, 1982), 46, 76; Gordon W. Bailey, "Dry Run for the Hangman: The Versailles-Leipzig Fiasco, 1919–1921: Feeble Foreshadow of Nuremberg" (PhD diss., University of Maryland, 1971), 77–80.

## CHAPTER THIRTEEN: CAN THESE BE MEN?

316 **"the body keeps the score":** Bessel A. van der Kolk, *The Body Keeps the Score: Brain, Mind, and Body in the Healing of Trauma* (New York: Viking, 2014).

318 **"worn down with sickness":** U.S. Congress, House, Special Committee on the Treatment of Prisoners of War and Union Citizens, Report No. 45, *Report on the Treatment of Prisoners of War by the Rebel Authorities, During the War of Rebellion* (Washington, D.C.: Government Printing Office, 1869), 1138.

318 **a speech in New York City in May:** "Cruelties to Union Prisoners in the South," *New York Times*, May 12, 1865, 8.

318 **published an etching of a skeletal January:** "Rebel Cruelties," *Harper's Weekly*, June 17, 1865, 380.

318 **"Can these be men":** Walt Whitman, *Complete Prose Works* (Philadelphia: David McKay, 1892), 70.

319 **"is looked upon as public property":** A. F. Hill, *John Smith's Funny Adventures on a Crutch; or, The Remarkable Peregrinations of a One-Legged Soldier After the War* (Philadelphia: John E. Potter, 1869), 48.

319 **"exact facsimiles of photographs":** "Rebel Cruelties," 379–80.

320 **caught himself combing his food:** William Henry Lightcap, *The Horrors of Southern Prisons During the War of the Rebellion, from 1862 to 1865* (Platteville, Wisc.: Journal Job Rooms, 1902), 57.

321 **"the real thing":** Samuel H. Miller, ed., "Civil War Memoirs: 1st Maryland Cavalry, C.S.A.," *Maryland Historical Magazine* 58 (June 1963): 169.

321 **"Ambition has been my god":** Henry Lloyd White, "War Prison Diary of Major Harry White, 1863–1864," 7, White Family Papers, "Indiana, Pennsylvania in the Civil War Era" collection, Indiana University of Pennsylvania Special Collections, Indiana, Pa.

321 **"Turning myself into myself":** White, "War Prison Diary," 13.

321 **he returned home to his wife:** "Obsequies for Gen. White on Friday Afternoon," *Indiana (Pa.) Evening Gazette*, June 24, 1920, 1, 3.

322 **"activity and breadwinning":** "A Survivor from Stoneman's Raid," Washington *National Tribune*, April 10, 1890, 9.

323 **"chastened, humbled, and purified":** John England in Lydia M. Post, ed., *Soldiers' Letters from Camp, Battle-field, and Prison* (New York: Bunce and Huntington, 1865), 459.

323 **England attested that his "suffering":** For insight into nineteenth-century ideas on suffering, see Frances M. Clarke, *War Stories: Suffering and Sacrifice in the Civil War North* (Chicago: University of Chicago Press, 2011).

323 **a higher risk of death during the 1870s:** Dora L. Costa and Matthew E. Kahn, "Surviving Andersonville: The Benefits of Social Networks in POW Camps," *American Economic Review* 97 (September 2007): 1167–87; Dora L. Costa, "Scarring and Mortality Selection Among Civil War POWs: A Long-Term Mortality, Morbidity, and Socioeconomic Follow-up," *Demography* 49 (November 2012); 1185–1206.

324 **When Henry Lubker, a survivor:** James Marten, *Sing Not War: The Lives of Union and Confederate Veterans in Gilded Age America* (Chapel Hill: University of North Carolina Press, 2011), 88.

324 **he shot himself in the head:** "Failed with the Razor Then Shot Himself," *Detroit Free Press*, September 2, 1884, 4.

324 **"his friends claim it as due":** Affidavit, December 30, 1936, record of David Penman, 7th New York Heavy Artillery, ID 1311130751, Early Indicator Data Set, National Bureau of Economic Research. The losses of his unit were derived from the regimental roster in Robert Keating, *Carnival of Blood: The Civil War Ordeal of the Seventh New York Heavy Artillery* (Baltimore: Butternut and Blue, 1998), 357–532.

325 **"his mind began to give way":** Jeffrey W. McClurken, *Take Care of the Living: Reconstruct-*

*ing Confederate Veteran Families in Virginia* (Charlottesville: University of Virginia Press, 2009), 124–25.

325 **Jackson had witnessed firsthand:** For the timeline of Jackson's life, see https://www.ancestry.com/search/?name=John+E.+Jackson&event=lynchburg-virginia-usa24278&death=1873lynchburg-virginia-usa24278&count=50&deathx=0-0-0&namex=s1&searchMode=advanced, accessed May 15, 2025.

326 **"gloomy and depressing melancholy":** *Petersburg (Va.) Index*, July 29, 1873, 2, and July 30, 1873, 3.

326 **By one estimate, one million men:** Megan Kate Nelson, *Ruin Nation: Destruction and the American Civil War* (Athens: University of Georgia Press, 2012), 161.

327 **"despondent at being prisoners":** U.S. Surgeon General's Office, *The Medical and Surgical History of the War of the Rebellion, (1861–65)*, ed. Joseph Janvier Woodward (Washington, D.C.: Government Printing Office, 1879), pt. 2, 2:326. See also Shauna Devine, *Learning from the Wounded: The Civil War and the Rise of American Medical Science* (Chapel Hill: University of North Carolina Press, 2014), 46.

327 **"while Infinite Mercy slept":** Horace P. Porter, "The Common Nervous Trouble of Old Soldiers," *Leonard's Illustrated Medical Journal* 10 (1889): 22.

328 **"to show treatment where none":** "Prisoners' Pensions: An Eloquent Appeal for the Passage of the Robinson Bill," Washington *National Tribune*, March 27, 1884, 7.

328 **"was in itself calculated":** "The Robinson Bill," Washington *National Tribune*, May 15, 1884, 3.

328 **"a miracle of bodily and mental endurance":** "Prisoners' Pensions," Washington *National Tribune*, March 27, 1884, 7.

329 **provide evidence of their physical "soundness":** "Justice for Our Ex-Prisoners," Washington *National Tribune*, April 10, 1884, 4.

329 **It was no small matter:** "A Sad Roll Call at Andersonville," Washington *National Tribune*, July 26, 1883, 7; Wesley S. Thurstin, *History of the One Hundred and Eleventh Regiment O. V. I.* (Toledo: Vrooman, Anderson and Bateman, 1894), 8–12.

329 **"has not been marked, as such struggles":** Government Hospital for the Insane, *Report of the Board of Visitors*, H. Ex. Doc. 1, 38th Cong., 1st sess. (1863–65), 696–97.

329 **dismiss veterans' claims of mental trauma:** On Civil War–era terminology for psychological disorders, see Eric T. Dean, ***Shook over Hell**: Post-Traumatic Stress, Vietnam, and the Civil War* (Cambridge: Harvard University Press, 1997), 115–34.

330 **Many Democrats:** John William Oliver, "History of Civil War Military Pensions" (PhD thesis, University of Wisconsin, 1917; published in *Bulletin of the University of Wisconsin*); "Pensions to Prisoners of War," Washington *National Tribune*, September 3, 1881, 5.

330 **"a history of great suffering":** Record of Michael Nellis, 27th New York Infantry, ID 1311116366, Early Indicator Data Set, National Bureau of Economic Research, https://www.nber.org/research/data/union-army-data-andersonville, accessed March 27, 2025.

330 **"his nervous system":** Affidavit, August 1, 1886, and Surgeon's Certificate, November 23, 1898, record of George W. Farrar, 4th Massachusetts Cavalry, ID 0311117504, Early Indicator Data Set, National Bureau of Economic Research, https://www.nber.org/research/data/union-army-data-andersonville, accessed March 27, 2025.

331 **"from abuse while in prison":** Compiled Military Service Records, Private James Myers, Company E, Forty-Third U.S. Colored Infantry.

331 **Myers lacked witnesses:** Caroline Newhall, "'Under the Rebel Lash': Black Prisoners of War in the Confederate South" (PhD diss., University of North Carolina at Chapel Hill, 2020), 184–85.

331 **Nine years after filing:** Newhall, "Under the Rebel Lash," 186–88.

331 **"no other comradeship":** "Ex-Prisoners of War," Washington *National Tribune*, December 9, 1886, 6.

332 **"when their circumstances demand it":** "Meeting of the Andersonville Prison Survivors Association in Washington," *Olathe (Kans.) News*, September 28, 1865, 2.

332 **that organization finally settled:** *Constitution and By-Laws of the National Association of Union Ex-Prisoners of War, Organized 1873* (Washington, D.C.: Bass & Simms, 1887), 1; Robert B. Beath, *History of the Grand Army of the Republic* (New York: Bryan, Taylor, 1889), 680–81.

332 **Of the twenty-five ex-prisoners:** "Andersonville: Reunion of the Survivors of the Rebel Prison Pen," *Chicago Tribune*, October 21, 1880, 12.
333 **new members were blindfolded:** *Proceedings of Enlistment and Muster of the Grand Army of the Republic* (Springfield, Ill.: B. Richards, 1866), 4.
333 **"who seemed to excite special enthusiasm":** Georges Clemenceau, *American Reconstruction, 1865–1870, and the Impeachment of President Johnson*, ed. Fernand Bladensperger, trans. Margaret MacVeagh (New York: Lincoln MacVeagh and Dial, 1928), 250.
334 **"the author, knowingly, deliberately":** "Soldiers, Choose!," Washington *National Tribune*, July 17, 1884, 6.
334 **"reciting anew in the face:** "Mr. Blaine's War: The Eloquent Words of the Maine Statesman Enthusiastically Received," *Chicago Daily Tribune*, October 21, 1888, 9.
335 **"made up the blackest pages":** "Ex-Prisoners of War," 6.
335 **"it has heard little of the still greater number":** McElroy, *Andersonville*, xv.
335 **"fortitude, courage and heroism":** Charles M. Smith, "From Andersonville to Freedom" (1894), in *Military Order of the Loyal Legion of the United States, Rhode Island* (1899; repr., Wilmington, N.C.: Broadfoot, 1993), 8:87–88.
335 **"To suffer day by day":** Quoted in *Memorial of Aaron Thomas Bliss, Governor of Michigan During the Years 1901–2 and 1903–4* (Grand Rapids: Michigan Legislature, 1908), 73–74.
335 **"When taken prisoner [I] was fleshy":** John L. Ransom, *Andersonville Diary, Escape, and List of the Dead, with Name, Co., Regiment, Date of Death, and No. of Grave in Cemetery* (Auburn, N.Y.: privately pub., 1881), 158–59.

## CHAPTER FOURTEEN: THE ONLY TRUE AND CORRECT PICTURE

336 **"nowise an exaggeration":** Robert H. Kellogg, *Life and Death in Rebel Prisons: Giving a Complete History of the Inhuman and Barbarous Treatment of Our Brave Soldiers by Rebel Authorities, Inflicting Terrible Suffering and Frightful Mortality* (Hartford: L. Stebbins, 1867), title page.
340 **"the brutalizing effect":** Alonzo Cooper, *In and Out of Rebel Prisons* (Oswego, N.Y.: R.J. Oliphant, 1888), 198.
344 **Sensing an opportunity:** Stephen Davis, "'A Matter of Sensational Interest': The Century 'Battles and Leaders' Series," *Civil War History* 27 (December 1981): 338–49.
344 **"The Southern side of prison life":** John A. Wyeth, "Cold Cheer at Camp Morton," *Century Magazine*, April 1891, 852.
344 **"the slanders against our Government":** J. William Jones, *Confederate View of the Treatment of Prisoners* (Richmond: Southern Historical Society, 1876), prefatory note.
345 **Wyeth described capricious and cruel:** Wyeth, "Cold Cheer at Camp Morton," 844–48. See also John A. Wyeth, "Prisoners North and South," *Southern Historical Society Papers* 19 (1891): 47–51; John A. Wyeth, "Rejoinder by Dr. Wyeth," *Century Magazine*, 1891, 771–75.
345 **"that human beings were actually starving":** Wyeth, "Cold Cheer at Camp Morton," 847–48. For similar arguments by Confederate memoirists, see Walter D. Addison, "Recollections of a Confederate Soldier of the Prison-Pens of Point Lookout, Md., and Elmira, New York," 10, September 30, 1889, Southern Historical Collection, Wilson Special Collections Library, University of North Carolina at Chapel Hill; Anthony M. Keiley, *In Vinculus; or, The Prisoner of War: Being the Experience of a Rebel in Two Federal Pens, Interspersed with Reminiscences of the Late War, Anecdotes of Southern Generals, Etc.* (New York: Blelock, 1866), 31; R. M. Gray Reminiscences, 50, 2445-z, Southern Historical Collection, Wilson Special Collections Library, University of North Carolina at Chapel Hill.
345 **"characterized either by indifference":** Wyeth, "Prisoners North and South," 48.
345 **"northern histories of the war":** Quoted in *Indianapolis Journal*, September 27, 1891, 12.
346 **"rescue his memory":** "Daughters of Lost Cause Seek to Restore a Name: Proposed Monument to Major Wirz, Commander of Andersonville Prison," *New York Times*, February 2, 1908, 10.
346 **Winslow Homer was an unlikely documentarian:** William R. Cross, *Winslow Homer: American Passage* (New York: Macmillan, 2022), 11.
346 **The female subject and her placement:** James Hall, *The Sinister Side: How Left-Right Symbolism Shaped Western Art* (New York: Oxford University Press, 2008).

348 **"full of significance":** *New York Evening Post,* April 19, 1866, quoted in Marc Simpson, *Winslow Homer: Paintings of the Civil War* (San Francisco: Fine Arts Museums of San Francisco, 1988), 245.

348 **The price of this comity:** Valuable discussions of the retreat from Reconstruction include David W. Blight, *Race and Reunion: The Civil War in American Memory* (Belknap Press of Harvard University Press, 2001), 31–139; Eric Foner, *Reconstruction: America's Unfinished Revolution* (New York: Harper and Row, 1988), 524–86; William Gillette, *Retreat from Reconstruction, 1869–1879* (Baton Rouge: Louisiana State University Press, 1979), 259–362.

350 **"the bitter psychosis of the Civil War":** William B. Hesseltine, "The Propaganda Literature of Confederate Prisons," *Journal of Southern History* 1 (February 1935): 57.

351 **"young and impressionable":** Bernard De Voto, "The Easy Chair," *Harper's,* February 1946, 124, 126.

351 **"devoid of humanitarianism":** Hesseltine, "Propaganda Literature," 58, 60, 61, 96.

352 **Hesseltine assured his readers:** Hesseltine, "Propaganda Literature," 59, 95.

352 **"found guilty of conspiring":** Hesseltine, "Propaganda Literature," 62.

352 **"their series of pension raids":** Hesseltine, "Propaganda Literature," 63, 64, 66.

353 **"it was a minor part":** Hesseltine, "Propaganda Literature," 99.

354 **"Andersonville was merely the worst":** Bruce Catton, "Prison Camps of the Civil War," *American Heritage,* August 1959, 4.

354 **"Whatever be the message":** J. G. Randall and David Herbert Donald, *Civil War and Reconstruction* (New York: D. C. Heath, 1969), 339.

354 **"fairly objective":** Frank Byrne, "Prisons and Prisoners of War" in *Civil War Books: A Critical Bibliography,* ed. Allan Nevins, James I. Robertson Jr., and Bell I. Wiley (Baton Rouge: Louisiana State University Press, 1969), 185–206.

## CHAPTER FIFTEEN: PLACES OF SHADOWS

357 **An act of Congress in 1903:** John R. Neff, *Honoring the Civil War Dead: Commemoration and the Problem of Reconciliation* (Lawrence: University Press of Kansas, 2005), 227–35.

358 **They were so conscientiously buried:** Clifton W. Potter Jr., *Yankees in the Hill City: The Union Prisoner of War Camp in Lynchburg, Virginia, 1862–1865* (Jefferson, N.C.: McFarland, 2024), 134.

360 **The work of compiling an accurate:** Edwin C. Bearss, *Andersonville National Historic Site: Historic Resource Study and Historical Base Map* (Washington, D.C.: Department of Interior, 1970), 144–50.

360 **as per Colonel William Hoffman's orders:** Alfred E. Lee, *History of the City of Columbus, Capital of Ohio* (New York: Munsell, 1892), 2:161; Roger Pickenpaugh, *Camp Chase and the Evolution of Union Prison Policy* (Tuscaloosa: University of Alabama Press, 2007), 145.

361 **described as a desolate "skeleton":** Columbus (Ohio) *Weekly State Journal,* May 3, 1866, 1.

361 **In 1905 a real estate company:** William H. Knauss, *The Story of Camp Chase* (1906; repr., Columbus: General's Books, 1994); Pickenpaugh, *Camp Chase,* 146–48.

361 **By 1878 a local history enthusiast:** William Bross, "History of Camp Douglas," in Mabel McIlvaine, *Reminiscences of Chicago During the Civil War* (Chicago: R. R. Donnelley, 1914), 164–66.

361 **"They were the sons of God":** "Pioneering Funeral Home Director," *Chicago Sun-Times,* March 12, 2017.

361 **"a symbol of respect":** "Patriot Flies Flag in Face of Threat," *Chicago Tribune,* February 16, 1994.

362 **"'We will pull it down!'":** David D. Potter, "President Lincoln's Entry into Richmond After the Evacuation of That Place by the Confederates," *Bedford's Magazine,* September 1891, 593.

362 **"picked it to pieces":** "Libby Prison, Chicago," *Chicago Tribune,* February 5, 1888, 9.

363 **"a rich growth of bushes":** Albert Webster Jr., "A Jaunt in the South," *Appleton's Journal,* September 13, 1873, 334. See also Mary A. Shearman, "A Visit to Andersonville," *Hours at Home: A Popular Monthly, Devoted to Religious and Useful Literature,* September 1867, 409–15; "Andersonville Prison," *West Branch [Iowa] Local Record,* March 10, 1881, 4; S. Creelman, *Collections of a Coffee Cooler* (Wilkinsburg, Pa., 1889), 37–41.

364 **These raucous celebrations of Union valor:** Bearss, *Andersonville National Historic Site,*

161–64; Robert Scott Davis, *Ghosts and Shadows of Andersonville: Essays on the Secret Social Histories of America's Deadliest Prisons* (Macon, Ga.: Mercer University Press, 2006), 37–45; Adam H. Domby, "Captives of Memory: The Contested Legacy of Race at Andersonville National Historic Site," *Civil War History* 63 (September 2017): 264.

364 **Grand Army of the Republic:** Bearss, *Andersonville National Historic Site*, 172.

364 **Under the auspices of the WRC:** James P. Averill, *Andersonville Prison Park: Report of Its Purchase and Improvement* (Atlanta: Byrd, 1899), 13–16; Bearss, *Andersonville National Historic Site*, 172.

365 **"the disorderly colored element":** *Americus (Ga.) Times-Recorder*, May 31, 1901, 3; "Crowd a Small One," *Americus Times-Recorder*, May 31, 1902, 3; "No More the Scene of Riot and Crime," *AmericusTimes-Recorder*, May 2, 1903, 4; "Excellent Order Is Preserved," *Americus Times-Recorder*, June 1, 1907, 1.

365 **"the role of prisoner-of-war camps in history":** Andersonville National Historic Site, *Andersonville National Historic Site Long-Range Interpretive Plan* (Harpers Ferry Center, W. Va.: National Park Service, 2010), 2.

366 **The museum's founding mandate:** Adam H. Domby, "Captives of Memory: The Contested Legacy of Race at Andersonville National Historic Site," *Civil War History* 63 (September 2017): 253–94.

367 **John Wool Bartleson**: *Wichita Eagle*, April 19, 1944, 1.

367 **"meaning of life and the value of faith":** *Indianapolis News*, January 5, 1949, 15.

368 **"the hauntingly possessive ghosts":** Dominic LaCapra, *Writing History, Writing Trauma* (Baltimore: Johns Hopkins University Press, 2014), xxxi.

369 **"we saw that we were":** U.S. Congress, H. Ex. Doc. 23, *Trial of Henry Wirz: Letter from the Secretary of War ad Interim, in Answer to a Resolution of the House of April 16, 1866, Transmitting a Summary of the Trial of Henry Wirz* (Washington, D.C.: Government Printing Office, 1868), 674.

# SELECT BIBLIOGRAPHY

A century and a half removed from the war itself, Civil War prisons are finally the focus of sustained interest. This bibliography is only a starting point for further reading in the history of Civil War prisons.

## PRIMARY SOURCES: OFFICIAL DOCUMENTS, MEMOIRS, AND DIARIES

Essential for any understanding of the experiences of Civil War prisoners are primary sources, many of them now accessible online. The compilation of Union and Confederate official documents gathered by the U.S. War Department is the mother lode: U.S. War Department, *The War of the Rebellion: A Compilation of the Official Records of the Union and Confederate Armies* (Washington, D.C.: Government Printing Office, 1880–1901). The first 111 volumes include scattered but important information on the capture and disposition of prisoners. The next eight volumes, the Second Series, are a storehouse of correspondence, orders, and reports relating to prisoners of war. Anyone consulting the "*OR*," as it is commonly known (and referred to in the Notes), should also read Yael A. Sternhell's *War on Record: The Archive and the Afterlife of the Civil War* (2023) for a fascinating analysis of what was included and left out of the *OR*.

Several other official reports are invaluable: see U.S. Congress, Joint Committee on the Conduct of the War, *Returned Prisoners* (38th Cong., 1st sess., 1864), Report No. 67; Confederate States of America Congress,

*Report on the Joint Select Committee Appointed to Investigate the Condition and Treatment of Prisoners of War* (1865); and U.S. Congress, House Special Committee on the Treatment of Prisoners of War and Union Citizens, Report No. 45, *Report on the Treatment of Prisoners of War, by the Rebel Authorities, During the War of the Rebellion* (40th Cong., 3rd sess., 1869). Of particular importance is U.S. Congress, House, Executive Document 23, *The Trial of Henry Wirz: A Congressionally Mandated Report Summarizing the Military Commission's Proceedings* (40th Cong., 2nd sess., 1867).

The United States Sanitary Commission, which enjoyed a quasi-governmental status, published several reports related to the treatment of Union prisoners of war as well as to the condition of prisoners exchanged by the Confederacy. See U.S. Sanitary Commission, *Narrative of Privations and Sufferings of United States Officers and Soldiers While Prisoners of War in the Hands of the Rebel Authorities* (Philadelphia: King and Baird, 1864); Austin Flint, ed. *Contributions Relating to the Causation and Prevention of Disease, and to Camp Diseases; Together with a Report of the Diseases, etc., Among the Prisoners at Andersonville, Ga.* (1867); and U.S. Sanitary Commission, *Sanitary Memoirs of the War of the Rebellion: Collected and Published by the United States Sanitary Commission* (1867).

Prisoners of war themselves left unvarnished commentary on almost every aspect of captivity. Their postwar memoirs still carry some of the undeserved stigma attached to them by William Hesseltine and others during the early twentieth century. Those of John McElroy and John Ransom rank with the finest writings on the conflict and endure as essential texts on the prisoner-of-war experience. Whenever possible, I have relied on the prisoners' contemporaneous diaries. Written in forthright prose, the now published diaries kept by Charles Smedley, Frederic James, Charles Mattocks, and many others reveal in poignant detail their authors' physical and mental anguish during captivity.

Especially valuable dairies and memoirs include: Robert D. Allen and Cheryl A. Allen, eds., *A "Guest" of the Confederacy: The Civil War Letters and Diaries of Alonzo M. Keeler, Captain Company B., Twenty-Second Michigan Infantry Including Letters and Diaries Written While a Prisoner of War* (2008); Leon Basile, ed. *The Civil War Diary of Amos E. Stearns, a Prisoner at Andersonville* (1981); Robert Knox Sneden, *Eye of the Storm: A Civil War Odyssey*, ed. Charles F. Bryan Jr. and Nelson D. Lankford (2000); Andrew Jackson Campbell, *The Civil War Diary*, ed. Jill Knight Garrett (1965); Jacob Osborn Coburn, *Hell on Belle Isle: Diary of a Civil War POW*, ed. Don Allison (1997); Donald F. Danker, "Imprisoned at Andersonville: The Diary of Albert Harry Shatzel, May 5, 1864–September 12, 1864," *Nebraska History* 38 (1957): 81–126; Michael Dougherty, *Prison Diary, of Michael Dougherty, Late Co. B, 13th., Pa., Cavalry: While Confined in Pemberton, Barrett's, Libby, Andersonville and Other Southern Prisons* (1908); Ted Genoways and Hugh H. Genoways, *A Perfect Picture of Hell: Eyewitness Accounts by Civil War Prisoners from the 12th Iowa* (2001); Randal W. McGavrock, *Pen and Sword: The Life and Journals of Randal W. McGavock*, ed. Herschel Gower and Jack Allen (1959); Jefferson J. Hammer, ed., *Frederic Augustus James's Civil War Diary* (1973); Anthony M. Keiley, *In Vinculis; or, The Prisoner of War: Being the Experience of a Rebel in Two Federal Pens, Interspersed with Reminiscences of the Late War, Anecdotes of Southern Generals, Etc.* (1866); Charles Mattocks, *"Unspoiled Heart": The Journal of Charles Mattocks of the 17th Maine*, ed. Philip N. Racine (1994); Henry C. Mettam, "Civil War Memoirs of the 1st Maryland Cavalry, C.S.A.," *Maryland Historical Magazine* 58 (June 1963): 137–70; George C. Osborn, ed., "Writings of a Confederate Prisoner of War," *Tennessee Historical Quarterly* 10 (March 1951): 74–90; B. Yancey Malone, *The Diary of Bartlett Yancey Malone*, ed. Sam J. Ervin and William Whatley Pierson (1919); Howard O. Pollan and Randal B. Gilbert, eds. "The Camp Ford Diary of Captain William Fortunatus McKinney," *Chronicles of Smith County, Texas* 25 (Summer 1996): 15–25; George Haven Putnam, *A Prisoner of War in Virginia, 1864–65* (1914); John L. Ransom, *Andersonville Diary, Escape, and List of the Dead, with Name, Co., Regiment, Date of Death, and No. of Grave in Cemetery* (1881); William B. Styple, ed., *Death Before Dishonor: The Andersonville Diary of Eugene Forbes, 4th New Jersey Infantry* (1995)—interested readers might also consult a newer edition of Forbes's diary, edited by Mary Elizabeth Reynolds and Rosemary Wiseman Seal, and published in 2014 as *All for the Flag: The Civil War Diaries of Eugene Forbes*; Ezra Hoyt Ripple, *Dancing Along the Deadline: The Andersonville Memoir of a Prisoner of the Confederacy*, ed. Mark A. Snell (1996); Lyle G. Adair, *They Have Left Us Here to Die: The Civil War Prison Diary of Sgt. Lyle Adair, 111th U.S. Colored Infantry*, ed. Glenn Robins (2011); Alfred S. Roe, *The Melvin Memorial: Sleepy Hollow Cemetery, Concord, Massachusetts, a Brother's Tribute* (1910); Charles Smedley, *Life in Southern Prisons: From the Diary of Corporal Charles Smedley of Company G, 90th Regiment, Penn'a Volunteers* (1865); and Timothy J. Williams and Evan A. Kutzler, *Prison Pens: Gender, Memory, and Imprisonment in the Writings of Mollie Scollay and Wash Nelson, 1863–1866* (2018).

Wartime prison diaries and postwar prison memoirs have yet to receive the careful attention they warrant. The best extant analysis of prison memoirs and their debt to nineteenth-century literary conventions is Ann Fabian's *The Unvarnished Truth: Personal Narratives in Nineteenth-Century America* (2000).

## SCHOLARSHIP ON CIVIL WAR PRISONS

Several excellent general histories have now dislodged William B. Hesseltine's *Civil War Prisons: A Study in War Psychology* (1930). Lonnie R. Speer's *Portals to Hell: Military Prisons of the Civil War* (1997) has been a catalyst for the recent reevaluation of the history of Civil War prisons. Charles W. Sanders Jr., in *While in the Hands of the Enemy: Military Prisons of the Civil War* (2005), stresses the deliberate mistreatment of prisoners of war. Two admirably researched and crafted volumes by Roger Pickenpaugh are *Captives in Gray: The Civil War Prisons of the Union* (2009); and *Captives in Blue: The Civil War Prisons of the Confederacy* (2013). James M. Gillispie's *Andersonvilles of the North: The Myths and Realities of Northern Treatment of Civil War Confederate Prisoners* (2008) debunks many of the postwar accusations against Union prison camps. A concise recent survey is Paul J. Springer and Glenn Robins, *Transforming Civil War Prisons: Lincoln, Lieber, and the Politics of Captivity* (2015).

Several recent works have far broader implications than their titles may suggest. Lorien Foote's *The Yankee Plague: Escaped Union Prisoners and the Collapse of the Confederacy* (2016) is a revelatory study of the failing of the Confederate prison system and its consequences. Angela M. Zombek's *Penitentiaries, Punishment, and Military Prisons: Familiar Responses to an Extraordinary Crisis During the American Civil War* (2018) provides a provocative consideration of the carceral impulse evident before and during the war. For an unsurpassed evocation of the prison-camp experience, see Evan A. Kutzler, *Living by Inches: The Smells, Sounds, Tastes, and Feeling of Captivity in Civil War Prisons* (2019).

These overviews can be supplemented with case studies of individual prison camps. The three best works on Andersonville are Robert Scott Davis, *Ghosts and Shadows of Andersonville: Essays on the Secret Social Histories of America's Deadliest Prison* (2006); Ovid L. Futch, *History of Andersonville Prison* (1968); and especially William Marvel, *Andersonville: The Last Depot* (1994). Despite the notoriety of Belle Isle and Libby Prison, neither is the subject of a robust history. The best extant work on Richmond's prisoner-of-war facilities is Sandra V. Parker, *Richmond's Civil War Prisons* (1990). The Cahaba prison is addressed in William O. Bryant, *Cahaba Prison and the Sultana Disaster* (1990). Florence prison has yet to attract the scholarship it warrants; the fullest account of the prison is in Roger Pickenpaugh's *Captives in Blue*. Clifton W. Potter Jr.'s *Yankees in the Hill City: The Union Prisoner of War Camp in Lynchburg, Virginia, 1862–1865* (2024) offers a thorough account of a major transit site for Union prisoners. The Millen prison is the subject of an excellent study by John K. Derden, *The World's Largest Prison: The Story of Camp Lawton* (2012). The best work on Salisbury prison remains Louis A. Brown's *The Salisbury Prison: A Case Study of Confederate Military Prisons, 1861–1865* (1992).

Several Union prisons have been the subject of excellent histories. Roger Pickenpaugh's *Camp Chase and the Evolution of Union Prison Policy* (2007) is a case in point. On Camp Douglas, see George Levy, *To Die in Chicago: Confederate Prisoners at Camp Douglas, 1862–1865* (1994). The history of Camp Morton is traced in James R. Hall, *Den of Misery: Indiana's Civil War Prison* (2006); and Hattie Lou Winslow and Joseph R. H. Moore, *Camp Morton, 1861–1865: Indianapolis Prison Camp* (1940). Elmira prison is the focus of Michael P. Gray's excellent *The Business of Captivity: Elmira and Its Civil War Prison* (2001). For a contrasting interpretation, see Michael Horigan, *Elmira: Death Camp of the North* (2002). Fort Delaware's stint as a prison is ably traced in Dale Fetzer and Bruce Mowday, *Unlikely Allies: Fort Delaware's Prison Community in the Civil War* (2000). Johnson's Island is the subject of Charles E. Frohman, *Rebels on Lake Erie* (1965); and Roger Pickenpaugh, *Johnson's Island: A Prison for Confederate Officers* (2016). Rock Island is the focus of an outstanding study: Benton McAdams, *Rebels at Rock Island: The Story of a Civil War Prison* (2000). Point Lookout badly needs study; at present Richard H. Triebe's *Point Lookout Prison Camp and Hospital: The North's Largest Civil War Prison* (2016) is a useful compendium of materials related to the site.

Several of the major figures responsible for prisoners of war have been the subject of biographies. Leslie Gene Hunter's "Warden for the Union: General William Hoffman (1807–1884)" (Ph.D. diss., Arizona State University, 1971), is an excellent overview of Hoffman's wartime career. Hoffman deserves a modern biography. Arch Frederic Blakely's *General John H. Winder, C.S.A.* (1990) provides a measured portrait of a man who aroused strong opinions among his contemporaries. For a surprisingly positive account of the actions of the general responsible for feeding the Confederacy and its prisoners, see Jerrold Northrop Moore's *Confederate Commissary General: Lucius Bellinger Northrop and the Subsistence Bureau of the Southern Army* (1996). Edwin Stanton has been the target of many biographers, few of them sympathetic. The best is Walter Stahr's *Stanton: Lincoln's War Secretary* (2017). Joseph Jones, the Confederate doctor who visited Andersonville, is treated fully, and favorably, in James O. Breeden, *Joseph Jones, M.D.: Scientist of the Old South* (1975). Several important figures in the history of Civil War prisons are virtually unstudied. James Seddon, the Confederate secretary of war who tenaciously refused to exchange Black prisoners of war, remains an enigma. Likewise, Ethan Allen Hitchcock, as fascinating a man as ever donned Union blue, warrants the attentions of a biographer.

During the past quarter century, historians of the Civil War have debated whether the conflict crossed the threshold and became "a total war." This new focus has provoked interest in the prevailing laws of war and ideas about the conduct of warfare. Two provocative examples of this "dark turn" are Megan Kate Nelson, *Ruin Nation: Destruction and the American Civil War* (2012); and Michael C. C. Adams, *Living Hell: The Dark Side of the Civil War* (2014). David Silkenat's *Raising the White Flag: How Surrender Defined the Civil War* (2019) deftly explains the protocols and circumstances that generated the prisoners who would populate the wartime prison camps. The essential work on the origins, logic, and impact of Francis Lieber's General Orders No. 100 is John Fabian Witt, *Lincoln's Code: The Laws of War in American History* (2012). For a contrasting interpretation, see D. H. Dilbeck, *A More Civil War: How the Union Waged a Just War* (2016). Two works that brilliantly explore the logic of retaliation that dictated the conduct of the war and the treatment of prisoners of war are Aaron Sheehan-Dean, *Calculus of Violence: How Americans Fought the Civil War* (2018); and Lorien Foote, *Rites of Retaliation: Civilization, Soldiers, and Campaigns in the American Civil War* (2021).

The fate of Black soldiers is at the very center of the story of Civil War prisons. Seven decades after its first publication, Dudley Taylor Cornish's *The Sable Arm: Black Troops in the Union Army, 1861–1865* (1956) remains an essential work. More recent works include Noah Andre Trudeau, *Like Men of War: Black Troops in the Civil War, 1862–1865* (1999); John David Smith, ed., *Black Soldiers in Blue: African American Troops in the Civil War Era* (2002); and Evan Kutzler, Julia Brock, Ann McCleary, Keri Adams,

Ronald Bastien, and Larry O. Rivers, *In Plain Sight: African Americans at Andersonville National Historic Site* (2020). The essential work on the Black prisoner-of-war experience is Caroline Wood Newhall, "'Under the Rebel Lash': Black Prisoners of War in the Confederate South" (PhD diss., University of North Carolina at Chapel Hill, 2020).

The Union blockade of the Confederacy figures prominently in Confederate excuses for the hardships endured by Union prisoners. Only a few works have delved into food shortages in the Confederacy; they include Mary Elizabeth Massey, *Ersatz in the Confederacy: Shortages and Substitutes on the Southern Homefront* (1993); Andrew F. Smith, *Starving the South: How the North Won the Civil War* (2011); and Joan E. Cashin, "Hungry People in the Wartime South: Civilians, Armies, and the Food Supply," in Stephen Berry, ed., *Weirding the War: Stories from the Civil War's Ragged Edges* (2011), 160–75.

The medical history of Civil War prisoners of war has yet to be written. Valuable works that touch on medical care in the prisons include Glenna R. Schroeder-Lein, *Confederate Hospitals on the Move: Samuel H. Stout and the Army of Tennessee* (1994); Frank R. Freemon, *Gangrene and Glory: Medical Care During the American Civil War* (1998); and especially Margaret Humphreys, *Marrow of Tragedy: The Health Crisis of the American Civil War* (2015). Valuable studies that shed light on the mental health effects of the war are Eric T. Dean Jr., *Shook Over Hell: Post-Traumatic Stress, Vietnam, and the Civil War* (1997); Dillon J. Carroll, *Invisible Wounds: Mental Illness and Civil War Soldiers* (2021); and Robert D. Hicks, *Wounded for Life: Seven Union Veterans of the Civil War* (2024).

How Civil War–era Americans came to terms with suffering and death is addressed in Drew Gilpin Faust, *This Republic of Suffering: Death and the American Civil War* (2009); and Frances M. Clarke, *War Stories: Suffering and Sacrifice in the Civil War North* (2011). For a thoughtful reflection on Civil War artifacts and the war's meaning, see Jennifer Raab, *Relics of War: The History of a Photograph* (2025).

Among the valuable books on the experiences of Civil War veterans, including some prisoners of war, see Donald R. Shaffer, *After the Glory: The Struggles of Black Civil War Veterans* (2004); James Marten, *Sing Not War: The Lives of Union and Confederate Veterans in Gilded Age America* (2011); Brian Matthew Jordan, *Marching Home: Union Veterans and Their Unending Civil War* (2014); Paul A. Cimbala, *Veterans North and South: The Transition from Soldier to Civilian After the American Civil War* (2015); and

Bradley R. Clampitt, *Lost Causes: Confederate Demobilization and the Making of Veteran Identity* (2022). A careful study of veteran prisoners of war is badly needed.

The historical memory of Civil War prisons has only recently attracted notice. Benjamin G. Cloyd's *Haunted by Atrocity: Civil War Prisons in American Memory* (2010) is an exceptionally crafted meditation on the persisting shadows of the camps. John R. Neff's *Honoring the Civil War Dead: Commemoration and the Problem of Reconciliation* (2005) sheds light on the origins of the Civil War national cemeteries, including at Andersonville. Adam Domby provides a wide-ranging survey of Andersonville's evolving meaning in "Captives of Memory: The Contested Legacy of Race at Andersonville National Historic Site," *Civil War History* 63 (September 2017): 253–94.

Consideration of the Civil War prisoner-of-war experience in the visual arts is long overdue. To date only Winslow Homer's *Near Andersonville* has attracted sustained interest. On this extraordinary painting, see Marc Simpson, ed., *Winslow Homer: Paintings of the Civil War* (1988); Robert Scott Davis, "'Near Andersonville': An Historical Note on Civil War Legend and Reality," *Journal of African American History* 92 (2007): 96–105; and Peter H. Wood, *Near Andersonville: Winslow Homer's Civil War* (2010).

# INDEX

Page numbers in *italics* refer to illustrations.